MANCHESTER UNITED

IN EUROPE

MANCHESTER UNITED

IN EUROPE

David Meek
and Tom Tyrrell

Hodder & Stoughton

Copyright © 2001 by David Meek and Tom Tyrrell

First published in Great Britain in 2001
by Hodder and Stoughton
A division of Hodder Headline

The right of David Meek and Tom Tyrrell to be identified as the
Authors of the Work has been asserted by them in accordance with the
Copyright, Designs and Patents Act 1988.

1 3 5 7 9 10 8 6 4 2

A CIP catalogue record for this title is available from the British Library

ISBN 0 340 81938 3

Typeset in Plantin Light by
Rowland Phototypesetting Ltd,
Bury St Edmunds, Suffolk

Printed and bound in Great Britain by
Mackays of Chatham plc, Chatham, Kent

Hodder and Stoughton
A division of Hodder Headline Ltd
338 Euston Road
London NW1 3BH

Contents

Acknowledgements

This is a first-hand history because we have both been involved in writing and broadcasting about Manchester United since the early days of Sir Matt Busby's venture into European competition, and our book has been based on the reports and interviews which have been the mainstay of our professional lives.

So we must firstly acknowledge the help of the players who naturally have been the main focus of our story. Without their cooperation over the years we would have a much more limited tale to tell. We would therefore like to say thank you to the footballers who have walked the big European stage at Old Trafford but still found time to talk to us.

We would also straightaway like to express our appreciation to the managers who have found Europe the exciting challenge it is, and shared their hopes and ambitions with us. This has been especially true of Sir Alex Ferguson who has taken United to new heights and given us generous insight into his management on the European trail. Sir Alex, in addition, has been kind enough to write a foreword to the book and set out what, we think, everyone feels about the championship of Europe.

The book conceived some three or four years ago, has been a long time coming to fruition because our initial publisher went into receivership, leaving the project in no man's land. Roddy

Bloomfield, Editor of the Year following his successful publication of Sir Alex's autobiography, came to our rescue with Hodder and Stoughton. We are more than grateful to him and for enabling us to renew helpful editorial work again with Marion Paull, and for the invaluable photographic research by Gabrielle Allen.

We also much appreciate the unsung contribution of Peter Evans, a long-time friend, who has been in on the book from the start and who read the original manuscript so carefully that we were able to correct more errors than we expected!

Photographic acknowledgements

The author and publisher would like to thank the following for permission to reproduce photographs:

Action Press (Germany), Allsport, Associated Press, Colorsport, EPA (Holland), Steve Hale/Kenneth M. Ramsay, Hulton Getty Picture Collection, Mark Leech Sports Photography, Manchester Evening News, Popperfoto, Rex Features, Peter Robinson, Sport & General, Topham Picturepoint, Paul Windridge/Michael Craig.

Foreword

by Sir Alex Ferguson

Euuropean football is stitched into the history of Manchester United, providing a challenge that drives us all on at Old Trafford, and forming a bewitching tapestry that offers immense satisfaction in victory but considerable misery when things go wrong.

In my time as manager at Old Trafford we have experienced all the emotions. We were certainly on a high with the supreme moment in 1999 when we beat Bayern Munich in Barcelona to complete a unique treble. That was an unforgettable achievement and I felt so proud of the players who had been outstanding in both the Premiership and the FA Cup while at the same time finding the resources to crown their efforts by going all the way in Europe. Its significance was huge as all United supporters, who had waited since the triumph of Sir Matt Busby's team in 1968, appreciated on that magical night in the Nou Camp Stadium.

Success at this élite level doesn't come easily, as we know only too well after our efforts to taste again the delights of European glory. Twice now we have fallen short, failing to get past Real Madrid in the quarter-finals of the millennium season, and then the major disappointment of losing to Bayern Munich at the same stage last season. Our hopes were high for both attempts and we operated from a solid platform. You can't build a much better basis than winning your domestic League by a record 14 points, unless it is to wrap up the title by Easter which is what we did this year.

I confess I was stunned by the way we lost to Bayern, albeit by two close scores. I knew it would be difficult to pull the game round in Munich after losing the first leg 1–0 at Old Trafford, but we set out with every confidence. Defensive mistakes cost us the game in Germany, uncharacteristic lapses I might add, and we staged a grandstand finish with the kind of spirit that has become a highlight of so many of our performances.

We had a team that tried its best without being able to reveal its best, but then that's the challenge and romance of our game. We have already picked ourselves up and dusted ourselves down, ready for another bid, and committed to trying even harder.

I know we can improve. This summer we have taken Ruud van Nistelrooy on board, a transfer that I think signals our intentions quite clearly, and I know the players have lost none of their hunger and ambition for more success.

This season is a critical one for me because it's my last as manager before I step back from the front line, and naturally I would dearly love to make a final mark in Europe as well as in the domestic competitions. Four successive championships has never been done before. There is plenty to aim for and I would like to write a last successful chapter in the history of Manchester United in Europe.

It's a story that goes back a long way of course. The first chapter came when Matt Busby defied the authorities to lead Manchester United into European competition in 1956 and first introduced fans to the artistry of Real Madrid.

It's been a gripping story ever since and I'm glad that David Meek and Tom Tyrrell have put it all down in this book because their work in writing and broadcasting about our club has provided them with an understanding and appreciation of Manchester United's great adventure in Europe.

1

INTO EUROPE

THERE is a special magic about European football for Manchester United. It's woven into the history of the club and appreciated by their huge following of fans. Right from the beginning, the idea of competing against the giants of Europe fired ambition at Old Trafford and caught the imagination of the supporters. It's an arena that has brought both tragedy and triumph but nothing has dimmed the attraction of European competition.

The story starts in the promising pioneering days of the Busby Babes, encompasses the tragedy of the Munich air crash, takes in Sir Matt Busby's 1968 European Cup triumph, touches the heights with Sir Alex Ferguson's success in the Champions League of 1999 and continues in the new millennium.

Europe became a holy grail for Busby and there is no doubt that Europe latterly became the driving force for Ferguson in his career as manager at Old Trafford. As he summed it up before achieving his dream against Bayern Munich in Barcelona's Nou Camp Stadium, 'It's the one trophy we have still to win. In the past we have let ourselves and our fans down quite badly but we have improved. We know what playing in Europe entails these days and the Champions League figures high on our list of priorities. It is the next logical step for us and we are not far away.'

Martin Edwards, the chairman of United, has always shared

the excitement of the challenge, and as he puts it, 'A clear winter's night, a big crowd, the floodlights shining on the stage, the atmosphere electric, strange foreign names lining up against us . . . it has never failed to thrill me.'

The compulsion of Europe burned particularly fiercely in the minds of the players who survived the Munich crash, and despite their awful experience, they were committed in their desire to see Matt Busby win the European Cup. The team had been wiped out on their way home from competing in the quarter-finals against Red Star Belgrade.

The Munich disaster undoubtedly added to the fascination of Europe, both inside and outside the club. For Busby, the European Cup became a personal crusade. It became very special for the supporters, too, and not just for the club loyalists. The sheer enormity and drama of the accident on the Munich runway struck a chord with people in many parts of the country, and was a major factor in Manchester United and their players becoming probably the best-known football club throughout the world.

But the appeal of Europe was there right from the start. Their entry into the European Cup competition was surrounded by controversy and involved an act of defiance which in itself immediately won the interest and admiration of not only their own supporters but a much wider audience.

Gabriel Hanot, football editor of the French daily sports paper, *L'Equipe*, and a former French international player himself, advanced the concept of European club football. He had nursed the idea for many years but the advent of air travel and floodlighting made his ideas more practical. He wrote an article in 1954 and received an encouraging response. The paper, along with the weekly *France Football*, took the initiative of proposing that the champion league club of each of the European Football Associations should take part in a championship of champions.

2

In April 1955, representatives from sixteen nations met in Paris at the invitation of *L'Equipe* to launch an official UEFA competition to start in season 1955–56. Further discussions took place in Vienna at the congress of the European Union and the rules were drawn up.

Chelsea, English league champions for the first time in their history, entered but later withdrew 'on advice' from the Football League. The League's argument was that they couldn't allow it because of fixture congestion and dislocation of the domestic programme, but in private, they were probably fearful of their own competition being overshadowed. By a strange coincidence, Joe Mears, whose family had founded Chelsea and built their ground at Stamford Bridge, was chairman of the Football League. Maybe he found it difficult to wear two hats and use his league influence to help his own club. More likely, he came under pressure from the then powerful Alan Hardaker, the league secretary, who once told Brian Glanville, *The Sunday Times* journalist, in an unguarded moment that he didn't much enjoy dealing with football on the Continent: 'Too many wogs and dagoes!'

Hardaker was a law unto himself, but his was the prevailing view at the time. English football was in isolation after refusing to join FIFA in 1903, which meant that when the World Cup was introduced in 1930, England could not take part because they were not members of FIFA.

In the face of this insular attitude, Hardaker was probably just reflecting the mood of his league masters. The Scottish FA proved much more far-sighted and allowed Hibernian to enter the inaugural European Cup. Indeed, the Scots reached the semi-finals where they lost to Reims who were beaten in the Paris final 4–3 by Real Madrid. The Spanish club came to dominate the first few years of European football.

Sixteen clubs made up the competition in the inaugural

season: Rot-Weiss (Germany), Rapid Vienna (Austria), Anderlecht (Belgium), Servette (Switzerland), Djurgarden (Sweden), Partizan Belgrade (Yugoslavia), Aarhus Forening (Denmark), Stade de Reims (France), Voros Lobogo (Hungary), AC Milan (Italy), FC Saarbrucken (Saar), Gwardia (Poland), Real Madrid (Spain), Hibernian (Scotland), Philips Vereniging (PSV Eindhoven) (Holland), Sporting Club Lisbon (Portugal).

The success of his fellow countrymen from Edinburgh was noted by Matt Busby who, in any case, had a far more visionary feel for football than the administrators. When Manchester United won the League in season 1955–56 and were invited to enter the following season's European Cup, there was a different outcome. Busby persuaded his board of directors that, unlike Chelsea, they should accept the invitation. As the United manager later explained, 'I was very keen on the idea and at one of our board meetings early in May 1956, Harold Hardman the chairman asked me if I thought it wise that the club should go in for the added commitment.

'My reply was, "Well, Mr Chairman, football has become a world game. It no longer belongs exclusively to England, Scotland and the British Isles. This is where the future of the game lies."

'Mr Hardman replied, "All right, if that's what you really feel."

'I said, "Yes, I do. I think we should try it."

'It was at that point that a letter was received from the Football League forbidding us to enter. At our next board meeting I repeated my keenness to take on the challenge and once more proposed that if the Football Association were willing to accept and back us we should enter.'

United met with a much more encouraging response from the FA. The secretary, Stanley Rous, had a broad outlook and ultimately he became Sir Stanley, President of FIFA.

There has long been tension between the two governing

bodies of English football, demonstrated by the fact that the FA has its headquarters in London while the League has stuck to its Lancashire roots. When a move was made from its offices in Preston, it was to St Annes on Sea, near Blackpool. It later returned to Preston.

With the FA encouraging United to go ahead and take part, the decision was finally made at the board meeting on 22 May. Busby commented some years afterwards, 'When I led Manchester United into Europe in 1956 in the face of league opposition, some people called me a visionary, others a reactionary, while a few thought me just plain awkward and stubborn.

'Certainly I was eager to be part of this new European challenge and the reasons were many. There was money to be made for the club, there was a new kind of adrenalin-inducing excitement for the players and there was the opportunity for the spectators to enjoy the skills of continental players. It always seemed to me the logical progression that the champions of England should pit their abilities against the best of Europe. You cannot make progress standing still.

'Looking back now, I can see that our resolve to enter into European competition was a significant milestone in the history of the game,' he declared.

Of course, Matt Busby needed a strong board of directors behind him when he decided to defy authority and he was fortunate to have a chairman small of stature but large of heart in Harold Hardman.

Hardman's contribution has never been properly acknowledged because he preferred to stay in the background unless it was important for him to play a more dominant role. He was to prove an indomitable figure during the crisis of Munich some two years later and he was just as determined as his manager on the issue of entering European football.

He became a director under James Gibson before being

elected chairman and was on the board for a total of fifty years. He was an amateur outside-left in the Everton team that won the FA Cup in 1906 and he had won four amateur caps for England. A solicitor by profession, he had simple Spartan habits, as Jimmy Murphy once recalled. 'We were returning to Old Trafford from an away match when we spotted the chairman standing at a bus stop wearing a pack-a-mac and his inevitable trilby hat in the pouring rain. I asked him why he didn't get a taxi but all he said was that he didn't need one and that the bus was good enough. He added that if it didn't come soon he would probably walk home, a distance of four or five miles! That was the sort of man he was and everyone respected him.'

The chairman was not going to give way on the European issue. The clash caused a strain in relationships between Manchester United and the Football League for years, which showed itself the season after the Munich accident. Because United had suffered such a grievous blow with the air crash on their way home from playing a European Cup tie in Belgrade, UEFA invited them to play in the competition the following season. Their depleted team had finished ninth in the League but as a gesture of sympathy and respect, UEFA extended an 'honorary' invitation to take part along with Wolves, the champions. The organisers no doubt also felt that they were offering practical help with finance; even in those early days European football was a lucrative exercise. United eagerly accepted. They received confirmation from the Football Association that they had no objection but were stunned by a letter from the Football League forbidding entry. Hardaker had not forgiven United for their original act of defiance, and was not going to be beaten a second time. He argued that UEFA were infringing their own rules which set out that the competition was for league champions and holders. United were neither but UEFA were surely entitled to waive their own rules if they so wished.

United appealed to the FA who ruled against the League. This time it was the League who protested and Hardaker insisted that the matter should go to a joint committee of League and FA for a final judgement. The joint commission sided with the league view and United received a letter signed by Stanley Rous as secretary, baldly stating, 'The committee is of the opinion that, as by its name this is a competition of Champion Clubs, Manchester United FC does not qualify to take part in this season's competition. Consent is therefore refused.'

It seemed a churlish decision, as if someone somewhere was determined to cut Manchester United down to size.

United wrote back to the FA pointing out the contradictions but had no alternative to accepting the decision of the consultative committee. The situation was both frustrating and poignant for Busby, the man who had set out to conquer fresh fields only to find that he had led his club and his players into the calamity of Munich. He admitted that he had had to do a lot of heart-searching after the crash, and a few years before he died he said:

The pursuit of the European challenge led down a road that encompassed great glory and terrible tragedy. I need no reminding of the bitter sadness and suffering of Munich. I still grieve for my fine young players who lost their lives.

For a long while the responsibility of urging us down that road to Europe weighed heavily on my mind, but of course no one was to know the catastrophe that lay ahead. Like the rest of life, we just have to do our best and do what seems right at the time.

There was no alternative really in 1956 but to join the rest of Europe. It was inevitable at some stage, with the forces at work that later made this country partners in the Common Market of Europe.

Even after Munich we had to go on, if only out of respect for those who had perished in the cause of Manchester United, and ten years after the accident we had the great satisfaction of becoming the 1968 champions of Europe.

The European path has not been easy in many respects. Different styles of play and culture, varying interpretations of the laws of the game by the referees and, of course, the glittering prizes at stake for success have resulted in some stormy encounters over the years.

We have had our share of controversy, too, especially when we played for the World Club Championship against Estudiantes. Other teams subsequently refused to play the South American teams but that was never my way. Despite all the problems, I always felt that the only way we would reach a better understanding was to continue to meet and play. It's been done at international level competing for the World Cup, and even after the upset of Estudiantes, I was always willing to try again if the opportunity arose.

European football brought us a second horror when Liverpool met Juventus in the final of the 1985 championship. A long history of crowd misbehaviour reached an awful climax in Brussels in the inadequate Heysel Stadium when thirty-nine people died. English clubs paid the penalty with a ban from playing in any European competition.

I don't want to strike too unhappy a note, though, because the European arena has brought pleasure and widened the experience of thousands of football followers. The excitement and electricity that flows at a floodlit evening game between two crack championship teams has an atmosphere and beauty all of its own. To take part in it is a rare privilege and our hopes were high and our hearts were beating faster at the prospect of our baptism in Europe in 1956.

Busby was excited because in his heart he felt he had a team ready to play on a higher level. He was sure of it, but you never really know until the whistle blows and your players are put to the test. He had good cause for quiet confidence, after ten years in which he had shaped a new concept and produced a side in his own image.

The team was tagged by the sportswriters 'the Busby Babes' because it was a side made up mostly of boys who had joined United straight from school. Along with his assistant Jimmy Murphy, Busby had developed them to play in the way he wanted the game to be played. And could they play? Starting in 1955, they were moving swiftly to dominate English football and the margin of successive championship wins in 1956 and 1957 told its own success story – 11 points ahead of Blackpool in 1956, 8 points ahead of Spurs in 1957.

Introducing the new wave of talent took courage because Busby already had a good side. They had won the FA Cup in 1948 and had gone on to win the League in 1952, but the manager had some gems he had been polishing in the reserves and he knew they were ready to sparkle at first-team level. Only skipper Roger Byrne and winger Johnny Berry bridged the four-year gap from the championship side of 1952 to the team that won the League in 1956 with an average age of twenty-two. This was the encouraging background against which the decision to play in Europe was taken and there was swift confirmation that his players were ready for it. The following season as they plunged into Europe to reach the semi-finals, they raced away with the League again and for good measure reached the final of the FA Cup.

Little wonder Matt Busby was excited about Europe and felt ready to take on the English football establishment as well as the continental giants.

2

SIR MATT BUSBY

S IR MATT BUSBY became a legend in his own lifetime as he steered his beloved Red Devils to the summit of Europe. With Sir Matt at the helm, Manchester United became the first English club to win the European Cup when they beat Benfica at Wembley in a pulsating final in 1968. It was the pinnacle of his career and not long after, he brought down the curtain on a distinguished twenty-five-year reign as manager. It was a natural moment for him to choose to step back from the firing line and he moved upstairs to become general manager, then a director and finally the club's first President.

In his time, he had created three great sides – the one that gave him his first honours in his early days of management just after the war, the richly rewarding Busby Babes so sadly destroyed at Munich, and finally the team of the swinging sixties featuring Charlton, Law and Best that delivered him the Championship of Europe. It would have been unreasonable to expect more. Even though his going plunged the club into some managerial disarray, his mind was made up. He no longer had the hard-hearted resolve he knew would be required to break up the team that had completed his life's work.

The team was growing long in the tooth. As individuals they all had more mileage in their tanks but collectively they needed an injection of youthful endeavour. But who to leave out? Sir

Matt couldn't face bringing down the curtain on the careers of Bill Foulkes and Bobby Charlton, two of the crash survivors who had travelled the same bitter road from Munich, or the likes of Pat Crerand, Alex Stepney and Denis Law. By this time they were friends as much as footballers and their manager had become a father figure as well as the boss.

He had nothing left to prove. His warmth of character was reflected in the manner of his retirement. Success didn't spoil him and he retained a modesty and humility, a friendliness and goodness that made him loved as well as admired.

He ended his days as Sir Matt Busby, probably Manchester's most famous citizen, but it was not like that when he first came to the city as a hesitant young footballer. He had humble origins growing up in Bellshill on the outskirts of Glasgow, the son of a miner who was killed in the First World War when Matt was six years old. But for a visa hold up, his mother might have taken him to a new life in America, following his sisters. While they waited, he needed to work and ended up following his father down the pit, a job he needed no encouragement to leave when he was spotted by Manchester City playing for Denny Hibs.

He had a few other offers but Manchester appealed to him, he couldn't explain why, and so he arrived at Maine Road early in 1928 aged seventeen. He was hardly an overnight success; in fact, he struggled to make progress, which may explain why he was always so patient with youngsters, especially those from far away.

Although he made little impact at first, he stuck it out and a fluke change of position from inside-forward to right-half in the reserves seemed to settle him and he established himself in the first team. He played in two FA Cup finals, losing to Everton in 1933, but returning to Wembley the following season to share in a 2–1 win over Portsmouth. One of his team-mates in that era was Alex Herd whose son David he later signed from Arsenal. David Herd was in the Manchester United team that won the Cup against Leicester in 1963.

By 1936, Matt was the captain. After being out of the side for a spell through injury, the chance came for him to go to Liverpool. He felt like a change and so made the move, playing at Anfield until war broke out in 1939. Nearly the whole team joined up. He joined the 9th Battalion of the King's Regiment in Liverpool and was stationed there until he was transferred to the Army Physical Training Corps as a sergeant instructor.

He played a lot of football for army teams, touring with the likes of Joe Mercer. He met Jimmy Murphy in Italy.

At the end of the war, he was still on Liverpool's books and the club wanted him to return as a player and as assistant to the manager, George Kay. But Manchester United had also been attracted by his potential, probably advised by their old scout Louis Rocca who knew everything there was to know about football in the north west. His old fondness for Manchester, where he had brought his young wife Jean to live, swayed the choice and he accepted an offer from chairman James Gibson to become manager of United.

His insistence on a five-year contract, rather than the one for three years he had been offered, gave an early indication of Busby's inner strength and confidence. James Gibson was a man accustomed to getting his own way but he backed down, doubtless recognising in Busby the strength that he was going to need in management.

When Matt first reported to Old Trafford it was to find a bombed and blitzed ground, the offices elsewhere and the team forced to hire Manchester City's ground for matches. The club overdraft was £15,000 and a lot of the senior players were still away in the services. But he was undeterred and set about the job in a revolutionary way by putting on a tracksuit and getting out with his players. Busby was the first of a new breed. His predecessor, Scott Duncan, wore spats and a rose in his buttonhole.

When Busby brought in Jimmy Murphy to look after the reserves, he also set up a youth development policy based on the pre-war MUJACS (Manchester United Junior Athletic Club) which within a few years started to produce a plethora of talented youngsters.

Busby was good with older players, too, and shaped a sound team out of the players he inherited, including Johnny Carey, Henry Cockburn, Jack Rowley, Johnny Morris, Stan Pearson, Allenby Chilton, Joe Walton, Johnny Aston and Jack Crompton. He made some shrewd moves, such as switching Carey and Aston from inside-forwards to full-backs, and demonstrated that he was not afraid to buy when he paid £4,000 to Glasgow Celtic for Jimmy Delaney. The football world were staggered that he should pay what was then a princely sum for a winger whose nickname was 'old brittle bones' because of the frequency of his injuries. But even in those early days he knew what he was doing, and Delaney was the final piece in the jigsaw. Busby won his first trophy when United beat Blackpool 4–2 in the 1948 final of the FA Cup. The team lined up: Crompton, Carey, Aston, Anderson, Chilton, Cockburn, Delaney, Morris, Rowley, Pearson, Mitten.

For years afterwards the match was dubbed the finest ever Cup final. Busby put his stylish stamp on the way the team played and revealed his ability to inspire players in the heat of battle. As his captain, Carey, put it afterwards, 'We were a goal down at half-time but Matt assured us that if we kept playing football we would win. He made us believe in ourselves. He always had the right words for the right time.'

Throughout his career, especially on the European scene, he was to show the same masterly touch. He could also show who

Matt Busby

was the boss. At the start of the following season he was confronted by a players' strike. They wanted some kind of bonus for winning the Cup. Instead of going in for training, they gathered in a coffee house in Manchester. Busby met them and quickly ended what he saw as nonsense. The players all trained the following day. As one of the rebels, Jack Crompton, goalkeeper and later the team trainer, said in later years, 'At the time it was a big test for a comparatively new boss and it was probably only due to his great ability as a manager of men that he was able to bring everyone back on line.

'The following year he transferred Johnny Morris, one of our leading forwards, to Derby County on a point of principle, and to my mind if Johnny had stayed we would have won the Cup again. Naturally, all the players thought the club should have kept him. I thought so, too, at the time, but this is where you live and learn. I can appreciate now that Matt was right to let an unsettled player go and it was this uncanny foresight and judgement, even when it involved an unpopular decision, that kept United at the front in post-war football.'

Busby was definitely on the right track and although they didn't win the Cup the next year, he built on four seasons of finishing runners-up in the League to win the championship in 1952, the first time United had won the league title for forty-one years. They did it with what was to become a typical flourish, beating Arsenal 6–1 in the decisive fixture at the end of the season.

Busby had also managed the Great Britain team at the 1948 Olympics in London, taking them to the semi-finals, and as his stature in the game increased he had received an offer to manage Spurs, which he turned down. There had also been an approach to see if he was interested in coaching the Italian national squad but Matt was planning long-term at Old Trafford and he knew his investment in youth was ready to pay a dividend.

As his championship team began to fade, he started to inject some of his home-produced youngsters into the side, as well as making a few positional changes and filling one or two gaps from the transfer market.

Duncan Edwards, the powerhouse taken as a boy from under the noses of Wolves, much to the annoyance of Stan Cullis, was introduced to the half-back line along with Eddie Colman, the local lad with a delightful shimmy. Roger Byrne had been switched from the wing to left back, and Dennis Viollet, Billy Whelan and David Pegg began to make their mark. Mark Jones and Jackie Blanchflower competed for the centre-half position as the Busby Babes were created, leaving just three positions to be filled by players bought from other clubs.

Johnny Berry had been recruited from Birmingham City to fill the outside-right position while Ray Wood came from Darlington to take over from Jack Crompton in goal. Then, in one of their shrewdest moves, Busby and Murphy persuaded Barnsley to sell them Tommy Taylor for the unusual fee of £29,999, an odd sum agreed by the two clubs in an effort to avoid a round figure of £30,000 and undue publicity. The missing £1 was given to the tea lady at the Oakwell ground in appreciation of her efforts during the negotiations! Taylor quickly justified the time and cash Busby had spent getting him to Old Trafford as he settled at centre-forward for both United and England.

Taylor led an attack with a real cutting edge in front of goal. When they won the League in 1957, they topped the hundred-goal mark. Taylor scored twenty-two to go with a incredible twenty-six from Whelan and sixteen from Viollet. Also thrusting his way forward in that season was yet another youngster. The dashing Bobby Charlton scored ten goals from only fourteen appearances, an auspicious start to a wonderful career.

Busby's team for the 1957 championship mostly lined up:

Wood, Foulkes, Byrne, Colman, Jones, Edwards, Berry, Whelan, Taylor, Viollet and Pegg, with Charlton, Blanchflower and Wilf McGuinness the leading reserves.

The destruction of that team in the Munich air crash was awful to contemplate. It was a long hard road back for Busby. It was three weeks before his wife could tell him about the players who had been killed. It was another two months before he was able to leave the Rechts der Isar Hospital and take the train and boat back home to Manchester.

He arrived still in considerable pain and able to walk only short distances with the aid of two sticks. He was back in time to watch the painfully patched up United play Bolton in the final of the FA Cup after being swept along to Wembley on a tide of emotion. Bolton won as United finally found their true level after playing out of their skins. One can only hazard a guess at Busby's thoughts as he watched the match and remembered the players he had lost, except to say that for a long time after Munich he used to tell friends, 'Sometimes I still see them play.'

Then he faced a different kind of challenge, almost as tough, as he asked himself whether it was right and whether he had the will to start all over again. Jean Busby urged her husband to return to football to honour the memory of those who had died. It wasn't easy, as Matt confessed to David Miller in his book *Father of Football*:

Deep down the sorrow is there all the time. You never really rid yourself of it. It becomes part of you. You might be alone, and it all comes back to you, like a kind of roundabout, and you weep . . . The first time was when I went back to the ground at Old Trafford after the accident. I just looked at the empty field, and in all my life I have never felt such an empty vacuum. And so I cried, and afterwards I felt better for the tears, and because I had forced myself to go back there. It was something I had done, something I'd conquered. The first rung of the ladder . . .

Busby had to fight to regain full physical fitness and it took all his formidable spirit to make it. Jack Crompton, brought back from Luton after the crash to become the first-team coach, described it thus:

I remember driving him to Blackpool and he must have shifted his position in the seat a dozen times a mile to try and get some relief from his injured back. He would also give me his crutches and walk down the corridor to his office door using the walls for support as an exercise. He was so determined to make it.

We all wondered whether he would pick up the threads after his injuries, but knowing him, I believed he would not let things go until he had got the club moving again. I also knew that if he couldn't do it, no one else could.

By 1963 – just five years after the crash – Matt had put together a side good enough to win the FA Cup by beating Leicester City 3–1 at Wembley, even if they did flirt with relegation for a while. Naturally, he had been forced to explore the transfer market more extensively than before with the result that Albert Quixall from Sheffield Wednesday, Noel Cantwell from West Ham, Maurice Setters from West Bromwich Albion, David Herd from Arsenal, Denis Law from Torino and finally Pat Crerand from Glasgow Celtic had been bought.

The success put United back into Europe in the Cup-Winners' Cup which was followed by a season in the Fairs Cup. Then a new wave of youngsters began rolling off the conveyor belt as Nobby Stiles and George Best made their debuts and

Busby's third great team took shape. They were back in the big time with championship wins in 1965 and 1967 and consequently two more seasons in the European Cup building up to the great triumph of becoming European champions in 1968.

Bill Foulkes, Munich survivor, described Busby's moment of joy after beating Benfica at Wembley like this:

> I had come the whole way with the Boss trying to become champions of Europe. I thought the destruction of our team at Munich would have been the end of it, but he patiently put together another team. I'm proud to have been a part of it and for those of us who had lost our friends coming home from a tie in 1958 it seemed the right tribute to their memory.

For Matt Busby the success had given a tragic story new meaning. He had walked through a vale of tears and he embraced each player in turn at the end of an epic 4–1 victory against the Portuguese champions in extra time.

In all, Busby won the league championship on five occasions, he collected the FA Cup twice out of four finals, won the FA Youth Cup six times and then added the crowning glory of Europe. Soon after the European success he was knighted, following the CBE he was awarded in 1959 and the Freedom of Manchester in 1967. Pope Paul VI made him a Knight Commander of St Gregory the Great, one of the highest civil decorations of the Roman Catholic Church.

He took the honours comfortably in his stride and never lost his common touch. He was at ease with humble folk as well as with the famous. His players respected him as a man as well as a manager because his authority was always wielded with courtesy and dignity.

His family was always a source of inspiration to him – his

wife and their two children, Sandy and Sheena – as he freely admitted when he and Lady Jean celebrated their golden wedding in 1981 and he said, 'Jean has been my strength on many occasions in my life. And she is a love, a real love.'

Lady Jean died in December 1988 after a long and trying illness which eventually confined her to a nursing home. Every day Sir Matt was a visitor, and even though, through a mist, he was no longer recognised, his love and loyalty never wavered.

Matt died in January 1994, aged eight-four. Old Trafford was turned into a shrine as the first fans arrived at dawn to lay bouquets on the forecourt beneath the Munich clock memorial. By the end of the day there was a carpet of red and white as admirers of the grand old man of English football came with more and more flowers and to lay their scarves and flags in his memory. One message in particular summed up the feelings of many: 'You planted the seeds that have made Manchester United the greatest team in the world. Rest in peace Sir Matt, you have left us all in safe hands.'

From Europe came a tribute from Lennart Johansson, President of UEFA, who wrote from Berne to say:

Sir Matt was a man of dignity, courage and warmth, who experienced both triumph and tragedy in the service of his club. He will be remembered for having built the wonderful Busby Babes team of the 1950s, and who knows what that team might have achieved in European football but for the Munich air disaster in 1958, which cost so many talented young footballers their lives.

Sir Matt himself was seriously injured in the accident, but it was a mark of his great strength of character that he survived his injuries and returned to the game he loved despite the ordeal he had suffered. Within ten years, Sir Matt had built a second great United team, which went on to win the Champion Clubs' Cup against Benfica on a night of high emotion at Wembley.

This was perhaps Sir Matt's finest hour as a manager. His teams always embodied what is best about football, style, panache and above all entertainment. These attributes made Manchester United loved by millions throughout the world.

After his retirement as a manager, Sir Matt continued to give valuable service not only to United but also to the European Football Union as an advisor and expert. His opinions always deserved the greatest respect. He was, quite simply, a giant of a man.

Those who follow European football with never forget his achievements, and European football will be poorer with his passing. We shall all miss him.

Sir Matt's funeral procession stopped for a few moments beside Old Trafford, which chairman Martin Edwards believes will be a permanent memorial to his achievements as the architect of the Manchester United we know today.

'To gauge the life and work of Sir Matt you have only to look at the magnificent stadium and think back to how it was at the end of the war, bombed and derelict,' he declared.

With the road beside the ground now renamed Sir Matt Busby Way, a huge bronze statue stands outside looking across to his adopted city of Manchester, a fitting tribute to a great man of football.

George Best

Sir Matt Busby became almost a father to me. I must have sorely tried his patience as a young man but he never abandoned me. The older I get, the more I appreciate what he did for me.

He became larger than life but not to himself or to those

closely associated with him. Legendary figures are often disappointing when you come to meet them, especially in football.
But I have never heard anyone who met Sir Matt disagree with
the view that he was an outstanding man. It isn't just the big
things that he did, but the little things that leave an imprint on
another person's life.

When I first went to Old Trafford the young lads all knew
their place. We were part of the family but there was a hierarchy
to be respected. We were encouraged to mix but there was never
any cheeking of the élite players and there weren't any cliques,
at least not until things went wrong at the end.

This great team spirit was Sir Matt's influence and my other
abiding memory of him is his capacity to remember people and
things about them. For instance, the first time my father went
over to Old Trafford to see me play, he brought a couple of his
pals with him. The next time he went to a game he had one of
these friends with him again, and Sir Matt not only remembered
his name but where he was from and what he drank!

One thing he wasn't, though, was soft, despite what many
people thought about him being easy on players, especially me.
I saw players go in to see him, fully determined to demand this
and that and tell him exactly what they felt they were worth.
Time after time they came out with a sheepish smile on their
faces, but not feeling put down. In that respect he was tremendous. You might be called into his office for a dressing down –
it happened to me on numerous occasions – and he would really
get stuck into you. Then just as you were getting up to go he
would wink at you.

That's how he managed to keep everyone so happy. It was
his personality and understanding, and that's why I loved the
guy.

3

A TEAM FOR ALL

N<small>O DOUBT</small> there were some who secretly hoped that Manchester United would come a cropper in Europe after daring to defy the authority of the game's rulers. There was a feeling around at the time, in 1956, that Matt Busby and his club were getting a little too big for their boots and perhaps even the manager and his directors wondered privately if they had bitten off more than they could chew. They were taking a step into unknown territory and judging by the performances of the England national team against foreign opposition, the standard on the Continent was pretty tough. Indeed, there were strong indications that Europe had progressed while English football had largely stood still.

This was the period when our international teams were in the doldrums. Hungary had shocked everyone in 1953 by coming to the home of football and winning 6–3 at Wembley, like soccer creatures from another planet. It was the first time a foreign country had won in England and to show that it had not been a fluke, the Hungarians repeated the medicine with a 7–1 win in Budapest six months later.

This followed the stunning blow at the 1950 World Cup when England failed to get beyond the first-round group games because of 1–0 defeats against Spain and the United States of America of all countries! So Busby and his boys were certainly sticking their necks out. They were confident enough in domestic football after running away with the championship, but nobody was quite sure how they would measure up as they prepared for their debut in the European Cup. The first leg of their opening preliminary round tie against Anderlecht was to be played in Brussels on 12 September 1956.

The Belgian champions were well regarded, even though they were a team made up of amateurs and part-time professionals playing under an English coach. Their key players were Jef Mermans, an attacking goal-scoring forward, the clever right-half Lippens and at left-back the tall slim Culot.

They opened brightly, a piercing run through the middle by Mermans bringing Ray Wood into action. United were unfazed, and put together some sound football. Dennis Viollet's blistering shot after a long run gave the visitors the lead. The second half was closely contested and Anderlecht had the chance of an equaliser when Mark Jones was penalised for hand-ball. Lippens struck the penalty against the post and Wood saved Van den Bosch's shot from the rebound.

Duncan Edwards was missing through injury but his replacement at right-half, Jackie Blanchflower, emerged as the man of the match. His shooting always worried the Belgians; and they had no answer to a fine centre from winger David Pegg which was headed home by Tommy Taylor with a superb and typical leap.

The *Manchester Guardian* writer, Old International, summed up the game:

Among the heroes of United's well-earned victory, Wood must be given the high place. He made three saves of superlative skill and importance. Blanchflower covered himself in glory. Jones, too, rarely put a foot wrong and the Belgian folk must have thought he possessed as many heads as the hydra-headed monster so often did he get in the way.

Colman, in this high pressure football, had scarcely time to air his graces, but he fought gallantly nevertheless. Some of the forward moves tonight were exquisitely pretty; some devastatingly swift; and if Viollet, Taylor and Pegg collected most of the honours, this is not to say that Berry and Whelan, who are a little quieter, played badly. On the whole, it was a triumph of team spirit and a credit to all concerned.

Nowadays a two-goal lead from the away leg would be regarded as such an advantage as to make the return a formality, but as Matt Busby was to comment some years later:

It was a useful start but of course Europe was new to us then and no one was sure whether a 2–0 lead was as commanding as we would regard it now. So we were all keyed up for the return match, and also a little anxious because we, too, were playing away from home. We had to stage the match at Maine Road because Old Trafford did not then have floodlighting.

The conditions were also a little unsettling. It had rained heavily and the pitch was covered in pools of water. We needn't have worried, though. The boys won 10–0, an incredible score which possibly had some people assuming that Anderlecht were a poor side.

But this was no little team from Malta or Iceland. Belgium were a strong soccer nation and Anderlecht were their champions. I have just got to say that we ran up what has to be regarded in football circles as a cricket score because we played darned well.

I was becoming accustomed in those days to seeing a great team playing well, but they excelled themselves that night. It was in fact the finest exhibition of teamwork I had ever seen from any side at either club or international level.

In spite of the score building up, I can still see young Eddie Colman running to collect the ball for a throw-in with only two or three minutes remaining as if we were losing and his life depended upon it. His appetite epitomised the keenness of the whole team that night.

Colman's urgency might have been prompted by the fact that every forward, bar David Pegg, was on the scoresheet and the players were desperate to get the winger on as well. His team-mates wanted a goal for him because he had been the outstanding attacker with a devastating display at outside-left. He had repeatedly turned the opposition defence and had created seven or eight of the chances as Dennis Viollet had helped himself to four goals, Tommy Taylor to three, Billy Whelan to two and Johnny Berry to one.

United broke the backs of the Belgians after nine minutes when Roger Byrne got Pegg away for the winger to find Taylor for a headed goal which on aggregate put United three goals up. Taylor scored again and then Viollet grabbed a hat-trick to establish a 5–0 interval lead.

There was no respite for the Belgians as Taylor, then Colman, Viollet again, Colman and finally Berry produced the spectacular ten-goal result. Anderlecht had passed prettily at times but had been completely crushed. They kept their tempers and their cool, rather as Old International summed up when he concluded his second-leg report: 'Finally, a word of thanks to the losers for their sportsmanship in circumstances which could not fail to be a little wounding to their self-esteem. They received an ovation due to a gallant band of gentlemen.'

Mermans, their captain and a distinguished Belgian international, conceded, 'After United had scored their sixth goal, they still ran as hard as they had at the start. We have played against the best teams of Hungary and Russia and never been beaten like this. Why don't they pick this team for England?' he asked.

The line-up for the historic match in Brussels, with a fit again Edwards replacing Blanchflower, was: Wood, Foulkes, Byrne, Colman, Jones, Edwards, Berry, Whelan, Taylor, Viollet, Pegg.

The Welsh referee, Mervyn Griffiths, joined in the tributes and said, 'I have never seen football more deadly in execution.'

Everyone at Old Trafford, including the supporters, had been thrilled by the quality of the football and the overwhelming scoreline, but the ripples of the victory were far more significant. For a start, the decision to enter the European Cup had been vindicated. The domestic fixtures had been completed on time and there had been no problem involved in a midweek flight abroad. The club had taken Europe in their stride on the field, and there was no possibility of recrimination from the Football League. They had answered all the questions and there were none left for the League to pose.

Even more important perhaps was the feel-good factor that United had brought back for English football after the disappointment of the national team. At last football followers, and not just United fans, had a team to be proud of and worthy of allegiance. This was undoubtedly one of the earliest factors in Manchester United acquiring supporters all over the country. It was a team for all. Those early days in Europe created a special glamour and stature that ensured United became the best known and widest supported club, even during those periods when there was an absence of trophies!

A fuse had been lit and had caught the imagination of the Manchester public. For the next round, a visit from Borussia Dortmund, the crowd at Maine Road zoomed from an already impressive 43,635 to an incredible 75,598.

United opened with the same kind of enthusiasm, especially Viollet, who twice flitted through the German defence to put his team into a 2–0 lead in the first twenty-seven minutes. Pegg forced a third goal past Kwiatowski in the Dortmund goal with the help of a deflection. Although the team never quite acquired the domination of their Anderlecht performance, they nevertheless jumped firmly into the driving seat and at half-time there were expectations of another runaway score.

But German teams are invariably made of stern stuff and sure enough they did not give up. A rare error by Roger Byrne was punished by Kapitulski and then Preissler scored to pull the score back to 3–2. The recovery put the tie back on a knife's edge for the second leg and was a sharp reminder about counting chickens before they were hatched. The players were glad of the support of the national servicemen stationed in the Ruhr who came to cheer them in the second leg. Borussia attempted to run United off their feet but Colman pulled out all the stops and Wood settled quickly to make two important early saves from Kelbassa and Preissler. At the other end, Duncan Edwards, who was playing at inside-left in the absence of Dennis Viollet, laid on a good chance which was muffed by both Taylor and Whelan. Fortunately for the visitors, Borussia were mangling their chances even more regularly. Towards the end of the first half, Mark Jones, Bill Foulkes and Roger Byrne had to use every trick in the defender's armoury to peg back the speedy Germans.

United were lucky to finish the match 0–0 and so go through on the first-leg result of 3–2. As Old International acknowledged:

Here was history repeating itself: the Thin Red Line against the German hosts. Twenty-five minutes still remained for play when Kelbassa missed the sitter of a lifetime in the very jaws of United's goalmouth. After that we felt that even Wotan must be playing for England.

So, after many alarms and excursions, and a spate of

incredible misses by Kelbassa and Preissler, ended a tremendous battle in which only United's perspiring defence came
through with honours. Except in the matter of shooting,
Borussia were easily top dogs.

But if Dortmund had proved a narrow squeak, the next tie
looked like bringing the end of the European road. The quarter-
final draw pitted them against Bilbao in Spain where they slipped
three goals behind by half-time. They clawed back to 3–2 in
a great recovery before an incredible game finished in a 5–3
defeat.

Roger Byrne, the captain, said that the pitch, a swamp following heavy rain and snow, was the worst he had ever experienced.
The Spanish champions went ahead with two goals from Uribe
and, just before the interval, Marcaida scored another. Taylor
and Viollet put United back in the game with goals scored in
the first eight minutes of the second half.

Bilbao restored their three-goal advantage to lead 5–2 but
United roared back again and produced a splendid goal from
Billy Whelan after the Dubliner had beaten three men, dragging
the ball through the slush and mud. It was an inspiring moment
and at least gave United a chance for the second leg, albeit a
tough one.

First, though, they had to get home and when they arrived
at the airport it was to find their Dakota plane covered in ice
and snow after being left out on the runway all night. Nobody
was to know it, but it was an eerie, grim foretaste of the problems
that were to prove so calamitous the following season at Munich.
On this occasion, the players joined the crew brushing off the
snow while Billy Whelan took photographs. United were under
pressure to fly out that night in order to fulfil their Saturday
fixture and avoid a 'we warned you' reaction from the Football
League.

There was even a refuelling scare. A difficult landing at Jersey in a gale threw the plane about before bouncing down to land, leaving Mark Jones in particular scared out of his wits.

Looking ahead to the return at Maine Road, Ferdinand Daucik, the Czech manager of Bilbao, announced that no team ever scored three goals against them. His confidence seemed justified when the German referee twice disallowed United goals for offside. Viollet scored just before the interval but the score wasn't level on aggregate until Taylor struck six minutes from the end. Now quite inspired, Taylor worked the winner for Johnny Berry to put away. United were in the semi-finals against the mighty Real Madrid.

The colourful Henry Rose – like Old International and six other journalists, he was to lose his life at Munich – wrote in the *Daily Express*:

My hands are still trembling as I write. My heart still pounds. And a few hours have passed since, with 65,000 other lucky people, I saw the greatest soccer victory in history, ninety minutes of tremendous thrill and excitement that will live for ever in the memory. Salute to the eleven red-shirted heroes of Manchester United. The whole country is proud of you.

Hammering in my brain almost shattering my senses is the still fresh memory of the spectacle of eleven brave, gallant footballers battering, pounding until they had them on their knees almost crying for mercy, a team of Spaniards ranked as one of the best club teams in the world.

This was another of the games that won friends and admirers for Manchester United in places far removed from the city itself, but when they came up against the holders in the semi-final they found there was still a gulf between the very best of English football and the cream of the Continent. That, of course, was why Busby was so convinced from the start that it was necessary to take up a more global challenge. Real Madrid were in a class of their own with players such as Alfredo Di Stefano, described by Busby as the best he had ever seen, and Gento, their stocky left winger, the fastest Busby had ever seen.

The first leg in the Bernabeu Stadium, watched by 120,000 people, belonged to the men from Madrid. United matched their opponents for an hour but then Rial scored, quickly followed by one from Di Stefano. The always dangerous Taylor pulled one back but the game went 3–1 to the men from Madrid after Mateos had rounded off a sweeping move through the middle.

Bobby Charlton came in for the second leg at Old Trafford, following the installation of floodlighting, and he marked his European debut by scoring the final goal in a 2–2 draw. Whelan was the other scorer for United, and it was a rousing finish, but by the time United had found their way to goal, Real Madrid had scored through Kopa and Mateos.

So Real went through to the final on an aggregate 5–3 victory, and by beating Fiorentina they successfully retained their European crown. From United's point of view, to have drawn level on the night against the top club of that era after being two goals down, stamped them as a team starting to get to grips with the special demands of playing in Europe. As Busby summed up at the end of this first campaign, 'A great, experienced team will always triumph over a great inexperienced one, but our time will come.'

United were encouraged by the general reaction. They received a handsome letter from the Foreign Office following the match in Bilbao for instance, which said their Consul had reported:

As we know only too well, international sport can so often engender bad feeling instead of good. I believe on this occasion

Bobby Charlton

we have every reason to be well content at the conclusion of a British team's visit to a foreign country, and for this happy result, the Manchester United representatives – players and non-players – who by their bearing and behaviour during an arduous visit, proved themselves first-class 'unofficial ambassadors of Britain' must take their full share of the credit.

Retaining their league title meant United qualified for the competition again in 1957–58. They started with another scoring spree, beating Shamrock Rovers 6–0. Billy Whelan was the star in his native Dublin. The preliminary round was completed with a 3–2 victory at Old Trafford, closer than expected thanks to a carefree display by the Irishmen, but at 9–2 an impressive enough aggregate scoreline.

United were in sterner mood for their next tie, a home leg against Dukla Prague which was won decisively 3–0 in front of a 60,000 crowd. Colin Webster, a Welsh international and generally a reserve, scored the opening goal, and he was followed on to the scoresheet by Taylor and David Pegg.

By this time they were acquiring a good understanding of the two-leg system of Europe, and they adopted a defensive approach for the return in Prague. Eddie Colman was outstanding, despite a 1–0 defeat, as they moved through on aggregate 3–1 for a quarter-final home leg against Red Star Belgrade.

The team had been changing with Harry Gregg, bought from Doncaster for £23,500 and still wearing his old joiner's cap as a good luck mascot, now in goal for Ray Wood. More Busby Babes were coming off the assembly line, too. Eighteen-year-old Welshman Kenny Morgans was on the right wing for Johnny Berry, and local lad Albert Scanlon replaced David Pegg on the left for a spell.

Tasic gave the Yugoslavs the lead but Charlton and Colman replied for a 2–1 win which kept the overall tie on a knife's edge. Boosted by a superb performance at Arsenal four days before playing in Belgrade, a match still talked about for the way United took a three-goal lead, lost it but came back to win 5–4, they produced a storming display. They raced into a half-time lead of three goals through Viollet, Charlton and Charlton again. The tie seemed safe but Kostic scored two minutes into the second half, Tasic hit a penalty after being flattened by Bill Foulkes and then three minutes from time Kostic scored from a free kick after Gregg had rolled out of his area with the ball in his arms. Red Star, needing one goal for a replay, had their tails up and went hell for leather but United hung on for a 3–3 draw and a 5–4 aggregate victory which put them into the semi-finals for the second successive season.

Tragically, that team was never to play again, decimated by the crash at Munich on the way home, and the semi-final against AC Milan had to be tackled by a much different side as the Reds fought to recover from the disaster.

The line-up against Red Star in Belgrade was: Gregg, Foulkes, Byrne, Colman, Jones, Edwards, Morgans, Charlton, Taylor, Viollet, Scanlon.

Jackie Blanchflower was a spectator at this last fateful match before the accident. He lost his place after dropping out to play for Northern Ireland in a World Cup qualifier. The trip cost him dearly. His injuries included a fractured pelvis and badly mangled arm. They were so severe that he never played again. He looks back . . .

Jackie Blanchflower

I played in the reserves against Barnsley just before the Belgrade trip and I think we had nine internationals in the team. The quality of the squad and the depth of it was frightening. But for the accident, I think Manchester United would have gone on to dominate European football like Real Madrid did for many years and Benfica after them.

I also believe that England with Tommy Taylor, Roger Byrne and Duncan Edwards would have won the 1958 World Cup. Taylor had just scored a hat-trick against Brazil and was destined for great things internationally. If all those players who were killed and injured had been spared, the course of football history would have been very different.

The quarter-final against Red Star illustrated the power of the club, which was just getting into its European stride. It was such a young team, but learning so fast. We had won the first leg in Manchester 2–1 with goals from Eddie Colman and Bobby Charlton. One goal was not a big advantage to take away, but the mood of the players was one of confidence. They had just beaten Arsenal 5–4 at Highbury while I was losing 6–5 in the reserves against Barnsley. We always felt we could go up a gear if it was necessary.

I remember it was a pea-souper on the day we were flying out and I thought we would never get off but the fog cleared. It was Bobby Charlton's first European trip and he had been kidded about the shortage of food in Eastern Europe. He packed his suitcase with biscuits and sweets.

He might have been a kid but there was nothing of the novice about him once the game had begun on a freezing cold day. We made a great start with Tommy Taylor forcing an early error for Dennis Viollet to score after only a couple of minutes.

I recall Sekularac as a danger, a busy little man who also chopped people. He got Kenny Morgans high on the thigh, but Charlton was the star of the show. He scored with the kind of rocket that was to become his speciality, and he also nicked in another to give us a three-goal lead and a 5–1 advantage on aggregate.

It looked as good as over, except of course Red Star were a

great team as well and they got back into it with a goal from Kostic, a penalty and a free kick from just outside the box. The match ended 3–3 but we were safe at 5–4 and celebrating a semi-final appearance for the second year running. It was the last match for so many, a long time ago now, but not so easy to forget for those of us still bearing the scars.

4

THE BUSBY BABES

M ATT BUSBY was creating a team in his own image when he embarked on the youth policy that produced the legendary Busby Babes. He had this idea that if he could get hold of footballers young enough, he could bring them up to play the game the way he wanted. He gave priority to the finding the raw material, setting up scouts in the two Irelands, Wales and Scotland with instructions to pick out the likely lads while they were still at school and then bring the best to Old Trafford.

He appointed as his chief scout the avuncular, rosy cheeked Joe Armstrong who was not only a shrewd judge of a player but had a genuine interest in the welfare of the boys he wanted to bring to Manchester United. Billy Behan in the Republic of Ireland, Bob Bishop in Northern Ireland, and all the other scouts, were people capable of winning the trust of parents. In those early days, many of the youngsters had never been out of their hometown before, let alone crossed the Irish Sea to a far away place like Manchester.

This emphasis on the well-being of the boys is still a keynote of the policy. Under the present-day regime of Alex Ferguson, their Academy has been expanded to include an education officer, a chaplain and all kinds of welfare advice from dietitian to chiropodist.

In Busby's early days, it was pioneering stuff. When the

youngsters first started their training, they soon came under the eye of Jimmy Murphy who was another great believer in catching 'em young. One of his favourite sayings was that out of little acorns grow big oak trees, and their early work bore fruit when their junior teams won the FA Youth Cup for five successive years from its inception in 1953.

Those boys grew stronger until suddenly, over the course of a couple of seasons, they began to flood into the senior team with such dramatic effect that they were tagged the Busby Babes, not an expression welcomed by Busby but nevertheless one which caught the imagination of the fans.

By the time of the Munich crash in February 1958, the Babes had virtually taken over the first team with more jostling for places in the reserves. There was one little acorn who had grown into a massive oak to become the apple of Jimmy Murphy's eye. Duncan Edwards, who died from his injuries fifteen days after the crash, had a massive physique and a talent to match. He was the giant of the team that led English football into Europe and made such a tremendous impact on the domestic game. Until the day Jimmy Murphy died he used to talk about the player like a lost son, and his eyes would glisten with tears as he told how he could still see the boy leaping into the air as he ran out for the start of matches. As he once put it:

Duncan was the Kohinoor diamond among our crown jewels, the greatest of them all. If I shut my eyes I can see him. Those pants hitched up, the wild leaps of boyish enthusiasm as he came out of the tunnel, the tremendous power of his tackle – always fair, but fearsome – the immense power on the ball.

In fact, the number of times he was robbed of the ball once he had it at his feet could be counted on one hand. He was a players' player. Ask Bobby Charlton and he will tell you Duncan was the greatest. When I hear Muhammad Ali proclaim on television and radio that he is the greatest, I have to smile, because there was only ever one and that was Duncan Edwards.

Any manager lucky enough to have him had half a team and that is why, when I heard the sad news of his death on the morning of Friday, 21 February 1958, I broke down and cried. The club and England had lost a great footballer and I had lost a friend, a very dear friend.

From the first time I saw him as a boy of fourteen, he looked like and played with the assurance of a man with legs like tree trunks, a deep and powerful chest and an unforgettable zest for the game. He played wing-half, centre-half, centre-forward and inside-forward with the consummate ease of a great player. He was never bothered where he played. He was quite simply a soccer colossus.

It's difficult to visualise the honours that could have come Duncan Edwards' way if he had been spared to play a normal span in the game. His achievements by the age of twenty-one were already phenomenal.

He was a natural for the FA Youth Cup and played in it for three seasons, including the first year of the competition, 1952–53, when United beat Wolves 9–3 in the final over two legs. No wonder Wolves boss Stan Cullis was cross about failing to sign him – he lived just down the road from Molineux at Dudley. Edwards rubbed more salt into the wound in the following year's final, scoring two goals against Wolves who lost again, this time 4–5 on aggregate. By the time of his third year, he was well established in the first team but there was nothing he liked better than to play with his contemporaries and he was again outstanding in a 7–1 win over two legs against West Bromwich Albion, another Midlands club.

Despite the fact that Wolves were a top club in that era, Cullis never had a chance of signing Edwards. The schoolboy had made up his mind that Old Trafford was the place he wanted to be. There was a last-minute scare when United heard a rumour that a rival club were planning to move in. United coach Bert Whalley drove through the night to the Edwards home and knocked the family up in the early hours. Duncan came down in his pyjamas.

'What's all the fuss about?' he said. 'I've already said Manchester United are the only club I want to join.'

He duly signed on the dotted line, and he developed quickly to become United's youngest ever first-team player when he made his debut against Cardiff City at Old Trafford on 4 April 1953 at the age of sixteen years and 185 days. The game was lost 4–1 and he didn't play again that season but it was a start and there was no holding him the following season when Busby unveiled the full extent of his precocious Busby Babes.

Edwards won championship medals in 1956 and 1957, played in the 1957 FA Cup final and impressed in Europe. On the international front, he was the youngest to play for England when in April 1955, at the age of eighteen years and eight months, he was given his first cap, against Scotland at Wembley. It was an auspicious debut. He shared in a 7–2 victory and his performance was such that he went on to make eighteen international appearances after captaining the England schoolboy team and the Under-23 team. He was the obvious choice to follow Billy Wright as a senior captain, but it was not to be.

Everyone who knew him speaks of his unassuming nature, his modesty, his shyness and the easy way he handled his early acclaim. It's clear he had the temperament and character as well as the talent to sustain a career, and his loss was England's as well as United's.

But the excitement that surrounded the Babes was not centred on just one person. The beauty of the team was that it was exciting in every department, especially up front with a free-scoring forward line led by Tommy Taylor and featuring two brilliant inside-forwards, Dennis Viollet and Billy Whelan.

Viollet was a local boy born in the shadow of Manchester City's ground but he always had wide horizons. Indeed, he has spent much of his life in the United States. He survived Munich with relatively light injuries and he played again before the end of the season. The ghastly experience did nothing to blunt a sharp sense of humour and a jaunty approach to life. Those players who knew him before and after the crash say that afterwards he seemed to be even more determined to squeeze the last drop out of life. As fellow 'Busby Babe' John Doherty, who grew up with him at Old Trafford, put it, 'The effect of Munich on his life was that he mustn't waste a minute of what was left.' Tending to live in the fast lane was not conducive to married life and his first marriage broke up, but he married again and lived very happily in the States, where he died in 1999.

One can never be certain if Munich took anything away from Dennis Viollet as a player. A mere two England caps suggests he did not fulfil his early career promise as a schoolboy inter-national and captain of Manchester Boys. He certainly made a dashing start in senior football. His silky, sharp and stealthy approach made him a perfect foil for Tommy Taylor in the swashbuckling attack, but Munich took Taylor's life and per-haps at the very top level something went from Viollet's game. Nevertheless, two seasons after Munich, as part of an attack featuring Bobby Charlton, Alex Dawson and Albert Quixall, he scored thirty-two league goals from just thirty-six appearances, a club record which still stands today.

It makes you wonder what he would have gone on to achieve with a maturing Taylor by his side, for United and perhaps England. Perhaps the selectors were put off by his seemingly slight physique. Thin faced and slim, he never appeared to have the strength for a robust game but there was steel in that wiry frame and he had an electric burst of speed to go with an astute mind, good timing and instinctive vision.

In league and cup competitions, Dennis made 291 appearances for United and scored 178 goals. He left Old Trafford to play nearly 200 games for Tony Waddington at Stoke City, had a spell with Linfield in Northern Ireland and played for Ken Barnes when his great Manchester City friend was manager of non-league Witton Albion. He enjoyed brief coaching spells at Preston and Crewe before joining the fashionable exodus to America where he numbered Baltimore Bays, the Washington Diplomats and Richmond, Virginia among his clubs. He also coached university soccer at Jacksonville in Florida where he finally settled.

His scoring record for United still speaks for itself, and his former playing colleagues have nothing but admiration for his prowess. Doherty went on to say, 'He would always be in my all-time best United eleven. The lack of caps was an insult.'

Liam – or Billy as he became in England – Whelan joined as a shy eighteen year old from Home Farm in Dublin, a club which practically became a nursery for United. He soon made his debut and in season 1956–57, when United won the second successive championship, he was the team's top scorer with twenty-six league goals, even more than Tommy Taylor. In all he chalked up seventy-nine league appearances and scored forty-three goals. Harry Gregg remembers his poignant last words as the plane tried fruitlessly to get off the slush-covered runway at Munich. Always religious and reported at one point to be considering training as a priest, Billy said, seconds before the end, 'If the worst happens, I am ready for death. I hope we all are.'

Naturally, forwards thrive on good service, be it from midfield or from the flanks and Busby always set great store by fast, penetrating wingers. The first player he ever signed was Jimmy Delaney, ignoring the fact that the Scot was already thirty-two because he knew he was speedy, direct and could shoot. He also went into the transfer market to find a successor for Delaney when he bought Johnny Berry from Birmingham City for £25,000 in 1951.

Berry, who had always impressed playing against United, took over from Delaney at outside-right and contributed a touch of experience as the first wave of Busby Babes reached the team. He was a regular until he also felt the impact of the youth explosion with the emergence just before Munich of Kenny Morgans, an eighteen-year-old Welsh Babe from Swansea. Morgans was a crash survivor but afterwards never fulfilled his potential, perhaps the result of his terrifying experience. He played at a lower level back home in Wales where he still lives.

Berry suffered badly in the crash with head injuries which affected his personality and he never played again. He returned to his native Aldershot where he had a sports shop with his brother for a number of years before his death in 1994.

When Charlie Mitten, he of the sweet left foot, defected to South America to play for Bogota, a succession of players including Roger Byrne, Jack Rowley and Harry McShane all did duty at outside-left, but then the youth programme produced two brilliant young challengers for the position.

David Pegg had joined from Doncaster Technical School after playing for Yorkshire Boys and in a junior international match at Oldham. He made his first-team debut at the age of seventeen and had made 127 senior appearances before his death at Munich at the age of twenty-two.

He had already played for England at a time when the wing positions were dominated by Stanley Matthews and Tom Finney, but like so many of the other Babes, his best was undoubtedly still to come.

Even so, he had a major rival at Old Trafford with the emergence of Albert Scanlon, a local boy who had starred in the
FA Youth Cup victories of 1953 and 1954 before making his
league debut as another talented seventeen year old. Nicknamed
Joe Friday after the cool detective in the television series *Drag-
net*, he recovered from a fractured skull sustained in the crash
to play again, but the spark was missing. He moved first to
Newcastle and then to Lincoln and Mansfield before returning
to the Manchester area where he had a succession of jobs in a
bakery, as a docker on Salford docks and then as a security
guard.

The attack wasn't entirely made up by Busby Babes. In the
middle was Tommy Taylor, the dashing centre-forward signed
from Barnsley for £29,999. The manager had set out to nurture
his own players but he did not allow his policy to blind him to
weaknesses and he knew he didn't have anyone ready to lead
his attack following the great days of Jack 'Gunner' Rowley. He
had his youngsters in plenty of other positions but he needed a
strong centre-forward to make the most of them.

Busby listened to Jimmy Murphy, who used to reckon that
he must have worn a path across the Pennines going to watch
Taylor play in Yorkshire. He wasn't alone, as Murphy explained:

I should imagine that Big Tommy was one of the most sought-
after players of all time. The more I saw of him, the more I
realised that he was a must for us.

He was a superb mover, a man who possessed a grace and
athleticism not normally found in tall men. He could crack a
ball with either foot and when it came to heading you could
put him alongside Tommy Lawton and Nat Lofthouse. Of
the centre-forwards at that time, probably only John Charles
could climb higher.

From the very start we were in for this boy with his mop

of black hair and the perpetual smile which caused one sports-writer to christen him 'The Smiling Executioner'.

There were twenty other league clubs interested in Taylor when Barnsley finally decided to sell their twenty-one-year-old York-shireman in 1953, and despite his reluctance to leave his home-town, United were always favourites to get him. He settled quickly, but Henry Rose wrote: 'If Tommy Taylor is England's best centre-forward then I'm Father Christmas.' The contro-versial *Daily Express* writer had to eat his words the following week after Taylor had starred in an international. Rose did so graciously at the next United match, acknowledging the crowd's good-natured jeers by standing up in the press box and raising his Homburg to them.

Journalist and footballer, both perished at Munich, Taylor aged twenty-six after playing 166 league games for United with a return of 112 goals. For England he had scored sixteen goals in nineteen appearances. The football world had lain at his feet.

Taylor was arguably even more effective in European combat as Jimmy Murphy claimed when he said:

He played some of his best games in the European Cup and one of them was the second leg against Bilbao when we had to come back from a 3–5 defeat in Spain. We had to score three goals in Manchester to win. By half-time only Dennis Viollet had scored. I was sitting with Matt surrounded by a pile of half-smoked cigarettes when, in the seventieth minute, Tommy pivoted like a ballet dancer round Jesus Garay, one of the best centre-halves in Europe, to smash a shot into the roof of the net.

Now we were level on aggregate and nerves were jangling like mad when Tommy hit the post and the Spaniards just managed to scramble the ball away. Five minutes from the

Tommy Taylor

end, with his hair streaming in the wind, he raced out wide to the right wing. He sped past Garay and was lining himself up for an angled shot at goal when he paused and then casually flicked a pass into the middle for Johnny Berry to score.

Although a lethal finisher himself, he was completely unselfish, as became even more evident when a youthful Bobby Charlton came into the side and he nursed him along like a veteran.

Only John Berry and skipper Roger Byrne from the 1952 championship-winning side had held their places to play in Europe. Bill Foulkes had become a regular at right-back and by the time of the crash, Wood had given way to Harry Gregg, signed from Doncaster, but there seemed no end to the talented youngsters streaming off the assembly line for other positions.

Eddie Colman from Archie Street, Salford, had such a cheeky young face that at one match at Blackpool the doorman wouldn't let him through the players' entrance and directed him to the kids' turnstile. He was often described as having snake-hips and he certainly had a brilliant body swerve developed in three FA Youth Cup-winning teams. He made his senior debut and won a championship medal in season 1955–56. He died at the age of twenty-one after playing 107 games for United.

There were so many Babes they couldn't all get into the team. John Doherty, another local boy and a skilful inside-forward who played in the successful youth teams, had moved on to Leicester by the time of the crash. The powerful Mark Jones from just outside Barnsley competed with Jackie Blanchflower for the centre-half position. Mark was killed with 127 league appearances to his name while Jackie, a Northern Ireland international like his brother Danny, was so badly injured he never played again and had to be satisfied with 116 outings made over five seasons.

Geoff Bent from Swinton was on the trip and perished. Such was the competition for places that while he would have walked into the first team at most clubs, he had made only twelve league appearances.

Bobby Charlton was the last of the youngsters to force his way into the reckoning before the team was decimated at Munich. Bobby, of course, survived and became a major player at Old Trafford with the kind of long and illustrious career tragically denied to so many of his friends and team-mates.

Leading all these exciting youngsters to their league successes and into Europe was the captain, Roger Byrne, almost a veteran by their standards. Born in Gorton, he went to Burnage grammar school and had done two years National Service in the RAF before joining United as an outside-left. Converted to full-back by Busby, he played 246 league games for United and won thirty-three England caps before Munich claimed him at the age of twenty-eight. His wife, Joy, was waiting at home to tell him that he was to become a father. He was a natural skipper for the young side, respected and admired, and his influence on the Babes was incalculable.

As Albert Scanlon puts it, 'The man I admired most at United was Roger Byrne. I had always been a little afraid of our previous captain, Johnny Carey, and I never spoke to him unless he spoke to me. It was quite different with dear old Roger. Although he was just as much a gentleman, we always felt that Roger understood us as well as he understood football. One of the things that I think is wrong with football today is that there doesn't seem to be discipline and respect commanded by men like Roger.'

The football world had been astonished when Busby broke up his successful post-war side but the manager knew the prodigious talent he had waiting in the wings. He had sowed and he was ready to reap. The result was a marvellously gifted team that will forever occupy an important place in the history of Manchester United. The tragedy was that they played together so briefly.

5
MUNICH

THE FOOTBALL WORLD lay at the feet of Busby's Bravehearts as they readied themselves for the journey home from Belgrade. They had resisted a terrific onslaught from Red Star to come out with a 3–3 draw, good enough on aggregate to take them through to the semi-finals of the European Cup.

They also had high hopes of retaining their championship, especially after thrilling everyone with their 5–4 victory at Arsenal prior to flying to Yugoslavia. So no sooner had they quietly celebrated their progress in Europe with a few drinks after the match than thoughts were turning to their challenge in the League and Saturday's match against title rivals Wolves.

They had everything to play for, everything to live for, as their Elizabethan aircraft headed for home and the fateful refuelling stop at Munich. Where they chose to sit on the plane largely dictated whether they lived or died. They landed in a snowstorm and hurried quickly into the terminal building for tea and coffee. The refuelling did not take long and they were soon back on the plane, ready for take-off and the flight home.

The airfield was covered in snow and all the survivors spoke afterwards about the slush on the runway. Later there would be a big debate about ice on the wings but in the meantime at 14.19 hours, Captain Ken Rayment, the pilot for the flight, with Captain James Thain the Commander sitting alongside him, requested permission to taxi out for take-off. At 14.30 Radio Officer Bill Rodgers told the control tower that 609 Zulu Uniform was rolling and a horrific drama had begun.

Some forty seconds later the plane pulled up. The pilots were concerned that the engines were giving out an uneven note. Power surging was not uncommon with Elizabethans and apparently the pilots were not unduly worried. They requested permission for a second attempt. Another charge down the runway began but again Captain Thain abandoned the take-off after thundering half its length. He was not satisfied with the pressure reading from the port engine.

The aircraft returned to the terminal building and the passengers went into the lounge while the pilots conferred with the station engineer, William Black. The question of an overnight stop cropped up but no one really wanted that kind of inconvenience and everyone trooped out for a third attempt. Alf Clarke, the *Manchester Evening Chronicle* reporter, was nearly left behind because he had been on the phone to his office with the story of the delay. He dashed out just in time and at 14.56 the plane taxied out to the runway. At 15.03.06, Zulu Uniform started a third attempt to take off and this time there was no pulling up.

Frank Taylor, the only football writer to survive, described graphically what happened next in his book *The Day a Team Died*. He wrote:

Suddenly, there was a thunderous roar as the engines burst into life. I listened intently. Not a cough or a splutter, as the motors throbbed louder and louder, until they had reached their familiar high-pitched whine . . . then we started to move.

Slowly at first, then faster and faster, racing down the runway like a high-powered car . . . 70 knots, 80 . . . 100 knots an hour.

Those were the figures which flashed before the expert eyes of Commander James Thain as he monitored his instruments. He saw the needle reach 117, then as he told the official German inquiry into the accident . . . the needle inexplicably dropped back to 105 . . . What the hell had gone wrong again? For the first time on that fateful run, he allowed his eyes to look up from his instruments and realised the aircraft was running out of runway! In that nerve-shattering split second he heard his co-pilot, Captain Ken Rayment, cry out, 'Christ . . . we're not going to make it.'

By this time, even we passengers realised something had gone drastically wrong. Peter Howard (*Daily Mail* photographer) says he thought he heard the starboard engine make a noise like a car changing gear. Harry Gregg had the same impression. Sitting as I was on the other side of the aeroplane from these two, I didn't notice any change in the note of the engine. But I was now becoming slightly alarmed at the huge wave of slush being thrown backwards by the port wheel, as we ploughed along that runway. We zipped past a red building away to my right, which I remember quite clearly because of its prominent colour, and the fact that on our two previous runs, we had slowed and stopped almost opposite this landmark.

I was sure we had already gone past the point of no return, although it was quite impossible, because of that wave of brownish slush, to make out whether or not the wheels had actually left the ground.

My heart froze when I saw the perimeter fence rushing towards us. Like Ken Rayment, I knew in that chilling split second that we were not going to make it. I felt the machine suddenly lurch off the concrete runway to the right, on to the grass, with the landing lights flashing by. I felt a sickening blow behind the left ear . . . and I could feel my senses slipping away.

Then there was a horrendous bang, and in my dazed state I thought I saw the port wheel crashing through a crumpled fuselage. The bulkhead behind me was caving in, with cases and other items of luggage hurtling around in the cabin.

There was a kind of green haze sweeping up in front of my eyes, like a huge tidal wave engulfing me. Everything was becoming hazy, even though I kept shaking my head in a desperate attempt to stay conscious; I was like a drowning man fighting to keep his head above water. I had never been knocked out in my life, and I was fighting against that awful feeling of just fading into oblivion.

This couldn't be happening to me. This was crazy. I could hear, as though far away in the distance, a tremendous rending and grinding of metal, and it was only when the airliner started to buck like a wild thing that I realised it was our aeroplane which was being ripped apart, as it slid helplessly along the ground. There was a tremendous hammering on the fuselage near my head, as though a giant was getting to work with a sledgehammer . . . Then mercifully my eyes closed.

A wing of the plane hit an isolated house, setting it on fire, but Mrs Anna Winkler and her children miraculously escaped unhurt. Then came an impact with a hut and a truck carrying fuel which exploded as the rear section of the fuselage was torn off and was caught up in the fire. Journalists travelling with football teams invariably sit at the back to leave the main section free for the players. Those at the back on this occasion had little chance.

Frank Taylor was the one sportswriter who was sitting further to the front, and although he was seriously injured, his freak decision undoubtedly saved his life. Fate worked the other way for David Pegg who had been sitting towards the front in a card school until suddenly announcing before the third attempt to take off that he was going to the rear because he felt it was safer there. David died but the card school he left, Bill Foulkes, Kenny Morgans and Albert Scanlon, all survived.

Meanwhile, the front half of the plane careered on, now spinning wildly and throwing out several of the passengers through the gaping hole where it had been ripped in two. Others were trapped inside. Matt Busby was one of those flung out on to the snow.

Goalkeeper Harry Gregg was one of the first to stumble from the wreckage and as he stood bewildered he was ordered to run clear by Captain Thain who feared an explosion. But the United goalkeeper had heard the cry of a baby and plunged straight back in to bring out twenty-two-month-old Vesna Lukic, daughter of the Yugoslavian air attaché in London, travelling with her mother courtesy of a lift on United's charter plane. Moments later the player went back into the plane to rescue Mrs Vera Lukic.

The people involved all talk about Captain Thain going back to the flight deck for the portable fire extinguisher to put out a blaze in one of the engines, promising to return for his friend and co-pilot, Ken Rayment, whose feet were trapped and who had received what proved to be a fatal blow on the head from a tree which had smashed through the cockpit.

Peter Howard and Ted Ellyard were also heroes who risked the plane going up in flames to free Ray Wood and Albert Scanlon who had been trapped in the tangled mess inside. Then they pulled Frank Taylor clear and as Frank himself says in his book, it couldn't have been a pretty sight. He writes:

The left side of my head had been sliced open, creating a wound which eventually needed twenty-one stitches; I was breathing with difficulty as a result of a double fracture of the collar bone and nine broken ribs; my left arm hung helplessly from a smashed elbow joint; and my right leg above the ankle was crushed, with the foot bent backwards to expose the broken tibia and fibula protruding through the dark grey cloth of the trouser leg. As gently as they could, they pulled me outside the aircraft. Howard was trying to comfort me, but I just stared at them without saying a word.

My senses had flown, so I do not know who put me on the stretcher, but I do remember quite clearly trying to sit up on it, and Harry Gregg coming over to push me gently in the chest. 'Don't worry Frank, you are going to be all right,' he said.

With great presence of mind, Harry Gregg used his tie as a tourniquet to put round Jackie Blanchflower's mangled arm which was bleeding badly. Kenny Morgans, trapped under a wheel, was freed by Peter Howard and Radio Officer George Rodgers, who, along with Harry Gregg, Ted Ellyard and the stewardesses, Margaret Bellis and Rosemary Cheverton, ignored the dangers to help their fellow passengers.

Bill Foulkes recalls seeing Matt Busby trying to sit up after he had been flung out of the plane. 'I remember kneeling down by the Boss, and he kept saying, "it's my side, it's my side." I wrapped him in my jacket and sat holding his hand. Then suddenly Bobby Charlton [who was lying nearby] woke up, as if he had just been enjoying a nap, and without a word walked over to us, took off his jacket, and put it underneath the Boss, who was lying in the slush.'

The survivors were rushed to the Rechts der Isar Hospital in Munich and into the care of a highly organised and expert medical team headed by Professor Georg Maurer, the Chief Surgeon, who had planned for just such an emergency. The Professor knew all about major disasters from his previous life as a doctor under fire. He was awarded the Iron Cross for his work on the beaches of Dunkirk during the war. Critically injured survivors, including Matt Busby and Frank Taylor, all subsequently paid tribute to the skill and care of the doctors and nurses, especially Herr Professor Kessel, Herr Professor Thysinger, Herr Doktor Lechner, Frau Doktor Schmidt and Frau Doktor Jacques. As Frank Taylor puts it, 'Professor Maurer and his Angels of Mercy set to work.'

Frank Swift died almost as soon as they got him to hospital. Captain Rayment was in a coma from his fearful head injury and never came out of it before he died. The football world held its breath while Duncan Edwards fought bravely, kept alive on a kidney machine flown to the hospital, but he didn't make it either. He died fifteen days after the accident on 21 February, but not before he had asked Jimmy Murphy, 'What time is the kick-off against Wolves on Saturday, Jim? I mustn't miss that match.'

Harry Gregg and Bill Foulkes both played in United's next match. Bobby Charlton came back into the side after a short break, Dennis Viollet just in time for the Cup final. Albert Scanlon returned the following season.

The bodies of the unlucky ones were flown home. Some of the coffins were put into the gymnasium at Old Trafford. Jimmy Murphy attended every one of what seemed to be a never-ending series of funerals.

Of the forty-three people on board the Lord Burghley, twenty-three died either in the crash or soon afterwards as a result of their injuries: players Roger Byrne, Geoff Bent, Eddie Colman, Mark Jones, David Pegg, Tommy Taylor, Liam (Billy) Whelan and Duncan Edwards; officials Walter Crickmer (secretary), Tom Curry (trainer) and Bert Whalley (coach); journalists Alf Clarke (*Evening Chronicle*), Don Davies (*Guardian*), George Follows (*Daily Herald*), Tom Jackson (*Manchester Evening News*), Archie Ledbrooke (*Daily Mirror*), Henry Rose (*Daily Express*), Frank Swift (*News of the World*) and Eric Thompson (*Daily Mail*); crew Captain K. G. Rayment (co-pilot) and W. T. Cable (steward); and B. P. Miklos (travel agent) and Willie Satinoff (United supporter). The survivors were Matt Busby; players Johnny Berry, Jackie Blanchflower, Bobby Charlton, Bill Foulkes, Harry Gregg, Kenny Morgans, Albert Scanlon, Dennis Viollet and Ray Wood; journalists Ted Ellyard and Peter Howard (*Daily Mail* photographers) and Frank Taylor (*News Chronicle*); crew Captain James Thain (pilot), George Rodgers (radio officer), Margaret Bellis and Rosemary Cheverton (stewardesses); and Mrs Vera Lukic and baby Vesna, Mrs Miklos and N. Tomasevic.

Jimmy Murphy hardly knew which way to turn as he faced the most appalling of burdens. His friends the coaches Bert Whalley and Tom Curry had been killed, and the administrative heart had been ripped out of the club with the death of the long-serving and dedicated secretary, Walter Crickmer. He had no team and Matt Busby lay terribly ill in hospital.

The nightmare task of bringing some order out of the chaos fell to him and he grappled with the problems not just of raising a team but of coping with the anxieties of relatives, going to funerals, meeting the demands of the media and coming to terms with his own immense grief. Supporters gathered outside Old Trafford, waiting for news or perhaps simply hoping for some miracle.

With the death of Walter Crickmer, who had been with the club from 1919 and secretary from 1926, Les Olive had to take on the role of secretary. Les was a young man who had joined as office boy and a player for the Colts team. Later he was officially appointed secretary until his retirement in 1988 and subsequent election to the board of directors, but it was a tremendous responsibility to thrust on to young shoulders. He rose to the occasion and helped steer the club through the most exacting period of its history.

Tony Stratton Smith, a sportswriter with the *Daily Sketch*, captured the mood of the time when he wrote, 'At Old Trafford, dozens of people on the car park, just waiting and among them many young faces begging to be told it wasn't true. Inside, Les Olive, a still, pale mask beneath his reddish hair, standing beside a mound of telegrams, coping manfully, because all the men had gone.'

Jimmy also turned for help to Jack Crompton, United's goalkeeper in the 1948 FA Cup final who had joined Luton as trainer in 1956. He readily accepted the invitation to return to help in the emergency, and became a key figure at Old Trafford for many years.

The chairman, Harold Hardman, had quickly grasped the situation and made it clear that Manchester United had no intention of surrendering to the calamity that had overtaken them. Saturday's match against Wolves was called off, but they were back in business on 19 February playing their postponed FA Cup fifth-round tie against Sheffield Wednesday and three days later on the Saturday they faced Nottingham Forest at Old Trafford. They drew 1–1 with a goal from Alex Dawson, but the real significance was the message from the chairman printed on the front page of the *United Review* programme. Under a headline 'United will go on', Harold Hardman wrote:

On 6th February 1958 an aircraft returning from Belgrade crashed at Munich Airport. Of the 21 passengers who died 12 were players and officials of the Manchester United Football Club. Many others still lie injured.

It is the sad duty of we who serve United to offer the bereaved our heartfelt sympathy and condolences. Here is a tragedy which will sadden us for years to come, but in this we are not alone. An unprecedented blow to British football has touched the hearts of millions and we express our deep gratitude to the many who have sent messages of sympathy and floral tributes. Wherever football is played United is mourned, but we rejoice that many of our party have been spared and wish them a speedy and complete recovery.

Words are inadequate to describe our thanks and appreciation of the truly magnificent work of the surgeons and nurses of the Rechts der Isar Hospital at Munich. But for their superb skill and deep compassion our casualties must have been greater. To Professor Georg Maurer, Chief Surgeon, we offer our eternal gratitude.

Although we mourn our dead and grieve for our wounded we believe that great days are not done for us. The sympathy and encouragement of the football world and particularly of our supporters will fortify and inspire us. The road back may be long and hard but with the memory of those who died at Munich, of their stirring achievements and wonderful sportsmanship ever with us, Manchester United will rise again.

United had paid a heavy price in pursuit of their European dream but from the heart-searching and the agonising sprang a commitment and determination to ensure that, like the Phoenix they wore as a badge on their Cup final shirts three months after the tragedy, they would recover to play football once more.

Their resilience and courage was well reflected by their goalkeeper Harry Gregg. He had been the final piece in Matt Busby's jigsaw, his last signing before Munich to complement his babes. He represented Northern Ireland at school and youth levels, and played for Linfield and Coleraine before joining Doncaster Rovers where he spent five years until recruited by United in December 1957. In all, he played for United for ten years and won twenty-four caps for Ireland, excelling in the 1958 World Cup in Sweden. Stoke City launched him into management and later he returned to Old Trafford as Dave Sexton's goalkeeping coach. Harry Gregg marked the fortieth anniversary of the Munich air crash by putting into words the anguish that is still very much part of his life.

Harry Gregg

We landed at Munich for a refuelling stop. It was snowing slightly and there were footprints in the snow as we made our way into the terminal. We got back on and there was nothing untoward as we set off down the runway.

I watched the telescopic leg of the wheel on my side extend as we went towards lift-off. I watched the wheel lock and unlock with the plane swerving about a little bit. Then the aircraft stopped and someone came on to say we would be going back to make another attempt. I just supposed it was a technical hitch.

We set off again, going a little bit further this time. It was like a speedboat at sea with a bow wave as the snow got deeper. We pulled up again and it was quite unnerving. This time they said we would be going back into the terminal and the party would disembark.

In less than five minutes we were called back on and we boarded again. I watched the steward belting himself in and I thought it was perhaps more serious than I had realised. So I made a point of getting well down in my seat, undid my collar and tie, and put my feet on the chair in front.

We started to roll until someone said we were one short. It

was Alf Clarke from the *Evening Chronicle*. He came on board and we set off once again. I was reading a book which wasn't too kind to the way I had been brought up so I put it down. I thought if I get killed reading a book like that I'll go to hell, which was the way of life in those days.

I kept watching the wheels and I thought we were away this time because we were going past places I had not seen before. I couldn't see the fence because you can't see ahead from inside a plane. I thought we had lifted until all of a sudden there was this horrendous noise. It felt as if everything was upside down, one minute daylight the next darkness, with the awful sound of tearing, ripping, smoke and flames.

The first thump I got was on the back of the head, then on the front of my head. I felt something going up my nose and I just didn't know what was going on. I had not long joined Manchester United. I was married and had one child, and in my simple mind I thought I had done well for the first time in my life and now I wouldn't see my wife, little girl and parents again. I also worried that I couldn't speak German. Why I thought that I have no idea. Everything seemed to be in slow motion.

All of a sudden it all stopped. There was nothing but darkness and I thought it must be hell because of the blackness. I just lay there for a while and felt the blood running down my face. I was afraid to reach up for fear of what I would find.

Then I realised I couldn't be dead. There was some burning and sparks from wires. Above me to the right was a hole and daylight. I started to crawl towards it and in the darkness went over one or two people. I looked out of the hole and lying directly below me was Bert Whalley, the team coach, wearing an airforce blue suit. His eyes were wide open and he hadn't a mark on him.

I made the hole bigger and dropped down beside Bert. In the

distance I could see five people running through the snow and shouting, 'Run, run, it's going to explode.' I just stood there. I think the fear factor had gone, I really don't know, but from around what was left of the cockpit came the pilot, Captain Thain, and he also shouted, 'Run, you stupid bastard, it's going to explode,' and ran back the way he had come.

Just then I heard a child crying and I shouted. 'There are people still alive in here.' I crawled back in terrified of what I was going to find. I found the child under a pile of rubbish and crawled out. The radio operator came back and I gave him the child. I went back in and found the mother. She was in a shocking state and I had literally to kick her through the hole to send her on her way.

I found Ray Wood and was sure he was dead. I couldn't get him out. I saw Albert Scanlon and he looked even worse. I tried to drag him out but he was trapped by the feet and I had to put him down.

I got out and went round the back of the aircraft where I found Bobby Charlton and Dennis Viollet hanging half in and half out of the stump of the plane. I dragged them clear by the waistbands of their trousers and left them about fifteen yards away.

I got round the other side and at that point realised how bad it was with the rest of the plane sticking out of what I later learned was a fuel store and it was on fire. Between that and the part of the plane I had come out of was the Boss. He was sitting up on his elbows with his hands across his chest and moaning a terrible, 'Aargh.'

He had a bad cut behind his ear and one of his feet was bent back the wrong way but he didn't look too bad compared with what I had seen. I thought I could leave him. I put something behind him to support his back and said, 'You're OK, Boss.'

I went another twenty yards and found Jackie Blanchflower.

The snow was melting around him because of the heat and the burning part of the aircraft. He was crying out that he had broken his back and was paralysed. I looked and saw Roger Byrne lying across him and I don't think Jackie had realised that it was Roger's body that was holding him down.

Roger didn't have a mark on him. He was a handsome fellow, handsome in life and handsome in death. I kept talking to Blanchy. His right arm was almost severed and I took my tie off to tie round his arm. I pulled so hard I tore the tie. I looked up and one of the stewardesses was standing there. I asked her to get something to tie his arm with but the poor girl was in shock, so I just used what was left of my tie.

I stayed with him until a fellow in a tweed coat turned up with a medical bag and carrying a syringe. There were explosions going on and one made him jump so much he ended up on his backside but still holding the syringe up in the air.

People came from across the fields, ordinary people, not rescue people. I didn't see any of those at all. Eventually a Volkswagen arrived which was a coal van. Jackie was put into it, also Johnny Berry who I didn't even recognise as a player until I saw the badge on his blazer. Myself, Billy Foulkes and Dennis Viollet were also put in and we were driven to the hospital.

I remember breaking down and crying when we got there and I saw Bobby Charlton, Peter Howard, Ted Ellyard and a big Yugoslav. I was just relieved that there were more of us alive. Some of us were asked to identify people they were working on. Ray Wood was lying on the floor as they attended to his eye.

They gave us a bowl of soup and the Yugoslav collapsed. He just slid down the wall. He had been walking around with a broken leg which suddenly gave way. They started to give us injections. Bobby fainted and so he was kept in hospital. Billy Foulkes, Ted, Peter and I were taken to an hotel where the people looked after us wonderfully.

Jimmy Murphy turned up the following day with Jean Busby, Sandy Busby, Duncan's father, Gladstone, Jimmy Payne, Duncan's best friend, Jackie's dad and the other wives. Jean Busby was remarkable. She took care of everyone and encouraged the other wives while all the time her own husband was upstairs fighting for his life. She was strong, very, very strong.

I had to go back to the hospital the next day. I could hardly get out of bed because of my back. They gave me injections to the point where I said that's enough because the injections were worse than the bad back. Jimmy Murphy asked Bill and I to stay for a few days so that those lying in hospital wouldn't realise the full extent of the accident.

Eventually Professor Maurer took Jimmy, Bill and myself round the wards. We stopped at the foot of each bed and he told us the chances of survival. The Boss was fifty-fifty because he was a strong man, Jackie Blanchflower OK, Duncan fifty-fifty but when he got to little Johnny Berry he whispered, 'No, no, I am not God.' Johnny survived of course but unhappily died a year or two ago.

Duncan Edwards woke up when we went into his room and he asked us, 'What time's kick-off?' Quick as a flash Jimmy Murphy told him, 'Three o'clock, son.' Duncan responded, 'Get stuck in.'

Bill and I came home and I remember about ten days afterwards all the newspapers in my house kept disappearing. I couldn't figure what was going on until I realised they were being hidden from me. Big Duncan had died. I found that hard. It hit me terribly. Yes, that was Munich.

A lot of people wondered where Matt Busby got the strength from to return to football and start all over again. I went to see him shortly after he got back to England. He had aged terribly and he told me that the hardest part for him after the crash was the way Johnny Berry kept coming to his room to say, 'Tommy

Taylor's some friend of mine, he hasn't even been to see me.'
Johnny didn't know the full extent of the crash and Matt said
he just didn't know what to say to him.

He told me, 'Son, they couldn't give me an anaesthetic to set
my broken foot because of my chest injuries, so they set it a
bone at a time, one every day. It was cruel, but it didn't hurt
me like Johnny Berry coming into my room every day to say
Tommy Taylor was a poor friend.'

It was awful for Jimmy after the crash, too. He had so much
to do. I remember in Munich walking up the stairs to my room
and I was one flight from the top when I heard this terrible
crying. At first I couldn't figure it out but as I got nearer I could
just make out Jimmy sitting in the dark on the empty staircase
crying his eyes out. I just quietly walked away.

Matt and Jimmy were oil and water as people but they were
a wonderful partnership. I believe the greatness of Manchester
United was founded on their strength and friendship, but after
Munich it was the strength of Matt's wife, Jean, which enabled
him to carry on.

6

JIMMY MURPHY

LYING GRIEVOUSLY INJURED in his hospital bed in Munich, Matt Busby whispered to his second in command, 'Keep the flag flying, Jimmy. Keep things going until I get back.' With those words to concentrate his thoughts and inspire him, Jimmy Murphy faced up to the most daunting task of his career. The team had been destroyed, the management and coaching structure had been well nigh wiped out and Busby, the architect of the club's achievements and ambitions, lay at death's door fighting for his life in an oxygen tent and twice given the last rites.

United's assistant manager had missed the trip to Belgrade for the European Cup quarter-final against Red Star because of his part-time post as manager of the Welsh national team. He had stayed at home to steer Wales through to a World Cup group qualifying win against Israel in Cardiff. News of the crash was given to him by Alma George, the manager's secretary, on his arrival back at Old Trafford. He was greeted with the terrifying message as he hurried to his office: 'The United plane has crashed at Munich.'

Murphy recounts his reaction in his book *Matt . . . United . . . and Me* with the words: 'My feet stopped. So did my heart. The fingers of the clock on the wall pointed to four o'clock . . . but time now meant nothing. The numbing horror of that moment will live with me till I die. I dashed into my office and picked up the phone.'

The weight of the burden handed to Murphy that day must have seemed intolerable. For here was a man overwhelmed with anguish for personal friends and many of his beloved players either killed, dying or suffering injuries that would end their careers. Simply to cope with what had happened was asking a great deal – and to think Kenny Dalglish and Kevin Keegan left clubs due to stress – but to be charged with restoring order out of such tragic chaos and keep Manchester United playing football was a frightful challenge. The hurdles ahead were enormous. Not only was there the league programme to complete, United were still in the FA Cup, and thanks to their 3–3 draw against Red Star in Belgrade just hours before the crash, they were through to the semi-finals of the European Cup with a daunting draw pitting them against AC Milan on the horizon. The fact that United battled on to finish a respectable ninth in the First Division, reach Wembley to play Bolton in the final and give the Italians two fair games, including a 2–1 victory in the first leg at Old Trafford, says it all for Jimmy Murphy.

Always a shy, retiring man as far as the public were concerned, he rose to the occasion to reveal a strength of character and wisdom that had been somewhat hidden by his role as number two to the much more outgoing and genial Matt Busby. But cometh the hour, cometh the man and the Welshman who had perhaps been rather taken for granted made sure that Manchester United not only survived but did so with pride and surprising success. Jimmy Murphy has probably never been given the acknowledgement he deserves for his superhuman contribution after Munich, partly because he never wanted it. Perhaps it was ever thus for a number two, in all walks of life.

The grand European adventure had exacted a terrible price but Murphy had one staunch ally left at the club, a tough little old man too frail to have gone on the trip himself, but resilient and clear thinking. Harold Hardman was determined that the club would survive and he told Murphy, 'You have got to keep it going, Jimmy. Manchester United is bigger than you, bigger than me, bigger than Matt Busby. It is bigger than anybody. The club must go on.' They were noble words, but where was Murphy to start, just who was there left capable of playing for Manchester United?

Murphy hurried back to Manchester after Busby's whispered plea, heartbroken and empty. He did not know whether he would see Busby alive again and he was fearful for the dying Duncan Edwards, the player he well nigh worshipped. As the Rhinegold Express thundered out of Bavaria, Murphy says he sat numb while the wheels of the train drummed into his tired brain, 'Where do you find the players? Where do you find the players?'

With him were two of the survivors, goalkeeper Harry Gregg and defender Bill Foulkes. They had escaped the destruction with hardly a scratch, though nobody was sure they wouldn't suddenly collapse from delayed shock. Both men showed signs of claustrophobia, insisting that the windows of the train were kept open and they travelled from London to Manchester by taxi.

They went home to join their families but Jimmy Murphy had to wrestle with the problem of trying to raise a team good enough to represent Manchester United. Gregg and Foulkes were the only players from the squad immediately available.

The crash happened on a Thursday. The league fixture on the Saturday was quickly postponed while their FA Cup fifth-round tie against Sheffield Wednesday due the following Saturday was delayed until the Wednesday. It was a welcome breathing space but still cruelly short with little over a fortnight to find a team. Murphy described his task:

To start with I was in a mental turmoil through sheer sorrow. I also felt completely on my own. Not only was Matt not there, but my great friend, Bert Whalley our coach, had been killed and so had Tom Curry the trainer. I was going to funerals and at the same time trying to sort out what to do.

My first move was to call on Joe Armstrong, our chief scout and an old faithful, to draw up a complete list of our remaining players. When I looked down the list at those left I groaned. It read like a team of schoolboys. There was plenty of promising talent which might, and indeed did, show itself in two or three years' time, but I needed people immediately.

I had plenty of letters expressing sympathy from other clubs but I had to learn the hard way that practical help was another matter.

Only two clubs promised players, Liverpool and Nottingham Forest, but Murphy refused to panic and just take anyone. He didn't want to complicate the future because he knew that eventually their own injured players would return to action. For a time he contemplated trying to sign Ferenc Puskas, the 'Galloping Major' from Hungary who had starred against them for Real Madrid, but eventually decided against because it seemed contrary to their efforts to make their own players. He decided that at the end of the day British players and British guts would see them through.

Nowadays, with the English game almost taken over by foreign stars, that may seem an old-fashioned viewpoint but that's how it was in the fifties, and who's to say he was wrong because he produced a team that, given the circumstances, pulled the club through in a quite astonishing fashion.

He made just two immediate ventures into the transfer market. Ernie Taylor was unsettled at Blackpool and wanted to move back to his native north east, but with the help of a mutual friend and United enthusiast, Paddy McGrath, Taylor agreed to answer the SOS. He was thirty-one, took size four in boots, but had been a key man in Newcastle United's FA Cup final victory in 1951. He had also schemed Blackpool to their Wembley triumph two years later in the Stanley Matthews final against Bolton.

Murphy paid £8,000 for Taylor and looked round for a harder man to help him in midfield. He remembered Stan Crowther playing against them for Aston Villa in the previous season's final at Wembley and doing equally well in that season's league fixture at Old Trafford. The hard-tackling Crowther cost £24,000. He was granted special permission to play for United in the FA Cup after appearing for Villa in a third-round defeat against Stoke City. The deal was rushed through but the dispensation for him to play against Sheffield Wednesday did not arrive until the afternoon of the match.

Gregg was in goal, and Foulkes was in his normal right-back role. Ian Greaves had a little first-team experience and was a natural at left-back. Another reserve, Freddie Goodwin, who like Greaves went on to a career in senior management, was picked at wing-half with the newly signed Crowther on the other flank. Colin Webster, a Welsh international, and Taylor, went into the forward line but that was the extent of players with a modicum of experience – and there were still four more places to fill.

Murphy called up Ronnie Cope from the A team to play centre-half and selected three other unknown teenagers for the remaining places. Mark Pearson, small but sturdy, was brought in at inside-forward. He was from the Sheffield area. Alex Dawson, a brawny centre-forward, powerful in the air, was to lead the attack while a slightly built youngster with an Irish background from Manchester, Shay Brennan, nominally a full-back, was put on the left wing to make up the numbers. Boy

Brennan, a dark-haired stripling, emerged the hero in that first match after Munich, scoring twice in a 3–0 win.

Sheffield Wednesday faced a 60,000 human tide of emotion as well as a patched-up football team. Bill Foulkes, promoted to captain in place of Roger Byrne, said, 'I felt very sorry for Sheffield Wednesday. They were never in the game with a chance, for I'm sure that everyone who took an interest in football, and even those who didn't, were willing us to win that night.'

There was an extraordinary atmosphere, frightening in its intensity. The poignancy of the occasion was illustrated by the match programme. Underneath the numbers for the United team were lines of dots and the crowd had to write in the names themselves when the team was announced over the loudspeakers. That first team lined up: Gregg, Foulkes, Greaves, Goodwin, Cope, Crowther, Webster, Taylor, Dawson, Pearson, Brennan.

The makeshift team went on to become 'Murphy's Marvels'. They drew 2–2 at West Bromwich in the next round and Colin Webster scored the only goal in the replay. For the semi-final at Villa Park Bobby Charlton returned to the team instead of his pal, Brennan, and he scored both goals in a 2–2 draw. Murphy brought Brennan back for the replay at Highbury and this time left out Pearson to make room for Charlton in a thrilling high-scoring match. Alex Dawson scored a hat-trick and Charlton and Brennan scored one each. The 5–3 victory took them to Wembley and an all-Lancashire final against near neighbours Bolton.

Dennis Viollet was back in time for this one and on paper the team looked its strongest since the crash but it was as if the tide of emotion had exhausted itself and, of course, Bolton had their own agenda. A fortnight before Munich, United had beaten Bolton 7–2 in the League but as their rugged England centre-forward, Nat Lofthouse, put it, 'All that mattered from our point of view was that Bolton should win the FA Cup.'

Matt Busby, not fully recovered, was at Wembley but he left it to Jimmy Murphy to lead out the team. Lofthouse scored twice in a 2–0 win, his second the result of charging Gregg in the middle of the back and knocking the ball and player into the back of the net, a foul even in those days, but in truth United were never really in it.

Even reaching Wembley had been a miracle and the point had been well made. United had survived the greatest misfortune ever to befall an English football team and that they had was testimony to the inspired leadership and superb organisation of Jimmy Murphy.

Their amazing recovery had been reinforced on the European front with a spirited display in the first leg of their semi-final against AC Milan, a 2–1 win for the United youngsters. The Italians scored first when Bredesen intercepted a pass for Schiaffino, the talented Uruguayan international centre-forward, to glide the ball round Gregg after twenty-four minutes.

Milan deserved the lead but five minutes before half-time Dennis Viollet put United back in the fight by snapping up a half-chance in the box from a mishit back pass. With Murphy no doubt winding up his players during the interval, United came out to launch themselves into the Italians with a blazing fury.

Schiaffino was now sporting a big plaster over a cut eye, the result of a collision with Gregg, and his team began to waver. Goodwin and Taylor forced Buffoni to make great saves and Webster shot high as the Reds tore into the opposition. United grabbed their winner eleven minutes from the end after Viollet had been brought down by Maldini. The centre-half flung himself to the ground in anguish as Danish referee Helge awarded a penalty and his team-mates protested violently. All that meant nothing to little Ernie Taylor who stayed cool amid the scenes of excitement. He smashed his spot kick into goal off the underside of the crossbar.

The slender lead proved far from enough as United crashed to a 4–0 defeat in the second leg. Little went right for them. To start with, for obvious reasons, they had travelled overland by boat and train to Milan rather than by air, not ideal preparation for an examination in the mighty San Siro Stadium. They couldn't even gain entry to the ground as their coach was turned away from a succession of gates as not being the right entrance. They didn't reach their dressing-room until twenty-five minutes before the kick-off in a ground filled by a volatile crowd. The players felt it was gamesmanship to upset them and they also had to deal with some surprising decisions from the German referee, Albert Deutsch, but Harry Gregg admitted, 'Milan were really a class above us.'

United withstood the pressure in the first half, but the fact that it took them until nearly half-time to win their first corner tells the story. Four minutes into the second half Schiaffino lobbed over Gregg. Ronnie Cope saved on the line but conceded a penalty for handling which Liedholm converted. Schiaffino went on to score twice with the other goal coming from Danova.

United's line-up for both legs was: Gregg, Foulkes, Greaves, Goodwin, Cope, Crowther, Morgans, Taylor, Webster, Viollet, Pearson.

Young Kenny Morgans had recovered from his injuries in time to play in the European semi-final but that didn't compensate for the absence of Bobby Charlton who was somewhat harshly taken by England for an end of season tour involving friendly matches. Bill Foulkes found the game in Milan an intimidating experience:

The Italian crowd didn't show us much sympathy. As we walked out we were bombarded with vegetables. I remember

73

being hit by cabbages and the biggest bunch of carrots I have ever seen. It was very hostile with all the flares and fireworks. Milan had a good team, too, with players like Schiaffino and Liedholm and they crushed us in the second half.

It was a sad end to a horrific season but inevitable when you think about it. Emotion and spirit had kept us going for a long time, but after a while it was not enough. I know that in the summer I was happy just to rest and count my good fortune that I was at least playing football while so many of my friends and team-mates just hadn't made it.

Jimmy Murphy had certainly earned the right to relax for a spell. He had indeed kept the flag flying and Matt Busby was always quick to acknowledge the contribution of his assistant in a long and creative partnership which had turned a blitzed and bankrupt club into a dynamic force in football and then ensured its survival through the dark days of Munich.

In later years Sir Matt said, 'I saw Jimmy Murphy talking football to a crowd of players when we were both in the army during the war in Italy and I decided then that if ever I needed someone to help me in management he was my man.

'We had a wonderful and happy relationship. He was never a yes man which was a good start and our natures seemed to join to produce common sense. He was straight, honest and loyal.'

Murphy and Busby were totally different people, even as players. Both were wing-halves after failing as forwards, but that was the end of their resemblance. While Matt was the gentle giant, his right-hand man was the archetype Welsh dragon, breathing fire and fury. Perhaps the choice of Jimmy as his lieutenant was an acknowledgement by Matt of the lack of aggression in his own make-up. It was Jimmy who taught the youngsters of Manchester United the physical aspects of the game. Bobby Charlton believes he might not have made it to the top without the toughening up process of going through Murphy's mangle on the training pitch.

'When we played in practice matches he used to come up behind me and kick me. I used to think what's going on here. I couldn't always understand what he was trying to do but now of course I realise he was teaching me what to expect from the harsher side of professional football,' Charlton explained.

'Jimmy was so intense he used to frighten me. He was hell to work for but everything was done for a purpose and I owe more to Jimmy Murphy than any other single person in football. I shall always be grateful to him. The success of Manchester United over so many years was a testimony to his work.'

Wilf McGuinness, another of Murphy's favourites from the sixties, agrees. 'Without him a lot of us would never have made it as professional footballers. At times we almost hated him because he drove us so hard but it was always for our own good and we certainly respected him.'

His team-talks were vintage stuff and watching from a distance it seemed he was conducting some Welsh choir with his arms and hands punctuating the air to emphasise the effort needed for victory. It was undoubtedly his skill as a motivator that took Wales through to the quarter-finals of the World Cup in 1958 where they lost narrowly 1–0 to Brazil, the ultimate winners of the tournament. That run has never been bettered, nor is it likely to be.

Sometimes he was not too fussy how he motivated his teams. His players tell of one Welsh game against Germany, a friendly after the war, when he delivered the usual talk on tactics and wished them luck. Then just as they were about to walk out of the dressing-room he called after them, 'And don't forget it was Germans shooting at your fathers not so long ago!'

The son of a Welsh mother and an Irish father, Jimmy was

brought up in a little village called Pentre in the Rhondda Valley and as a young man when he wasn't playing football he could often be found playing the organ in Treorchy Parish Church.

He played for Wales Schoolboys and when he helped beat England 3–2 at Cardiff and draw 2–2 with Scotland at Hampden Park, he came to the attention of English League clubs. He joined West Bromwich Albion where he played from 1928 until the outbreak of the war, which signalled the end of his playing career. He was the youngest player in the Welsh team of his day at the age of twenty-one and in all he was capped twenty-two times as well as captaining his country.

Jimmy was a Desert Rat during the war, serving with the Royal Artillery and going through the North African campaign before arriving at Bari transit camp in Italy where he took over from Stan Cullis as the sergeant in charge of sport and where he met Matt Busby.

Recalling those days when he teamed up with Busby at the end of the war, he said, 'Old Trafford was bombed out and was little more than a rubbish dump. The club didn't have any money either. We used to give the team their lunch on a match-day, across the bridge in an old wooden hut called the United Café. They used to get a poached egg. As we progressed we started to have lunch at the Trafford Hotel and the food went up the social scale as well with boiled chicken on the menu. Later we moved to Gorse Hill and really went up in the world with lamb cutlets, even a steak, but it still wasn't like eating in the Old Trafford Executive Suite.'

Looking for players and developing the youngsters in the reserves was Jimmy Murphy's special responsibility and he was the key element in the emergence of the Busby Babes so that when the crash came it hit him hard. They were his boys and as he was always fond of saying, he had watched these little apples grow. He used to tell you that the sun was always shining

. . . and even if you couldn't actually see it, it was still shining behind the clouds! Even Jimmy must have wondered, though, in the aftermath of Munich whether the sunshine would ever return to warm his soul.

His work did not go unrecognised in the outside world. Juventus sent John Charles to sound him out about becoming manager of Juventus. Brazil made him an offer and after Munich there were overtures from Arsenal. He turned them all down. Perhaps he felt he had found his life's work at Old Trafford, although in later years as his career came to a close, he did wonder whether he should have cut loose from Manchester United and Matt Busby. He said at the time, 'Looking back, I wonder if I would have been better served had I taken one of those opportunities. Loyalty in football is not always as generously rewarded as one would hope, but then that's another story.'

Nothing dimmed his enthusiasm, though. He retired from full-time work when Matt did in 1971 but continued to scout for the club under a succession of managers. It was just four days after representing United at a match that he collapsed and died as he walked in a park near his home. It was 14 November 1989, and he was seventy-nine.

Sir Matt once said about his partner, 'We worked together to bring greatness to Manchester United and no one outside the club will ever know how important he was to our success. Jimmy Murphy . . . the best friend, helper, companion and right-hand man any manager would wish for in this great but risky business of football management.'

Murphy's Marvels undoubtedly did uncommonly well, bridging a horrendous gap to ensure the future, but few would rank his makeshift team alongside the all-time great sides of Old Trafford. However, Michael Parkinson, television presenter and sportswriter, feels strongly that Murphy's achievement has never been awarded the accolade it deserves and that his players should be elevated to a place among the élite. He wrote:

> I think it is time that Jimmy Murphy's team were included on the roll of honour. They might have lacked the glitter of the others but it would be difficult to name another who so courageously battled overwhelming odds. More than that, they were responsible for the special link which exists to this day between Manchester United and a tribal following encircling the world. I was once in the Arctic Circle making a documentary when a peasant guarding a herd of reindeer approached. 'Manchester United,' he said, nodding in my direction. I indicated that was my name. Satisfied I knew what he was talking about, he said, 'Bobby Charlton, Number One.' So when we talk about the future of Manchester United, let us remember the team who gave them a future to look forward to.

A writer who recognised immediately the greatness of Jimmy Murphy and who did not hesitate to say so at the time was Keith Dewhurst, who took Alf Clarke's place on the *Evening Chronicle*. Keith, in later years a playwright and novelist, paid tribute to the club's emergency manager in an illuminating piece he wrote for his Manchester paper on the eve of the FA Cup final against Bolton, just a few weeks after the accident. It read:

> Manchester United's Jimmy Murphy is a short, explosive character who hates crowds and publicity, and people who do not know him well think that he is hard and difficult to approach. When they know him a little better they think that he is a kind of spectacular joker. His team-talks are epics of colourful language and wild gestures, far removed from the calm analysis of Matt Busby. His stock greeting of 'Hello, my

old pal' – equally effective for handling pressmen, players, genuine old pals, barmen, waiters and the people who pretend to be genuine old pals in the hope of scrounging tickets – has in fact become a joke among the team. Everyone is 'old palling' everyone else.

The players may smile at Jimmy's jokes and mannerisms, but they know that these mask one of the shrewdest soccer brains of all time. When you really know Jimmy Murphy you know a man of deep feelings and sympathy which he does not choose to expose all the time for the world to knock around. You know a masterly talker and story teller. You know perhaps the best football coach Britain has ever seen.

Murphy has the managerial flair, too. His handling of the Manchester United team since Munich has been superb. He has had only a handful of players, and some of those are not really up to first-team standards. Yet look at the way he has used them. Look at the hunch that paid off when Shay Brennan hit two goals in the Sheffield Wednesday Cup tie. Look at the dropping of Mark Pearson and the restoration of Brennan in the Highbury (semi-final) replay – another match-winning move. Look at the switching of Ken Morgans to the left wing, a move which has at least solved a desperate problem, and may yet win the Cup.

Look at Murphy, buffooning to keep the players' morale up, and yet all the time thinking, thinking. Staying up all night in London before the semi-final. Deciding on the Morgans switch when everyone thought he was asleep in the corner of the train compartment.

I know what he will say to skipper Billy Foulkes before the Cup final. I can only say the same to Jimmy – best of luck, my old pal.

7

THE WAY BACK

JIMMY MURPHY had worked wonders after Munich with such an assortment of players, but it was of course only the start of the recovery. Matt Busby returned to the helm the following season and he wasted little time in strengthening the team from the transfer market. The 1958–59 season was only a few weeks old when he paid a then record fee of £45,000 to bring Albert Quixall to Old Trafford to replace the emergency signing Ernie Taylor. Quixall, a skilful inside-forward in the United tradition, had impressed Murphy when he played for Sheffield Wednesday against United in their first match after the crash. Helped by the new addition, and the fact that to a certain extent the team was still running on spirit and adrenalin, United scored a hatful of goals that season and finished runners-up to Wolves.

Wilf McGuinness became a regular in the side and it was a golden season for Bobby Charlton who scored twenty-nine league goals. Dennis Viollet scored twenty-one and there were twelve from Warren Bradley, a right winger signed from amateur club Bishop Auckland. Warren, later a head teacher and treasurer of the club's Former Players Association, went on to become a full England international.

The following season, 1959–60, was notable for Viollet's club record thirty-two league goals from thirty-six appearances. They ran up some big scores, helped by eighteen goals from Charlton, fifteen from Alex Dawson and thirteen from Quixall but they were erratic and slipped to a finishing place of seventh.

Maurice Setters was signed to help bolster the defence and full-back Noel Cantwell arrived in season 1960–61 but again they finished seventh. David Herd was signed from Arsenal for the following season and obliged by becoming top scorer with fourteen goals but the team didn't click and slid to fifteenth place. This was too much for Matt Busby who sprang into more transfer action, pulling off a great coup by working with Gigi Peronace, the Italian agent, to bring an unhappy Denis Law home from what he had increasingly felt was exile in Turin. United paid a record £115,000 for the former Huddersfield and Manchester City striker in a deal which would eventually prove a bargain – not immediately, though. Midway through season 1962–63, the manager realised he needed someone to deliver the ammunition for his star-studded forward line with a little more guile.

He went to Glasgow Celtic to sign Pat Crerand for £56,000 and although it wasn't apparent in the league performance, he had assembled the basic parts of what was to become a great side.

The team continued to plunge down the table, raising the spectre of relegation. There was paper talk posing the question of whether United would want to continue with Busby at the helm of a team in the Second Division. Happily all such questions were rendered irrelevant thanks to a splendid run in the FA Cup as the newly built side at last produced convincing displays to beat Huddersfield, Aston Villa, Chelsea, Coventry and Southampton. They were to meet Leicester in the final. So awful had been United's league form that Leicester started favourites but Wembley soon brought out United's best and they won convincingly 3–1. The team lined up: Gaskell, Dunne,

Denis Law

Cantwell, Crerand, Foulkes, Setters, Giles, Quixall, Herd, Law, Charlton.

Denis Law put United ahead from Crerand after half an hour. David Herd increased the lead when Gordon Banks failed to hold a thunderbolt from Bobby Charlton. Ken Keyworth pulled a goal back for Leicester but Herd scored again. The victory put Manchester United back into Europe for the first time since their fateful Munich season.

It had been a gruelling five-year fight-back and prompted Donald Saunders of the *Daily Telegraph* to write:

Manchester United, who only a few weeks ago had fallen so far from glory that they looked like slipping ignominiously out of the First Division, will be back in Europe next season as worthy representatives of British football. A thoroughly merited, handsomely achieved victory over disappointing Leicester at Wembley on Saturday has earned United, the first English team to follow the European Cup trail, a place alongside Spurs in the Cup-Winners' Cup competition.

And no one who saw them rise brilliantly to the challenge of Saturday's big occasion will doubt their ability to make Manchester United as great an attraction on the Continent as they were in the fifties.

A series of spiritless, unenterprising performances spread over a number of years had convinced me by Saturday morning that United were a poor side, content to live on the glittering reputation of their predecessors. By teatime that same day such thoughts seemed ludicrous.

As Cantwell led his troops on a lap of honour, everyone knew that here were a team of spirit, pride, skill and intelligence, a team, indeed, of true thoroughbreds, that fully deserved to climb up beside the Busby Babes of the forties and fifties.

It didn't seem quite so promising in the first tie of their return. A five-year absence seemed to have left them decidedly rusty on the European stage as they struggled to hold the Dutch Second Division club, Willem II Tilburg, to a 1–1 draw in Holland. Louer scored for the Dutchmen after ten minutes, and although David Herd managed an equaliser, the expected easy win became a dour struggle in midfield. Louer appeared to have snatched a late winner when his shot almost squeezed under Harry Gregg's dive and indeed many thought the ball had, for a moment crept over the line.

Ten minutes from the end, United's embarrassment was completed by the French referee's dismissal of Herd for a foul on Brooymans. It was a dismal return to the European scene, but perhaps the players realised it, for in the second leg at Old Trafford they came out with all guns blazing to register a crushing 6–1 win for an aggregate 7–2 victory.

The Dutch defence was breached early by Maurice Setters who scored after seven minutes. Denis Law, bounding back after injury, dominated the match, scoring in the twelfth and thirty-first minutes. Then in a dramatic four-minute siege in the second half, Bobby Charlton, Phil Chisnall and Law again, piled in three more goals. Willem's goal came with the help of Noel Cantwell, who unaccountably slammed the ball past his own goalkeeper.

The hopes of the United fans soared after this display until the day of the second-round draw. They were paired with Spurs who were playing in the competition as holders. It was the last draw English football needed, but at least it guaranteed national representation in the next round.

After the first leg at White Hart Lane, it looked as though Spurs would go through. They took the tie 2–0, although it wasn't until the sixty-seventh minute that they scored their first goal. United defended splendidly but they had little answer to

These young hopefuls straight from school were destined for greatness until the Munich air crash: Albert Scanlon, Eddie Colman and Duncan Edwards.

The FA Youth Cup winners of 1955 pose with their trophy after beating West Bromwich Albion 3–0 at the Hawthorns for an aggregate 7–1 victory. *Back row:* Duncan Edwards, Terry Beckett, Shay Brennan, Tony Hawksworth, Alan Rhodes, John Queenan. *Front row:* Peter Jones, Dennis Fidler, Eddie Colman, Wilf McGuinness, Bobby Charlton.

Ray Wood dives to push a shot from Bobby Smith, the Spurs centre-forward, round his post at White Hart Lane.

The Busby Babes of April 1957. *Back row:* Bill Inglis (assistant trainer), Geoff Bent, Ray Wood, Mark Jones, Bill Foulkes, Dennis Viollet, Tom Curry (trainer). *Front row:* Jackie Blanchflower, Colin Webster, Wilf McGuinness, Tommy Taylor, Billy Whelan, David Pegg. *Sitting:* Johnny Berry.

Carmelo punches clear under challenge from Dennis Viollet but Bilbao still went down 3-0 in this pulsating European Cup quarter-final at Maine Road in 1957.

Goalkeeper Pavlis and defender Borovicka keep David Pegg (No.11) at bay against Dukla Prague in the Strahov Stadium in season 1957–58.

United practise on a waterlogged pitch at the Yugoslav Army stadium before the second leg of their European Cup quarter-final in Belgrade in February 1958.

The final line-up before the kick-off against Red Star Belgrade and the tragedy of the Munich crash on the journey home. *Left to right:* Duncan Edwards, Eddie Colman, Mark Jones, Kenny Morgans, Bobby Charlton, Dennis Viollet, Tommy Taylor, Bill Foulkes, Harry Gregg, Albert Scanlon and Roger Byrne.

Skipper Roger Byrne *(left)* exchanges pennants with the captain of Red Star in front of the Austrian referee.

A newspaper front page delivers the horrific news from Munich the following morning.

Jimmy Murphy brings home two of the survivors, Harry Gregg (*left*) and Bill Foulkes (*right*), on the Rheingold express from Munich four days after the crash.

Two minutes' silence was observed before the kick-off against Sheffield Wednesday at Old Trafford in honour of those killed. Directors Louis Edwards, Bill Petherbridge and Harold Hardman (Chairman) stand with Les Olive who had taken over as secretary.

Matt Busby *(left)* and Jim Murphy anxiously watch their Munich-ravaged team in the final of the FA Cup against Bolton.

Harry Gregg wins the challenge with Schiaffiano as United beat AC Milan 2–1 in the first leg of their European Cup semi-final three months after the air crash.

The rebuilt Reds after Munich. *Back row:* Bobby Harrop, Ian Greaves, Freddie Goodwin, Harry Gregg, Stan Crowther, Ronnie Cope, Shay Brennan, Bill Inglis (assistant trainer). *Front row:* Jack Crompton (trainer), Alex Dawson, Mark Pearson, Bill Foulkes, Ernie Taylor, Colin Webster.

The FA Cup final victory over Leicester put United back into Europe. Maurice Setters, Noel Cantwell, Pat Crerand, Albert Quixall and Bobby Charlton run a lap of honour.

Denis Law scores the opener in a 4–1 win in the first leg of the European Cup-Winners' Cup quarter-final against Sporting Lisbon at Old Trafford in 1964.

a great move down the left between Dave Mackay and Cliff Jones. The battling Scottish wing-half, Mackay, scored. United closed ranks and with four minutes remaining it was still 1–0. Then the normally immaculate Tony Dunne made a weak pass back to David Gaskell in goal. The ball never reached him as Terry Dyson nipped in to grab a goal which had the Tottenham fans thinking they were as good as through to the next round.

Their confidence rose even higher when Denis Law and Nobby Stiles both missed the return leg, David Sadler and Phil Chisnall standing in, but fate dealt Tottenham a bitter hand at Old Trafford. After eight minutes Mackay had to be stretchered off with a double fracture of the left leg after a tackle and collision with Noel Cantwell. The United captain was quickly back on his feet but the Spurs player lay unmoving. Cantwell took one look and waved frantically for the stretcher bearers.

United went on to win the match 4–1 and so go through to the quarter-finals, 4–3 on aggregate, but the tributes went to the Londoners for their stirring display with ten men. United had pulled one goal back through David Herd just before Mackay was carried off but they couldn't put another past the heroic visitors until ten minutes into the second half. Herd made sure after Setters had headed a Quixall corner back into the goalmouth for an aggregate equaliser.

Spurs were playing like men inspired and they pulled away again through Jimmy Greaves. They finally crumbled in the face of two rip-roaring goals from Bobby Charlton in the last quarter of an hour, the second one and overall winner coming three minutes from the end.

The quarter-final brought Sporting Lisbon to Old Trafford for the first leg and had the Portuguese beating a hasty retreat following a 4–1 defeat. Denis Law grabbed a hat-trick, even if it was with the help of two penalties.

Silva hit a glorious goal to make it 3–1 and the Portuguese

perhaps thought they were on their way back into the game. Dutch referee Johann Martens ended that hope when he ruled that Charlton had been illegally felled and Law obliged with his second successful penalty.

United should have had a few more and they were criticised for not being ruthless enough. Nevertheless, they were in a strong position for the second leg in Lisbon, one foot seemingly already in the semi-finals. They were in a championship-challenging position in the League and heading for the semi-finals of the FA Cup, and so were campaigning for a treble.

How dangerous it is to count chickens before they are hatched in football. They lost their FA Cup semi-final 3–1 to West Ham at Hillsborough and four days later collapsed in Lisbon, losing 5–0 and going out of Europe 6–4 on aggregate. That turn-around is still Manchester United's greatest ever humiliation in Europe. It wasn't a fluke, either. Questions were asked about David Gaskell's goalkeeping. Sporting got off to a dream start with a penalty from Silva when the game was two minutes old after Tony Dunne handled. After twelve minutes, Silva wove his way through the panic-stricken United defence to make it 2–0. It was still 2–0 at the interval but not for much longer as the Lisbon club scored three goals in the opening nine minutes of the second half. First Geo found the net to level the aggregate score, then Morais the winger put the Portuguese in front with Silva scoring again to make it an embarrassing 5-0.

The Times reported:

Manchester United's hopes of keeping the European Cup-Winners' Cup in England crumbled in an avalanche of goals. United were but a shadow of the side that tore the heart out of Sunderland just one week ago in the FA Cup. Crerand and Setters were completely unable to get to grips with Silva and Geo, and the Sporting attack, which had seemed so naive at Old Trafford, suddenly burst into life. Sporting dominated entirely, with Law and Charlton reduced to nonentities. United's tackling in defence drew whistles from the crowd and was sluggish and ready prey for the lightning Portuguese forwards. Their attack was innocuous.

United had just one change in Lisbon from the first leg, Phil Chisnall replacing Nobby Stiles so that the quarter-final team read: Gaskell, Brennan, Dunne, Crerand, Foulkes, Setters, Herd, Chisnall (Stiles), Charlton, Law, Best.

The five-goal hammering in Lisbon was a blow to David Gaskell's hopes of replacing Harry Gregg as the regular goalkeeper. Gaskell had been in keen competition all year, with the shirt regularly changing hands, but Gregg was back for the closing stages of the season. Matt Busby lost faith with both of them, though, and the following season he brought in a relatively unknown Irishman from Dublin, Pat Dunne. In a brief but spectacular United career, Dunne kept goal in the championship season of 1964–65. The next year all three competed for the position until Alex Stepney was signed from Chelsea and helped win the 1967 league title.

Pat Crerand still winces when he recalls Matt Busby's anger at the Lisbon defeat.

Sir Matt Busby was renowned for his dignity and cool head but he ranted and raged at us after throwing away what should have been a big enough lead to have seen us through to the semi-finals of the European Cup-Winners' Cup. He had waited five years to get back into Europe after the awfulness of Munich. He had rebuilt the team bit by bit and though he had struggled in the League, everything had come together in the FA Cup. After our Wembley performance everyone was confident we were ready to make an impression on the

European scene again, and we were ... until that terrible 5–0 crash!

What Matt was going to do to us was nobody's business. He said our performance was an insult to the people of Manchester and that we had let him and ourselves down badly. We were in disgrace all right and there were dire warnings about what was going to happen to us when we got back to Manchester.

I think we made matters worse by trying to drown our sorrows afterwards and coming back to the hotel late. I know he said he was going to fine me and about five or six of the other lads for missing the curfew.

Normally Matt would accept defeat with good grace, no matter how disappointed he was. He always stayed calm and even if he was angry he never lost his temper. He did this night though, and I can't say I blame him. We really did make a mess of the second leg after taking a 4–1 advantage in the first leg at Old Trafford.

It should have been a cakewalk and maybe that was the attitude we adopted. It was our big mistake but who could blame us because the first game had been so easy and I remember thinking that they were a really poor side. Denis Law had scored a hat-trick and Bobby Charlton had hit a great goal. It all looked so easy for us and the trip to Portugal a formality.

What we didn't appreciate in those early days in Europe was the way the continental teams varied their tactics and style for two-legged ties. When they travelled away they sometimes didn't seem to offer much resistance and they simply concentrated on defence to keep the score down. You didn't see them in attacking mood.

Sporting Lisbon were a bit like that. We had so many chances we could easily have doubled our score. In Portugal it was a different story of course and we had a rude awakening. They came out with all guns blazing and it was such a surprise that I think our goalkeeper froze, though I don't single him out particularly for blame because the rest of us never got going either. We were two goals down before we knew what had hit us! Our start to the second half was just as bad when we conceded another quick couple of goals. Silva went on to score a hat-trick and we never looked like pulling anything back.

I am ashamed to talk about it even now and it remains a nightmare memory. Our only excuse was that we had had a very exhausting spell prior to the tie in Lisbon with three tough ties in the FA Cup against Sunderland before we were able to knock them out of the quarter-final. We won easily enough in the second replay at Huddersfield when Denis Law got a hat-trick but the grounds had been very wet and heavy.

We were in three competitions right to the death that season which meant playing ten games in March, including three in four days. So it was an extremely busy spell and the Lisbon game fell in a particularly hectic week, four days after losing the FA Cup semi-final to West Ham. I suppose the disappointment of missing out on Wembley didn't help Matt Busby's mood when we did so badly just afterwards.

But we still had the champanionship to play for, and from Lisbon we went straight to London to play at Tottenham. Fortunately we hit form again and got a great 3–2 win which pleased the Boss. We all went to the House of Commons for dinner that night and Matt was so pleased with the result at White Hart Lane that he told us we could forget all about the fines he had been threatening.

He actually apologised for losing his temper, which says a great deal about Matt Busby's character and his stature as a man. In actual fact he had no need to apologise because we had deserved every word of his criticism and we had deserved to be shouted at.

Beating Spurs kept us on the title trail but we finished runners-up four points behind Liverpool. Harold Wilson said a week was a long time in politics but it can be just as dramatic in football. One moment we were chasing glory in three competitions and the next we were out of the lot. It had been a shattering experience, especially our disgrace in Lisbon.

The return to Europe had ended in tears but finishing second in the League at least ensured they stayed in continental combat for season 1964–65 with a place in the Inter Cities Fairs Cup, forerunner of the UEFA Cup. Busby signed John Connelly from Burnley, where he had won a championship medal, to play at outside-right in a two-winged attack which produced another high-scoring season. This time, with a tighter defence behind them featuring new goalkeeper Pat Dunne, they won the championship, reached the semi-final of the FA Cup again and produced another exciting season in Europe all the way to a dramatic semi-final.

Denis Law was again top man near goal with twenty-eight in the League, backed up by David Herd's usual twenty, along with ten apiece from Bobby Charlton and George Best while new boy Connelly weighed in with fifteen.

The campaign in Europe was also notable for some high scoring, although it wasn't evident in the opening leg of the preliminary round against Djurgaarden in Sweden. United made a cautious start and had to wait until three minutes from the end for David Herd's equaliser after Johansson had given the Swedes an eighth-minute lead. It certainly gave little indication of what was to come from the Manchester team in the second leg at Old Trafford.

Denis Law scored in the first half and then the roof fell in as far as Djurgaarden were concerned. United scored four in ten minutes as Law went on to complete a hat-trick, with the other goals coming from Bobby Charlton (two) and George Best in a handsome 6–1 victory (7–2 on aggregate).

They stayed in the scoring groove to beat Borussia Dortmund 6–1 in the opening leg of the next round in Germany. Ronnie Crowther described the display in the *Daily Mail* as a 'bombshell burst of brilliance' and at the end hundreds of Dortmund fans poured on to the field to applaud the visitors for their verve and skill. Bobby Charlton hammered a personal three-goal rebuke to England manager Alf Ramsey for leaving him out of his side but the star who stole the show was eighteen-year-old George Best. He scored the most exciting goal and played a big part in the build-up for three others. David Herd and Denis Law got the other goals and Matt Busby proclaimed, 'This is our greatest show in Europe for many years. I am delighted with such a team performance against a side that went to the European Cup semi-final last season and I am only sorry that more of our fans couldn't have seen it.'

The Old Trafford leg was a formality, especially after United scored in the opening minute, and they ran out comfortable 4-0 winners for the impressive overall tally of 10–1. Charlton (two), John Connelly and Law were the scorers.

The next round produced an all-English draw with Everton the opposition and a return to normal goal levels. Fred Pickering gave Everton the lead in the first game at Old Trafford with John Connelly grabbing an equaliser. Pickering scored for Everton in the game at Goodison Park but United went through 2–1 on the night with goals from Connelly and Herd.

United travelled to play Racing Strasbourg in the first leg of the quarter-final and quickly found the scoring pace that had been such a feature of the earlier rounds. Seemingly casual but always classical football ensured they won 5–0. The scorers were Law (two), Connelly, Charlton and Herd. The return at Old Trafford was disappointingly poor fare but it was now the middle of May and the players were perhaps feeling the effects of a long and testing season. They could do no better than a no-score draw, but the game had been won in France, and after the other scoring extravaganzas nobody could really complain as the Reds steadied themselves for a semi-final against Ferencvaros.

United were on song in front of goal again with two goals from Herd and one from Law in the first leg at Old Trafford. But the Hungarians were quite the best side they had met in the competition and they scored through Novak and Horvath (penalty) to leave the Reds with a 3–2 win, a slender lead indeed to take to Budapest.

Ferencvaros won the second leg 1–0 with a penalty from Novak after Nobby Stiles had handled, leaving the overall score level at 3–3, which meant a play-off with the venue to be decided on the toss of a coin. This was before the days of away goals counting double. United lost the spin and ten days later they set off for Budapest. By now it was 16 June, a month after the normal end of a season, and summer soccer obviously didn't suit United as they crashed to a 2–1 defeat.

The Hungarians delighted a 75,000 crowd with controlled intelligent football which enabled them to take a two-goal lead through Karaba and Fenyvesi. United pulled a goal back through Connelly but could do no more and their long, long season was finally over as Ferencvaros went through to a one-match final against Juventus in Turin.

The team for all three of the semi-final ties was: Pat Dunne, Brennan, Tony Dunne, Crerand, Foulkes, Stiles, Connelly, Charlton, Herd, Law, Best.

It had been a great season for United with their first championship win since Munich and football rated by Nobby Stiles as their best ever.

Nobby Stiles

Everyone remembers our team for winning the European Cup in 1968 but as far as I am concerned we hit a peak in 1965 playing in the Fairs Cup. We dished out some cracking football, scoring five or six goals in every round, even away from home.It made us very optimistic about our semi-final with Ferencvaros, but it had been an extremely long season. I played sixty-six games, taking in England Under-23 appearances, and we even had a replay with Leeds United in the FA Cup semi-final.

We seemed to be OK when we went into a 3–1 lead against the Hungarians in the first leg but then we gave away a silly goal. Goalkeeper Pat Dunne misjudged a long lob and it bounced over his head into the net, which left us with a narrow advantage of just one goal. It was always going to be difficult and the journey to Budapest didn't help. We were delayed in London by a strike and then had another hold-up in Brussels.

They had a good player in Florian Albert who had a real tussle with Bill Foulkes. Just before the interval he got the ball to Vargo who let fly with a hard shot. I flung myself to block it and stopped it with my shoulder. To my astonishment the referee gave a penalty against me which Novak scored. I thought it was a harsh decision.

We tried hard in the second half but ended up losing 1–0 which meant a 3–3 draw on aggregate. We had to go back to Budapest for a play-off. I felt awful as the one responsible for the penalty which had forced us into a third match.

By now it was the middle of June and most footballers were on holiday. I remember we played well, indeed we paralysed them, but we lost 2–1 because we simply couldn't put the ball into the net. So success in Europe eluded us for yet another season. I still look back proudly on that period, though, because we had won the championship with a team dripping with scoring power. We had five players in double figures with league goals alone and Denis Law had a grand total in all competitions of thirty-nine goals. It was a very good team and great to be a part of it. People said we used to play off the cuff but in reality we were well organised and had some very good players.

8

EL BEATLE

MANCHESTER UNITED did extraordinarily well in season 1964–65 and it is little wonder that Nobby Stiles picks out that year as the peak of his era. It's only in recent times that the Reds have pulled off a league and cup double, yet not only did they reach the semi-finals of both the FA Cup and the Fairs Cup in 1965, they won the league championship as well.

It was a magnificent all-round effort on three fronts, and despite the long and gruelling finish to the season they were able to clinch their championship by reeling off seven successive wins with the help of a flush of goals. Denis Law led the way in their powerful scoring finish with six while Bobby Charlton smashed a hat-trick along with goals from George Best, David Herd and John Connelly. As Stiles described it, their forward line was dripping with goals!

The real bonus was that United were back in the top European competition for the first time since the Munich season and what's more they had a good team which gave them every hope of a successful European Cup campaign in season 1965–66. Matt Busby and Jimmy Murphy had been back to the drawing-board in the eight years since the crash and, with the help of some notable transfers plus the fact that their rebuilt assembly line was again supplying talented youngsters, they were back in business.

They started impressively against Helsinki HJK in the first leg of their preliminary round in Finland. The game was only thirty seconds old when David Herd scored after a typical burst by Denis Law. In fifteen minutes a centre from Herd enabled John Connelly to increase their lead. John Aston, making his first appearance in a European tie, repeatedly outpaced Jalava, the Helsinki captain and right-back. The first time Jalava succeeded in stopping Aston, the home crowd applauded ironically.

The Finnish amateurs pulled a goal back through Pahlman, a band leader and television entertainer, but Law scored for a half-time lead of 3–1. United relaxed in the second half and paid for their casual approach by conceding another goal to close at 3–2, a scoreline which proved more than adequate for the second leg. The match at Old Trafford turned out to be a stroll. The Finns never looked like scoring and United cruised to a 6–0 win with a hat-trick from Connelly, two goals from Best and one from Charlton.

In the first round proper, United were drawn against the East German army team, ASK Vorwaerts, clearly a harder task if only because of the unknown nature of the opposition. United flew to Berlin and then went by bus through Checkpoint Charlie into East Berlin where even the street lights seemed to be on half power. The match conditions did little to lighten the mood. Sleet was falling on the huge bowl of a ground and the pitch was frozen hard. Only the band was under cover and the game was played in the afternoon because there were no floodlights.

United won the match 2–0 with a cautious performance. Both their goals arrived in the final quarter of an hour. The first was a flowing move through Best, Law, Herd and back to Law, who in the meantime, seemed to have climbed an invisible ladder to hang in the air and head over Weiss in the German goal. Law initiated the second goal by sweeping in from the right for Connelly to flick in his pass.

Although the German team must have felt the writing was on the wall for them, they still went out of their way to be hospitable and after the match their players took the United team and press out to a club for a memorable late night of drinks and toasts.

The second leg was a comfortable exercise for United. Stiles and Law gave Herd an early goal and the centre-forward scored again just before half-time. Piepenburg pulled a goal back for the visitors but it was too late to affect the outcome. As if to demonstrate United's control, Herd promptly hit back to complete his hat-trick for a 3–1 win. The decisive 5–1 aggregate victory put them into the quarter-finals against the big guns of Benfica.

United knew they were in for a more searching examination against a team who had reached the final of the European Cup four times in the previous five seasons, winning twice. The Portuguese champions were unbeaten in European competition on their own ground, so United also knew they had to make the most of home advantage in the first leg at Old Trafford. The match more than lived up to expectations with a 64,000 crowd enjoying it so much that they applauded both teams back on to the pitch for the second half and again as the players went off at the end.

Benfica started and ended with a flourish. They scored first when Eusebio bent an inswinger from the corner flag on to the head of Augusto. United responded with goals from Herd and Law for a half-time lead and with half an hour left, Noel Cantwell crossed a free kick for Bill Foulkes to head the Manchester team into a 3–1 advantage. Then with a touch more magic from Eusebio, the towering Torres scored to reduce United's lead to one goal.

As the headline in *The Times* summed up, 'Precarious lead plucked from magnificent match'. The newspaper's association football correspondent, the late and great Geoffrey Green, enjoyed the game and the rich contribution of individuals from both teams. He wrote:

Here was a match played at a sizzling speed, full of creation and movement. For Manchester, Charlton was in world class, the equal on this occasion of Eusebio, who needs no space in which to move, a dark flash who shoots like a thunderbolt from all angles and at any range. For United, too, Herd was a bombardier, pressed on by the fluid movement of the darting Law and a delicate Best.

For Benfica there was, of course, Eusebio, lazy, almost casual, in movement, but eating up the ground as he changed direction, sending the defence one way and moving the other; little Simoes also jinking down one flank; and the long-striding giant Torres, at centre-forward, another player with lazy strides, but seven league boots and a head that can almost reach a ball from the overhanging clouds.

One goal perhaps in the bank may not be enough for Manchester United. But at least this night cannot be taken away. It was something to remember.

But *The Times* could not have got it more wrong. Manchester United went to Lisbon and won the second leg 5–1, standing normal football logic on its head. The most optimistic United supporter could not have foreseen such a dazzling display against the mighty Eagles who had a fine unbeaten record of nineteen European games on their own ground.

On this night of Wednesday, 9 March 1966, Benfica were not just beaten, they were pulverised. All expectations and sense of planning indicated that United would open cautiously in an effort to safeguard their slim lead but they were three up on the night after just fourteen minutes. George Best, the

George Best

nineteen-year-old Belfast genius touching new heights in his already meteoric career, scored the first two in the sixth and twelfth minutes, and then two minutes later sent John Connelly in to slot home the third.

There were 80,000 people crammed into the Estadio de Lus, most of them expecting to hail a Benfica triumph, and why shouldn't they have anticipated victory after winning eighteen and drawing one of their European contests, scoring seventy-eight goals in the process and conceding only fourteen? Never had a visiting foreign side scored more than two goals on Benfica's ground and the mood of the home crowd was one of noisy confidence as the 10 p.m. kick-off approached. Rockets shot into the night sky to celebrate the presentation of a statuette to Eusebio to mark his selection as European Footballer of the Year. Within twelve minutes he should have handed over his award to the brilliant Best, a stripling playing in only his third season of league football, who had produced such shimmering skills and spectacular craft to plunge the Stadium of Light into gloom.

He scored his first goal with a header, from Tony Dunne's pinpoint free kick, leaving goalkeeper Costa Pereira stranded. His second followed a huge goalkick from Harry Gregg which Herd headed back and down into the path of the Irish youngster. Best streaked away past two white-shirted Benfica players as if they were statues before slamming a swift right-foot shot low into the corner of the goal.

Law masterminded the third, working the ball in from a deep position and drawing two defenders before slipping a pass to Best who promptly played it further across to present Connelly with a goal. United even had two efforts which found the net disallowed, so dominant were they in the first half.

Early in the second half Benfica got a goal back, but only with the help of Shay Brennan slicing the ball into his own net as he tried to clear, and even then it failed to fire the Portuguese into anything like their normally incisive form. It was as if they were still confounded by the visitors' opening onslaught.

Law laid on the fourth goal, finding an unmarked Pat Crerand on the penalty spot, and near the end Charlton sailed through for a fine fifth goal. Revenge for the five-goal drubbing they had received in Lisbon two years previously in the Cup-Winners' Cup was now complete. Back home, the fans prepared to hail a new hero and salute El Beatle, the accolade bestowed on the player by the Portuguese press.

As for the team tactics, Matt Busby laughed afterwards and said, 'George must have had cotton wool in his ears when we made our plans. I told them to play it tight for a while, for twenty minutes or so, until we got their measure. George just went out and destroyed them. I couldn't believe it and Benfica most certainly couldn't until it was too late. They were also prepared to play it tight for a while. After all, that is always what happened in European Cup games.

'Then out comes this kid as if he's never heard of tradition and starts running at them, turning them inside out. I ought to have shouted at him for not following instructions. But what can you say? He was a law unto himself. He always was. I was cross with him . . . almost!'

The player himself described the match in one of his books:

I felt superb. The atmosphere sent the blood coursing through my veins, adding power to my muscles, imagination to my brain.

Why I played the way I did that night is one of those inexplicable things. Genius, and I believe on the football field I had it, is something you simply can't begin to explain. I've been interviewed by American journalists to whom analysis is of the greatest importance. Why do you do this, and how?

It all seems so important to them, whereas to me it's natural. Football is a simple game.

Perhaps in Lisbon I fell in love with the place where we stayed, Estoril. Sunny, beautiful sandy beach, lovely park, luxurious hotels. I just felt good all the time we were there. Even the jeering Benfica fans before the game didn't upset me, holding up five fingers to the coach windows as a sardonic reminder of our 5–0 defeat by Sporting Lisbon two years earlier in the Cup-Winners' Cup quarter-final. We gave them five goals all right, and we put a stop to their damn firecrackers and rockets. They had been masters of Europe but we showed them how to play the game.

The morning after the match every bikini on the beach wanted my autograph, some wanted a snip of my hair. The men were just as bad. I was having my first taste of adulation, and I'd be a liar if I said I didn't enjoy it.

I had a feeling of total warmth afterwards. That is the only way I can describe how I felt when I walked off the field at the end of the game, knowing I had done something that no one else could have done or is ever likely to do again. I was labelled El Beatle and I was suddenly the best-known sportsman in Britain.

There is no doubt that George Best had instinctive flair off the field as well as on it. Hunting for souvenirs the morning after the match in Estoril, he bought himself a huge floppy sombrero. He carried it through all the airport formalities and stuck with it on the journey home. Then as the team walked off the plane in Manchester, he put the hat on his head. The press photographers were already looking for the game's scoring hero and now they were being presented with a publicity dream, an unusual and distinctive picture opportunity which duly hit the next day's papers in a big way. The *Daily Mirror* had him on both the front and back pages. George later admitted that it was in his mind that he was due to open a boutique in a few weeks' time and he thought the sombrero would be good publicity. He was right – the picture went round the world!

The team that startled Europe in Lisbon was: Gregg, Brennan, Dunne, Crerand, Foulkes, Stiles, Best, Law, Charlton, Herd, Connelly.

After their dazzling feat in Lisbon, United were immediately established as favourites to go all the way and become the champions of Europe, but fate had a cruel trick to play. The hero of Lisbon twisted his leg in a tackle in an FA Cup tie against Preston a fortnight later. He had a cartilage problem in his right knee and without warning it would lock. It needed an operation but Busby asked the player to carry on playing for as long as they remained in the European Cup. He was rested for one league fixture and then brought back for a run-out which persuaded the club he was worth a gamble for the first leg of their European Cup semi-final against Partizan Belgrade in Yugoslavia.

He was strapped up and sent out against a team that proved to be far more accomplished than had been acknowledged. They had seven internationals in their side and a record for springing shock results. In the quarter-final, for instance, they had lost the first leg against Sparta Prague 4–1 but roared back to win the second game 5–0.

United found them a tough nut to crack, although as early as the fifth minute Best missed a chance and Law hit the bar from only five yards out. It was downhill soon afterwards when Best felt a stab of pain return to his knee and he faded to become little more than a limping passenger, although many people at the match thought that overall he was still United's most dangerous player. It didn't say much for the rest, and indeed, as Peter Lorenzo put it in the *Daily Herald* 'The same team whipped

Benfica 5–1 in the last round but tonight they had no punch, sparkle or rhythm.'

Law hammered another cross against the crossbar but in the second half they were made to pay for their careless marksmanship. Two minutes after the interval, a long cross from right-back Jusifi seemed to catch Harry Gregg in two minds and he was beaten by a fierce header from Hasanajic. Partizan, through to the semi-finals for the first time, clinched their 2-0 win after an hour when Vasovic fed the ball forward for Becejac to hit a sharp low shot into a corner of the net.

The Yugoslavs had acquired a useful lead for the second leg but just as big a blow for the Reds was that it had become pointless to persevere with the injured Best. As soon as the team got home he was sent to hospital for a cartilage operation and it seemed that when Best dropped out, the magic went with him.

Partizan defended powerfully at Old Trafford and although United won 1–0 on the night they were beaten 2–1 on aggregate. Tension rose as the game dragged on with United unable to score. In the seventieth minute Pat Crerand and Mihaslovic were sent off after exchanging blows and United's goal didn't come until three minutes later when Nobby Stiles crossed from a short corner, catching Soskic unawares. The goalkeeper could only palm the ball into his own net. United redoubled their efforts but there was precious little time for the further goal they needed to force a play-off.

Partizan went on to lose in the final against Real Madrid who exposed the limitations of the Yugoslavs and Manchester United were left regretting even more deeply their failure to account for them after their heady success against Benfica.

Busby was devastated because he knew his team was at a peak and that after finishing fourth in the League it would be at least two more seasons before he could make another attempt to conquer Europe. He said, 'I was at the lowest ebb since the Munich air crash and it was in my mind to turn my back on football altogether. It seemed the fates had conspired against the club and me and I remember telling Paddy Crerand, "We'll never win the European Cup now."'

Crerand recalls that his reply to his manager was a promise – 'We'll win the League next season, Boss, and the European Cup the season after.' He later admitted that he had said it more in hope than judgement and because he realised Matt Busby had been so utterly depressed by the defeat against Partizan. In actual fact, it turned out to be a brilliant forecast but more significantly it also reflected the team's determination to let nothing stand in the way of making Busby's big dream become a reality.

Denis Law scored twenty-eight goals in thirty-three European games for Manchester United and was voted European Footballer of the Year in 1964. Here he recalls the bittersweet season of 1965–66.

Denis Law

Benfica in 1966 were the cream. They had been in three European Cup finals and had taken over from the legendary Real Madrid as top dogs. We beat them 3–2 in the first leg at Old Trafford but as they left the field their players were smiling because they didn't think one goal would be enough for us in the second leg in Lisbon against the most powerful team in Europe.

Two years previously we had been beaten 5–0 by Sporting, the other Lisbon team, and when we went out on to the pitch all the Portuguese fans were holding up their hands with all five fingers sticking out giving us the salute.

Matt Busby had made tactical plans for a careful start because we could ill afford to give away an early goal that would wipe out our slender advantage. To say we were keyed up would be an understatement. There was an 80,000 crowd packing the famous Stadium of Light, and I wasn't exactly pleased when Pat Crerand, kicking a ball about in the dressing-room, banged it against a mirror. The glass shattered and though no one said anything, I imagine everyone was thinking about seven years bad luck. It certainly didn't help our nervous mood, yet we went out and were three goals up on the night in the first quarter of an hour. It was incredible and the best performance in my view from a United team in Europe. It was a beautiful experience and a joy to share in that splendid team effort.

George Best, only nineteen at the time, grabbed the headlines and no one begrudged him that; after all, it was cheeky George who scored the first two goals and helped lay on the third for John Connelly. In the last quarter of an hour we rubbed in our superiority on the night when I put Pat Crerand in for a goal and Bobby Charlton waltzed in for the fifth.

My name was missing from the scoresheet, but it was of no consequence because I knew I had played well, just like everyone else in the side. It was unusual for the three so-called stars, Charlton, Law and Best, all to turn it on in the same match, but we did that night. So did Nobby Stiles, John Connelly and the rest of them.

Everything came off for us. By rights we should have gone on to win the European Cup that year, but we played badly in the semi-final against Partizan Belgrade. So we missed out on final glory and Matt Busby was bitterly disappointed, but it was nevertheless an exciting period in the club's history. Those were the days of the swinging sixties in soccer, as well as in music, and I think we saw football at its best. I was privileged to play in a great side. Matt Busby had recovered after Munich and I came home from Italy to join the team he had rebuilt. It was a splendid team, too, with Pat Crerand, Bobby Charlton, Nobby Stiles and George Best. Over a period of five years United were outstanding for entertainment and goals.

We always felt that if the opposition scored one, we could score two, if they scored two we could get three. It didn't always work out that way, but that was the feeling, and it was all very special for me.

9

THEIR FINEST HOUR

S O BACK to the drawing-board and Matt Busby had to pick himself up yet again after the crushing disappointment of European defeat. Finishing fourth in the League was not good enough to qualify for the Fairs Cup, so it meant a Europe-free season in 1966–67. They were at least able to concentrate on a championship campaign without distraction.

In fact, the League was the only competition on their plate. A shock home defeat against Norwich in the fourth round put them out of the FA Cup and, in an even bigger surprise, they were on the receiving end of an opening round 5–1 thumping at Blackpool in the League Cup.

There was no slip-up in the First Division, though, and they roared to the title on the back of a searing run after Christmas in which they played the last twenty games without defeat. Denis Law scored twenty-three goals but again they were firing on all cylinders with sixteen from David Herd, twelve from Bobby Charlton and ten from George Best. The defence was also stronger with Alex Stepney signed from Chelsea to take over in goal from David Gaskell. Asked at the end of the season for the most important factor in their success, Busby had no hesitation saying, 'Signing Stepney.' Away games which in the past might easily have been lost often finished as a low-scoring or no-score draw. It made a big difference as they crossed the finishing line four points ahead of Nottingham Forest and Spurs, opening the way for another attempt to win the European Cup.

This time there was no mistake; 1967–68 was the season when they finally reached their Holy Grail and became the champions of Europe. To win the ultimate trophy at any time is a marvellous achievement, but to do so against the background of Manchester United's history was little short of miraculous, especially considering the manner of their campaign, the teams they played and the results they gained.

The first round was not particularly testing. Hibernians, a team of Maltese part-timers coached by a local priest, Father Hilary Tagliaferro, even lost one of their players on the way to Manchester for the first leg. They broke their journey in London to take in an Arsenal match. Seventeen-year-old winger Francis Mifsud went to buy an ice cream and got lost. The party had to travel on to Manchester without him. He couldn't remember the name of his hotel in London but he knew they were on their way to Manchester so he caught a train to Piccadilly on his own. With the help of a girl he met on the journey he was eventually reunited with his team-mates and Scotland Yard were able to call off their hunt.

Denis Law and David Sadler scored two goals apiece in a 4-0 win and Father Hilary said he was happy to have kept the score so low. He added that the United players might find the conditions in Malta a bit of a shock.

He was right about that. The Gzira pitch in Valletta had a rock-hard surface of sand, gravel and lime. The ground had few facilities and the *Manchester Evening News* correspondent watched the match from the roof of a nearby house in order to have access to a phone for his running report back to England.

It was also extremely hot. That and the pitch conditions perhaps accounted for United's stilted display in a goalless game.

The Maltese spectators, many of them United fans, didn't know whether to laugh or cry. On the one hand they were pleased that their team had held the mighty Manchester to a draw but at the same time they were disappointed that such distinguished visitors had failed to thrill and entertain them.

However, there was no doubting the warmth of the welcome which started with a cavalcade of cars and motorbikes, horns blaring, escorting the team bus at breakneck speed from the airport to the Hilton Hotel with yet more enthusiastic supporters throwing flowers at the players. The United Supporters Club, which has always thrived on the island, threw a big party for the officials, players and press and they still dream about a repeat fixture one day.

The next round brought more serious opposition and pitted them against the champions of Yugoslavia, Sarajevo. The first leg was to be played in that ancient historical city where Archduke Franz Ferdinand had been assassinated, triggering the First World War. The United party were charmed by the meeting of western Europe and the Moslem world. In fact, as the world now knows, it was a deadly cocktail which eventually resulted in a brutal nationalistic war.

The Yugoslavs proved to be a tough and ruthless team. They dished out some fearsome treatment but United's response was mature. The players kept their heads in face of scything tackles on Francis Burns, George Best and Brian Kidd. Trainer Jack Crompton was on the field so often treating injured players that Pat Crerand commented afterwards, 'I bet half the crowd thought Jack was playing.' The composure, as much as the goalless result, was an indication of United's growing experience and as Matt Busby summed up, 'I was pleased with the result but even more with the way the players behaved under extreme provocation.'

United returned home quite confident about the second leg. Sarajevo, who had played for an hour with ten men and had

had what they considered a good goal disallowed, were equally optimistic. The first capacity crowd of the season, with 62,801 inside Old Trafford, saw United open the scoring in the eleventh minute through John Aston after George Best's header from a Brian Kidd cross had been palmed out by goalkeeper Muftic. The Yugoslavs were slowly getting back into the game when, in a decisive moment in the second half, Best took a swipe at Muftic after the pair of them had collided. Best lost his cool because as the goalkeeper helped him up he dug his nails into him and George explained afterwards that it had hurt. The irony was that it looked like an ungracious gesture to an opponent offering a helping hand and the Yugoslav players clearly didn't like Best's reaction. The result was that they lost their heads. Fahrudin Prljaca hunted Best down in revenge and kicked him so blatantly that referee Roger Machin had no option but to send him off.

Yugoslav tempers were even more inflamed when Best made the score 2–0 after it looked as though the ball had gone out of play. Eventually the visitors got back to playing the ball rather than the man and even pulled a goal back through Delalic but it was too late and United emerged 2-1 victors.

The nastiness spilled over as the players went up the tunnel and when it looked as if Muftic was coming for Best, Pat Crerand intercepted and, in his own words, 'I gave him such a clout I nearly broke my hand.'

Busby stepped in to sort things out in his usual diplomatic way. He was cross with the players over the tunnel incident but couldn't conceal his satisfaction at winning through to the quarter-finals as he switched back to the domestic programme during the European midwinter break of three months. In January he saw his team knocked out of the FA Cup in a third-round replay at Tottenham but with his boys going well in the League and looking forward to resuming battle in the European Cup it was proving to be a good season. Shortly after the domestic

Cup knock-out, United took revenge on Tottenham by beating them in the League and moving into a five-point lead at the top of the First Division. Realistically speaking they had enough on their plate without an FA Cup run, so nobody was complaining!

Back on the European trail in February, United were up against Gornik Zabrze, the dark horses who had knocked out Dynamo Kiev, conquerors of Glasgow Celtic, the European Cup holders. At the end of the first leg in Manchester, which United won 2–0, the home players stopped at the top of the tunnel to applaud their opponents off the pitch – a gesture later to be repeated in Poland – because it had been that kind of game, a refreshing tonic after the previous round.

George Best got the first goal after an hour's play when Florenski turned his shot into his own net. The second came when Brian Kidd flicked in a drive on goal by Jimmy Ryan. It looked a comfortable lead until United arrived in Silesia for the second leg to be greeted by biting cold and snow.

Busby toyed with the idea of asking for a postponement because he said they had not come this far in the competition to go out on a farce of a pitch. His hand was forced, though, when Concetto Lo Bello, Italy's top referee, went missing on the day of the match. The players waited and consoled themselves with another brew of tea in Room 905 of the Katowice Hotel – they took their own kettle and tea-brewing equipment with them. Pat Crerand had remembered a trip there with Scotland three years before and had unhappy memories of being unable to get a decent cuppa!

But the tie had to be played and in the event United performed brilliantly on a snow-covered pitch and for half the time in a mini-blizzard. John Fitzpatrick, replacing Jimmy Ryan for the second leg in the absence of the injured Denis Law, gave the team a more defensive plan which was put into operation with great discipline.

Danger man Lubanski, who had played for Poland at the age of sixteen, scored for Gornik twenty minutes from the end. They won the match 1–0, but lost overall 2–1, giving Manchester United their fourth appearance in the European Cup semi-finals.

The semi-final brought them up against much respected adversaries from their early days in Europe. In United's eyes, Real Madrid, under their great President, Don Santiago Bernabeu, were the team that had set the standards. There had developed between the two clubs a close sporting friendship and the Spanish club had been particularly sympathetic after the air crash. It was practical sympathy, too, waiving their normal match fee to play a friendly at Old Trafford to help ease United's financial strain and keep alive the tradition of European football in Manchester. Later on, when the club celebrated its centenary in 1978, there was only one choice to bring as opposition to mark the occasion and that was Real Madrid. But in 1968 it seemed appropriate that United should be meeting the club that, pre-Munich, had proved a step too far for the newcomers to the European scene.

The first leg was played at Old Trafford in front of a full-house 63,000 crowd who constantly roared their side forward. Indeed, United supplied most of the attacking play but, for all their possession, they could do no more than force a 1–0 win. The goal came ten minutes from the interval when Brian Kidd got John Aston away down the left wing. As the winger pulled the ball back from the bye-line, it was met with a thundering left-foot shot from George Best into the roof of the Real net.

Pat Crerand had already hit the woodwork but, against some masterly defensive play by the visitors, there were few real chances. It was a nerve-tingling match of high technique and played in the kind of spirit associated with a club who were friends as well as foes. The Russian referee commented later,

'The number one footballer and gentleman on the field for me was Bobby Charlton and I have never had more pleasure in taking such a match.'

The Spaniards, so well versed in the arts of two-legged ties in Europe, were quietly confident about overhauling Manchester's slender lead in Madrid. Their optimism seemed quite justified as they went into a 2–0 lead and then, after United pulled a goal back, increased it to go off at half-time 3–1 up.

Their first goal came after half an hour when link man Pirri headed in Amancio's cross. Ten minutes later, Gento, the left-wing flier, came off the blocks to beat Shay Brennan and score from a very narrow angle. The lifeline for United came just before half-time when Zoco panicked under pressure from Brian Kidd and turned the ball into his own net.

United were no sooner back in the hunt when Amancio made it 3–1 and not many in the crowd of 120,000 would have given a peseta for Manchester's chances of recovering from that kind of deficit in the second half. The fainthearts had not allowed for the shrewdness of Busby under pressure. The manager made good use of the few minutes he had at his disposal during the interval. As he explained later, 'Although we were 3–1 down on the night, I reminded the players that the aggregate score was 3–2 and that we were in fact only one goal down. I told them that if they were 3–2 down at half-time in an FA Cup tie they wouldn't consider that the match was over and that they had no chance. I told them simply to go out and play.'

And this is what his team did with such flair and force that the Spanish champions crumbled and lost their grip on the game. With attack once more at the forefront of their tactics, United were a different proposition. David Sadler left his defensive duties and started to advance upfield to such telling effect that in the seventieth minute he was on hand to turn in a header from George Best following Pat Crerand's free kick.

Level now on aggregate, United had their tails up and just five minutes later they stunned Real with a winner courtesy of the player least likely to score. Bill Foulkes played first-team football for eighteen seasons at Old Trafford and in all competitions played around 700 games. In that time he scored just nine goals, none of them as important as this one.

He rarely strayed over the halfway line but something dragged him forward as Best began a run down the right wing. As Best jinked his way closer to goal Foulkes steamed down the middle of the pitch and when Best turned the ball back he sweetly sidefooted it home. As Best described it, 'I saw a red shirt on my left and just pushed the ball inside. When I saw it was Bill Foulkes I wished I had hung on to it because I expected him to lash at it. I was quite wrong. He was really calm and just placed his shot past the goalkeeper.'

Pat Crerand said, 'Bill Foulkes of all people – goodness knows what he was doing so far upfield. All I know is that people have talked about providence and about fate evening things out after Munich ten years previously.'

What was hard fact was that United had become the first English club to reach the final of the European Cup and take Matt Busby even closer to his dream of conquering Europe. Bill Foulkes had been in at the start of Matt Busby's European quest and it was entirely fitting that he should score the winning goal to take the Reds to the final against Benfica at Wembley. It was his second goal playing in a total of fifty-two European games.

Bill Foulkes

I still don't really know what possessed me to go forward. After so many games with no thought of scoring it seems unbelievable as I look back.

I was lucky to be playing. I was rarely injured but that season

I was out from about January. I had missed the first leg against Real Madrid and had played only two league games when the manager picked me for the return in Madrid.

I think Matt went for my experience because I wasn't really fit. My knee had blown up at Sunderland on the Saturday and the European tie was just four days later. My knee was strapped up and I seemed to be hobbling everywhere. I think I only got by thanks to some brilliant defending and covering by Nobby Stiles and Tony Dunne.

We had gone to Spain with that precious one-goal advantage and at half-time when we were 3–1 down on the night, it didn't seem anything like enough. We were struggling. George Best was double marked, Bobby Charlton and Pat Crerand, who normally ran the games for us, hadn't shown and at half-time we were all a bit depressed.

But Matt with his typical logic pointed out that on aggregate we were only one goal behind and that at least a replay wasn't beyond us. His reasoning made an impression and we went out again thinking, 'We can do it.'

Perhaps Real Madrid sat back a little as well and gave us more room to play. For suddenly George began to figure, and Brian Kidd, too. We got a corner which hit David Sadler's heel to go in for an aggregate equaliser.

It seemed to me then as if both sides stopped playing, perhaps too frightened of making a mistake and losing. Nothing much happened for us until we got a throw-in on the right. Paddy Crerand was taking it and nobody seemed to want the ball. I shouldn't have done, but I called for it. Paddy looked and decided not to bother, sensibly perhaps. He threw it to George instead who promptly shot off down the wing, eluding three or four tackles. Perhaps it was moving slightly forward to call for the throw-in that prompted me to keep running forward.

Anyway I reached the corner of the box and again found

myself calling for the ball. George saw me and I thought I was going to be ignored again – you must appreciate I was never renowned for my attacking and shooting skills. So I thought George was going to do what he usually did and have a shot, but instead he cut back the most beautiful of passes to me. It was perfect and I just had to sidefoot the ball in at the far side.

There wasn't a sound from the Spanish crowd. My first thought was that it was so quiet that it wasn't a goal, but I realised it was when all the lads piled in and I was trying to get out from beneath all the bodies.

There was still ten minutes to play but we hung on and scoring that goal remains probably my most precious moment in football. It opened the door to the final for us, the beginning of the end of the rainbow for us.

I had come the whole way with the Boss and I thought the destruction of the team at Munich would have been the end of it but he patiently put together another team. When we finally did it, I thought that for those of us who had lost our friends at Munich coming home from a European tie, it was the right tribute to their memory.

The European Cup was finally won as much by character as ability. Matt Busby described it as heart, the kind of fighting spirit that his team had shown to pull the game out of the fire in Madrid, and he found it significant that only two men in the final line-up had come to Old Trafford on big fees. That is not to belittle Denis Law or Pat Crerand, recruited in the transfer market, but to recognise that the bulk of the side were fashioned in his own image.

Even before the match, in their hotel in Egham, Surrey, as they prepared for their big night against Benfica at Wembley, Busby quietly summed up, 'Their heart is right and that is the important thing.' His belief was to be tested and proved right in every respect.

It was hard going against the Portuguese champions, tension seeming to cramp the style of both teams. Perhaps because the match was being played on home soil, United were the first to settle and establish themselves as the team taking the game to their opponents.

Crucial duels were taking place all over the field. Bill Foulkes knew he had to win the aerial battle with the towering Torres, and Nobby Stiles was aware that his marking of the elusive Eusebio was critical. Benfica knew they had particular players to mark and the rugged Cruz became George Best's watchdog, several times bringing him down without hesitation. When Cruz missed him on one occasion, Humberto sailed in and was booked.

United's persistence in attack took a long time to find a chink in the visitors' defence but in the fifty-third minute David Sadler crossed from a deep position on the left for Bobby Charlton to jump and glance the ball over the goalkeeper into the far corner of the net. That was the signal for Benfica to throw caution to the winds. They stepped up their own forward momentum and drew on the experience garnered from playing in five European Cup finals. Nine minutes from the end they pulled level through a finely worked goal. Augusto put the ball in for Torres to nod down. Eusebio made a run which drew the defence and it was Jaime Graca who latched on to the ball and scored with a fierce shot from a narrow angle.

This was the moment when United needed all the heart they could muster. Benfica stepped up the pressure and twice Eusebio broke through to test Alex Stepney. His last effort brought him face to face with the United goalkeeper and he unleashed a rocket which Stepney saved with such effect that even his opponent applauded!

United were faltering and as Stiles put it later, 'If the game had had another ten minutes without a break I think we would have lost. We suddenly realised how tired we were. For me it was like the World Cup final all over again when Germany pulled level just before the end. It came close to knocking the heart out of us.'

It might have been close, but there was still something there and when the whistle came for the completion of normal time, Busby seized his chance to massage the heart back into active life again. 'I told them they were throwing the game away with careless passing and hitting the ball anywhere. I said they must keep possession and start to play their football again,' he explained.

They all immediately raised their game, none more so than John Aston who made his critics eat their words with a dashing display down the left wing. Although Eusebio was always a threat, Nobby Stiles came out on top in his fourth game against the Portuguese star – three for United and one for England – and what's more he played him cleanly.

'One newspaper said Eusebio had asked for more protection from the referee but I don't believe he ever said it. I never went out to kick him. I respected him and found him all right,' said Stiles.

Extra time opened dramatically as United played with renewed heart, sweeping forward and scoring twice in two minutes. In only the third minute, Brian Kidd headed on Alex Stepney's clearance to Best who immediately took off for goal. He took the ball round the defenders in a splendidly curving arc and then past the goalkeeper before popping it into the empty net.

It was Best at his best and Kidd was quick to match him with a goal to mark his nineteenth birthday. Kidd whipped in a close-range header from David Sadler's cross, which was blocked by Henrique, but as the ball came out the youngster got in a second header which this time looped over the goalkeeper. Kidd laid on a goal for Bobby Charlton and United triumphed with a 4–1 victory.

Denis Law watched the game from his hospital bed in Manchester, recovering from a knee operation. He had had a frustrating season and at one point the club thought the pain he complained about was more in his head than his knee. After his operation, Law couldn't resist having the offending piece of irritant bone pickled in a jar and labelled 'From my head'!

Although the injury-hit Law had inevitably been subdued all season, his place had been more than adequately filled by the dynamic Best, who in addition to his exploits in Europe, scored a magnificent twenty-eight league goals to help the Reds finish First Division runners-up. Still only twenty-two, he was voted Footballer of the Year by the sportswriters of England and soon afterwards he was named European Player of the Year as well.

Brian Kidd, the baby of the side, said, 'I honestly felt it was something that was meant to be. We knew we had to do it, if only for Sir Matt Busby. My treasured moment of glory is one I will never forget.'

The teams in the European Cup final at Wembley on 29 May 1968, with United wearing an all deep blue strip, were:

Manchester United: Stepney, Brennan, Dunne, Crerand, Foulkes, Stiles, Best, Kidd, Charlton, Sadler, Aston. Sub: Rimmer.
Benfica: Jose Henrique, Adolfo, Humberto, Jacinto, Cruz, Jaime Graca, Coluna, Jose Augusto, Torres, Eusebio, Simoes. Sub: Nasimento.

Bobby Charlton was unashamedly in tears at the end of the game. Like Bill Foulkes, he had survived Munich to fight back with Matt Busby. Later that evening he missed the celebration party at the team's London hotel, too exhausted to attend, physically and emotionally.

Sir Bobby Charlton

My thoughts on the day of the European Cup final were that we just wouldn't lose. I can remember thinking that we had come too far and had been through too much for us to fail in that final match.

The European championship had become like a mission for Manchester United and I think the older players felt as if we had been pursuing a sort of golden fleece of football. We had everything going for us, of course, playing on our own patch at Wembley. We also had a good record against teams from Portugal, and after coming from 3–1 down in Madrid to win the semi-final I thought it would be impossible for us to get beaten.

It was very humid during the day and I knew it would be hard work, but I also knew that we would find something extra. That's something British teams have always had, this resilience, especially in extra time. This is what England had produced to win the World Cup two years previously.

We should have been dead and buried against Real Madrid when we were losing 3–1, and the fact that we had come from so far behind to beat them gave us all an invincible feeling.

I thought there was no point me worrying because Benfica had a lot more to worry about. I knew it would come one day, but it was in the nick of time. Without being disrespectful to the players involved, the 1968 team was probably no longer at its best. We had faded in the League to let Manchester City win the title and a lot of us were past our peak. I knew I for one wasn't going to get another chance and about half the team were in the same boat.

So we were all pretty determined and, as I say, defeat was

never in our minds. Our first goal confirmed that idea because I scored it with a header – and that didn't happen very often!

We felt some despair when they equalised to force us into extra time, but even then I thought our background of stamina training would stand us in good stead. We knew they must be tired as well.

Then came that sparkling ten minutes in which we scored three goals – George Best, Brian Kidd and myself.

Benfica were a formidable side going forward but I thought their defence might creak, and that's how it worked out. Our own defence rose to the occasion with some key saves from Alex Stepney against Eusebio, and steady displays from Bill Foulkes, Shay Brennan and Tony Dunne.

Nobby Stiles was an important cog in the team, too. He used to tidy up for us. He seemed able to sense trouble and where danger was going to come from. So he was always there ready and waiting, a great reader of the game. He was a bit like a sheepdog keeping everything under control. If one of the sheep tried to break away he would dart into action and put the break-away back in the pen.

Johnny Aston had a particularly good game in the final, running the legs off their full-back down his wing to produce some great crosses. At the same time he was pulling their defence wide, which gave the rest of us more room.

When the final whistle went I remember thinking that it was the ultimate achievement, not just for the players but for the club and Sir Matt Busby. I suppose I can't speak for everyone, but I think I probably do when I say that we felt winning the European Cup had been a duty to Manchester United. For some of us it had become a family thing. We had been together so long.

I missed most of the celebrating that night. I was absolutely drained and kept fainting. My wife Norma told me the next day that Matt had got up late in the evening to sing 'What a Wonderful World' and I guess that just about summed it up for all of us.

10

THE GLORY BOYS

M ANCHESTER UNITED had an awesome trinity of players during the swinging sixties – the names of Charlton, Law and Best trip off the tongue in a familiar football litany. Every member of the team in the European Cup-winning year of 1968 was an outstanding player in his own right, but these three were the superstars who dominated their era. They are recalled by football followers who never even saw them play. Each was totally different in temperament, style and what they contributed to the team, but they shared a quality that dusted the football of their day with magic. Sir Bobby Charlton, knighted in later years, sportsman supreme, was majestic and graceful. Denis Law, the Demon King, was all fire and brimstone. George Best was simply dazzling, a fantastic footballer.

They said that when Best retired, Slack Alice had got her man early! The Irish genius was twenty-eight when he turned his back on playing serious football to open a nightclub in Manchester with the trendy but questionable name of Slack Alice. It was a typical Best gesture and a reflection of his life at the time, which focused a great deal on birds and booze. He was in the fast track all right with a stunning girlfriend – Carolyn Moore, the reigning Miss Great Britain – on his arm when he decided to walk away from Manchester United. This slip of a boy who had become a household name reckoned at the time that he couldn't go on any longer. As he put it himself after fleeing to Spain, 'Mentally and physically, I am a bloody wreck.'

The rest of us found it hard to comprehend. Why should a young man who seemed to have everything want to throw it all away? United, while becoming increasingly distraught at how to deal with his wayward behaviour, were reluctant to lose his great talent and a lot of fans were angry that they would no longer have the pleasure of seeing such a great player in action. They had watched him blossom into a rare performer who, in the view of many older fans, still stands alone as the most gifted and exhilarating player they have ever seen. But once you thought about it, you forgave him his early departure for a life with Slack Alice and her pals, because when you stood back, you realised George Best had more than paid his dues to the game. He might have left it young, but he started young, and played for eleven seasons in the First Division, packing more into his football career than the majority of professional players. If he had got into the first team at twenty-one and retired eleven years later at thirty-two nobody would have turned a hair. George just happened to live his career a little sooner than most. So when people say that he threw away a great career, they should remember that by the time he quit Old Trafford aged twenty-eight, he had played 466 league, Cup and European games and scored 178 goals.

The other significant fact is that once he had established himself in the side he rarely missed a game. In fact, in six of the seasons when he was in full flow, he made forty, forty-one or an ever-present forty-two league appearances each year. That's hardly the career of a fly-by-night. After the knocks he took and the magic he so often created, he was entitled to call it a day when he felt he had had enough.

In terms of entertainment he definitely delivered more than most. He transported so many to the heights of delight – and that doesn't include the girls, Miss World as well as Miss Great Britain, who flocked to swoon at his feet. He became a cult figure who led soccer into the sixties. In 1967–68 George enjoyed his best-ever scoring year with twenty-eight league goals from forty-one appearances, and proved an inspiration in Europe. He was voted Player of the Year in Northern Ireland, the English writers gave him their award and, six months later, he was voted European Footballer of the Year, the youngest ever. The following season was the beginning of the end. Busby retired. Wilf McGuinness, Frank O'Farrell and finally Tommy Docherty took up the managerial reins but found George increasingly difficult to manage.

Pity the predicament of young McGuinness who caught Best in his hotel room with a girl a couple of hours before an FA Cup semi-final. The situation called for disciplinary action, but should you really leave your best player out of such a vitally important game? Wilf didn't, but they lost anyway.

George's behaviour didn't help team spirit. Willie Morgan, the Scottish international winger signed from Burnley, once said, 'George had everything he wanted – money, girls and tremendous publicity. He lived from day to day and until right to the end he got away with it. When he missed training or ran away, people made excuses for him. He didn't even have to bother to make them himself. He just didn't care.'

It was a sad ending accompanied by trouble with referees and lengthening suspensions. On one famous occasion, Matt Busby arranged to meet him at Piccadilly Station in Manchester to accompany him to a disciplinary hearing at the FA in London. George failed to show. Matt waited for a couple of trains and then had to go to London on his own in support of a player who couldn't even be bothered to turn up for his own case. How embarrassing for the grand old man of football!

So it all ended in tears as George slid down the slippery slope, playing for Hibs, Dunstable, Stockport County, Fulham and in America, although he still produced many dazzling displays. He certainly continued to pull in the fans, as he went on to do as a television pundit and after-dinner speaker.

Most of those who marvelled at his play in the sixties readily forgave him his latter day slip-ups because he was always such a pleasure to watch. We remembered that he gave far more than he ever took during his eleven seasons with Manchester United before Slack Alice got hold of him.

If Best was the magician, Denis Law was the king and the Stretford Enders his worshipping subjects. No player until Eric Cantona commanded more allegiance from the terrace fans. They loved his prolific and dramatic scoring but they also liked the streak of villainy, which undoubtedly ran through his football.

The Stretford End found it easy to identify with a player whose commitment and aggression were so obvious. He was slightly built but there was a venom in his play that frequently brought him into confrontation with opponents, and at times, referees. The crowd liked his willingness to fly into the thick of the action with no holds barred.

Denis Law was daring, cocky, impudent and abrasive which, along with his great talent, made him an explosive player who became the people's champion. Few who watched him in the sixties will forget the Law trademark as he signalled his goals, punching the air and then running with one arm raised, finger pointing to the sky as he clutched his cuff with the rest of his hand. He was the first player to salute the fans in that way and the crowd would rise to him as to a gladiator of old.

It became a familiar sight because Denis Law is still in the record books as the most deadly marksman ever to play on the Old Trafford stage with a total of 171 league goals scored in 305 games, well over a striker's usual target of a goal every two games. Bobby Charlton thundered some marvellous goals in a tally of 199 in the League, but it took him 604 appearances, and for all his scoring wizardry, George Best's ratio in the League was 137 goals in 361 matches. They were splendid scoring returns but Law left them all standing with outstanding figures which were even more amazing in cup competition.

In Europe he scored twenty-eight goals in thirty-three matches and in the FA Cup he totalled thirty-four goals from forty-four ties. Eric Cantona led the scoring way and was the inspiration behind United's marvellous success under Sir Alex Ferguson, but even the Frenchman's scoring figures don't quite add up to the Law ratio.

Figures tell only half the story of course. It was the way in which Law scored so many of his goals that played a big part in his popularity, his spectacular overheads, his scissor kicks and his whiplash headers. Lightning over two or three yards, his reflexes were razor sharp.

Yet looking at him as a youngster, few would have predicted such a glittering career. Born in Aberdeen, the youngest of seven children, he arrived for a trial at Huddersfield hardly expecting to be taken on. As he later said himself in his book: 'I couldn't really believe Huddersfield Town were going to be impressed when they actually saw me. After all, I was only a skinny bit of a kid weighing little more than eight stone. I still had my squint and my owl-like glasses, although by then I did have my name on a waiting list for an operation to correct the squint.'

Andy Beattie signed him and passed him to Bill Shankly who was then in charge of the reserves. Says Shankly, 'He looked like a skinned rabbit and my first reaction was to say get him on the next train home, but from the first moment I saw him play I realised that here was something special. There was never any danger about him not making it.'

Matt Busby tried to sign him after United had played

Huddersfield in an FA Youth Cup tie but his £10,000 offer was turned down. He was given his league debut at the age of sixteen years ten months and his career quickly took off via a season and a half at Manchester City and then an unhappy year in Italy with Torino.

'It was like a prison,' said Denis. When Torino refused to release him to play for Scotland, he simply walked out, paving the way for his £115,000 transfer to Manchester United.

His scoring peak came in season 1963–64 with a startling goal-a-game return of thirty in thirty league appearances. When United won the championship the following year he contributed twenty-eight goals in thirty-six games. He was top scorer again in the championship season of 1966–67 and his biggest disappointment came when injury and a knee operation stopped him playing in the great European Cup final victory of 1968.

Tommy Docherty ended his United career by giving him a free transfer at the end of season 1972–73. He went back to Manchester City but he will always have a special place among United legends for the qualities which were well described by Matt Busby when he said:

The Italians dragged me and my chairman all over Europe before we were able to complete the transfer with Torino. At one time I was so angry I almost pulled out of the deal. I was always extremely glad that I didn't because when we had got him, I knew we had the most exciting player in the game. He was the quickest thinking footballer I ever saw, seconds quicker than anyone else. He had the most tremendous acceleration, and could leap to enormous heights to head the ball with almost unbelievable accuracy, and often with the power of a shot.

He had the courage to take on the biggest and most ferocious of opponents and his passing was impeccable. He was also one of the most unselfish players I have ever seen. But when a chance was on for him, even a half-chance, or in some cases no chance at all for anyone but him, whether he had his back to goal, was sideways on, or the ball was on the deck or up at shoulder height, he would have it in the net with such power and acrobatic agility that colleagues and opponents alike could only stand and gasp.

No other player scored as many miracle goals as Denis Law and he soon became what the crowd called him – the king.

Bobby Charlton also thrilled with his goal scoring and the sight of him in full stride, his cheeks puffed out with the effort, before unleashing a thunderous shot, was a picture. He was also an idol without feet of clay, a hero who represented all the good Corinthian things of professional soccer. He played the game well, but he also played the game. As Geoffrey Green timelessly expressed it in his book:

His flowing movements when surging into attack suggested a hidden poetic line: the ceaseless support for each colleague on the field, while he was rotating as the midfield hub of the wheel, reflected a selfless loyalty to a cause; his high standard of behaviour on stage still remains an example and a reproach to others in a game of violence, and as such remains a mirror of deeper values.

Born in Northumberland, the son of a miner in the coal-pit village of Ashington, his mother, Cissie, came from the well-known Milburn soccer family. Three uncles, Jack, Jim and George Milburn, played for Leeds United. Uncle Stan was with Leicester City and his mother's cousin, Jackie Milburn, was Newcastle's legendary centre-forward of the 1950s. Football was certainly in the family and while Bobby enjoyed his distinguished career with Manchester United, brother Jack found fame at Leeds and together they helped England win the World Cup of 1966.

Bobby came through as a Busby Babe and marked his debut on 6 October 1956, against Charlton Athletic at Old Trafford, by scoring twice in a 4–2 win. Such was the competition that he was dropped for the next game to make way for the return of Tommy Taylor, but he had established himself as a regular by the time of the Munich air crash. He escaped with only superficial injuries and many would say that he flew out to Belgrade a boy and came back a man. Certainly he had a much more important role and greater responsibilities to shoulder in the dark days after Munich but he faced up to them with a dedicated determination. As Matt Busby summed up, later in his life, 'When things looked their blackest after the Munich accident and there were times when I felt great despair, I was cheered enormously to think that Bobby Charlton was there. He was one of the foundation stones and his presence was a great source of inspiration to keep working for the restoration of Manchester United.'

In all, Bobby enjoyed seventeen seasons of First Division football with Manchester United before a two-year spell as a player and then manager at Preston. When he played his final game for United, against Verona in the Anglo-Italian tournament of 1973, he had set a club record of 604 league appearances (199 goals), played in 79 FA Cup ties and appeared in 45 competitive European matches. It added up with League Cup games to an incredible 752 (plus two sub) appearances with a total of 247 goals. It is difficult to see anyone breaking his record.

On the international front spanning twelve seasons, he held the England appearances record with 106 caps until Bobby

Moore went two better. He still holds the England scoring record with 49 goals, one more than Gary Lineker, five more than Jimmy Greaves.

After his 1966 World Cup success, Bobby was voted Footballer of the Year, quickly followed by the European award ahead of Eusebio and Franz Beckenbauer. He was awarded both the OBE and the CBE before being knighted in the birthday honours of 1994, ten years after being made a director of Manchester United, the club he still serves as a board member.

While the household names of Charlton, Law and Best gave the European Cup-winning team a distinctive aura, they would be the first to acknowledge that the other positions were filled by players of great ability. Every team needs a Nobby Stiles, for instance, a defensive player who could win the ball as well as give it. He was a terrier of a player, once described in South America as El Bandido. In many ways that description is not far off the mark! He was short in stature and his eyesight was not good – his tackling improved after he had been introduced to the advantages of contact lenses – but he was effective. Alf Ramsey recognised his gritty qualities and played him just in front of the two centre-backs. He wore the number four shirt right the way through the World Cup triumph of 1966. Later, he played for Middlesbrough and Preston, and then in Canada, before taking up management and coaching posts, including a spell back at Old Trafford on the youth-team staff.

Nobby, or Norbert to give him his Sunday best name, was a local Collyhurst boy, the son of an undertaker. He went to St Patrick's, a school famed for producing good footballers under teacher Laurie Cassidy. Brian Kidd was another member of the successful European team from St Pat's. At eighteen he was the youngest player in the side and became one of their heroes in his first season at senior level. The son of a Manchester bus driver, he joined the club at the age of fifteen and replaced

David Herd in the attack at the start of the successful European season.

Brian, another product of Busby's youth philosophy, was an accomplished forward, strong and capable of a shot with either foot. He won two full England caps before being transferred to Arsenal for £110,000 in 1974 by Tommy Docherty. He went on to play for Manchester City, Everton, Bolton and in America before having spells in management with Barrow and Preston. He returned to Old Trafford in 1989 to work for the club's Football in the Community scheme. He was back home and such was his enthusiasm for the job that Alex Ferguson soon had him working on a wider front as he overhauled the youth scouting system. Kidd became a key figure in Fergie's junior revolution, and later moved up to replace Archie Knox as first-team coach when the Scot left to join Glasgow Rangers. He became an integral part of United's phenomenal wave of success before moving to Blackburn to try management as a number one. Relegation followed a trying time at Ewood Park but he surfaced again at Leeds United where, after working with the young players, David O'Leary made him first-team coach.

If Brian Kidd was the baby of the European Cup, there was no doubting who was the daddy of the side. Bill Foulkes, a traditional stopper, was the linchpin for Matt Busby for eighteen years involving nearly 700 competitive games. Born in St Helens, Lancashire, he was recruited from Whiston Boys Club after starting his working life down the pit, and was one of the stalwarts who bridged the gap between the Busby Babes and the teams after Munich.

A one-club man as a player, he went on to manage and coach at home and abroad, including a spell as a coach at Old Trafford. He was elected the first chairman of the Association of Former Manchester United Players, the first old boys' organisation in football. It was set up under the leadership of the tireless secretary, David Sadler, former Busby Babe John Doherty, Warren Bradley and Alan Wardle.

A former England amateur international from Maidstone in Kent, David Sadler was a versatile player who could operate in both defence and attack. He proved to be a pivotal figure in the European Cup final, moving forward into a decisive role in extra time, which tipped the balance United's way. An athletic performer, he provided the midfield with momentum in contrast to Pat Crerand whose strength was his vision and shrewd passing. It was always said that if Crerand played well, then United played well. Busby brought him to Old Trafford to improve the service to his front players, which he did with a creative spirit that was particularly welcomed by Denis Law. Crerand was not the speediest of men but it never seemed to matter because his football intelligence and use of the ball more than made up for a lack of pace.

Pace was the name of the game as far as John Aston was concerned at outside-left. A local boy, his father was the John Aston who was in Matt Busby's 1948 FA Cup-winning team. Young John sometimes seemed to run into trouble more often than creating chances, but he will be remembered for his performance in the European Cup final when he ran Benfica ragged down the left flank. His direct dashing style made a fine contrast to the wandering, mesmeric dribbling of George Best, United's notional winger on the right.

Pace was also the significant quality of United's full-backs. Tony Dunne was a modest investment from Shelbourne in the Republic of Ireland but he developed into a speedy and much admired defender for both club and country with thirty-three caps. He played for thirteen seasons in the first team, making over 500 competitive appearances.

Shay Brennan, Manchester born of Irish parents which led to nineteen games for the Republic of Ireland, was an overnight sensation after Munich. He was pulled up from the depths of the A team to star as a winger in the fraught weeks after the crash until the emergency was over. He returned to the senior scene two years later and played for another ten seasons, making nearly 300 league appearances. One of the quiet and unassuming men of the team, rather like his Irish full-back partner, he blended perfectly into the framework by linking together the more famous names. Shay later settled in Waterford in Ireland and died on a golf course from a heart attack in 2000.

Behind them all stood Alex Stepney, still talked about for his saves against Eusebio in the final against Benfica and regarded by Matt Busby as the final piece in that particular jigsaw. He was a long-serving master of his trade, making more than 500 appearances for United over a period of twelve years. His transfer to Old Trafford had been a complete surprise to the player because he had only just moved to Chelsea from Millwall. Chelsea already had Peter Bonetti and so Matt Busby asked for either one of them. Tommy Docherty decided to move Stepney out, even though he had played only one game for them. He wasn't a flashy goalkeeper but one who struck the highest of standards in all departments of his game, be it as a shot-stopper or coming out for crosses. A Londoner born and bred, he nevertheless stayed in the area and eventually became Manchester City's goalkeeping coach.

Matt Busby looked around Scotland, Ireland, the north east of England, London, Kent, St Helens and, of course, the schools of Manchester as he slowly and patiently built his great team of the sixties. Most of his 1968 team settled in or around Manchester, at the end of their playing days, the place they now call home and where their destiny was fulfilled.

11

SOUTH AMERICAN WAY

WINNING the European Cup brought entry into the World Club Championship, a competition played home and away between the champions of Europe and the winners of the Copa Libertadores in South America. This meant a match with Estudiantes of Argentina and an experience as novel as it was shocking for Manchester United and their players.

The first leg, played in Buenos Aires, was summed up the following night by the headline in the *Manchester Evening News* – 'SAVAGERY'. The *Daily Mirror* carried the banner 'THE NIGHT THEY SPAT ON SPORTSMANSHIP', and a sub-head which declared 'Estudiantes were set on treachery, provocation and violence'. Perhaps United should not have been surprised because this inter-continental competition between the winners of UEFA's Champion Clubs' Cup and the Copa Libertadores had a dark history.

The original idea for an annual challenge match between the northern and southern hemispheres came from Henri Delaunay, the general secretary of UEFA, and the first encounter – played in 1960 between Real Madrid and Penarol – was a great success. The match in Uruguay was goalless but the Spaniards romped home 5–1 in the Bernabeu Stadium. That game was refereed by England's Ken Aston. Penarol regained their pride the following year. Although they lost the first match 1–0 in Portugal, they beat Benfica 5–0 on their own ground and went on to win the play-off 2–1 in Montevideo two days later. Santos also figured in a high-scoring match in those early years, winning 3–2 at home before putting five goals past Benfica in the second match as the Brazilians demonstrated their world class.

But in 1963 the competition started to turn sour with violence in the game between AC Milan and Santos. Then matches between British and Argentinian clubs in 1967 and 1968 really plunged the competition into controversy. Argentina had been badly hurt by England manager Sir Alf Ramsey during the 1966 World Cup when he described the players in their national team as animals. The quarter-final when England knocked out Argentina and their captain Rattin was sent off provided a provocative background. Heads were completely lost in the 1967 play-off between Glasgow Celtic and Racing Club. Basile spat at Lennox and the result was a wholesale fight. Five players were sent off.

Then came Manchester United's two bad-tempered matches with Estudiantes in 1968. Everything started well enough with United's arrival in Buenos Aires marked by presentations of flowers, great hospitality, and even a specially staged polo match for the players, officials and English press to watch. The first indication that the South Americans meant business came on the eve of the match when both teams were invited to an official reception. Sir Matt Busby wasn't keen on taking his players to what he expected to be a long drawn out affair and hardly the best preparation for a big game, but he agreed in the interests of goodwill and courtesy to the hosts.

His unease was confirmed when the Estudiantes team failed to turn up and their coach, Osvaldo Zubeldia, said the next day: 'This is a game for men. I see no point in teams kissing each other.' The United manager became even angrier when he had the local newspapers translated to discover Benfica manager Otto Gloria had been quoted with some hardly welcoming comments. Gloria was reported as saying that Nobby Stiles was 'an assassin' and Estudiantes even ran an article in their match programme by the Benfica chief saying that Stiles was 'brutal, badly intentioned and a bad sportsman'.

Stiles had been in the England team that beat Argentina in 1966, and as subsequent events confirmed, he was the focus and hate target for the Estudiantes supporters. The hostility for Stiles actually started as he walked off the plane in Buenos Aires and an excitable commentator was announcing the arrival of the United players over the loudspeaker system as they walked through the airport – 'Bobby Charlton – El Supremo,' he shouted. 'George Best – El Beatle,' he declared. Then his voice went up an octave and there was a great answering roar as he went on 'Nobby Stiles – El Bandido!'

The pre-match scene was surreal with steel-helmeted riot police armed with batons and tear-gas guns waiting behind the goals while out on the pitch pretty girls in colourful national costume gave delightful dancing displays. As the players came out, a bomb releasing a thick cloud of dense red smoke lent a nightmarish touch as the United players struggled to retain their composure.

It was always going to be difficult because provocation was rife as Estudiantes set the attacking pace to force the visitors into a largely defensive position. Bill Foulkes and David Sadler were outstanding in the centre of defence, while Tony Dunne at left-back gave danger man Ramon 'The Witch' Veron hardly a kick of the ball. Francis Burns, the full-back on the other flank, hit top form. Pat Crerand was pushed back to help the defence but came forward at every opportunity to try to spark the attack into life.

Stiles, considering the pressure he was under, did marvellously with a disciplined performance as he tried to harass the

Nobby Stiles

South Americans into making mistakes. He was a marked man, though, and in the fourteenth minute he was head-butted by Carlos Bilardo, an assault which opened a gash over his left eye. It also left him with double vision in the damaged eye and it was perhaps significant that it was only quarter of an hour later when Estudiantes scored the goal for their 1–0 win. Certainly the goal was badly defended in the twenty-eighth minute when Conigliaro headed in a corner from Veron at close range. United tried hard for an equaliser and it seemed to have come in the thirty-eighth minute when Sadler flicked Bobby Charlton's free kick through a crowd of players into the goal. The referee, Señor Sosa Miranda of Paraguay, at first awarded a goal but then changed his mind after spotting the linesman's flag up and speaking to him.

Bobby Charlton insisted, 'It was a bad decision. I had to hit the ball round a wall of three players for David Sadler to run on to so it was ridiculous to say he was offside.'

United had few other chances against some ruthless tackling in midfield which effectively broke up any sustained attacking, and playing football was not easy against a team that kicked and spat at them for the entire ninety minutes. Bobby Charlton needed two stitches in a shin wound in the early stages and the miracle was how Stiles kept control in face of brutal tackling for as long as he did. He didn't snap until ten minutes from the end, and then just made a gesture of no real significance. A linesman flagged him for offside and, in the way of players, he flung his arm into the air. Considering the way he had been knocked about, it seemed a trivial offence but the referee saw it as dissent and he was sent off. The real price to pay was an automatic suspension for the game in Manchester.

Stiles was jeered as he trudged off, but he was certainly not blamed by his manager who said later, 'Bilardo behaved worse than Nobby has ever done in his life. I object to his sending-off because it was based on a false reputation of being a tough player. What do you expect of a man who was butted in the eye a few minutes after the game had started?

'They are crucifying Nobby Stiles because of a reputation he has been given which is quite unfair. He was sent off in this match simply because of a reputation and build-up around him in Argentina which has been quite disgraceful.'

Team-mate David Sadler also sympathised. 'Nobby was great,' he said. 'He turned his back and walked away from everything. He was butted, punched, pushed and kicked and then got sent off for getting offside.'

Skipper Bobby Charlton summed up, 'Their ideas and interpretation of football are just different from ours. We didn't really get a chance to play.'

Under the circumstances, United counted themselves fortunate to escape with such a narrow defeat and they were certainly not depressed about their chances in the return at Old Trafford. They also drew great satisfaction from knowing that if it hadn't been for their discipline and control, the game could easily have exploded into a mass riot.

As Sir Matt said, 'I was extremely proud of the way the boys accepted every provocation with hardly a murmur. This was the most trying game I have been involved in. Holding the ball put a player in danger of his life. It was disgraceful. After what we experienced, it was a very good result for us. The lads defended magnificently.'

The teams in Buenos Aires lined up:

Estudiantes: Poletti, Malbernat, Aguirre-Suarez, Medina, Pachame, Madero, Ribaudo, Bilardo, Togneri, Conigliaro, Veron.

Manchester United: Stepney, Dunne, Sadler, Foulkes, Burns, Stiles, Crerand, Charlton, Morgan, Law, Best.

The second leg came three weeks later at Old Trafford on 16 October in front of a 64,000 crowd who watched in frustration as their team took the game to the visitors but could do no more than draw 1–1 to lose the series. They pressed hard for a winner on the night, which would have brought a play-off in Amsterdam three days later, but Estudiantes were not only good in the dirty tricks department, they were brilliant defensively.

They rocked United by scoring as early as the fifth minute when Veron got on to the end of a curling free kick from Madero at the far post. United, who had Shay Brennan and Brian Kidd replacing Francis Burns and the suspended Stiles, were not helped by an injury to Denis Law. He had to have four stitches in a gashed knee and took no further part in the game. Carlo Sartori came on as substitute to find his team-mates dictating the course of the match but unable to create any serious chances until the closing stages.

In the last ten minutes the game exploded into action. First George Best retaliated after being heavily tackled by Medina. He swung a right which floored his opponent with the result that the pair of them were sent off. The pot really boiled over with two more Argentinians, Bilardo and Echicopa, booked, as United made a last ditch effort to save the match.

Hopes soared three minutes from the end when Willie Morgan crashed in an equaliser from Pat Crerand's smartly taken free kick. In one final fling, Brian Kidd slammed home a cross from Morgan and thousands thought their team had forced a third game, but the Yugoslav referee had blown for time a good couple of seconds before the goal.

Estudiantes hadn't played with the cynical approach that marked their play in Buenos Aires, but that hadn't stopped the United following gaining their revenge with continual baiting of the visitors, chanting 'animal' taunts at them. The first game left a nasty taste but in the second Estudiantes showed their considerable ability and the fact of the matter was that United had failed to rise to the occasion.

Skipper Charlton was utterly honest when he said, 'We can't blame them this time. The game was not anything like as tough as it was in Buenos Aires. They gave us the chance to play and we just didn't take it. They went in for time-wasting and obstruction but they weren't bad. We can have no quibbles. We have played teams ten times better and beaten them, but we failed to get going. Their early goal killed us.'

So United lost. They were sadder and perhaps wiser, but a lot of their supporters wondered if it had been worth it. While not enjoying the experience, Sir Matt Busby still felt pleased to have taken part. He made it clear that if the opportunity arose again to enter the competition he would do so. He reasoned that only by continuing to meet South American teams would a better understanding be reached and common ground between two cultures be found. A man whose imagination right from the start of the European adventure had been fired by a global vision saw no reason to turn parochial.

But even the enlightened Sir Matt must have questioned the wisdom of the annual affray the following year when Estudiantes played Milan and three of their players ended up in jail for their acts of hostility in the second leg in Italy. A number of European clubs took the huff and in the next few years Ajax, Bayern Munich, Liverpool twice and Nottingham Forest all refused to take part. It wasn't until Japan stepped forward in 1980 with an offer to host a one-game final sponsored by Toyota that the World Cup Championship regained its stature. Perhaps one day FIFA might expand the idea and bring in the champions from Africa, Asia and Central America to make it a truly world contest.

Nobby Stiles

Carlos Bilardo became famous as a football manager when he guided Argentina to victory in the World Cup of 1986 played in Mexico. I am sure he was a shrewd coach with great ability who deserved his success, but I remembered a very different man.

I knew Carlos Bilardo as a player from the time in 1968 when Manchester United played Estudiantes for the World Cup Championship, and I have got to admit that I did not care for the guy I knew in those days. I mean you don't particularly strike up a friendship with someone who head-butts you in a match. That's what he did to me in the first leg in Buenos Aires and we had only been playing for a few minutes. The 'nutting' was bad enough but what made it worse was that after he had done it, he threw himself down to try and kid the referee that it was me who had hit him. I think the referee was going to send me off until I was able to point to the blood running down the side of my face from a cut eye and he changed his mind.

In actual fact I did get sent off in that first game, but not until near the end and then for something which left me feeling pig sick. Paddy Crerand and I had talked at half-time about how we should try to beat their offside trap which kept catching us out. We agreed that if our forwards came back as their defence ran out then I should make some runs from midfield to try to catch them offguard and going the wrong way.

We tried it once or twice and on this occasion I thought we had caught them out but the linesman signalled I was offside. I didn't think I was, and so I just threw my hand up in the air as a natural gesture. The referee sent me off for dissent, which was ridiculous after what had gone on in the game with kicking, spitting and me on the receiving end of a butting. To be sent off for waving your arm was a bit silly.

I was still very upset, though, because I thought I had let the side down. Mind you, the referee was a funny chap. He was smoking a cigarette when we all came down the tunnel to go out on to the pitch. A lot of people smoke, of course, but you don't expect to see the referee having a puff like that!

It was a different world in South America. Before the kick-off there were all these girls folk dancing watched by riot police wearing helmets and carrying guns. It was quite incongruous, especially when we actually walked out with clouds of red smoke billowing from a bomb someone had let off.

I suppose even before the game had started I was targeted as the villain of the piece. I always had a reputation as a fairly aggressive player but the South American press really went to town. They called me an assassin and even in the match pro-gramme I was described as brutal. I could hardly expect the home fans to be on my side after that – and they weren't of course! Bilardo was clearly out to get me and I think the referee must have read the programme notes as well because I certainly didn't get much sympathy from him.

The situation had its lighter moments. I remember coming out of the dressing-room after the match and walking alongside the stadium towards the team bus. It was dark and shadowy when I suddenly felt something thrust into my back with a voice whispering into my ear, 'Now then, El Bandido.' I thought my end had come until I realised it was Brian Kidd!

12

FOLLOW THE MASTER

W HO could have predicted the bleak years that lay ahead as Bobby Charlton held aloft the European Cup on that unforgettable night in May 1968? No one expected thirty-one years to pass before the name of Manchester United was engraved on that famous trophy for a second time, certainly none of that ecstatic, celebrating mass packed into Wembley Stadium. None but the most gifted oracle could possible have foreseen the troublesome period that would follow the club's finest hour and anyone making such claims would have been scornfully disregarded.

Manchester United had reached nirvana. As the players paraded victoriously, posing for photographs, embracing one another, the supporters joined in a dance of joy that shook the famous old stadium to its foundations. The durability of Wembley's concrete terracing was tested to the limit as it vibrated under the pounding of tens of thousands of feet.

It was a scene of glorious realisation, a moment when the club and its supporters enjoyed the present as some certainly thought of the past. Tears of joy mingled with those of sadness as older fans recalled the players who made the ultimate sacrifice in their bid to win that giant glistening trophy being carried around below them.

What about the future? What was next for Manchester United? Surely that would take care of itself. Winning the European Cup marked the end of a long journey. Success in Europe meant Matt Busby had realised his dream. Thoughts of starting again, building another side to continue the club's reign at the top were doubtless far removed from his mind as he watched his players enjoying their moment of glory. The European Cup was his, the trophy he had coveted for more than a decade. Yet, as the cheers echoed around the stadium on that humid night, the manager knew the day would be not too far away when he would be faced with the task of breaking up the side that had won two championships and reached the ultimate goal. Would he have the heart to do it?

He was nearing sixty years of age – the European Cup was won two days after his fifty-ninth birthday – the pressures of the job, and the torment he had lived through after Munich, had taken their toll. No matter how calm and collected Matt Busby appeared on the surface, life for the past ten years had been an ordeal. To replace one important player is often a difficult task; to be forced through tragedy to find a whole new team must have placed immense pressure on the man who almost died along with his young stars.

He also wanted to spend more time with Jean, who had been forced to sacrifice many of the moments married couples took for granted during a lifetime together because of the demands of football management. A strong reason why he was prepared to relinquish his role as manager was to make up for all that time he had spent away from home.

There was good reason to expect more success in the years ahead. Had his team not proved they were the best in Europe as well as winning the league championship twice in three seasons? Before his inevitable retirement, Busby believed he would see his players bringing more trophies to the club. There seemed no indication of the stormy waters ahead, but did his choice of words give a clue that perhaps all was not well, when shortly after the European final he said, 'Let us hope this is not the end, just the beginning.'

United had dominated domestic football for the previous five seasons. As champions of Europe, they were ready to go on to greater things. New players would be brought in, merging with established stars, the club's youth system would continue to produce more talented youngsters, fresh horizons would be reached. Between what was contemplated and what occurred there was a sharp contrast. The glory years of the sixties led into the sparseness of the early seventies. The cause is difficult to fathom. Supreme success was followed by desperate decline, and the theory that one contributed to the other is difficult to contradict.

The win over Benfica brought a feeling of satisfaction as well as relief to everyone connected with the club, from chairman Louis Edwards, his directors and the management team of Busby and Murphy, down through the players young and not-so-young, to those ordinary folk who paid their shillings to stand and cheer. There was satisfaction because United had at last claimed what they regarded as their rightful place among the élite of football, and relief because a struggle had come to an end. A burden had been lifted, the albatross was finally taken from their shoulders. Now they could relax. To sit back once the job was done might seem unwise, but that is what appeared to happen at Manchester United once the Champions Cup was theirs.

For twelve years the club and its followers had shared the joys, and endured the sorrows as Busby tried to climb a seemingly unconquerable peak. Time and again he took the club close to the summit, glory seemed to be within reach, only for him to fail a few strides from the top and slide back to where he had

nter Cities Fairs Cup action against Ferencvaros in Budapest in 1965. A team wall consists f John Connelly, Shay Brennan, Nobby Stiles, Denis Law, Bobby Charlton, Bill Foulkes, at Crerand, David Herd and George Best. Pat Dunne is in goal behind and Tony Dunne on he extreme right.

Iarry Gregg punches clear from Vogt on a wet and freezing afternoon in East Berlin against he German Army team ASK Vorwaerts in the European Cup campaign of 1965–66.

Denis Law in white *(right)* beats Germano to score United's second goal in a 3–2 win over Benfica in the first leg of their European quarter-final in 1966.

John Aston flies through the air with Denis Law to his left, against Real Madrid. United are on their way to the 1968 final of the European Cup.

Bobby Charlton lets fly against Benfica in the final of the European Cup at Wembley.

Brian Kidd marks his nineteenth birthday with a goal against the Portuguese champions in the 1968 showdown.

George Best scores the killer goal in extra time which put United on the path to European victory.

Left Nobby Stiles, Bobby Charlton and Bill Foulkes celebrate as United become the first English club to win the European Cup.

Below More joy from Pat Crerand, George Best and a delighted Matt Busby.

obby Charlton proudly displays the European Footballer of the Year award he won in 1966.

eorge Best receives his European trophy in 1969 from Max Urbini. Denis Law won it in
964, so this completed a United hat-trick.

Ramon Veron, father of the Argentinian star United signed in summer 2001, was the player who did the damage when United lost the World Club Championship against Estudiantes. He laid on the goal when Estudiantes won 1–0 in Buenos Aires and here he scores the decisive goal in the 1–1 draw at Old Trafford.

Willie Morgan in action against Rapid Vienna as United defend their European crown in season 1968–69.

rian Kidd goes close with a header in the semi-final second leg against AC Milan. United
on 1–0 but went out on aggregate, 2–1.

Vilf McGuinness, the Busby Babe who became manager of Manchester United, shakes hands
ith Sir Stanley Rous, President of FIFA, at the start of the Watney Cup final against Derby
ounty in 1970.

United turned to the UEFA Cup in 1976. Lou Macari tests Schrivers the Ajax goalkeeper in the opening round.

The Reds came to grief in the next round against Juventus despite this brave diving header from Gordon Hill between Italian defenders Tardelli and Cuccureddu.

started. His idea was to create a side capable of facing every challenge in Europe. Now that was done he had to ask himself if he still had the appetite for more. United had already paid a far greater price than any other club to attain European recognition.

The thought of pulling apart his masterpiece and assembling another squad of players did not appeal to Busby, so as United prepared to defend the trophy he decided that the next season would be his last in charge of the club. After reaching the summit, he could prepare to stand down. To have retired before that would have left a job unfinished.

Would Europe still hold the same challenge? In the formative years of the European Cup, fans had been curious to see how their heroes would fair against the top sides of the continent. Shortly before the competition was launched, television audiences were given a taste of what was to come when friendly matches between English and continental sides were screened. As they watched the black and white pictures of the floodlit games, it was apparent that commentators regarded the foreign sides, and their temperamental stars, as something of a novelty.

Tradition dictated that any English team was expected to do well when playing European opposition – had we not invented the game? It was only after humiliation at the hands of the Hungarians in the mid fifties that those in authority reluctantly admitted football was developing abroad. Even the flair of the Brazilians was ignored by the establishment who claimed that while some nations might be our equal, they would never be considered our betters.

Matt Busby realised much was to be achieved by playing beyond our shores. As far back as the early 1950s he had spoken of his visions of top British sides competing in a European League. He could see football was being taken to new levels in countries such as Italy and Spain where the approach was more technical, more analytical, and much more professional. There players were rewarded with vast sums of money and in return were happy to sacrifice much of their freedom. Matt Busby's aim, and it became his obsession, was winning the European Cup. Thirteen seasons after the competition was launched, he achieved that but while winning it was one thing, Manchester United were soon to realise that retaining the trophy was a very different story. No longer were they regarded as the famous English challengers, full of hope. Now they were the champions of Europe. Busby's team had earned the right to be mentioned in the same breath as Real Madrid, Benfica and AC Milan. They were the side to be beaten.

During the summer United enjoyed their moment – the players were hailed as heroes, and Matt Busby was knighted for his services to football. Shortly before the campaign in defence of the trophy began, fate once again struck a cruel blow. John Aston, the unexpected hero of Wembley, broke his leg during the derby clash with Manchester City at Maine Road. It was an incident that typified the almost modest approach the young player took to the game, and which football appeared to take to him. He was hurt in a challenge just before half-time and was left lying on the field, receiving attention from Jack Crompton and physiotherapist Ted Dalton, while the rest of the players from both sides trooped off at the interval.

Aston was stretchered away to some sympathetic applause but the injury virtually signalled the end of his career at Old Trafford. He stayed with the club for a further three seasons, but never reached the standard of play of those weeks leading up to the European final and eventually joined Luton Town.

That derby game played on 17 August 1968 was a unique occasion. City were league champions; United, their neighbours and biggest rivals, held the European crown. Manchester had every reason to enjoy its moment as the nation's football capital and it was hardly surprising that a massive 63,052 turned up to watch the game.

A month later United faced Irish minnows Waterford in the first round of the European Cup. Aston and full-back Shay Brennan were the only players missing from the previous season's trophy winning line-up. Denis Law returning in place of the unlucky Aston, and Brennan losing his place to the youthful Francis Burns.

The Irish were not a real match, but the game provided Waterford with the biggest moment in its history. Their little ground on the Republic's south coast was deemed unsuitable for such an event, and in the knowledge that United had a massive following in the Emerald Isle, the fixture was switched to Dublin's Lansdowne Road. So it was that Manchester United's defence of the European Cup began in a stadium more often used for rugby union internationals, and when Law scored as early as the eighth minute there was good reason for many in the huge crowd to expect a scoreline more akin to the fifteen-a-side game.

The Irish were well beaten, but not humiliated in that first leg. Law completed a hat-trick, even though he missed a penalty, United won 3–1 and the crowd went home happy. Waterford's players felt satisfied that they had competed against the best and the club's loyal band of supporters had every right to be proud of their heroes, even though they knew the second leg was going to be a formality.

The Irish part-timers faced United at Old Trafford on 2 October 1968 and the game was in sharp contrast to the ill-tempered clash with Estudiantes which followed two weeks later. Even the Stretford Enders, not renowned for such hospitality, went out of their way to be sporting and friendly towards Waterford, probably because they felt they were no real match for Busby's thoroughbreds. Their chanting inspired other sections of the crowd to get behind the underdogs and the cry of 'Water-ford! Water-ford!' came from most of the 41,000 throats and gave the Irish players heart as well as a moment to savour.

United strolled through the early stages. The home supporters good-humouredly turned against their favourites. Cries of dissent came from the terraces and the slow hand-clap was an illustration of their dissatisfaction. The ploy worked. The protests brought United and the game to life and suddenly it was no contest. Four more goals from Law gave him his second hat-trick of the round with Stiles, Charlton and Burns also contributing to a 7–1 rout.

Befitting the occasion, the biggest cheer of the night was reserved for Al Casey, Waterford's right-winger, who got their consolation goal in the seventieth minute, and the Irish part-timers were cheered warmly as they left the field. They had enjoyed their moment on such a massive stage. There they were, the minnows of the Irish League, being feted not just by the crowd but by the European champions themselves, who formed a guard of honour to applaud them from the pitch on their way to the dressing-room.

After the first phase of the competition, the two previous winners, United and Glasgow Celtic, were Britain's remaining representatives. The claim by Manchester City's coach Malcolm Allison that his players would terrorise Europe proved way off the mark. The league champions fell at the first hurdle, losing 2–1 to Fenerbahce in Turkey, after a goalless opening leg at Maine Road.

Also out were Northern Ireland's champions Glentoran, beaten 5–2 by Belgium's Anderlecht, the 3–0 deficit from the first leg being too much to overcome on their own ground. Had they got through, they would have faced United, because it was Anderlecht who provided the opposition in the second round.

Memories of the first meeting between the clubs came flooding back. Newspapers recalled 1956 and the start of the European journey when United won 12–0 on aggregate. They were clear favourites to get through this time as well, but football is never as simple as that.

United's form in the League seemed affected by their concentration on Europe. The first cracks were beginning to show. They had started the season with a win against Everton but this was followed by defeat at West Bromwich Albion, then a 0–0 draw in the Maine Road derby. By the time they faced the Belgians in the first game, five more First Division fixtures had been lost, as many as in the whole of the previous season. Chelsea won 4–0 at Old Trafford, Sheffield Wednesday 5–4 at Hillsborough, Burnley beat them 1–0 at Turf Moor, Liverpool 2–0 at Anfield, and Southampton surprisingly won 2–1 at Old Trafford. It was hardly the form expected from Europe's top side.

Sir Matt had made few changes to his side. The backbone remained the same with the players who had won at Wembley being joined by youngsters John Fitzpatrick and Carlo Sartori, plus centre-half Steve James. Frank Kopel a full-back from Falkirk played a handful of games, Alan Gowling a lanky student from Manchester University broke into the squad, and occasionally young Scottish winger Jim Ryan deputised for George Best.

There had been just one major signing after the European final when Sir Matt captured Willie Morgan, Burnley's Scottish international star, for £100,000, adding another of football's pop-star generation to his cast. Like George Best, Morgan was a player whose picture adorned the bedroom walls of teenaged girls, part of the new support attracted to games not perhaps for the excitement and skill of the contest, but simply to be close to their favourites.

The new signing's debut came in the 3–1 win over Tottenham on 28 August 1968 but, because he was signed after the

European transfer deadline, Morgan was ineligible to play until the quarter-final stages of the competition. He was forced to watch from the wings as United faced Anderlecht three months after his arrival.

United had to make changes from their regular line-up. George Best was suspended so Ryan and Sartori were in the side. David Sadler moved to centre-half replacing the veteran Bill Foulkes, and Brennan took over from Burns at full-back. There was to be no 10–0 this time, but two more goals from Denis Law took him to a remarkable nine in three rounds. Another from Kidd gave United a 3–0 advantage for the second leg in Belgium.

Before the return game, United drew both their domestic fixtures without scoring a goal. They dropped a home point to Ipswich, and were held at Stoke. The signs that all was not as it should have been were evident to anyone willing to look. There seemed good reason for the critics to point accusing fingers, but the more faithful sportswriters assured everyone the League was not the prime target. Sir Matt was focusing on Europe and who could doubt his wisdom?

With Best still unavailable, the manager adopted a defensive approach for the return game. Stepney had Kopel and Dunne as his two full-backs, Foulkes returned at centre-half, Crerand and Stiles were the wing-halves. The forward line was Fitzpatrick, Law, Charlton, Sadler and Sartori. Ryan stepped down to make way for Fitzpatrick and Foulkes replaced Kidd in the eleven. Sadler's role was to help Foulkes in defence with Fitzpatrick slipping in alongside Crerand.

At the start of the previous season, UEFA had made changes to its competition rules. Up to the quarter-final stage, a goal scored away from home now became of extra value. If the scores were level at the end of two legs, the away-goal rule was used to settle matters rather than the tie going to a third game. The side scoring most away goals would be deemed the winner if the aggregate remained level at the end of extra time in the second leg. If both sides were equal on every count, a decision would be reached by the toss of a coin. Heads you win, tails you are out of the European Cup!

Such matters seemed of little significance when Carlo Sartori gave United the valuable advantage of an away goal after just seven minutes. They led 4–0 on aggregate, but Anderlecht, with nothing to lose, decided to gamble. They threw everything into attack and made the champions look extremely vulnerable.

After eighteen minutes Jan Mulder scored with a ferocious shot. The goal inspired the home side. With the fans screaming for more, United found themselves under siege. Stepney was forced to make save after save but was beaten twice by Bergholtz and suddenly, with the aggregate score on 3–4, Anderlecht realised they were in with a chance. They stepped up the fight, knowing a major upset was possible. Determined to make their own niche in European football history, and perhaps take revenge for that humiliation at the hands of the Busby Babes, they pushed United back. But the Belgians needed to score twice to win and it proved too much for them. It was a close call, but United went through.

If their pride was dented it didn't show. Three days later, they found their scoring touch again. With Best available once more, they beat Wolves 3–0 at Old Trafford.

Then came the break between the European rounds. The modern-day United has often used the Champions League winter lay-off to step up its challenge for the Premiership, but in 1968–69 any hopes of being involved in the championship race were fading fast. December was a bleak month. United won just one game, against Liverpool, but lost three others to Leicester, Southampton and Arsenal.

When they were beaten 2–1 by Leeds at Elland Road in early

January, it was their third successive league defeat, something they had not experienced since March 1963, and that season they came close to relegation. Three days after the Leeds defeat and eight months since the victory over Benfica, Busby decided to make his plans for the future public. The club issued a statement which read:

> Sir Matt has informed the board that he wishes to relinquish the position of team manager at the end of the present season. The chairman and directors have tried to persuade him to carry on, and it was only with great reluctance that his request has been accepted. The board fully appreciates the reason for his decision and it was unanimously agreed that Sir Matt be appointed general manager of the club, which he is very happy to accept.

Busby wanted to step into the background, staying with the club but leaving team matters to another. He felt it was time for a younger man to take over. Immediately the back-page speculation began. Who would take over Manchester United's throne? Who could follow the master?

Don Revie of Leeds United, Ken Furphy successful manager of Third Division Watford, and Brian Clough, who was about to bring Derby County up from the Second Division, were among the names put forward. Jock Stein of Celtic was another but, as with Jimmy Murphy, such an appointment was thought unlikely because of his age. Could the new man be Noel Cantwell, the former United skipper, perhaps partnered by Malcolm Allison, the Manchester City coach? The guessing game threw up a wide variety of potential candidates.

The press ran the story for weeks and touched on two men already ensconced at Old Trafford, Bobby Charlton (to become player-manager), and Wilf McGuinness. Charlton was a legend, his performances for club and country were second to none, but could he handle such a dual role? The promising playing career of McGuinness had been seriously affected when he broke a leg. Eventually, he joined the club's coaching staff and had been in charge of the youth team and United's reserves as well as the England Under-21 side. He had the credentials, but was he perhaps too young for such a task? The guessing continued as United prepared to play Rapid Vienna in the first leg of the quarter-final. By this time they were well behind Leeds, Liverpool and Everton, the sides setting the pace at the top of the First Division. They had lost eleven games, but more to the point had won just eight of the twenty-eight league fixtures they had played. The best they could hope for was a mid-table spot by the end of the season. Their chances of success lay in the FA Cup and in Europe.

The Football Association did nothing to ease the pressure by insisting they played an FA Cup fifth-round replay against Birmingham City forty-eight hours before the first of the European Cup quarter-finals. United kept hopes alive, dispatching Birmingham 6–2 with yet another Law hat-trick. Two nights later, with Morgan now available and Best free from suspension, they beat the Austrians 3–0. Best scored twice and Morgan, on his European Cup debut, got the other.

Between the two quarter-final games, Everton stunned Old Trafford by winning a sixth-round FA Cup tie 1–0, so now just one prize remained within United's reach.

In another of the quarter-finals, Celtic had drawn 0–0 with AC Milan in the San Siro, putting the British clubs on a collision course. What a perfect ending it would be for Sir Matt to lead out his beloved Manchester United side to face the former European champions from the city of his birth, but it was not to be. As United drew 0–0 in Austria in the second leg, Celtic lost 0–1 to the Italians. It would be United versus AC Milan in the semi-final, a repeat of the game played in 1958 in the aftermath of Munich.

Following the quarter-final, form at home took an upward turn but only after Manchester City had beaten United by a single goal at Old Trafford and Chelsea had won 3-2 at Stamford Bridge. The supporters were far from happy. Some made their feelings known by staying away from Old Trafford with just 36,638 turning up to witness the next home game. It was a meagre crowd by United's standards but those who stayed away missed a remarkable result as Queen's Park Rangers were beaten 8–2. Morgan scored his first (and only) league hat-trick for United, Best added two more and Kidd and Stiles also scored. The other scorer was John Aston, playing in his first home game since breaking his leg.

The win sparked off the best run of the season, seven games without defeat, five of them victories and it was during this spell that the club issued another statement putting an end to all the speculation about who would succeed Sir Matt. The final whistle was blown on the guessing game:

> The board has given further consideration to the changes which will occur at the end of the season and has decided to appoint a chief coach who will be responsible for team selection, coaching, training and tactics.
>
> Mr Wilf McGuinness has been selected for this position and will take up his duties as from June 1, and in these circumstances it is not necessary to advertise for applications as was first intended. Sir Matt will be responsible for all other matters affecting the club and players, and will continue as club spokesman.

Busby's final season was coming to an end as the club prepared for the semi-final. The first leg was in Milan but United made football and television history by screening the game at Old Trafford. Supporters watched the action on giant screens mounted on the pitch. Almost 23,000 turned up, cheering and chanting at the huge black and white images as if watching a live game at the stadium. It was a bizarre evening. The Stretford End was packed. The masses screamed their encouragement as though convinced the players could hear their shouts hundreds of miles away in Italy. They urged their side on, baiting the opposition and hurling abuse at the Czech referee when he allowed the first Milan goal.

Things did not go United's way. Sormani scored after appearing to handle and later in the game Jimmy Rimmer, in goal following an injury to Stepney, could do little to stop Milan's second. Fireworks exploded on the terracing in the San Siro and missiles were hurled at the British players but if things were bad, they got worse when Fitzpatrick was sent off for kicking Kurt Hamrin, Milan's Swedish midfielder.

Back in England, the Old Trafford crowd erupted as Fitzpatrick left the field in tears. He knew that even if they reached the final he would miss the game. His European Cup was over and three weeks later so was United's.

The 2–0 deficit did not seem impossible to overturn, and there lingered a faint hope that United might manage to reach the final in Madrid. What better game to provide the setting for Sir Matt's last in charge? Memories not just of 1968 and that semi-final victory over the Spaniards returned, but also of those closely fought contests between the two clubs in the years before Munich. Before that, though, came Milan.

On the night of the second leg, the Italians looked well organised in defence. With their lead from the first game they were understandably favourites to get through and the fact that Cudicini their goalkeeper had not conceded more than two goals in a game for over two years illustrated the magnitude of United's task. The Italians' plan was to play a formation which would stifle United in midfield, but some of their other tactics annoyed the English fans. At the slightest sign of physical contact the Milan players would go down and lay writhing on the ground, making the most of the situation and, more to the point, wasting valuable time.

United were up for it. Four times in the first half they almost scored but seventy minutes had gone before Bobby Charlton struck the winning goal. It was not enough to take United through. The goal was United's one hundredth in the Champions Cup. It was created by George Best but it was fitting that Charlton should score it, a player who linked the pioneering side of the fifties with the team that won the European Cup.

United needed a second and fought hard to get it. In the event of the score being level at the end of the two games, plans were already in hand for a third encounter. The decider would take place in the Heysel Stadium in Brussels, but hopes of reaching the comfort zone of a play-off began to fade as the minutes ticked away.

Then came the moment fate decided Manchester United would not be going to Madrid. Shortly before the end of a passionate encounter, Denis Law thought he had scored the equaliser but the referee ruled that the ball had not crossed the line. Law's stab was dragged back by an outstretched Italian leg but Willie Morgan, who was following up and the closest United player to the ball, claims to this day that it was a goal. This view was backed by BBC Television whose cameras were at the game, and later that evening *Sportsnight With Coleman*, broadcast live from Old Trafford, carried pictures of the ball crossing the line.

So United were out of the European Cup, and ended the season eleventh in the First Division. Wilf McGuinness took charge and Sir Matt stepped into the background, expressing his relief to be free from the pressures of the job:

My trouble is that it is almost impossible to forget football for a minute of my waking life. I have it for breakfast, dinner and supper. Driving the car I am thinking of it. If I go out socially, everybody wants to talk football. The only time I get a break is on the golf course. I'd like to read but I don't get the time. Really it is football all the way, other people's football too. Sometimes I go to another match and they start speculating about who I have come to see, but I haven't come to see anybody. I've just come to look and listen and enjoy a match and know what's going on.

This would be the burden the young Wilf McGuinness now had to shoulder.

13

UNLUCKY FOR SOME

AFTER twenty-three years in charge at Old Trafford, Sir Matt Busby stepped into the background as the young Wilf McGuinness began his job. Both men knew it would not be easy. Busby's was a hard act to follow and McGuinness had to handle things tactfully. There was a general feeling that some players in his squad might consider themselves equal if not superior to the new coach. This and the caution shown by the club in its reluctance to give him the title of manager made it hard for McGuinness.

As general manager, Sir Matt remained the overlord. He had his own office and secretary at Old Trafford, while as Chief coach, McGuinness spent the majority of his time three miles away at the training ground, supervising practice sessions.

McGuinness set about the task with enthusiasm. He was aware that the years were catching up on the European champions and the time had come for some of those players to be eased into the background. The first seeds of doubt about how everything would work out were sown when the team struggled through the opening weeks of the season. First they drew at Crystal Palace, then lost 2–0 at home to Everton. Southampton came to Old Trafford for the third game of the season, and their striker Ron Davies had a field day scoring four times in a

4–1 victory, a result which signalled the end for centre-half Bill Foulkes, rugged hero of Madrid and Munich. His loyalty was rewarded with a place on the coaching staff. Shay Brennan was also dropped for a second encounter with Everton at Goodison Park three days later.

McGuinness began the season with the twenty-one-year-old Jimmy Rimmer in goal. The promising youngster had been substitute for the European Cup final and had played in the Central League side McGuinness coached. He replaced the experienced Stepney for the first three games but after conceding eight goals was left out for the trip to Everton and went back to the reserves. Charlton, Dunne, Stiles and Law were also missing. Stepney, Kidd, Best, Sadler, Aston and Crerand were the survivors of the side that had taken United to European glory in '68. Fitzpatrick and Burns were the fullbacks; Crerand, Paul Edwards and Sadler were in midfield; and Morgan and Aston were on each wing. Best, Kidd and Irish youngster Don Givens led the attack but it was another blow as United lost 3–0. By the end of this first month, McGuinness had just one victory to his credit when Sunderland were beaten 3–1 at Old Trafford, thanks to goals by Best, Givens and Kidd.

The first move to strengthen the side was made when experienced centre-half Ian Ure was bought from Arsenal. His arrival steadied the ship for a while but it was later revealed the Scot had been the choice of Sir Matt, and not McGuinness. Wilf McGuinness might be the potter, but he could not chose his own clay, and if he felt fresh material was needed from which to mould his side, it was not obviously forthcoming. Charlton and Law remained a part of the squad.

Charlton was virtually an ever-present celebrating his thirty-second birthday by helping United to a 2–1 win over Ipswich as he headed towards his hundredth appearance for England.

Law's appearances were few and far between; he featured in just eleven league games. Law was approaching his thirtieth birthday, Pat Crerand was in his thirty-second year, Dunne, Stiles and Stepney in their late twenties. There were younger players in the squad but it was around the familiar names from the championship sides of '65 and '67 that the team taking United into the seventies was built.

By the end of McGuinness's first season, United were eighth in the table. It was an improvement on the previous year, but once again it meant there was no European qualification. They had come close in the Cup competitions. In the FA Cup they reached the semi-final. It took three games against Leeds before they were beaten at neutral Burnden Park, by the only goal scored in 210 minutes of football. The trophy did come to Manchester that season, but only to be handed to Chelsea, who beat Leeds as Old Trafford staged the replayed final.

During the run in the competition, it seemed for a while that the good times had returned. After beating Ipswich at Portman Road, then Manchester City 3–0 at Old Trafford, they recorded a remarkable win at Northampton beating the home side 8–2 with George Best scoring six times. It was the Irishman's return to the side after a four-match ban. He was suspended following a controversial moment at the end of the first leg of the League Cup semi-final a month earlier. Manchester City stood in United's way, and when a hotly disputed penalty two minutes from time gave them a 2–1 advantage for the return game, tempers flared. After the final whistle the United players made their feelings known to referee Jack Taylor and as he approached the Maine Road tunnel carrying the match ball, Best flicked it from the official's grasp with the back of his hand. The display of petulance cost Best a £100 fine as well as the suspension.

United lacked consistency, an essential ingredient for a successful side. They had a long run of eleven games without defeat sparked off by a 4–1 win over Liverpool at Anfield, but ended the season on the rollercoaster losing 5–1 at Newcastle then followed that result with a 7–0 victory over West Bromwich Albion.

McGuinness knew he had to change things. Denis Law was put on the transfer list at £60,000 and nine other players were released. These included Shay Brennan, a close friend of McGuinness's. His managerial ambitions were put to the test when he was forced to tell the Irishman his services were no longer required. It was a difficult job. The two of them had been together at the club for sixteen years and each was the other's best man when they were married.

The club showed faith in McGuinness before the start of the 1970–71 season when he was given the title of manager, but it did nothing to change his luck. Players from the European Cup-winning side were still in the team as the campaign started – Stepney in goal, Dunne at left full-back, Sadler now preferred as a defender, Crerand and Stiles in the half-back line with Charlton, Kidd and Best in the attack. Law remained at the club but did not play in the opening game. Once again United got off to a bad start, losing at home 1-0 to champions Leeds. Then they drew 0–0 with Chelsea before being humiliated 4–0 by Arsenal at Highbury. Law played in that game, and in the next match scored twice to secure the first win of the season when Burnley were beaten at Turf Moor.

Behind the scenes at Old Trafford there were rumblings of conflict between some of the senior players and their new manager. Sir Matt was still in the background and it seemed his presence made it difficult for McGuinness to feel he truly was the man in control.

By Christmas his side had lost nine times and thoughts of winning the championship had long vanished. They had once again reached the semi-final of the League Cup, which provided a chance of qualifying for Europe's Inter-Cities Fairs Cup, but McGuinness was forced to endure the agony of watching his side going out to Aston Villa who a season earlier had been relegated to the Third Division. It was time for action.

On Boxing Day 1970, following a 4–4 home draw against Derby County, United's board met to decide on the next step. Sir Matt Busby was re-appointed manager, and told the media:

> The directors had a special meeting last night to discuss the performances of the team and decided to release Wilf McGuinness from his duties as team manager. As he did not wish to leave the club, and as the club felt he still had a part to play, he was offered his former position as trainer of the Central League side, which he has accepted. The board has asked me to take over team matters for the time being and until a new appointment is made in the close season.

It was back to square one. Amid allegations that McGuinness had been ousted by player power, Busby was in charge once more. According to Sir Matt, his successor – now his predecessor – never got the players on his side. Within two months, McGuinness walked out. He had a year or more left on his contract but could stand it no longer. He left the country to manage Greek side Aris Salonika. The shock of leaving his first love had a lasting effect on the thirty-three year old. Virtually overnight a nervous condition caused his hair to turn white, then fall out leaving him totally bald.

McGuinness stayed loyal to United throughout his career, finally retiring in 1991 after a spell as physiotherapist with Bury and other managerial and coaching posts in Greece as well as with York City and Hull City. Today he remains part of Manchester's footballing scene, working for Manchester United

Radio as a matchday summariser, and as an entertaining after-dinner speaker.

Busby was reluctant to return. The directors felt he could sort out the dressing-room problems before a new manager was appointed, but the troubles continued. George Best had proved difficult for McGuinness to handle. The player was living up to his pop-star image. His photograph appeared in newspapers virtually every day and he spent much of his free time in nightclubs. He was constantly surrounded by pretty girls and even part-owned a city centre nightspot. He also owned a boutique in partnership with Mike Summerbee of Manchester City. It was hardly the lifestyle of a sportsman, yet on the field Best remained brilliant.

It was only in later years that he revealed the extent of his drink problems, and with hindsight it is easy to understand his behaviour during the early seventies if alcohol was beginning to take a grip on his life. He skipped Christmas Day training the day before McGuinness's last game in charge because he was suffering from a hangover, but still scored against Derby. Then he allegedly missed the train taking United to London where they were due to play Chelsea at Stamford Bridge on 9 January, and this was Busby's first game after taking over again. It was hardly the way to impress his old boss. Best was eventually discovered holed-up in a girlfriend's flat and Sir Matt suspended him for a fortnight, then welcomed him back like the prodigal son. After that life was never the same for the footballing genius from Belfast.

With or without Best, the side showed signs of revival under Sir Matt. They lost just two of their next ten league games, but were knocked out of the FA Cup in a replay at Middlesbrough. The last chance of European qualification vanished by early April as United slipped down the table and once again eighth position in the League was all that could be achieved.

In May 1971 another of the European Cup-winning side bowed out. Nobby Stiles was transferred to Middlesbrough, leaving eight of the 1968 team at Old Trafford. Despite the efforts to sell him a year earlier, Law, who would have played in the final but for his injury, was still there as was Rimmer, the twelfth man at Wembley.

A month later a new manager was appointed. Perhaps United hoped the luck of the Irish would bring back the good times. Frank O'Farrell, soft-spoken boss of Leicester City, took charge. Leicester had just won the Second Division championship. Sir Matt, feeling his presence might hinder the new man, resigned as general manager and was given a seat on the board.

O'Farrell brought his assistant Malcolm Musgrove with him from Filbert Street, and clearly had his own ideas of how the club should be run. Using the players he inherited from Busby and McGuinness, he too set about the task enthusiastically. Six of the Champions Cup winners were in the line-up when the new man named his first side. Law, Best and Charlton formed their familiar strike force. Tommy O'Neill, a nineteen-year-old right full-back from St Helens, the hometown of Bill Foulkes, was the only fresh face. He had broken into the side at the end of the previous season and kept his place. The veteran Dunne was his partner.

The start O'Farrell made was nothing short of sensational compared with the two previous years. They drew their opening fixture but won the next three. By Christmas they had lost just twice in twenty-three league games and topped the table. They had a five-point lead and there was every reason to believe that the good times were back. Talk now was of winning the championship, perhaps even more, and Europe was just around the corner.

Nothing can be taken for granted in football and an eight-match unbeaten run was followed by seven successive defeats.

For no apparent reason, form took a dramatic dive. It was basically the same side that had taken United to the top, but now the players seemed unable to win a game.

Best started his tricks again, failing to turn up for training. O'Farrell responded by dropping him. He fined him two weeks' wages and cancelled the player's days off for five weeks. He made him report for extra training to make up for the time lost. George moved in with Pat Crerand and his wife Noreen, and the senior player acted as his chaperone for several months.

O'Farrell knew he had to invest in new talent and within the space of a fortnight bought Martin Buchan from Aberdeen for £125,000, then Ian Storey-Moore from Nottingham Forest for £200,000. Both were drafted into the side during March but the slump in form meant European qualification had once again been missed. The club had two defeats in the games up to Christmas, but eleven afterwards. They were eighth once again. It seemed nothing had changed after all.

Best was to make the news once more that summer. He was supposed to be on international duty with Northern Ireland but instead went to Spain living it up. He announced that he was quitting the game completely in the furore that followed, and Frank O'Farrell suddenly began to realise what life was like for the manager of Manchester United.

During his first season, O'Farrell had introduced more youngsters into the side, including another Irishman, Sammy McIlroy, who scored on his debut in a 3–3 draw at Maine Road. He was seen as one for the future and was given seven starts as well as many appearances as a substitute during that campaign. Pat Crerand joined Bill Foulkes on the coaching staff after retiring as a player midway through the 1971–72 season. John Aston was transferred to Luton Town in July 1972. Even so, four years on there were still six members of the 1968 Wembley side in the team as the 1972–73 season began.

These included Best who once again had begged, and been granted, forgiveness. He had decided not to retire after all and after a summer of drinking and high living, returned to the fold. His absence from the club's summer tour was overlooked in an effort to get him back on the rails. He joined Law and Charlton in the side but the three former European Footballers of the Year could do little to stop the slide which was coming.

As early as September the championship was a remote hope as United failed to win any of their first ten games. Five defeats and as many draws made it obvious all was not well. A year after heading the table, they were now at the bottom. The alarm bells were ringing but where could the club turn this time?

The directors handed the manager the chequebook and O'Farrell bought Wyn Davies, a thirty-year-old striker from Manchester City, and spent £200,000 on Ted MacDougall from Bournemouth, a prolific goalscorer from the lower divisions. Davies played and scored in the first win of the season against Derby County. MacDougall came into the side a week later and scored his first goal after a further two games when United chalked up their second victory of the campaign against Birmingham City. Between them Davies and MacDougall scored half a dozen goals before a 5–0 defeat at Crystal Palace signalled the end for O'Farrell. Six days before Christmas, Manchester United's directors issued a statement:

In view of the poor position in the League, it was unanimously decided that Mr O'Farrell, Malcolm Musgrove, and John Aston snr. [the chief scout] be relieved of their duties forthwith.

As if that was not enough, it was revealed that Best had written to the board saying he was retiring. The directors had other ideas. They put him on the transfer list. If he decided on another change of heart, he would find himself at another club.

Christmas 1972 was not really a time for celebration at Old Trafford. A home draw with Leeds was followed by a 3–1 defeat at Derby County. Then the third manager since Busby was appointed. A change of manager, a change of luck? Tommy Docherty was certainly a sharp contrast to Frank O'Farrell.

The Doc breezed into Old Trafford just before New Year, picked up his broom and began to sweep the club clean of the dust and cobwebs he felt it had collected over the past years. There was no time for sentiment in Docherty's eyes. Nostalgia was not for him. Players were told they had to earn their place in the side by performance not reputation. He had little regard for past achievements and began to change things from day one.

He bought George Graham from Arsenal for £120,000 and Alex Forsyth, a right full-back, from Partick Thistle for £100,000. Tommy Cavanagh, the Hull City coach, joined him as his assistant. Luck was on their side from the off.

Docherty's first game in charge should have been at home to Everton but the pitch was frozen and the fixture postponed. So United played their first game under his guidance at Highbury on 6 January 1973.

With Graham returning to his former club – which one day he would lead to glory as manager – and Forsyth replacing Tony Dunne at left-back, United approached the game with some optimism. Despite the changes, Arsenal won 3–1 and the performance made the problems abundantly clear to Docherty. He had given up the seemingly secure position of manager of Scotland's national side to take over a club which was now bottom of the First Division.

A week after the Arsenal game, United were knocked out of the FA Cup at Wolverhampton. Any hopes of Europe had once again vanished. Trophies could be forgotten, survival was now the prime target.

Docherty spent again. He bought Lou Macari from Glasgow

Celtic for £200,000, and Jim Holton, a big centre-half from Shrewsbury Town. Four new players, four Scots – it was obvious where Docherty's interests lay. He made one more purchase before the buying stopped, breaking his Scottish sequence by adding midfielder Mick Martin to his squad from Dublin club Bohemians.

All five new players were in the side for Docherty's second home fixture, the postponed clash with Everton. Like his first Old Trafford game against West Ham four days earlier, it ended in a draw. Charlton and Macari had scored against the Hammers, the old and the new, but the Everton game was goalless, a unique achievement for the United of 1973. It was the first time a home crowd had seen a game without a goal for twenty-one matches.

Just two of the European Cup-winning side started that first home game, Stepney and Charlton. Docherty was certainly ringing the changes. Altogether he brought in nine players before the end of the half-season he was given to rescue the club. Rimmer was recalled for four games, and from the youth team came Trevor Anderson, Peter Fletcher and the tall, red-headed Arnie Sidebottom, who was later to enjoy a first-class cricket career with Yorkshire.

Docherty was not a fan of Ted MacDougall and made that clear from the start. He played him in all but one of his first six league games in charge, then sold him to West Ham for £150,000.

Somehow United managed to survive, but only just. Wins over relegation rivals West Brom, Norwich and Crystal Palace earned them crucial points. United ended the 1972–73 season in eighteenth place, their lowest position for ten years, and when Tony Dunne and Denis Law were given free transfers during the summer and Bobby Charlton retired, it truly did signal the end of an era.

Docherty would start his first full season as manager of Manchester United with only three from Busby's 1968 side in his squad. Stepney, Kidd and Sadler remained, the rest had moved on.

14

DOCHERTY DAYS

THE GAME that ensured United's survival in the First Division at the end of Tommy Docherty's first four months as manager was the home game against Manchester City on 21 April 1973. The new look side needed a point for safety and got just that, but the afternoon ended in controversy when thousands of Stretford Enders climbed the perimeter fence and spilled on to the pitch. Hundreds more followed from other parts of the 61,676 crowd to join in the unwelcome celebrations – it would certainly prove an embarrassment to the club if such an event occurred today.

According to City officials, there were still two or three minutes remaining and some of their directors felt the game might be replayed. Certainly no one heard the final whistle but as far as United and the referee were concerned, the game was over, the 0–0 scoreline stood and the result provided the lifeline the Doc needed. It was a close call, but Manchester United remained in the top division.

However, those who felt the new manager had produced a magic wand and might have the solution to all the club's problems had another think coming. During the summer of 1973, another of the European Cup-winning squad left. Denis Law may not have played in the final, but his contribution to the success was unquestioned. He would return to haunt his former club. Amid bad feeling between the Scottish star and the new manager, Law joined Manchester City. The player claimed he knew nothing about the termination of his contract until he saw his picture on television while relaxing with friends in a bar in his hometown of Aberdeen. Because he had no idea why he was in the news, he asked the barman to turn up the television set's sound, only to learn he had been given a free transfer by United.

He opted for Maine Road so he could keep the family home in the Manchester area, returning to the club he had been with for a year before his move to Torino in 1961. United fans were angry at the thought of their hero playing for their rivals again, but Docherty was unmoved. Years in the game had taught him there was little room for sentiment.

The manager claimed that while keeping your place in the side might be a tough job for any player, it was even harder for those responsible to tell one of their squad he was surplus to requirements. Law felt Docherty avoided that issue by making the news public rather than telling him to his face.

Docherty had been successful as manager of a young side at Chelsea before taking charge at Rotherham, Queen's Park Rangers, Aston Villa, then FC Porto in Portugal. Before his move to Old Trafford he had been in charge of Scotland and was fully aware of the pitfalls of the managerial hot-seat. He had his own way of doing things and an incredible gift of saying the right thing to the media and winning over the fans.

Today in his retirement – apart from regular radio appearances and a full after-dinner speaking diary – he will joke about his regular clashes with chairmen, which so often led to the sack. One of his favourite lines is that during his managerial career he had more clubs than Jack Nicklaus. By the time he came and went at non-league Altrincham, long after his Old Trafford days and spells in Australia, he had passed the legal limit of the fourteen a golfer is allowed to carry!

Tommy Docherty

According to Docherty, his favourite club was and will always be Manchester United. He knew when he took over at Old Trafford he had reached the pinnacle of his career. 'You only go downhill when you leave here,' he would warn players. That same yardstick could also be applied to whoever occupied the manager's chair. Downwards may not have been a direction normally associated with the club but in Docherty's days times were changing.

When the 1973–74 season began, Law showed there was still plenty of life left in the old dog. He scored twice on the opening day, giving City victory. At the same time, United lost 3–0 away to Arsenal. It was a sign of things to come.

At Highbury, Gerry Daly made his United debut. He had followed Mick Martin across the Irish Sea from Bohemians and was the newest face on show. Goalkeeper Alex Stepney was now the sole survivor from the 1968 side.

Bobby Charlton had taken his first steps in management by moving to Deepdale, home of Preston North End. Many predicted he would use the job to hone his skills before one day returning to Old Trafford to follow in the footsteps of Sir Matt, his mentor. Charlton was quickly to learn that being one of the best players the country had produced meant little when it came to management.

With Law and Charlton departed, George Best asked if he could come back. United still held his registration so he asked Docherty to give him a chance, reported for training and, although not fully fit, was drafted into the side for the game against Birmingham City on 20 October 1973. He was greeted with rapturous applause by a crowd of just under 49,000. United won thanks to a goal from the unlikely source of Alex Stepney. He had been elected penalty taker and converted his second spot kick of the season to secure the 1–0 win. A bizarre statistic is that that goal made Stepney United's leading scorer alongside

Sammy McIlroy and Brian Kidd. The side had scored just ten goals in their first twelve league games.

Best featured in a dozen games under the Doc and scored twice. After a career now regarded as legendary, his final goal for Manchester United was scored not in front of a packed audience of 63,000 as he took centre stage on a major European night, but witnessed by just 28,589, the lowest home gate of the season, on Saturday, 15 December 1973. That day United lost 3–2 to Coventry City.

The Irish star played in four more games before his final goodbye and was on the winning side once – Ipswich were beaten 2–0 at Old Trafford on 29 December. The other games ended in defeats by Liverpool at Anfield and Sheffield United at Old Trafford before QPR humiliated United 3–0 at Loftus Road on New Year's Day 1974. Europe was but a dream.

Best's departure was a sad moment, not just for United but for football. Those who had seen him at his peak witnessed the skills of a rare footballing genius. George Best was special and should be remembered in that way. Those who only saw him at the end of his career caught a mere glimpse of what had gone before, a pale shadow of the player he had been.

With or without him, winning had become a rarity for Docherty's team. By Christmas, the traditional halfway mark of the season, United had won just four games. Ten defeats out of twenty made the record worse than any of the catastrophes under McGuinness or O'Farrell. The board realised it had to keep faith in Docherty and not let panic take over but there seemed little hope as the New Year began with the team in the bottom three. Relegation was a distinct possibility. Sack Docherty and appoint yet another manager – would that really be the answer?

Hopes of Cup success vanished before they even materialised. They were knocked out of the League Cup by Middlesbrough in October, then the FA Cup by Ipswich on 26 January, both defeats coming in front of the loyal but disillusioned fans at Old Trafford.

In his desperate bid to stay up, Docherty used twenty-five players during the season. He bought Jim McCalliog from Wolves, introduced Brian Greenhoff from the youth side and signed Stewart Houston from Brentford, the ninth Scot in the first-team squad.

Bad luck again played its part. Ian Storey-Moore was forced to quit the game because of injury and another of the 1968 side played his last game for the club, on 23 March 1974. Brian Kidd was later transferred to Arsenal and this was to prove a mistake by the Docherty–Cavanagh partnership. Kidd continued a successful career at the top level and after a good spell with Arsenal he moved back to Manchester and joined City, then went on to play for Everton and Bolton Wanderers.

By the time he was transferred, the fight to survive had been lost. United were relegated to the Second Division for the first time in thirty-seven years and there was a certain irony in how the end came.

Manchester City, including the ebullient Denis Law, faced Docherty's side on 27 April, the season's most decisive afternoon. Since then, it has been widely claimed that Law scored the goal that sent United down. Law did indeed score and it was the only goal of the game. However, Docherty's side would have been relegated even if they had won. Survival was out of their hands provided Birmingham City won their home game against Norwich. It was in fact a goal from Kenny Burns which kept Birmingham up that sent United down, not the much-publicised back-heeled strike from ex-King Denis eight minutes from time, which clinched victory for the Sky Blues.

That Law should deliver the *coup de grâce* was seen by some as sweet revenge for the way he had been treated the previous summer, but Denis did not gloat. As he flicked the ball beyond his friend Alex Stepney there was no elation. For once he did not raise his arm, one finger pointing to the sky in the familiar gesture he had made his trademark. Instead he turned, and walked towards the centre circle as if almost embarrassed about the deed he had done.

As in the previous year, the game ended with hundreds of supporters spilling on to the pitch as the blue half of Manchester celebrated the decline of its neighbours. It may have been United fans trying to disrupt the end of the game or the response of some to the taunts of others, but this time there was no cry for additional time to be played, or the game to be re-staged.

Law's goal was the last of his career, and although he remained at Maine Road the following season the game against United was his final league appearance.

Close to tears Docherty put on a brave face, promising United would bounce straight back. His critics felt it was bravado, he was being over optimistic on the evidence of that season's performance, but he was to prove them wrong.

Another period of re-building began. Striker Stuart Pearson was immediately added to the squad in a surprise signing from Hull City. The story stole the headlines on the morning the country prepared for the 1974 FA Cup final, and three months later the fans flooded back to watch a winning side. The new look Manchester United took the old Second Division by storm.

They topped the table for the whole season and as new players came in, others, including George Graham, faded into the background. He took up a managerial career, leaving the youthful United side to skip its way back to the First Division. The fans enjoyed every moment, flocking to watch displays of fast attacking football. Entertainment had once again become the keyword at Old Trafford.

The saddest blow during the promotion chase was an injury

to Jim Holton. The Scottish centre-half had established himself as a folk hero among the fans, but his career was badly affected when he broke a leg during a 4–4 draw with Sheffield Wednesday at Hillsborough. A repeat of the injury shortly after his comeback signalled the end of his days with United. Eventually he joined Coventry City then Sheffield Wednesday before retiring in 1982. Sadly, 'Big Jim' was only forty-two years of age when he died from a heart attack in October 1993.

As the 1975–76 season began, Docherty turned his attention to European qualification and added to the four Englishmen who were regulars in the side by signing Gordon Hill, a hyperactive left winger from London. Hill had played for Millwall, one of Stepney's former clubs, and immediately hit it off with the fans. With Coppell on the right and Hill on the left, Docherty defied the fashion of the day by playing down the flanks. Flair outstripped the planning of the tacticians, and the supporters loved it. For a while United topped the First Division, but slipped to third place in early April because of the pressures of a successful FA Cup campaign.

It was Hill who scored both goals in an FA Cup semi-final win over Derby County at Hillsborough, taking United to their first domestic final since 1963. Docherty had kept his promise to the fans by taking the club within reach of glory once again.

They were also back in Europe. Third place in the League meant qualification to play in the UEFA Cup. While victory over Southampton in the Cup final would secure entry to the more prestigious Cup-Winners' Cup, whatever the outcome at Wembley they were guaranteed a tilt at foreign opposition again.

As it turned out Southampton beat them 1–0, and once again one of Docherty's rejects came back to haunt him. The goal was scored by Bobby Stokes, but created by a pass from Jim McCalliog who had left Old Trafford and moved to the Dell a year earlier.

So it was to be the UEFA Cup and the first round of the competition brought together two European giants as United were paired with Ajax of Amsterdam. The Dutch club had dominated Europe in the early seventies, winning the Champions Cup three times between 1971 and 1973, and starting their run the season after Rotterdam's Feyenoord had beaten Celtic in the 1970 final. They would be a stiff challenge.

On 15 September 1976, Manchester United ended a bleak period of six years and four months without European football as Docherty's players stepped out for the first leg in the Olympic Stadium in Amsterdam. While the game was not as significant as Busby's first taste of European football twenty years earlier, the achievement of qualifying for the competition at least showed an upturn of fortune.

The eleven who started the game deserved their place in the club's history. The veteran Alex Stepney was in goal. He had been with United for ten years, and three days before his thirty-fourth birthday, he was able to keep the younger Paddy Roche out of the side. The full-backs were Jimmy Nicholl, an Irishman, and Stewart Houston, a Scot. Nicholl had joined United after leaving school in 1971. He was a product of the club's youth system and made his full debut in the 1975–76 season when he replaced the injured Alex Forsyth. Born in Canada, he was raised in Northern Ireland after his parents moved back to their homeland when he was a child. He captained the youth team, showing early signs of leadership which were to come fully to the surface once his playing days ended and he moved into management. Stewart Houston's playing career later took him to Chelsea, Brentford and Sheffield United but he found managerial success as assistant to George Graham during Arsenal's successful years in the early nineties.

Brian Greenhoff and Martin Buchan were paired as Docherty's central defenders from the start of the season.

Although neither possessed the physical attributes normally associated with players filling those positions, both used speed and skill to make up for any lack of height and strength. Barnsley-born Brian was the younger brother of Jimmy Greenhoff, who joined Docherty's side two months after the Ajax game. Brian was another to come through the club's youth system, a method of finding players which has paid massive dividends for Manchester United over the years. He went on to make 263 appearances for the club over a period of nine years before joining Leeds.

Martin Buchan's background was quite different. He had been the subject of a big-money transfer during Frank O'Farrell's time as manager after playing almost 200 games for Aberdeen, the club Sir Alex Ferguson was later to manage before his move south. He captained United and spent eleven years at Old Trafford before leaving to join Oldham in 1983. A short spell as a manager with Burnley followed, but he decided that life was not for him and he spent several years with one of the country's top sports equipment companies. Today he works as a player's representative with the Professional Footballer's Association.

Midfield in the 4-4-2 formation was made up of England wingers Steve Coppell on the right and Gordon Hill on the left, with an all-Ireland duo, Sammy McIlroy and Gerry Daly, in the central positions.

Coppell was one of a rare breed, a university graduate who made it to the top in football. He joined United from Tranmere Rovers and had entered the professional players' ranks while still studying for his BSc degree at Liverpool University. He was a revelation following the £60,000 move, going straight into the side for the run-in to the Second Division championship and remaining a regular for the next eight seasons.

His arrival meant the end of Willie Morgan's days at Old Trafford, and another of the links with the side that played in

Sir Matt's final campaign in Europe was broken. Coppell went on to set a club appearance record when he had an unbroken spell of 206 consecutive league games between January 1977 and November 1981. He would certainly have added to that number had he not been injured on international duty. He played forty-two times for England before the knee injury brought his career to a premature end.

Coppell became the game's youngest manager when he took charge of Crystal Palace during the 1983–84 season, leading them to promotion to the top section. He also had a short spell as manager of Manchester City in 1996, but returned to Palace a few months later, taking them to the Premiership. Today he is a director of the London club.

Gordon Hill was a very different person from the deep-thinking Coppell. Speedy and tricky with a fierce left-foot shot, Hill was the comic of the side and immensely popular with the supporters. Docherty spent £70,000 to bring him from his London roots at Millwall. He went on to play 132 games for United before moving on to Derby County in April 1978, for £250,000. A spell with Queen's Park Rangers followed before he went to the United States. He ended his playing days as player-manager with non-league Northwich Victoria.

Sammy McIlroy is today the popular manager of Northern Ireland, but at the time of the Ajax game he was playing for club and country in the heart of midfield. Often incorrectly referred to as 'the last of the Busby Babes', McIlroy arrived at Old Trafford in 1969 as a fifteen year old while Sir Matt was in charge, but the Northern Ireland midfielder did not play senior football under the legendary manager. He broke into the side in November 1971 by which time Frank O'Farrell was in charge, and his career could not have got off to a better start when he scored against Manchester City in a Maine Road derby which ended in a thrilling 3–3 draw.

McIlroy survived the set-back of serious injury following a car accident in 1973 and went on to make over 400 appearances for United and eighty-eight for Northern Ireland before moving to Stoke in 1982. His playing career also took in Manchester City, Bury and Preston before those first steps in management with Northwich Victoria then Macclesfield Town, which he took into the Football League at the end of the 1996–97 season.

Gerry Daly represented a shrewd £20,000 investment; he eventually established himself as the hub of United's midfield. Although Daly was popular with the fans, things were not so good with his manager. After a row early in 1977, he was sold to Derby County, the £175,000 fee making him Ireland's most valuable player at the time. Moves to Coventry (for £310,000), Birmingham City, Shrewsbury Town and Doncaster Rovers followed. Once his playing days ended, he too tried his hand at management with non-league Telford United.

Stuart Pearson and Lou Macari were United's strike force. They had been brought together during the 1974–75 season and by the September of 1976, the partnership had produced more than sixty goals. 'Pancho' Pearson was aggressive and fast. He soon began to pay back the £200,000 transfer fee Docherty invested and during his first season at Old Trafford helped win the Second Division championship in 1975, scoring the first of his seventeen goals of the campaign during his first home game against Millwall. A late entrant into professional football, he was an apprentice telephone engineer before joining Hull City, yet still went on to play for England fifteen times. His days with United were cut short by injury, but he joined West Ham and tasted more success as a member of their 1980 FA Cup-winning side.

West Ham also featured in Macari's career, but he was later to move to the London club as manager rather than player. Docherty had snatched the diminutive Scot from under the noses of Liverpool who were also trying to sign him from Glasgow Celtic in January 1973. By then Macari was an international and he went on to play twenty-four times for his country, eighteen of those games coming during his time at Old Trafford. Since retiring as a player, he has managed Swindon Town, West Ham, Birmingham and Stoke City as well as having a spell with Celtic in 1996. He took charge of his current club, Huddersfield Town, in 2000, as a replacement for another former Manchester United player, Steve Bruce.

That first step back into Europe in 1976 was to end in defeat, but not disaster for Docherty and his players. United lost the first leg against Ajax 1–0 with Dutch centre-half Ruud Krol scoring the winner. There was controversy when the officials ruled out what seemed a perfectly good equaliser, a Houston shot squeezing under goalkeeper Schrijvers. Many felt the ball had rolled over the line when he dragged it back, but referee and linesman ruled in favour of the home side.

Another young player, David McCreery, was introduced in that game. The Belfast-born midfielder came on as a substitute for Daly during the second half. The fresh-faced lad was given his first taste of European football the day before celebrating his nineteenth birthday.

With only a single goal deficit to pull back, United were reasonably confident of success in the second leg, but four days before the return game against Ajax they were struck a major blow when Pearson was injured during a 3–1 win over Manchester City at Maine Road. This time young McCreery was included from the start as Docherty shuffled his formation.

After a tense opening, Macari scored just before half-time. The scores were level on aggregate as the teams went off for the break. In the second half, United tried everything but the Dutch stood firm and the game seemed destined for extra time when Docherty decided a change of approach might swing things. Arthur Albiston, a Scottish youngster, came into the fray, replacing Daly in midfield. Brian Greenhoff was switched to striker. The move paid off. Within five minutes Greenhoff burst his way through the Dutch defence, rolled a pass into the path of McIlroy and the Irishman scored the winner.

So United's sixtieth game in Europe ended in victory, and their reward was a second-round tie against Italian giants Juventus. This would be the first competitive meeting between the clubs, and only the third time United had faced Italian opposition in any of the European tournaments.

In the years between the 1969 European Cup semi-final and that first game against Ajax, United had actually played in Europe. They had accepted an invitation to take part in the Anglo-Italian tournament, a competition designed to promote friendship, trade and the game itself between the two countries. It also gave those clubs that had failed to qualify for any of UEFA's tournaments an opportunity to compete against foreign opposition.

In February 1973, shortly after Docherty's arrival, United were hosts to Fiorentina. They drew 1–1 in front of a crowd of 23,951, more than 40,000 below Old Trafford's capacity and an illustration of how the Manchester public viewed the competition. Attendances deteriorated even further as United went on to draw 0–0 with Lazio in Rome, before beating Bari 3–1 at Old Trafford. This time 14,303 turned up.

The final fixture, in Verona on 2 May 1973, turned out to be an important milestone in the club's history although it passed without many realising its significance. It was Bobby Charlton's final game for the club. Britain's best-known footballer had officially bowed out four days earlier when United played Chelsea. That day 44,184 packed Stamford Bridge to bid United's loyal servant a fond farewell. It was his last league game for the club, but the curtain actually came down on that illustrious career in the historic city of Verona, a far cry from the cobbled streets of Ashington, County Durham, where Charlton first kicked a football. Verona provided a picturesque enough setting for a player of Charlton's stature, but sadly only 8,168 fans – the majority of them there out of curiosity – witnessed his grand finale as a Manchester United player.

Bobby bowed out on a high note, scoring twice in a 4–1 win. Amazingly, that remained United's only competitive victory on Italian soil until Sir Alex Ferguson's side beat Juventus in Turin in April 1999. Docherty's team chalked up a victory over Juventus on 20 October 1976, but the result was not as significant as the meeting between the clubs twenty-three years later.

The first leg was full of what was regarded was typically cynical stuff from Juventus. They used every trick in the book to prevent United from playing their normal style of open, flowing, fast football. Shirts were pulled, sly fouls committed off the ball and time wasted, but Docherty had known exactly what to expect. A month earlier Juventus had knocked Manchester City out in the first round, quite happily losing 1–0 at Maine Road, then using their vast European experience to overcome the English side in the second leg.

They used the same plan at Old Trafford, obviously hoping to hold United to a single goal, if any. They succeeded. Gordon Hill scored on a frustrating night and Juventus left the field with the chants of 'animals! animals!' from United's faithful falling on deaf ears. Those spectators sensed it could be the end of another European journey, and they were right.

In the second leg, Roberto Boninsegna and Romeo Benetti, two of Italy's longest serving internationals, played leading roles in the downfall of United's young side. Boninsegna scored twice, Benetti tied things up with a goal four minutes from the end and Docherty sadly accepted defeat in what turned out to be his final United game in Europe.

The club would be back in European competition the following season, but before then there were more traumatic times at Old Trafford.

Tommy Docherty

We were babes in Europe that season but I was glad to be able to bring back a taste of European action to Old Trafford.

During my time at Stamford Bridge, I had taken Chelsea to the semi-finals of the UEFA Cup but there was always something special about Manchester United's involvement in Europe. Our problem was that we drew two of the top sides in the competition, Ajax and Juventus, and we were short of experience at that level.

It had always been my policy to try to arrange as many games as possible against foreign opposition, to give the players a taste of what would come if we qualified for Europe. I used to collect the pennants they presented to us and hang them on the office wall, mentally ticking off each place we visited.

I was also determined that when we played in Europe we would stick to our normal attacking style, not adjusting to suit opponents. The Manchester United tradition is an adventurous approach to the game, bringing a smile back to football, and I think we succeeded in that aim against Ajax in that first round. It had not been too long since Ajax had won the European Cup three years in succession and victory over them meant a lot.

I was optimistic when Juventus came to Old Trafford and their manager Giovanni Trapattoni was full of praise for the way we played. He singled out Gordon Hill, who scored our winner, as our best player, but when it came to the game in Turin it was a case of men against boys and we were not the men.

My biggest disappointment was that the following season we

qualified for the Cup-Winners' Cup and I was not at the club to take us into Europe once again. Love of a woman caused me to lose my job but I have no regrets and Mary and I remain happily married to this day. I was sad to leave Manchester United at the peak of my managerial career and to hand over to another but that, as they say, is life.

15

TROUBLED TIMES

B Y THE END of the 1976–77 season United had secured a place in the Cup-Winners' Cup, but long before they played their opening game Tommy Docherty had left Old Trafford and Dave Sexton replaced him as manager. Once again the club was forced to endure another period of transition.

Docherty's dismissal was unique. He was sacked not because his team was performing badly, or because of a clash with his chairman, but on moral grounds. On the morning following United's victory over Liverpool in the 1977 FA Cup final, the Sunday newspapers revealed that the manager of Manchester United was having a love affair, and was about to leave his wife Agnes to set up home with a younger, already married woman. While those were fairly sensational claims and bound to raise an eyebrow or two among football's hierarchy, there was more to the story than that. The woman in question was the wife of the club's physiotherapist Laurie Brown. Had the Doc strayed further from home, he might perhaps have escaped retribution for his indiscretion but by becoming romantically involved with the wife of another member of staff, the club's board of directors were left with no choice but to get involved.

It was obvious that Docherty and Laurie Brown could no longer work together but the directors realised it would be unjust to dismiss the physiotherapist. They found themselves in a no-win situation and United were forced to part company with the first manager to bring them success since Sir Matt's retirement. Just as his team began to show its potential, Docherty was told his services were no longer required. He had become an embarrassment, and after being called to the Alderley Edge home of chairman Louis Edwards, secretary Les Olive announced that the manager's contract had been terminated.

Docherty bounced back and within weeks found a new job as manager of Derby County but his dismissal caused unrest among supporters. He was popular with the fans, who loved the style of football he promoted, and he left behind a squad of players that was a force to be reckoned with. The people of Manchester and the nationwide band of supporters who followed the club had taken to Docherty, a man whose charisma was infectious. They loved his sharp wit, his stand-up comic style wisecracks during television and radio interviews, as well as his down-to-earth approach to the job. The Doc was one of the lads, but he could mingle easily with the toffs as well.

In truth, Docherty manipulated the media to suit his needs. He had his favourites and gave them what they wanted, yet at the same time got his own message across. The day after his sacking he and Mary Brown, later to become the second Mrs Docherty, posed happily for photographers in their Lake District retreat. While this went on, the fans back home wrote letters of protest to the *Manchester Evening News*, aired their views on radio phone-in programmes, and came down firmly on the side of the now ex-manager. Gone, but certainly never to be forgotten – that was the Doc!

So, for the fourth time in eight years a new man had to take the helm at Old Trafford, and called in to fill the void was Dave Sexton, a man in sharp contrast to the effervescent Docherty. Sexton was quiet, thoughtful, almost shy, shunned publicity and hated being in the spotlight, which could never be said of his predecessor. Chalk and cheese, that was Docherty and Sexton. Chairman Louis Edwards handed Sexton the job as the dust was settling after Docherty's sensational revelations.

The club tried to hide its blushes but there were many who felt the action it had taken was out of touch with reality. It was, after all, 1977 – ten years since the heart of the swinging sixties when cohabiting outside marriage became the trend. Marriages were breaking up every day. Unmarried men and women were happy to live together; something that might have been frowned upon a generation earlier was now accepted practice. Why should a football manager lose his job simply because he had left his wife? Was this not over-reacting?

United were obviously embarrassed and many close to the club felt there was more to the situation than reached the surface. Were the directors looking for a reason to get rid of the manager? Was the affair with Mary Brown the final straw? Was there a hidden agenda? Whatever the truth, Sexton had to swim against a tide of opinion as soon as he took up his post. A large section of the club's support was already opposed to his appointment and he knew the way ahead would be tough.

Docherty's side had ended his final season on a high, beating Liverpool at Wembley. Goals from Stuart Pearson and Jimmy Greenhoff did the trick, even if the winner was a freak in-off from the striker's chest. What did coach Tommy Cavanagh often say? 'I don't care if the ball goes into the net off the referee's backside in the last minute of the game, as long as we win!' The goal wasn't quite as sensational as that but Lou Macari confesses his shot was going well wide of the mark until it struck Greenhoff and was deflected into the Liverpool net, way beyond the reach of goalkeeper Ray Clemence.

United's victory dashed Liverpool's hopes of completing an unprecedented treble of European Cup, league championship and FA Cup. It was another twenty-two years before a club reached such a pinnacle, and that honour went to Manchester United.

Martin Buchan collected the trophy and for the first time in fourteen years – and only the second in the club's history – United earned an entry into the European Cup-Winners' Cup.

So began a new season under a new manager. Sexton made few changes during his early weeks in charge but his first steps in Europe almost ended in disaster. United were drawn against French side St Etienne, at a time when the behaviour of English football fans was being put under the microscope.

The reputation of the English fan left a lot to be desired. Football hooliganism was at its peak and clubs tried their best to combat the problem. Tall perimeter fencing was erected at most stadiums not simply to prevent pitch invasions but to make it impossible for rival fans to get to grips with one another. Segregation was introduced, policing methods improved and Manchester United was one of the clubs to install closed-circuit television cameras to scan crowds in an effort to single out offenders. There were constant appeals for common sense, but equally regular clashes between groups of violent fans both inside and well beyond the boundaries of football grounds.

From a United viewpoint, the club felt it was winning the battle. At Old Trafford incidents were kept to a minimum with only the odd arrest, usually for drunken behaviour, and rarely a violent clash within the stadium. Reputations, though, are difficult to play down and when the French media learned St Etienne would be hosts to an English side, the locals were warned to be on their guard because 'Les Hooligans' were coming.

They were ready for it. The police presence in the town centre was at a premium. Any United fan who stepped over the mark, whether through high spirits or, more likely, over-indulgence in the local beer, sparked off an instant reaction. Offenders were immediately pounced upon and unceremoniously carted off in police vans, their chances of seeing the game disappearing as the doors were slammed behind them.

Those who made it to the Geoffrey Guichard Stadium were greeted by the sight of the French riot squad patrolling the perimeter of the pitch, their dogs barking threateningly at the packed ranks of Brits in their red and white scarves, huddled in the centre of the terracing behind one goal.

Surrounding the United section on three sides were French fans. Before the game started, some of these began to throw bread at the United fans. All hell broke loose. United supporters began to hurl back the chunks of baguette – some of it far from fresh – which was apparently being thrown because French newspapers had carried stories of the problems Britain was having with growing unemployment. The St Etienne fans were under the impression that these supporters from England represented a country with no money, no work and no food. They goaded 'Les pauvre Anglais' by throwing the bread. Once the United fans threw it back, the police rushed at the crowd.

English heads felt the force of French batons while it seemed the St Etienne followers escaped unpunished. Many United supporters tried to plead their innocence in the furore which followed the incidents but were hauled away along with those who had retaliated against the St Etienne fans.

UEFA were quick to point out it was the English who had the bad reputation, not the French, and they had plenty of examples to support such a statement. Was it not English supporters who had wrecked trains and ferries in the past when making their way to European games? Had not the English torn out seats in the famous Parc des Princes Stadium in Paris in 1975, when Leeds United supporters ran riot after losing to Bayern Munich, and in so doing wrecked the twentieth anniversary celebrations of UEFA as the final of the European Cup was staged at its original venue? Was hooliganism – which admittedly had spread to other countries – not known throughout Europe as the 'English disease'?

UEFA's feelings would become known after the game but, despite the distractions in the crowd, United gave a good account of themselves and drew 1–1 with Gordon Hill scoring the vital away goal. They had every reason to feel they might get through to the second round, but days later were told they had been ejected from the competition because of the crowd troubles. It was a sensation. The club had to react quickly and UEFA were asked to listen to the other side of the story.

United supporters came forward claiming they had been injured by over-enthusiastic policing or hurt by bottles – not pieces of bread – thrown by the French fans. They painted a very different picture from the one UEFA visualised. These included middle-aged men and women, married couples, and professional people as well as young football supporters, and all told the same story of how they had been attacked as they were doing nothing more than trying to get out of the range of a hail of missiles.

United secretary Les Olive took the offensive and blamed St Etienne for not separating sections of support and claiming this had contributed to the trouble: 'UEFA rules say there should be segregation of rival supporters. We repeatedly stressed the importance of this to the St Etienne officials when they visited Old Trafford, but they made no attempt to put the United fans together in one special section. They did not have any police on the terraces to keep them apart.

'Our people were in a group surrounded by French supporters who, I understand, objected to them being there, and tried to push them to one side.

'We warned St Etienne about the danger they were risking. They kept saying that they could not make any alterations to the stadium because it is a municipal ground and not their own. In any case, they said they never had any trouble on their own ground. Unfortunately, they were proved wrong.'

United's appeal, no doubt boosted by the presence of Sir Matt Busby at the hearing, was successful. The club was reinstated in the competition but conditions were imposed. UEFA fined United £7,500 and ordered them to play the return leg on a ground no less than 200 kilometres from Old Trafford.

How fully UEFA considered the implications of such a decision is not clear. With the behaviour of football fans the main problem, the critics argued that to take the game away from Old Trafford meant the authorities could be playing into the hands of those hoping to disrupt things. A missile thrown by a neutral, a French supporter attacked by any Englishman and Manchester United could be banned from Europe indefinitely. The club would certainly be walking a tightrope. Had the game been left at Old Trafford, United would have been able to take full responsibility for anything happening within their stadium. The directors felt that moving the game away from Manchester was asking for trouble. Any irresponsible hothead intent on making trouble for United would have the perfect opportunity to do just that. Finding a suitable venue was itself a problem. Glasgow was considered, as well as London, and even Newcastle.

Finally, they settled on Home Park, Plymouth Argyle's stadium on the south coast, where on 5 October 1978 they faced St Etienne for a second time.

Sexton was both angered and upset by the ruling. He felt he and his players were the innocents, yet he was forced to begin his first European campaign as the manager of Manchester United under severe handicap. If there was a ball and chain around every ankle, it did not show as United played superbly and every supporter within the Plymouth stadium behaved impeccably.

According to the number of tickets allocated to United, only one thousand 'official' fans were supposed to be in the crowd, but it was obvious to anyone in Home Park that the majority of the 31,678 there wore red and white. Many United fans had travelled south to buy tickets, either by posing as locals or obtaining them from Plymouth fans eager to cash in on their luck at having such a big game in their town.

Sexton used the occasion to introduce Chris McGrath to European football, bringing the Irish youngster into the game because Stuart Pearson was sidelined with a hamstring injury. In the first leg in France, Ashley Grimes had made his European debut as a replacement for the injured Sammy McIlroy.

The game at Home Park while no showpiece ended in a comfortable victory. United controlled it from start to finish and even the flamboyant Dominic Rochetau – the Cantona of the day – could do little to stop the flow of attacks. Goals from Pearson in the thirty-seventh minute and Coppell half an hour later took them through without the safety net of Hill's away goal.

Sexton was a relieved man, but there were more troubled times ahead. In the League, United's form was inconsistent. The first game against St Etienne was sandwiched between defeats by City at Maine Road and Chelsea at Old Trafford, and the second leg by victory over Liverpool, then a 2–1 upset at Middlesbrough which plunged United from fifth to tenth place.

The delay caused by the appeal against the ban meant that the draw for the next round had already been made before the game in Plymouth. United knew that victory over the French would pair them with one of Tommy Docherty's clubs, FC Porto of Portugal. Memories of the last time the club had played against a Portuguese side in the same competition came flooding back. Sporting Lisbon had left Matt Busby's side smarting in

1964 when, after taking a 4–1 first-leg advantage to Portugal, United sensationally lost 5–0.

The trip to Oporto was to prove just as big a disaster. Shortly before kick-off, Jimmy Greenhoff was taken ill and pulled out of the side. No one can say if his inclusion would have made any difference to the outcome as Porto ran rings round the United defence. Their Brazilian striker Duda was in superb form scoring a hat-trick as Sexton's side was hammered 4–0.

Greenhoff's illness was later diagnosed as a form of hepatitis brought on by eating seafood. His colleagues felt equally sick as they flew back to Manchester in the early hours to be greeted by newspaper headlines claiming it had been 'Duda's Day' in Portugal. The European game was followed by a trip to West Brom in the League three days later and yet another humiliation as Ron Atkinson's side, inspired by star midfielder Bryan Robson, ran another four goals past the hapless Stepney. United were now twelfth in the table and seemingly out of Europe.

The most optimistic fans felt there might be hope. If Sporting Lisbon could fight from 4–1 down to win 5–4, why not Manchester United thirteen years on? On the night of the second leg those dreams almost became reality in an incredible game.

With Stepney in goal, Sexton named Nicholl, Buchan, Houston and Albiston as his back four with Coppell, McIlroy, McGrath and Hill in midfield and Pearson aided by McCreery up front.

United threw caution to the wind. They knew they had to score five times to have a chance and went at the Portuguese with guns blazing. After eight minutes Coppell fired home a fierce drive to make it 1–0. Wave after wave of red-shirted attacks poured downfield but in doing so, left gaps at the back and Arsenio Seninho hit back after a breakaway in the thirtieth minute.

It turned out to be a crucial goal. Again United knew they

needed to score five times to get through and did their best to do so. A cross from Hill was turned into the Portuguese net by Murca, their big centre-back, and on the stroke of half-time Jimmy Nicholl scored with a powerful shot to make it 3–1. It was 5–3 on aggregate and there was still hope.

Early in the second half United were refused a penalty for what they felt was deliberate handball; then Coppell struck again following a Hill corner. Old Trafford went wild, two more goals and United would be through to the third round. But Seninho scored again after another breakaway and that was that.

Another mistake by Murca seconds from time gave United the five goals they set out to score, but it was too late. Sexton's side managed to win 5–2 on the night but went out of the competition, losing 6–5 on aggregate. Another European campaign was over.

During the rest of the season the team once again found Atkinson's West Bromwich Albion a stumbling block. They knocked United out of the FA Cup at the Hawthorns in a thrilling replay after a 1–1 draw at Old Trafford, and even though Sexton invested heavily in new players there was little he could do to stop the slide. Striker Joe Jordan and centre-back Gordon McQueen were bought from Leeds United but Sexton's side finished tenth in the League, outside a European qualification place.

The following season there was a vast improvement and the upturn was due largely to the emergence of a young goalkeeper named Gary Bailey.

With Stepney now in his thirty-seventh year, Sexton began the 1978–79 season with Paddy Roche in goal. The tall slim Irishman found it difficult to win over the fans. Many voiced a lack of confidence in him and this got through to the player. After a 5–1 defeat at Birmingham City, Sexton decided to make another move in the transfer market, this time for Coventry City keeper Jim Blythe. The deal was agreed and the player arrived at Old Trafford to be greeted by the media. Cameras were ready and reporters waited as a stony faced Sexton emerged to announce the deal was off. Blythe, like Ruud van Nistelrooy more than two decades later, had failed the club's stringent medical. United were back to square one.

Stepney had been confined to the reserves since the season began. Roche was devastated after being made aware he was no longer seen as first-team material, and that just left one route open to Sexton. He called up A team keeper Bailey. As if in a story from a boys' magazine, Gary, the son of Roy Bailey the former Ipswich keeper, found himself standing in front of a packed Stretford End, keeping goal against his father's old club.

Bailey had joined United after writing to the club for a trial while studying at Witts' University in Johannesburg. He and his family had emigrated to South Africa from Ipswich, where Gary was born, after his father retired as a player and took up coaching.

Three months after his twentieth birthday the English goalkeeper with the South African accent was plunged into top-level football. The pressure must have been immense, but the tall blond keeper took it in his stride. To give the story added impact, he kept a clean sheet and United won 2–0. It was the beginning of a fine career for Bailey who stayed in goal for the rest of the season as United finished ninth in the League.

Europe was within their grasp again as they reached the 1979 FA Cup final but they were beaten by Arsenal. The game was decided during a sensational period just before the final whistle. Arsenal had led 2–0 at half-time and seemed well in control until, as the end approached, McQueen scored and McIlroy grabbed an equaliser. The goals injected life into the side, building hopes of success in extra time. Right at the death Arsenal snatched the winner in a game remembered as 'the five-minute final'.

The result left United hungry for European football at a time when English clubs enjoyed a period of domination in the Champions Cup. In 1977 Liverpool became the second Football League side to take the trophy when they beat Borussia Moenchengladbach in Rome. Then they went one better than United, claiming the European title for a second successive year thanks to a 1–0 win over FC Bruges at Wembley. A year later, eighteen days after United had lost to Arsenal, Nottingham Forest beat Malmö in Munich. In three successive seasons, an English side had won the European Cup, and the run of domination by the founders of football would continue.

During the summer of 1979, Ray Wilkins moved from Chelsea to re-join his former manager in an £825,000 deal. His arrival coincided with a confident start to the season and by October United led the table.

A month earlier, Alex Stepney, who had retired from top-class football, was appointed player-coach of non-league Altrincham, the Cheshire town on Manchester's doorstep. It meant the final link with 1968 had gone and the fans said goodbye as Stepney held a successful testimonial at Old Trafford.

In the FA Cup, United's exploits did not compare with those of the previous season and they made an early exit, drawing 1–1 with Tottenham at White Hart Lane then surprisingly losing to an Ossie Ardiles goal during extra time in the replay at Old Trafford. As for Stepney's Altrincham, they got as far in the competition as his former club, before losing to Leyton Orient.

Three days after the Cup exit, United once again found itself at the centre of crowd controversy, this time when two Middlesbrough supporters were killed by a wall collapse at Ayrsome Park. A massive 30,587 had crammed into the stadium to watch Mickey Thomas, one of Sexton's signings from the previous season, score United's goal in a 1–1 draw. As the crowd left, visiting fans apparently found their way blocked by closed doors. Pressure built up. An outside wall of the stadium took the strain and fell outwards. As well as the two deaths several other spectators were injured, but it was not until more serious disasters several years later that the authorities began to pay attention to crowd safety.

As football moved into the eighties, the Sexton squad included eight of the players inherited from Docherty. Those he had introduced were Andy Ritchie, a young striker from the youth side, Nikola Jovanovic, a Yugoslavian defender signed from Red Star Belgrade to become the club's first foreign import, and Kevin Moran, an Irish defender who had a successful career in Gaelic football before crossing to England. Four defeats from twenty-five league games lifted expectations, but happenings off the pitch brought more trouble.

World In Action, an investigative programme produced by Granada Television, looked into the affairs of United and chairman Louis Edwards. It claimed he had been involved in irregular dealings to buy club shares, gain a majority holding, and make large profits. It also alleged the club kept a secret cash fund to offer payments to young players in an effort to persuade them to join United.

The Football Association launched its own investigation after the screening but the repercussions reached a much deeper level. Within a month of its transmission, Louis Edwards was dead. To this day, his son Martin, who succeeded him as chairman, claims the television programme contributed to tragedy for his family. Members of the media knew Louis Edwards as a larger than life, warm-hearted man, who enjoyed his wealth to the full. He was said to be devastated by the allegations which came at a time when he was not enjoying the best of health. He died after a heart attack at his Cheshire home.

On the football field, United and Liverpool fought a neck-and-neck race for the title. Sexton's side were beaten to the tape by two points. It was their highest position since finishing runners-up in 1968, and again provided the passport to Europe, although the next campaign left a lot to be desired.

Indifferent form caused restlessness both in the boardroom and on the terraces. The fans wanted more from the side, which was strengthened by the signing of Garry Birtles, a prolific goalscorer, from Nottingham Forest. He cost £1.25 million, a new club spending record.

Birtles was bought to increase the team's goal power after Andy Ritchie had been sold to Brighton and Jimmy Greenhoff faded into the background. Sexton felt he needed someone to help Joe Jordan in his lone quest up front but the idea did not work. Jordan was the only player to reach double figures in the League in the 1980–81 season; of the rest, Macari came closest with nine. After twenty-five appearances, Birtles failed to score a single goal. His only success of the season came in an FA Cup third-round replay against Ritchie's new club, Brighton, but in the following round there was little anyone could do to prevent a 1–0 defeat at the hands of his former club, Forest.

By then, the European campaign of 1980–81 was long forgotten. It is fair to say that the tie against Polish side Widzew Lodz cannot lay claim to a memorable place in the European history of Manchester United. The two legs came and went leaving little to remember as far as football was concerned, but their outcome was of lasting significance that season.

The Poles came to Old Trafford on 17 September 1980, and succeeded in frustrating not only the players but most of the 38,000 crowd, even though United got off to the perfect start with Sammy McIlroy tapping home a Coppell cross before many of the spectators had settled in their seats.

With just four minutes gone, Widzew Lodz were back in the game. They scored what was to prove the decisive goal when a fierce free kick from Jozef Mlynarcyk gave Bailey no chance. It hit the inside of a post and ricocheted into the back of the net, marking the final blow of the encounter. United dominated but were vulnerable to the breakaway. The Poles' star player, Zbigniew Boniek, had a quiet night and United knew their luck was out when first Coppell then Jimmy Greenhoff hit the framework twice in the dying minutes.

The second leg in Poland proved costly. Martin Buchan limped off with a hamstring strain which was to keep him out for three months, and the game ended scoreless, United losing under the away goal rule.

That European exit was the beginning of the end for Sexton and in April 1981, five days after the season came to a conclusion with United in eighth position, he was sacked. It was a sad ending for a man who had tried his best. 'How many managers have lost their job after finishing off the season with seven successive victories?' was his parting shot. This was true. The side had an unbeaten run of nine games including those seven wins, but the board of directors, now led by the ambitious Martin Edwards, felt it meant little.

In June 1981, Ron Atkinson became the new manager, leaving West Bromwich Albion to head north to Old Trafford. Here was another contrasting manager. Atkinson oozed confidence. He was showbiz, outgoing and ideally suited to satisfying the demands of a media that wanted more than the unfortunate Sexton could offer.

In the first weeks of Atkinson's management, John Gidman was bought to take over at right full-back, Remi Moses came from West Brom and home attendances soared to the 50,000 mark again after dwindling below 40,000 towards the end of Sexton's reign. When Garry Birtles finally scored his first league goal, thirty games after his arrival, United followers began to believe the troubled times were really over. Would Big Ron Atkinson be the man to bring back European glory?

16

CAPTAIN MARVEL

EUROPE had to be put to one side during Ron Atkinson's first season in charge, but he made his intentions clear from the moment he took over the managerial seat. Second best was not good enough for Big Ron, or for Manchester United. He wanted success at both domestic and European level and was determined to get it.

The re-building began immediately. Mickey Thomas went to Everton in an exchange deal that brought John Gidman to Old Trafford. Joe Jordan was at the end of his contract when Dave Sexton was sacked, refused to accept the new terms he was being offered, and was transferred to AC Milan.

In his place, Atkinson bought Frank Stapleton from Arsenal, a tribunal fixing a transfer price of £900,000 – three times the fee the club received for Jordan, and nine years after the Irish striker had been a United triallist. He could have joined the club during the days of Frank O'Farrell, but opted for life in the capital and became an outstanding striker for Arsenal and the Republic.

Atkinson had only been in charge for a few months when he made what was to be the most significant signing of his United career. He brought Bryan Robson to Old Trafford, after persuading his former club, West Bromwich Albion, to part with their influential midfielder.

The move for Robson was not unexpected. Immediately Atkinson was given the job, the tabloid press predicted he would return to the Hawthorns armed with the Manchester United chequebook, and make them an offer they could not refuse for the England international. West Brom banked £1.75 million, and United got both Robson and fellow midfielder Remi Moses, who arrived ahead of Robson and had played half a dozen games before the deal was fully completed and the players were together again.

The Robson signing was hyped-up to the delight of supporters who had gone to Old Trafford to watch the league clash with Wolves on 3 October 1981. He was introduced to the crowd of 46,837 and went through an on-the-pitch signing ceremony, flanked by a beaming Atkinson and chairman Martin Edwards. The trio posed for pictures and the razzmatazz appeared to pay dividends. Even though Robson was not in the side, his presence had an effect on the other players. The enthusiastic crowd drove United on, and Wolves were humiliated 5–0.

Sammy McIlroy, who realised his days at the club were numbered now Robson had been brought in, scored a hat-trick. If he was trying to show the new manager there had been no reason to establish a new transfer record, Atkinson was not convinced. Before the season was over, McIlroy joined Stoke City and another generation of players began to evolve.

Martin Buchan started to fade from the scene, and youngsters such as Scott McGarvey, Ashley Grimes and Norman Whiteside found their names on the teamsheet. Mike Duxbury was another who forced his way into the squad when injury sidelined Gidman.

Robson's arrival signalled an upturn in form. He and Ray Wilkins became a creative partnership for both club and country, and by the end of that first season the side finished third in the table, earning a qualifying place in the UEFA Cup.

Whiteside was a sensation. He was only seventeen when he made his first senior appearance in the league game, at Brighton, but immediately showed signs of what was to come. Tall, strongly built and full of powerful aggression, the youngster from Belfast was tested as a substitute and from that moment it was obvious to all who saw him that he was a player of immense potential. He was another who had come through the ranks, taken on board as an Associate Schoolboy and then an apprentice.

As Atkinson's second season began, Whiteside was a regular in the first team. He and Robson scored two of United's three goals in the whitewash of Nottingham Forest, the first away game of the new campaign. It followed a summer during which both players had established new milestones at international level.

Whiteside became the youngster player to appear in the World Cup finals when he was capped by Northern Ireland for their game against Yugoslavia in Zaragoza, Spain. He was seventeen years and forty-one days old, replacing none other than the legendary Pele who established the record when making his debut for Brazil in 1958. If Whiteside could follow in the footsteps of his predecessor, great things would lie ahead.

Robson won his place in the Hall of Fame when he headed home England's opening goal of the tournament, in their game against France. It came after just twenty-seven seconds play and ended years of controversy about who had scored the fastest World Cup goal. The dispute was between Olle Nyburg of Sweden whose goal against Hungary in 1938 was timed at approximately thirty seconds, and Bernard Lacombe the French star who scored against Italy in 1978 in a time of thirty-one seconds. Robson's more accurately timed record has stood for twenty years.

World Cup hosts Spain provided Atkinson's first European opponents when United were drawn against Valencia in the opening round of the UEFA Cup. There were to be no records broken this time, as once again it was a game marred by crowd trouble abroad.

Atkinson added more experience to his squad during the summer, signing Arnoldus Johannus Hyacinthus Muhren from Ipswich Town as his contract ended. Arnie Muhren was an outstanding player who had been in Ipswich's UEFA Cup-winning side in 1981. He had played over 200 games under Bobby Robson, including the unforgettable 6–0 hammering handed out to United at Portman Road during the 1979–80 season. Muhren and fellow Dutchman Frans Thijssen were the playmakers who that day made United look ordinary. Sir Matt was at that game and afterwards was glowing in his praise for Muhren and Thijssen saying, 'They showed us how football should be played. I hope that we learned something from what happened this afternoon.'

No doubt the former manager was delighted to see Muhren in a red shirt as the 1982–83 season began, and consecutive 3–0 victories, first over Birmingham City at Old Trafford, then Forest at the City Ground, certainly boosted confidence.

Unfortunately, Muhren was injured after five starts and missed the clash with Valencia. The first leg at Old Trafford was goalless but there was no lack of controversy. Missiles rained on to the pitch even before the half-time whistle, punches were thrown and the Spaniards felt the strength of the over-enthusiastic Whiteside, one of three players booked by the Czech referee.

The crowd trouble began after a challenge by Stapleton on goalkeeper Jose Sempere. The Spaniards piled in and there was a mêlée in the goalmouth which angered the fans. Players wrestled with one another, some lashing out at opponents, others trying to calm the situation, and in the end, out came the referee's notebook.

United should have scored early in the game when Gordon McQueen challenged the Spanish keeper, forcing him to punch out hurriedly to an unmarked Ashley Grimes, brought in to replace Muhren. It seemed a simple task for the Irishman to tap the ball home, but it took a wicked bounce, spinning away from him, and his shot went wide of the target.

Wave after wave of United attack was held off by ruthless tackling from the Spaniards who had decided their best chance of reaching the second round lay on home soil. Damage limitation was their objective in that first game, and the defensive tactics paid off. Robson went close with a flying header, which was brilliantly saved by the acrobatic Sempere. Arthur Albiston thought he had scored with a blistering shot which met a similar fate, and poor Grimes missed another before the final whistle.

The second leg in Valencia was Martin Buchan's last game in Europe, and it was a sad exit for the player whose behaviour both on and off the field set an example for any youngster to follow. Again the Spaniards tried to spoil the flow of the game and their supporters were extremely hostile.

Buchan had been replaced as captain by Ray Wilkins during Sexton's time in charge, but he was still very much an influence in the side. United were not short of leaders – Buchan, Robson, Wilkins were all experienced skippers, but even with the three of them in the side, little could be done to prevent a Valencian victory.

Chances were missed by United and a goal by Robson was disallowed after the referee ruled Whiteside had challenged the keeper dangerously. United did take the lead. A Wilkins cross and a typically brave header from Robson put them in front just before half-time, then things started to turn sour.

Violence erupted on the terraces as Valencia equalised

through a controversial penalty. It was conceded when Spanish substitute Ribes was challenged in the box and his dramatic dive was so obviously premeditated that the United players thought they had been given a free kick because of the Spaniard's gamesmanship. Not so, and it was Histrionics 1 Manchester United 1.

The penalty dealt a sickening blow to Atkinson's side. Four minutes later, as sporadic fighting continued among spectators and the police waded in, Valencia scored another and it was all over.

That explosive first leg at Old Trafford had provided the catalyst for Spanish retaliation and the ugly scenes continued after the game. Coach windows were smashed as the Valencians stoned United's motorcade when it headed for the airport, and apparently innocent fans were beaten up by groups of Spanish hooligans. Spectators were forced to run the gauntlet as they left the stadium and once again continental policing methods came under fire, but the British found it a difficult argument to win. The 'English disease' had spread to the continent.

Chairman Edwards realised that something had to be done. He and his board decided that in future United would not take any supporters to European away games:

Too many people abroad were trying to incite our supporters. Our people in Valencia got little protection from the local police, who subjected parties of United supporters to indiscriminate baton charges.

I believe our supporters are best off staying at home for their own protection. We cannot afford trouble which could lead to a ban on the team taking part in European competitions.

We have decided that the club will not take up any allocation of tickets for a match in Europe and will not run any tours. We simply want to discourage people from travelling abroad with us.

Dave Smith, the long-serving chairman of United's Supporters Club, was responsible for organising much of the club's travel, both home and abroad. He agreed with the move adding, 'I fear if things are allowed to continue, someone is going to lose his life, and I cannot take that responsibility.'

Sadly, Smith's predictions were to prove tragically accurate although Manchester United was not involved when death came to the terraces of the Heysel Stadium.

The defeat in Valencia left Ron Atkinson stunned and angry. He was furious his side had been cast out of Europe under such circumstances, feeling that the referee had been conned by the Spaniards.

'It was scandalous,' he fumed. 'We had everything under control when the penalty came. We had bossed the game in every department and looked to be on the brink of getting three or four. Our performance was so good, it was heartbreaking for everybody to have the game taken away from us like this.'

United's next meeting with a Spanish club was to leave much happier memories than the disastrous night in Valencia. Before then, the club had to qualify, and made doubly sure of European involvement in 1983–84 by finishing third in the First Division and beating Brighton in the FA Cup final replay, giving Atkinson his first trophy for the club.

The door opened once again. Could United get further than the opening round this time?

Injuries hit the club's run-in to the end of the 1982–83 season. Steve Coppell was hurt while on England duty and ruled out for the closing weeks of the season; Buchan played just three league games, so did Gidman who was recovering from a broken leg; and Macari was named substitute so often Atkinson tagged him 'The Judge' because of the length of time spent on the bench!

McQueen played most of the season as one of the two central defenders, but Paul McGrath was showing great potential. He was bought from St Patrick's Athletic in Dublin, and made fourteen appearances, partnering his fellow countryman Kevin Moran or McQueen.

As the FA Cup final approached, Atkinson brought Laurie Cunningham to Old Trafford. The England winger, who had been one of the manager's players at West Brom before being transferred to Real Madrid for £995,000, was surplus to requirements at the Bernabeu. He came to United on loan and it was touch and go whether he would face Brighton in the final. In the end, with Cunningham not fully fit, Atkinson opted for one of his youngsters, Welshman Alan Davies. Tragically, neither player is with us today. Cunningham died in a car crash in Spain in 1988, and four years later Davies committed suicide. He was thirty. He will be remembered by those who enjoyed the skills he displayed at United, Newcastle, Carlisle United, Bradford City and Swansea.

Davies had made just two full league appearances when Atkinson decided he was good enough to face Brighton in the Cup final. He did not let his manager down and his contributions in both the 2–2 draw and the 4–0 replay victory helped United to pick up their first trophy in six years. He broke an ankle during the pre-season build-up later that summer and it was this injury that prevented him making the progress expected, and eventually led to him leaving the club after thirteen games.

Coppell's injury was also serious, and in October 1983 he announced his premature retirement from football.

By then, the Cup-Winners' Cup campaign was under way. It began at Old Trafford when Dukla Prague provided the opposition and after the first game, it seemed that the journey would not take them much further than the second leg in Czechoslovakia. The first round first leg was almost a disaster.

United's unbeaten home record still stood. Since stepping into the unknown twenty-seven years earlier, they had held out against all-comers in Manchester, but when the Czechs took the lead on the hour through Tomas Kriz, doubts set in. Passes went astray, there was unrest on the terraces and nerves showed as the minutes ticked away. Then in the last minute, with defeat staring them in the face, Stapleton was pulled down *en route* for goal. The lifeline was thrown. Could United grab it?

The referee had no hesitation in awarding the penalty, but with the regular spot-kicker Muhren watching from the bench after being replaced by substitute Moses, who would shoulder such a huge responsibility? Ray Wilkins stepped up, and celebrated his twenty-seventh birthday by taking probably the most important shot of his career. The ball was driven beyond the dive of goalkeeper Karel Stromsik and Old Trafford breathed a huge sigh of relief.

The record remained intact, but how long Atkinson's side would survive in the competition was another matter. League form was no guideline. Between the two games, United lost 0–3 at Southampton, yet beat champions Liverpool at Old Trafford. That match was watched by a crowd of 56,121, the second highest league attendance since Atkinson became manager, and a figure which would be surpassed just twice more before the turn of the century, each time for a European tie.

So to Prague, and a tremendous display by United who were stunned to find themselves a goal down, despite dominating for the first ten minutes. Three times they went close before Dukla broke out of defence. Ladislav Vizek twisted and turned Mike Duxbury on United's right flank, picking out Frantisek Stambacher with a pin-point pass. The striker hit a powerful, accurate shot, which gave Bailey no chance. Once again it looked as if the European expedition would get no further than base camp.

United were winning the midfield battle. Muhren, Robson and Wilkins were in superb form and in the thirty-third minute Arthur Albiston made a break down the left wing. His cross eluded the Czech defence, and Bryan Robson running at the ball hit a rocket shot from twenty-five yards to level the scores.

Stapleton went close, Bailey made three good saves, and Whiteside was magnificent, fighting a lone battle up front as Stapleton limped through the game after twisting his ankle during the first half.

With twelve minutes left, full-back Albiston again found space to go forward. He took the ball into the corner, floated over a cross and Stapleton beat the pain barrier and the Dukla defence to head United in front for the first time in the two legs.

'I got hurt early in the first half and poor Norman Whiteside had to battle on his own. I didn't want to be taken off because we were doing so well,' said Stapleton. 'I had a feeling we could do it. As for the goal, I managed to get to the ball by jumping off my right foot, if it had been my left I would not have made it.'

It looked as if United were through, but with just eight minutes remaining, Vaclaz Danek scored. It was 2–2 and that was how it stayed after a frantic finish when both sides went so near to snatching another goal. The aggregate score was 3–3, but it was good enough. United won on away goals.

Round two was less frenetic. United were paired with Spartak Varna, taking another trip into the unknown but not the unexpected. Varna is a resort on the banks of the Black Sea, used mainly by Russian holidaymakers. The Yuri Gagarin Stadium where the game was played was no better than an English Third Division ground as far as facilities were concerned, but held a crowd of 40,000, curious to see what the star-studded Manchester United could offer. Spectators sat in the sun, with no cover apart from that provided for a privileged few. It was a far cry from Old Trafford but United's passage to the third round was booked early in the game.

Wilkins picked out Whiteside as he broke through Varna's square defence, and Robson hammered home the ball as it rebounded to him from the goalkeeper's dive. The value of an away goal had been made abundantly clear to United in the previous round, and Robson had again given them a push towards greater things. The already restless crowd was stunned to silence, but two minutes later the stadium erupted as surprisingly, the Bulgarians pulled level. Referee Walter Eschweiler, for reasons known only to himself, ordered that a free kick twenty yards out should be re-taken. With his second attempt, Dimov squeezed the ball past United's defensive wall and between the post and Bailey's outstretched arm to make it 1–1.

Despite this, United were unmoved and got their winner two minutes into the second half through Arthur Graham. A long clearance from Bailey bounced over the Varna defence giving Whiteside and Stapleton the chance to pile on the pressure. Stapleton headed down, and Graham, who had joined the club from Leeds at the start of the season, scored his only European goal.

United won the return leg 2–0 with Stapleton scoring both goals, his first after fifty-five seconds. During the game, a star of the future emerged. Mark Hughes, a young Welsh striker, took his first steps towards the senior side. He came on as a substitute for Whiteside; Mark Dempsey, another from the youth ranks, replaced Moran.

The draw for round three, put United back in the European big-time. After the competition's winter break, they would play Spanish giants Barcelona.

Between November and March, the side went through an impressive run of results, losing just twice in the League, both home games. First they were beaten by Aston Villa, three days after their return from Varna; then in early December, they lost 1–0 to Everton, one of the championship contenders.

United were doing well in the First Division but by the end of January were out of both Cup competitions. In the League Cup they fell at Oxford after three tough games. In the first of these, Hughes made his full debut and was outstanding, scoring at the Manor Ground in a 1–1 draw. The return at Old Trafford ended in the same scoreline despite extra time, but when the decider was staged at the Manor Ground, Gary Bailey had joined the injured list with Jeff Wealands taking over in goal. Second Division Oxford won 2–1.

In the FA Cup, the holders were beaten 2–0 at Bournemouth and by January Atkinson's injuries were building up. Robson had missed games because of a hamstring strain and Garth Crooks, who had arrived on loan from Tottenham, was out of action, but the most serious blow came when Gordon McQueen was badly hurt during a 1–1 draw at Anfield. He was ruled out for the rest of the season, and Graeme Hogg a nineteen year old from the reserve side was drafted in. The young Scot was to figure in the opening game against Barcelona in a manner he would rather forget.

Shortly before the trip, Whiteside was injured and when they faced the Spaniards on 7 March 1984, in the first leg of the quarter-final, Mark Hughes was in the starting line-up. Just twenty years of age, the quiet boy from Wrexham was starting out on an illustrious career. Later the Nou Camp was his home ground, before he made a triumphant return to Old Trafford.

Bailey was in goal, Duxbury and Albiston at full-back, and Moran partnered Hogg as the two central defenders. Wilkins, Muhren, Robson and Moses were in midfield, Stapleton and Hughes up front.

United held their own for thirty-five minutes when their luck turned and Hogg put the ball into his own net while trying to clear. The ball was running towards the better-placed Moran when Hogg intervened, giving Bailey no chance. Even so, it looked as if United would keep the deficit down to that single mistake until, in the dying seconds, Rojo fired in a fierce shot and Barcelona won 2–0.

So it was that Barcelona, with Argentinian superstar Diego Maradona in their side, came to Manchester on Wednesday, 21 March 1984 for a game which is remembered as one of the greatest nights Old Trafford has witnessed. Bryan Robson emerged as the Captain Marvel of Manchester United.

Robson promised, after the devastation of Nou Camp, that United would get through. Some thought he was the eternal optimist, others regarded it as brave talk from the England captain, knowing the odds lay firmly in the Spaniards' favour. Brave, bustling Robson was a man of his word.

In the twenty-second minute, United won a corner after persistence by Muhren. Wilkins took the kick and dipped the ball to the near post where Whiteside out-jumped the Spanish defence. His head flicked the ball across the goalmouth and Robson, running in, threw himself forward in a stooping run to force the ball home with his forehead. Old Trafford erupted and the noise sent shivers down Spanish spines. A massive 58,547 roared United on. It was fitting such a crowd should be treated to a game like this.

Compulsory introduction of all-seater facilities and ground development meant that Old Trafford would later reduce its capacity. Although they did not know it at the time, each one watching the game against Barcelona was part of the biggest audience the stadium would hold for at least sixteen years. Only when the capacity was increased to in excess of 61,000 in the late nineties was it possible for more spectators to watch a football match at the home of Manchester United. The volume of sound created by the massive turn-out, echoed into the night as every fan played his or her part in a great fight-back.

In the fiftieth minute Alonso, Barcelona's Spanish international full-back, tried to turn the ball towards his keeper Urruti. The pass lacked pace but Whiteside, Moses and Wilkins did not. They charged forward, creating panic, and Robson pounced again. This time he stabbed a foot at a loose ball and the scores were level.

Caution was crucial. Atkinson was off his seat along with assistant Mick Brown, urging the players on, yet warning them against the dangers of over-commitment. Two minutes after Robson's second, the wall of sound created by the crowd seemed but a whisper as Stapleton grabbed the winner.

Albiston broke forward, Whiteside met his cross and knocked the ball back inside to the Republic of Ireland striker. Stapleton's shot rocketed into the net and United had won 3–2.

As for Maradona, he was carrying an injury and was a shadow of his normal self. It is unlikely he would have made a bigger impact had he been fully fit because the night belonged to United. Atkinson's side won through to the semi-finals, where Juventus would be the opposition.

Bryan Robson

The night we beat Barcelona in 1984 has got to be one of the greatest moments of my footballing career, not just because of the result but for the way every United fan inside Old Trafford got behind the team and willed us to victory.

I have never heard a noise like it. It seemed to get louder as the game went on and it made us feel that there was no way we could let anyone down. Sometimes during a game there will be quiet moments, but not that night. I am sure the passion behind the noise had an effect on the Spaniards.

Barcelona may have been used to playing in front of bigger crowds – their own stadium held far more than Old Trafford – but they had never heard anything like the noise which greeted them that night. Because of this, we sensed from the start that we were in with a chance and we were right.

Although we were 2–0 down, and Barcelona had world stars Maradona and Schuster in their side, we knew they were not invincible. What we needed was an early goal, and once we got that, the advantage began to swing our way.

I thought Barcelona had been a bit lucky in the first leg. They took the lead through an own goal which left young Graeme Hogg devastated, and the rest of us felt the same way when they scored their second right at the death. Apart from that, we held our own in the Nou Camp, and I was the one with a guilt complex for throwing away two glorious scoring opportunities. I said afterwards that I owed the lads something after those missed chances and was delighted I was able to play my part at Old Trafford.

I was not alone. Everybody did their bit. From the fans who shouted until they were hoarse to the lads who ran themselves into the ground. Gary Bailey pulled off important saves, Arnie Muhren and Ray Wilkins controlled midfield, and Remi Moses kept such a close watch on Maradona I'm sure they had to stop him from boarding the plane back to Spain when the game was over!

I have many fond memories of my time at Old Trafford, and Barcelona figures in them more than once, but the magical night when we did what they all thought impossible will stay with me forever. If you were one of those who shouted us to victory that night, thanks for the memory.

17

ENTER ALEX FERGUSON

THE POSSIBILITY of Europe staging its first all-British final loomed large when United reached the semi-final of the 1984 Cup-Winners' Cup. Holders Aberdeen had aspirations of retaining the trophy and were also enjoying success on a domestic front under manager Alex Ferguson. The Scots were a game away from a second successive final and avoided United in the draw for the penultimate round, being paired instead with Portuguese side FC Porto. Could both the British hopefuls get through and make it a final to remember?

Britain – or perhaps more to the point, England – had become a force to be reckoned with in Europe since those tentative first steps in the fifties. The success of first Celtic then United in the sixties encouraged interest in foreign competition. In the seven years leading up to the far from Orwellian year of 1984, English clubs became the dominant force, sweeping all before them in Europe. Liverpool had won then retained the European Cup in 1977 and 1978. Brian Clough's Nottingham Forest repeated the feat over the next two seasons; Liverpool won the trophy for a third time in 1981; then it was Aston Villa's turn to be crowned champions of Europe.

When Villa beat Bayern Munich in the Rotterdam final of 1982, there was a link to the United squad of 1968. Jimmy

Rimmer, the young substitute for the game against Benfica at Wembley, collected his second European Cup winner's medal. The now vastly experienced goalkeeper, who had spent time at Swansea and Arsenal after leaving Old Trafford, helped the Midlanders lift the trophy fourteen years on.

As United reached the semi-final two years after Villa's success, Liverpool were heading towards a fourth success in the Champions Cup and Tottenham were on course to win the UEFA Cup. The possibility of a clean sweep by England's representatives was on the cards if Ron Atkinson's side could overcome Juventus – then perhaps Ferguson's Aberdeen.

The Dons had carried Scotland's flag in 1983, beating Real Madrid 2–1 in the Cup-Winners' Cup final staged in Gothenburg, and with Jim Leighton in goal and Gordon Strachan in midfield they had in their side players who would later figure in the Manchester United story. Their manager was to play an even greater role.

There could be no doubting the magnitude of Atkinson's task. To reach the final they had to overcome Juventus who were by far the most powerful of the four clubs left in the competition. Led by brilliant French star Michel Platini, their squad included many players from the Italian World Cup-winning side of 1982. There was Gentile, Scirea, Tardelli, Cabrini and Paolo Rossi, the young striker who had scored in the final as West Germany were beaten 3–1.

Despite the class of the opposition, United's hopes remained high following the breathtaking performance against Barcelona in the previous round, but football like life itself, can at times be exceedingly cruel. Nothing can be taken for granted.

Less than a month after Old Trafford's greatest night, Atkinson watched the opportunity to take the club to a second European final slip from his grasp. A dream was turning into a nightmare even before the two games against Juventus were played. The manager's plans for the first leg of the semi-final were shattered when the squad was hit first by suspension then by injury to key players.

Atkinson was aware that Wilkins faced a ban after picking up two bookings during the previous rounds, and was able to plan his approach to the game without involving the England star. When Muhren was injured, further adjustments had to be made, and just when it seemed things could not get any worse, the final blow came when Robson tore a hamstring in training.

The manager tried to put on a brave face. He also did his best to conceal the Robson problem from the media for as long as possible, declaring everyone but Muhren was available. The sight of the England captain limping to his car after staying behind for extra treatment was a big enough clue to tell waiting journalists something was wrong.

With the whole of his first choice midfield wiped out, Atkinson knew he was up against it when Juventus came to Old Trafford on Wednesday, 10 April 1984. Arthur Graham, Frank Stapleton and Norman Whiteside were the only recognised forwards in the side. John Gidman was at right full-back, Kevin Moran and Graeme Hogg in the central defensive positions and Arthur Albiston on the left. Paul McGrath stepped in to fill one of the midfield places along with Mike Duxbury and Remi Moses, but the injury jinx continued as soon as the game was under way.

In the opening minutes, as United launched a series of attacks, Gidman suddenly pulled up. The hamstring jinx had struck again and another of its victims limped away in agony. The Liverpudlian hobbled from the action to be replaced by Alan Davies, the youngster who had starred in the FA Cup final a year earlier. At least his arrival gave the side an extra forward but United had no answer to the pace of the Italians.

With a quarter of an hour gone, Zbigniew Boniek, who had previously played at Old Trafford with Polish side Widzew Lodz during the 1980–81 UEFA Cup campaign, broke through. He picked up the ball beyond the centre circle and sprinted forward, catching the home side's defence flat-footed. As they moved out hoping to catch the Italians offside, he laid off a perfect pass to Rossi and, to make matters worse, the striker's shot appeared to take a deflection from the outstretched leg of the unfortunate Hogg, before swerving beyond Gary Bailey's reach. The goal-keeper could only stand and watch as the ball rolled into the net.

It was the small contingent of Italian supporters who made their voices heard in the 58,171 crowd. The United fans' stunned silence signalled an awareness that this may not be their side's night. Then came hope.

Graham broke down the left, Stapleton headed the ball down and McGrath strode into the penalty area only to see his shot blocked by a tough challenge. Just as it seemed he might get the equaliser, the ball went spinning out for a corner.

Minutes later, Stapleton went crashing down in the penalty area amid wild appeals from the United players that he had been tripped. Television proved later that the referee had correctly ruled in favour of the defence when he rejected the claims.

More hope came after thirty-five minutes when Tacconi, the Juventus keeper, came off his line for a high cross, competing for the ball with Stapleton who was certainly making his presence felt. The centre from Albiston was placed perfectly, beyond the Italian's reach, and, put off by the Republic of Ireland striker's threat, the keeper missed the ball. It fell into the path of Whiteside. The bustling youngster charged in on goal and struck his shot well but Tacconi had somehow managed to regain his balance and got his body in the way. However, he could only deflect the ball away from goal and into the path of Davies.

The young winger had much in common with Ryan Giggs

who followed in his footsteps a generation later. Although Davies was Manchester born while Giggs was brought to the area as a child, Davies also opted to play for Wales when he had an opportunity to turn to England. Both his parents were Welsh and Davies found himself being capped by Wales at youth and Under-21 level before stepping into the United side. Comparisons between Davies and Giggs perhaps end there, but the two shared the delight of scoring important goals against Juventus.

Giggs would get his glory in years to come, but as Davies ran on to the loose ball and rammed it into the empty Italian net, it was a moment that provided the highlight of his short career. The scores level, the young hero turned to take the plaudits from his delighted colleagues and an equally grateful crowd. This was the only goal Alan Davies scored for Manchester United. No doubt the memory stayed with him until his tragic death less than eight years later.

The second half was goalless. Juventus used spoiling tactics to prevent United from adding to the score and Atkinson's European lifeline became a slender thread. When the party flew out to Turin for the return leg two weeks later, they were the outsiders.

Robson and Muhren were again missing although Wilkins was back, and Mark Hughes was brought in to add his power to the forward line. United knew the odds were against them and the sight that greeted the players as they entered the Italian stadium made each one realise he faced a test of nerve as well as ability. The night air glowed red and the Stadio Communale was filled with choking fumes as Italian fans sent fireworks soaring into the darkness. Hundreds held coloured flares above their heads with sparks spilling on those around them. Smoke spewed out to envelop one goalmouth. Explosions and coloured flashes greeted the United players as they took the field and the home supporters made it abundantly clear what was expected from their favourites. In such an intimidating atmosphere, United seemed like the Christians about to be thrown to the lions of Juventus. Would fate play Caesar and give the English side the thumbs down?

With eight minutes gone Hughes did his best to spoil the Italians' premature celebrations but his shot was parried away by Tacconi and as McGrath rushed in to finish off, Tardelli was there to boot the ball clear.

Then came the first blow. Platini placed a precise pass at the feet of Boniek and the pace of the Polish star was too much for United's defenders. They could not catch him as he ran half the length of the field. Bailey came out to narrow the angle but the shot was accurate and Juventus led.

Stapleton was again having trouble with his ankle and was forced to limp out after sixty-three minutes, making way for Whiteside. Atkinson had kept him on the bench, nursing a slightly injured knee. His introduction gave United a boost but the Italians were on top. United were defending desperately and Bailey was magnificent, stopping scoring chances from Rossi, Platini and Boniek.

Whiteside took his chance as Graham ran down the left. He crossed to McGrath who fired in a powerful shot. The ball came off the defence and ran towards Whiteside who bustled in and blasted home. The goal meant the tie was level. Both sides had scored an away goal and with twenty minutes to play United knew a second would surely put them through.

Bailey saved, this time from a Platini free kick, and with five minutes remaining confidence was growing in the United side. They attacked, and Juventus made mistakes but as extra time loomed the Italians pressed forward and were awarded a free kick. United pulled every player back and with just one minute of normal time remaining the ball was directed into their penalty area. Scirea held off two challenges and turned to shoot, but his effort struck Boniek. The ball rebounded from the Pole and as United's defenders turned to cover, Rossi ran in and fired a low shot past Bailey. The keeper dropped to his left in a vain bid to reach the ball but the noise which followed told everyone he had failed.

Relieved Italian cheers drowned the sound of the final whistle. It was a cruel way to go out. There had been just thirty seconds to play when the goal came. Juventus won the second leg 2–1. Once again the European dream had ended, and with Aberdeen also beaten by the Portuguese it turned out that neither of the British hopes got to the final.

Ray Wilkins, captain on the night in the absence of Robson, summed up the defeat by saying, 'I thought the difference between the two teams was the one moment of brilliance from Platini when he put Boniek through for their first goal. The man is a genius.'

It was the last European game Ray Wilkins played for United. Two months later he was surprisingly transferred to AC Milan when United accepted a £1.5 million offer from the Italian super club. Tommy Docherty's words that 'the only way is down' after leaving Old Trafford were proved wrong on this occasion.

The defeat in Turin had a drastic effect on United's league form. Before the second leg they trailed Liverpool by just two points. The first championship for seventeen years seemed a possibility, but after the disappointment of Juventus, Atkinson's side did not win another game before the season ended.

Liverpool took the title despite staggering to the finishing line. Had United managed to win more than the three points they collected from the five games played after Turin, they might have found themselves playing in the Champions Cup rather than the less illustrious UEFA Cup the following season.

Wilkins was not the only player to leave in the summer of

1984. Lou Macari moved to Swindon Town as player-manager. With doubts about the fitness of Stapleton, Atkinson strengthened his strike force by investing £625,000 in Alan Brazil from Tottenham Hotspur. Then he made a move for Danish winger Jesper Olsen, who had starred in the European Championship that summer. He agreed a fee of £700,000 with Dutch club Ajax for the speedy left-sided player.

Just before the new season started, the manager also persuaded Alex Ferguson to part with Gordon Strachan, Scotland's 1980 Player of the Year. Atkinson felt the diminutive midfielder, who stood just five foot five tall, could add another dimension – if not height – to his side.

Olsen on the left and Strachan on the right became instant hits with the supporters, especially when the Scot scored a debut goal from the penalty spot in the opening game of the 1984–85 season.

Despite the changes, the new look team, with Hughes and Brazil leading the attack and Whiteside as back-up on the bench, got off to a poor start. Four consecutive draws caused them to slip behind the early leaders. Then there was an upturn with a 5–0 home win over Newcastle followed by a 3–0 victory at Coventry which boosted confidence just as the UEFA Cup campaign began.

Once again United were drawn against lesser known first-round opponents in Raba Vasas ETO Gyor from Hungary who were easily beaten 3–0 in the first leg at Old Trafford. The trip to Gyor, an industrial town sixty miles west of Budapest, should have been a formality but United lived up to their reputation of never doing things the easy way. They drew 2–2. Brazil ended a nine-match run by scoring his first goal for the club and Muhren dashed Hungarian hopes with a penalty after the home side had taken a 2–1 lead. United were through but not without a scare.

So came the second round and Muhren was missing from the line-up when United visited his homeland for the first leg against PSV Eindhoven. Amid fears of serious crowd problems United travelled to Holland where PSV's supporters had a reputation for violent behaviour. The authorities had every reason to be concerned but there were no major incidents despite the presence of unofficial groups of United fans. The game ended in a goalless draw, leaving Atkinson's team favourites to reach round three.

Dogged defending combined with United's lack of finishing power meant the second leg went into extra time before another Strachan penalty, his fifth since his arrival, clinched victory.

The draw for the next round caused a stir on both sides of the border. United were paired with Scotland's Dundee United, the club's first-ever meeting with a Scottish side in Europe. It was also the first time since 1965, when Everton provided the opposition, that United had faced a British club in a European competition. Dundee United were fourth in their League and United third in theirs when the sides clashed at Old Trafford on Wednesday, 28 November 1984. Those in favour of the formation of a British League saw the confrontation as a step towards the inevitable. Those against the idea felt it would be a walkover victory for Atkinson's side.

What the game provided was a night of exciting football which left the home fans stunned as the Scots drew 2–2. Dundee's hero was their goalkeeper Hamish McAlpine. After failing to stop one Strachan penalty, he pulled off a remarkable save to keep out a second.

United led 1–0 at half-time, but the Scots hit back and equalised through Heggarty their centre-half. Three minutes later, Robson scored to make it 2–1 and it seemed just a matter of time before the issue would be put beyond doubt. Dundee United had other ideas, and after McAlpine pulled off his penalty save, diving to his left to turn the ball away from goal, Paul Sturrock scored the equaliser.

The city of Dundee prepared itself for a night to remember when Manchester United visited Tannadice Park. Ron Atkinson treated the game like a Cup final. The team flew north, checking in at the luxurious Old Course Hotel at St Andrews. The temptation to walk from the hotel and play golf on the Old Lady herself, home of the Royal and Ancient Golf Club, must have been immense for the golfers in the side when the players awoke on the morning of the game. That pleasure was reserved for the men of the media who took advantage of both the fine weather and the closeness of the legendary links before making their own preparations for the big game.

The morning mist had cleared by the time the players went through their light training routine, and Atkinson decided on his line-up. Bailey, Gidman, Albiston, Moses, McQueen, Duxbury, Robson, Strachan, Hughes, Stapleton and Muhren would start the game.

Muhren would finish it! Twice United led, first through Hughes, then a McGinnis own goal. Twice the Scots fought back, meaning both sides had scored two away goals as again the possibility of extra time loomed. Then in the seventy-eighth minute, Gordon McQueen fired in a shot and Muhren stuck his head in the way and deflected the ball beyond the keeper for a 3–2 win.

It was a relieved Atkinson who took his seat on the aircraft for the flight back to Manchester, and even though the departure was delayed as mist again descended, the manager had a clear view of what lay ahead in Europe. The quarter-finals beckoned, but before then would come UEFA's statutory winter break of just under three months. This gave United time to concentrate on the League and the FA Cup, Everton having ended any hopes of progress in the League Cup by winning 2–1 at Old Trafford back in October.

In the FA Cup the ghost of Bournemouth was exorcised as they were beaten 3–0 in the opening round followed by a 2–1 win over Coventry in round four.

Even in success the injury jinx remained. In round five Remi Moses was badly hurt during a 2–0 win at Blackburn, sustaining a knee injury which eventually ended his playing career. He was ruled out for the rest of the season, and appeared in only a handful of games before retiring three years later.

Everton led the championship race and provided opposition for the league fixture four days before the first leg of the quarter-final. The game ended in a 1–1 draw but it could hardly be seen as the best preparation for an important European tie. Perhaps it did take its toll because against Hungarian side Videoton, United seemed nothing like prospective winners of the competition. The Hungarians defended in depth, forming a ten-man barrier between United's forwards and their goal.

It was more than a game between two clubs from England and Hungary. Videoton, as the name implies, was run by the Hungarian video manufacturing industry. The rich westerners from Manchester were sponsored by Sharp Electronics, one of the world's leading producers of such consumer goods. Who would press the eject button to remove the other from the competition remained to be seen.

United got the only goal of the game in the sixty-first minute when Gordon Strachan sped down the right wing and Stapleton met his cross perfectly. In the second leg the Hungarians used the same defensive approach, but took the lead following a free kick in the nineteenth minute. The scores stayed that way until the end of ninety minutes as Videoton frustrated their opponents by wasting time and kicking the ball out of play as they stuck to their policy of blanket defence. Extra time failed to produce the decisive goal, United fully aware that they would have the upper hand if they could get just one more. After 120 minutes the Hungarians appeared to have achieved their aim. The game went to a penalty shoot-out and the Videoton players embraced one another as if the Cup was already won.

'In all my years I have never seen a team deliberately waste time hoping that the game would go to penalties. I suppose it must have seemed to them that this was their only chance of getting through,' said a dejected Bryan Robson afterwards.

If that was the plan, it worked. For the first time, United's European fate would be decided by a penalty shoot-out, but it would not be the last.

With the Hungarian crowd baying behind the goal, Whiteside scored with his spot kick, Olsen with his. Then Stapleton blasted his shot over the bar, but Borsanye did the same for Videoton. When each side had taken five spot kicks the score was 4–4. Now it was sudden death, one goal, one miss, and it would be all over.

Mark Hughes stepped up and hit the ball firmly but Peter Disztl pulled off a fine save – advantage Videoton. Gary Bailey had dived the wrong way for every Videoton attempt and once again chose to go in the opposite direction to Imre Vadasz's shot. Game, set and match!

The Hungarians won 5–4 and ended United's challenge for the UEFA Cup in what turned out to be Ron Atkinson's final game in Europe as manager of Manchester United.

Losing the tie left the United players feeling bitter. They could have accepted defeat had they been outplayed by a better side but Videoton's tactics left a sour taste in their mouths. It was all part of the learning process for the younger members of the squad and it might well have had a demoralising effect on the domestic front had it not been for the fine team spirit generated by Robson, Strachan and the young Whiteside.

Three days after Hungary, Atkinson's side beat Aston Villa 4–0 at Old Trafford. This was an important victory against a club that had tried to tempt the United manager to join them the previous summer. It was followed by a 1–0 win over champions Liverpool at Anfield, Leicester City were beaten 2–1 and Stoke 5–0 as United consolidated second place in the table. They could do little to catch runaway Everton who dropped only two points between January and May, but they kept up the fight.

The top two were also on a collision course in the FA Cup. To reach the Wembley final United first had to beat Liverpool in the semi-final, which they did with Robson and Whiteside clinching victory at Maine Road following a 2–2 draw at Goodison. They then found themselves standing between a Merseyside club and a unique treble for a second time.

In 1977 United had beaten Liverpool to win the FA Cup and so prevented them from taking the league title, European Cup and football's oldest trophy in the same season. Howard Kendall's Everton had easily taken the league title finishing thirteen points ahead of their neighbours Liverpool, with Tottenham third on goal difference and United a point behind the Londoners. They were also England's latest achievers in Europe having beaten Rapid Vienna to win the Cup-Winners' Cup three days before facing United in the Wembley showpiece. Victory over United would give them their third major trophy of the season, but Atkinson had other ideas.

The final turned out to be a dramatic affair won by a single goal in extra time but only after Kevin Moran became the first player to be sent off in the Wembley finale. He was ordered off for a challenge on Peter Reid, and while many have since judged the referee's decision to be harsh, there was little anyone could do about it. It was left to Norman Whiteside to score a sensational winner.

Down to ten men the odds were against Atkinson's side when the game went into extra time, but a move started by Hughes ended when Whiteside blasted a shot from the right-hand edge of the penalty area. United had won the trophy for a second time in three seasons and with it a passage into the Cup-Winners' Cup, but that was a ticket they never collected.

On 29 May 1985, the seventeenth anniversary of United's victory over Benfica, an English club was again in the European Cup final. Liverpool, looking for their fifth success in the competition, were due to face Juventus at the Heysel Stadium in Brussels, but the occasion is not remembered for the game. Before the kick-off, fighting broke out on the terraces. Eyewitnesses later said that as Liverpool fans threatened a section of Italian supporters behind one of the goals, the Juventus followers retreated. It led to disaster.

Under the pressure from the hundreds of fans pushing against it to avoid missiles being thrown in their direction, a wall above one of the entrances gave way and toppled on to people below. Some of the retreating fans were carried over the edge with the crumbling brickwork and in the mayhem below, thirty-nine supporters were killed.

In the aftermath of what became known as the Heysel disaster (perhaps 'riot' would have been a better description), FIFA intervened, banning all English clubs from European competition until further notice. The game's main governing body also decreed that Liverpool's punishment would extend beyond this period. Only when clubs proved that their supporters would not cause trouble would the ban be lifted, but even then Liverpool would remain outcasts.

So, as ever, because of the behaviour of the few the majority suffered. The innocents were punished along with the guilty and many clubs aired their anguish. They felt the ruling was unjust but if they were totally honest, there were few, if any, who could not have applied the words 'There, but for the grace of God . . .'

What had happened to Liverpool could so easily have

occurred when any English club had played abroad. United found themselves among the undesirables, exiled until FIFA saw fit to lift the ban, but it did not take much imagination to replace those scenes of bodies being stretchered away in Brussels, as weeping Italians stood in comforting groups, with what might easily have happened in St Etienne, Valencia or Eindhoven.

After a summer spent debating what could be done to improve the behaviour of those watching football, life went on without European involvement. A Super Cup competition was introduced in an effort to fill the gap, but it turned out to be nothing more than a meaningless exercise aimed at making up lost revenue.

Just after the season ended, Peter Barnes the former Manchester City winger, arrived at Old Trafford for a second spell after spending time with West Bromwich Albion, Leeds United and Spanish club Real Betis. Barnes had been on a loan spell two years earlier but in July 1985 made the move permanent when he was transferred from Coventry City.

Four months later, full-back Colin Gibson was signed and as 1986 arrived so did his namesake Terry from Coventry, signed in January of the new year, with Alan Brazil going in the opposite direction. In March, prolific goalscorer Peter Davenport, a self-confessed United supporter despite family roots in Birkenhead, was bought for more than half a million from Nottingham Forest.

Hopes of winning the championship that season had been given a major boost thanks to a record start. By the end of September, ten successive wins had opened a gap at the top of the table. Even United's greatest critics felt that at last this could be their year for the title, but the side could not maintain its consistency and slipped away. They ended the season in a disappointing fourth place, good enough for qualification for the UEFA Cup had it not been for the ban.

Then came a significant departure. Mark Hughes, who by this time had developed into a sensational striker, was sold to Barcelona. His all-round ability was unquestioned. He was a world-class player who was also immensely popular with the supporters. He had become a star at both club and international level and the news that Sparky was leaving caused a stir. Barcelona were willing to hand over a massive £2.5 million for the player, and United gave the impression that this was being accepted reluctantly. Were the club simply cashing in on his talent? In interviews, Atkinson said Hughes had made it clear he wanted to leave, but when the player spoke to the media it came across that he was being sold against his wishes.

In his book *Sparky* (Cockerel Books, 1989) Hughes revealed that in fact it was the club's refusal to treat him like the other front-line players that led to his going:

At the time I was picking up £200 a week. Not much for a so-called 'star'. I wasn't grumbling, the size of the pay packet was a legacy of my days in the reserves. I was clearly adrift of the other first-team players in the earning stakes.

All Hughes wanted was parity but sadly because he never really made his wishes clear to the club, they felt he wanted to get away.

Honestly, if the board or the manager had approached me with the kind of money the other top names were collecting, I would have snatched their hands off. Barcelona, or anybody else for that matter, could have taken a running jump.

Misunderstanding or not Hughes went, and three months later manager Atkinson followed. Had the sale of such an important asset played a part in his downfall?

During 1986, the manager's problems with injuries to key players had continued. Bryan Robson was one of the worst hit. His troubles began the previous season during a home league defeat by Coventry. A typical Robson dash at goal ended with his momentum carrying him towards the advertising boards which surround the pitch. He tried to stop himself going into the perimeter fencing by putting a foot on to one of the displays but his boot skidded off the painted surface and he fell heavily, dislocating his shoulder. The injury plagued him for a year but he played on without having surgery.

After a recurrence before Christmas 1985, he dislocated the shoulder for a third time during a Cup tie at West Ham in March 1986. This was World Cup year, and United's refusal to manage without their captain while he spent time in hospital to have the problem cleared caused a row between England manager Bobby Robson and the club. Matters came to a head when the shoulder went again during the finals in Mexico.

United had their own reasons for not helping England's cause. Gary Bailey had been hurt during international training in February and ruled out until the end of the season; and Steve Coppell's career had been cut short after he was hurt while on duty for his country. The loss of Bailey and its effect on United's title bid was not taken lightly at Old Trafford. Sadly, Bailey was forced to retire from the game, making just five more appearances for his club.

As for Atkinson, his reign came to an end in November 1986. By that time United had slid down the table and into the relegation zone and nothing seemed to be going right for them. The final nail was a 4–1 humiliation at Southampton in the fourth round of the League Cup. Two days later, on the morning after Guy Fawkes night, Martin Edwards called Atkinson and assistant Mick Brown to his office at Old Trafford and they were dismissed.

The chairman then flew north to Aberdeen and by the end of the day Manchester United had a new manager – Alex Ferguson.

Gary Bailey

Probably the best all-round team I played in came together in 1985 under Bryan Robson. We reached a peak with that marvellous run of ten successive wins at the start of the 1985–86 season after winning the FA Cup for a second time. It was a pity that we never quite made it in the League or succeeded in Europe but I still left the club with some great memories.

I was devastated when I had to retire but if I had continued there was always the danger that I could have aggravated the knee injury and ended up a cripple. Naturally at the age of twenty-eight, I felt that my best years were yet to come. I would like to have played longer and achieved my ambitions but it was not to be. I have to be grateful for ten fantastic years at Old Trafford.

There are moments I shall never forget – Jimmy Greenhoff's goal that gave us victory over Liverpool in the FA Cup semi-final in 1979; Joe Jordan taking us to within a whisker of winning the championship in 1982 thanks to his strength and tenacity; the organisational skills of Martin Buchan who controlled the defence in front of me; the subtle passing of Ray Wilkins and the footballing genius of Arnold Muhren.

Those are the kind of memories which live with me, rather than the bitter disappointment of going out of Europe in a penalty shoot-out to a Hungarian team we knew we should have beaten. We had done all the hard work before losing to Videoton, but that's football. It was not a very happy note on which to end my European career.

18

WREXHAM TO ROTTERDAM

I N THE TWO YEARS following the imposition of the ban on English clubs, all efforts to have it lifted failed. Claims that it was unjust fell on deaf ears. As far as the European football authorities were concerned, the English clubs were unwanted. They belonged to a forgotten nation.

The UEFA competitions continued but the exile of the English did not signal an end to hooliganism in Europe. There were regular newspaper reports of violence at grounds in Holland, Germany, Italy and Spain. There was football rioting in Greece and no doubt many other incidents went unreported in the British media. 'The English disease' was widespread but amazingly the violence did not merit a similar ban to England's.

It was during this period that Alex Ferguson began the journey that would eventually take him to Europe's summit and lead to him becoming the most successful manager in Manchester United's history, surpassing the achievements of the legendary Sir Matt Busby.

It was not plain sailing, far from it. At times it seemed as if the rough waters might overwhelm the Scot as his team hit peaks and troughs. One moment United would ride the crest of a wave but the next plummet to the depths. Ferguson described the inconsistency as 'a rollercoaster ride'.

He appeared to be enjoying it, but there were those within the media who used the sports pages to predict an early end to his reign at the club. Former Liverpool player Emlyn Hughes wrote 'Fergie will get the OBE – Out Before Easter' in an article that struck deep into the manager's heart. He craved success and set out to attain it, regardless of what the critics had to say.

Following his appointment, United survived the traumas of the 1986–87 season. They ended the campaign in eleventh place, an improvement considering they had actually hit the bottom at one stage of the season. Ferguson began to stamp his mark on the way things were done at the club. He restructured the youth system, having been shocked by the discovery that it was neighbours Manchester City who were taking the cream of young players from the area. He felt this was something which had to stop, and soon it did. During his first two years he brought Nobby Stiles and Brian Kidd back to Old Trafford. They began to organise youth development, assisting Eric Harrison, the man responsible for running the A and B teams.

The manager also bought experienced players to strengthen his side – Brian McClair the Scottish striker from Glasgow Celtic, Viv Anderson the England full-back from Arsenal and Steve Bruce of Norwich City, a rugged central defender whose passion for the club showed from the moment he first pulled on a red shirt.

There was an exodus, too. The first big name to leave was Frank Stapleton. He joined Ajax in the summer of 1987, before Ferguson's first full season in charge got under way. Several of the club's younger players were also surplus to requirements; by the end of that campaign, the new man's influence began to show and the club finished in second place in the League, good enough to qualify for the UEFA Cup again had it not been for the ban.

Injuries had once again hit the push for domestic honours.

First choice goalkeeper Gary Walsh was hurt shortly before Christmas and Chris Turner, who had been signed by Atkinson as a deputy for Gary Bailey, took over. By this time, Bailey had retired and within a year he was followed by Remi Moses who never fully recovered from the injury sustained at Blackburn.

In the summer of 1988, Ferguson made a move that won him a place in the hearts of tens of thousands of United supporters. He brought back Mark Hughes to Old Trafford. United discovered their former striker was unhappy at Barcelona. The Spaniards had farmed him out on loan to Bayern Munich and he had so impressed the Germans they wanted to sign him. However, when Hughes and his wife came to Old Trafford for Gary Bailey's testimonial game – Mark was playing – they made it clear they would be happy to return to England if offered the opportunity. The young couple had spent the first two years of their married life living in apartments in Spain and Germany. Despite the financial advantages a top-level footballer might have, they had nowhere they could call home. Once Ferguson was made aware of this, he made his move.

Like the Prodigal Son, the player who had left during Ron Atkinson's time in charge was welcomed with open arms by his former club. It was the best thing Alex Ferguson could have done and for once, the manager found the sports pages filled with positive rather than negative comments.

Ferguson also signed Scotland's regular first-choice goalkeeper Jim Leighton, from his former club Aberdeen. The new keeper got off to a great start with four clean sheets in his first five appearances as United set the early pace in the championship. Hughes was not as quick to make an impression and had to wait until 24 September before he scored the first goal of his second spell with the club. That opened the floodgates and began a run of twelve goals in fifteen league games, the best scoring spell of his career.

Despite the promise of such an enthusiastic opening, it turned out to be a mediocre season. United finished eleventh in the League and there was unrest both on and off the field as football found itself going through another traumatic period.

Heysel would not be forgotten. As a result of the troubles in Belgium, a group of Liverpool supporters appeared in court in Brussels and were found guilty of manslaughter. Some were given prison sentences, others heavily fined, but events thirteen days earlier overshadowed anything that happened in the courtroom.

Following the Heysel disaster, Margaret Thatcher's Conservative government had called for the introduction of more stringent controls over football supporters. Colin Moynihan, the Minister for Sport, led efforts to introduce an identity-card scheme, which was seen as a way of exercising control. The idea was for fans to register as official followers of their club. Only registered supporters would be allowed access to games and if anyone misbehaved they would have their membership cancelled.

Opponents – and the Football Association was among those against the idea – claimed it would remove freedom of choice from the casual supporter. Any law-abiding citizen wishing to watch a football match would be unable to do so without joining a scheme. Those who fancied an afternoon watching the local side in action would no longer be able to roll up, pay at the gate and enjoy the game.

There was much debating on the subject in the House of Commons and within football. Luton Town went further than most with the drastic step of banning all visiting supporters from its Kenilworth Road ground.

Others threatened to follow suit, while some erected fences up terracing to keep rival sections of support apart. Segregation became commonplace at most grounds and many clubs also prevented pitch invasions by erecting high barriers between supporters and the playing area. Fans were forced to watch like caged animals, looking out on the game through wire meshed fencing or – in Old Trafford's case – heavy steel bars.

It took another major tragedy before everyone realised the caging of spectators was dangerous, and positive action was taken to ensure crowd safety at all major sports stadia. Once again it was Liverpool supporters – who, ironically, were regarded by some as the best behaved and most sporting in the game – who found themselves involved.

On Saturday, 15 April 1989, the FA Cup semi-final between Nottingham Forest and Liverpool was abandoned after just six minutes play. Ninety-four Liverpool fans died on the terraces of Hillsborough, Sheffield Wednesday's ground. Over-crowding in one section of the Leppings Lane end of the stadium had led to a crush of fans going through one entrance. So-called safety fences prevented not only the trapped supporters being pushed forward by the weight of those coming from behind from finding a means of escape, but made it impossible for the emergency services to get to their aid. Thousands looked on helplessly as others died in the mêlée, the luckier ones being pulled to safety by those in an upper seated section of the grandstand.

Understandably, football was stunned. An official inquiry into the disaster led by Lord Justice Taylor came to the conclusion that the only safe way of watching top-level sport in future was in all-seater stadia. Any talk of a European return had to be forgotten, as even FIFA reacted to Hillsborough, deciding there would be no standing spectators during the 1990 World Cup finals in Italy.

At Old Trafford there were problems of a very different nature. Chairman Martin Edwards found himself the constant target of abuse from supporters. He had failed to win them over even though, time and again, he did his best to convince whoever would listen that his aim was to put Manchester United back at the top. He argued that he placed no financial restrictions on his manager, encouraged him to buy whichever players he might want, and yet it seemed to him that no matter what he did, it was wrong in the eyes of a hard core of fans.

This may have been one of the reasons behind events which marked the start of the 1989–90 season and a significant turning point in the Manchester United story. Chairman Edwards decided to sell his majority share-holding in the club for £10 million. The buyer was property developer Michael Knighton. It was officially announced that the new man would replace him as chairman, and was putting up the cash to develop the Stretford End where plans included the building of an hotel.

Before the kick-off of the opening game of the season against champions Arsenal came the bizarre scene of chairman-elect Knighton demonstrating his ball-juggling skills in front of a rapturous audience. At that moment the new man won over the masses in one fell swoop, although the events that followed changed many opinions.

On the day, the game matched the razzmatazz of the pre-match entertainment. United outplayed The Gunners, winning 4–1. It seemed the new era was off to a flying start but shortly afterwards things started to go wrong for Knighton, and eventually the deal was called off. The Knighton 'take-over' culminated in the flotation of Manchester United on the Stock Exchange as a public limited company. It led to some supporters and, perhaps more importantly, financial institutions buying shares in the business and opened the door to the club declaring record-breaking profits in the years that followed. At the turn of the twenty-first century the club was valued at more than £1 billion – a vast increase on the £10 million Knighton had been ready to pay for it – and there is every reason to believe that even more growth is possible.

Ten years earlier it was success on the field the supporters demanded, and that came through the FA Cup. Before the 1989–90 campaign began, Ferguson again invested in new players. He bought Michael Phelan from Norwich, and Neil Webb from Nottingham Forest. Webb was an established England international who got off to a fine start by scoring on his debut in the win over Arsenal before bad luck struck. Four games into the season Webb ruptured an Achilles tendon during an England appearance and was out of action for seven months – the international curse had again struck Manchester United.

A new transfer record was established by the signing of Gary Pallister from Middlesbrough. The tall central defender cost United £2.3 million and the spending did not stop there. Paul Ince arrived from West Ham, followed a short time later by Danny Wallace from Southampton. This took Ferguson past the £10 million spending mark since his arrival, but as yet there were no trophies to show for his investments.

There were outgoings, too. The popular Whiteside was sold to Everton, and his close friend and drinking partner Paul McGrath moved to Aston Villa. These moves did not go down well with the supporters and sparked off media speculation that Ferguson's days at the club were numbered. Reports claimed that unless United picked up a trophy by the end of the season, the manager would be on his way. This was – and still is – emphatically denied by Martin Edwards. 'I can honestly say that at no time did the directors ever discuss the issue,' he maintains. 'We could see what the manager was doing at the club and replacing him was not on the agenda.'

United did win a trophy, Ferguson remained at the club and success returned. United took their first tentative steps towards Wembley – and as it turned out, Europe – on 7 January 1990. In the FA Cup third round they faced tough opponents in Nottingham Forest at the City Ground.

United started as outsiders but after fifty-six minutes they scored the only goal of a tense Cup tie. It came when a cross from Hughes on the left was headed past Nottingham Forest goal-keeper Steve Sutton by Mark Robins, one of the few youngsters to survive Ferguson's early clear out.

Victories over Hereford, Newcastle and Sheffield United followed, despite the handicap of being drawn away from home in every round. The closest they came to Old Trafford was when the semi-final against Oldham Athletic was staged at Maine Road. Oldham under manager Joe Royle, were enjoying life as promotion candidates from the Second Division and stood between Ferguson and his first Wembley.

It took two games to overcome them and once again it was Robins who played a crucial role. Shortly after coming on as an extra-time substitute, the player, whose family home was within sight of Oldham's Boundary Park floodlights, ran on to a Phelan pass and scored the decisive ninth goal of the two encounters to give United a 2–1 win.

The final was against Crystal Palace and that too went to a replay. In the first game Mark Hughes scored twice following a first-half equaliser from Bryan Robson. Ian Wright got two for Palace and it ended 3–3. Five days later, Ferguson showed the first glimpse of the ruthlessness needed to succeed in modern football management. He dropped a bombshell by axing regular goalkeeper Leighton and giving his place to Les Sealey, the keeper who had been brought in on loan from Luton Town to act as a stand-by. It was a heart-rending move by Ferguson who put the success of his club before anything, even though it cost him a long-standing friendship with Leighton. As for the replay, Sealey kept a clean sheet, young full-back Lee Martin scored the only goal, and United's name went on the famous trophy once again.

Shortly afterwards came the news Ferguson had waited for.

The European ban was lifted. English clubs, with the exception of Liverpool, were allowed to play in UEFA competitions once again. United had qualified for the Cup-Winners' Cup, the trophy Ferguson had won during his days with Aberdeen, and were officially invited to take part. For the second time in the club's history, Manchester United were to become England's ambassadors abroad. After leading the way in 1956, they now had the responsibility of taking the first tentative steps of 1990 and knew they would find themselves under the microscope.

The historic return came on Wednesday, 19 September 1990 but fewer than 30,000 spectators gathered at Old Trafford. The ban had been imposed following the trip to play Videoton so it was fitting that Hungary again provided the opposition. This time Pecsi Munkas came to Manchester, and Clayton Blackmore found his way into the record books with a twenty-five-yard shot which bridged the years, United's first European goal since Frank Stapleton's strike against Videoton on 6 March 1985.

Blackmore was left full-back against Pecsi (pronounced 'Paich') and was partnered by Denis Irwin, a close-season signing from Oldham. Irishman Irwin had impressed Ferguson before the FA Cup semi-finals, but his performances in those games against United convinced the manager he was worth a £700,000 investment. The United boss was not impressed, however, by the attendance for that first European game in five years. 'I think one of the problems is after missing European football for such a period, a lot of fans have forgotten how exciting it can be,' he said. 'Some of the younger ones have never seen a European game at all. You get out of the habit.'

United won the first leg 2–0 thanks to a second goal from Webb, and followed this by taking the second 1–0, Brian McClair's header dashing any hopes the Hungarians may have had of pulling off a surprise.

Fears of possible crowd trouble were also quickly dispelled, even though hundreds of United supporters ignored the club's plea for them to stay at home. Those who made the trip were well behaved and one group provided plenty of entertainment for the locals by turning up in full Santa Claus outfits, a strange sight indeed on a warm evening in October!

When the draw for round two was made, United could have been forgiven for assuming Christmas had come early. They were paired with Fourth Division side Wrexham.

It was not Wrexham's first time in Europe, far from it, but although they had played in the competition before, they were regarded as one of the tournament's whipping boys. They qualified after winning the Welsh Cup for a remarkable twenty-first time but knew it would take a sensation to overcome United in a match played over two legs. Had this been an FA Cup game with United forced to make the trip to the Welsh club's Racecourse Ground, there would have been the possibility of a shock one-off victory. To come out winners over two games against the thoroughbreds from Manchester was asking too much.

The draw was greeted with mixed feelings. It was good news that a British club would go through to the quarter-finals but sad that another would go out. One player eager to see United through to round three was Mark Hughes because this particular European expedition took him to his hometown!

United won the home leg 3–0 with McClair, Bruce and Pallister scoring but Mark missed the opportunity of playing at the Racecourse Ground, where he watched his first professional football, because of a calf strain. There was a bizarre twist to that second leg. Because UEFA rules insisted the visiting club should check into the host country at least twenty-four hours before the game, the United squad had to board the team coach, travel south west for less than an hour and move into a country hotel half-a-mile on the Welsh side of the border. So they were based less than fifty miles away from Old Trafford as they completed a 5–0 aggregate victory.

Hughes may have been disappointed to miss out on playing in Wrexham, but he found himself in the thick of things in the next round. It came after the winter break when United met French club Montpellier.

The first leg of the third round was played at Old Trafford and by then interest in the competition had increased to such an extent that a crowd of just under 42,000 turned up to see United get off to a marvellous start. Within a minute McClair rifled home a Lee Sharpe cross after Hughes had found him with a pass wide on the left wing. Ferguson had asked for early pressure from his players and he certainly got it. Then in what the manager described as 'typical United fashion', disaster struck.

Lee Martin, the player whose goal had secured United's place in Europe, scored again – but this time he put the ball in his own net. Like Graeme Hogg before him, Cup final hero Martin accidentally flicked the ball past Les Sealey, who by this time had secured a permanent move to United after his Wembley success.

With only seven minutes gone the scores were level but, more to the point, the French had an away goal under their belts. It lifted the visitors who withstood everything United could muster. Then came the incident which marred the tie. Hughes fell to the ground after what appeared to be a head-butt from Pascal Baills, Montpellier's full-back. The defender screamed his innocence but was shown the red card and ordered off. Television proved the player deserved punishment for violent behaviour but there appeared to have been little, if any, contact with Hughes. The United striker later admitted, 'I went down as a reaction to the attack, and stayed down until the referee sorted it out.'

The incident did little to cement Anglo-French relationships and the comments of Montpellier's club president made matters worse. He said Hughes would 'not be welcome' in his town.

In the event, the broad-chested Welshman seemed unaffected by the furore, ignoring Montpellier supporter's chants. When the United players took an early walk on the pitch, he even showed his amusement as he pointed out to his team-mates the obscene slogans written in English on banners draped over the perimeter fence by French fans.

His fellow countryman Clayton Blackmore took a direct approach to the situation, firing home a free kick from what seemed an impossible distance for United's first goal. Later, he made such a dangerous run into the Montpellier penalty area that the only way to stop him was by foul means. Steve Bruce converted the resulting spot kick and United reached their eighth semi-final in European competition.

Just once had they managed to get beyond the penultimate round. Now Polish club Legia Warsaw stood between them and success. The Poles were the favourites to win the trophy after defeating Italian giants Sampdoria in the previous round, and Ferguson was fully aware of the magnitude of the task ahead.

Confidence within the side was growing and even though they were stunned in the first leg in Warsaw to find themselves a goal down when midfielder Jacek Cyzio scored in the thirty-sixth minute, United seemed unaffected. They hit back to win 3–1, McClair equalising within a minute of the Polish goal. Hughes made it 2–1 seven minutes into the second half, and Bruce added the third with a close-range shot following more good work from the Welshman.

After the thrill of hitting the heights that afternoon in Warsaw, Ferguson's rollercoaster plunged downwards once more.

Domestically, United lay fourth in the League and had reached the fifth round of the FA Cup before going out at Norwich. In the League Cup they had fared better, reaching the final which was due to be played three days before the second clash with Legia. United met Ron Atkinson's Sheffield Wednesday at Wembley and lost 1–0, but there was more to the game than the disappointment of defeat. While making an attempted save, goalkeeper Sealey badly gashed his knee and by rejecting efforts to have him replaced possibly made the injury much worse.

So Gary Walsh, whose career had been resurrected by revolutionary ankle surgery, found himself facing the Poles in the second leg. On the bench was rookie keeper Mark Bosnich, an Australian-born youngster seen as one for the future by Ferguson. Up to that time, Bosnich had made just two league appearances, separated by the summer break.

Ferguson got his wish for a bigger crowd – 44,269 turned up to see an edgy United do enough to get through to the final. Sharpe scored their only goal, meeting a Hughes pass with a fierce left-foot drive. The Poles equalised through striker Wojciech Kowalczyk but that was the only scare and the 4–2 aggregate was enough to secure United's victory.

For the first time since 1968, and only the second time in their history, Manchester United had reached a European final. Their opponents would be mighty Barcelona. The final in the Feyenoord Stadium in Rotterdam brought together the clubs that had met on that memorable night in 1984 in the quarter-final of the Cup-Winners' Cup, and for Mark Hughes it was the perfect way to make up for the disappointment of not playing in Wrexham. The Catalan club that had rejected him stood between United and European glory. If Hughes felt he needed to prove a point, this was the perfect opportunity for him to do so.

During the build-up to the game there was great concern about crowd control. Efforts to have the final switched to another venue failed and the Dutch authorities went out of their way to ensure an incident-free event.

United organised a massive airlift of fans from Manchester and on their arrival, the official parties were shepherded along with those who had travelled privately to a city centre park. Some fans had already set up camp there, sleeping in tents and campervans and everyone joined in a massive pop concert, which created the perfect party atmosphere. It set the mood for an enjoyable final even though a continual downpour threatened to dampen spirits.

Ferguson kept his team plans to himself, but followed the pattern he had set in the FA Cup final replay by leaving out one of his big-name players. This time it was Neil Webb. Three months earlier, Webb had been sidelined with cracked ribs. He had recovered and won his way back, playing in both legs of the semi-final, but his place against Barcelona went to Michael Phelan.

Ferguson gambled on Sealey's fitness and the senior keeper played with that injured knee heavily strapped, so United lined up:

Sealey; Irwin, Bruce, Pallister, Blackmore; Phelan, Robson, Ince, Sharpe; McClair, Hughes.

Media player profiles from the final described the United stars thus:

Les Sealey: found his way into the record books as the man who replaced goalkeeper Jim Leighton in the 1990 FA Cup final replay. Les was on his second loan period from Luton Town when he was drafted into the side in April 1990 for the vital games against QPR and Aston Villa. He gave two excellent displays to help keep United in the First Division. A Londoner who was born in Bethnal Green, he began his career with Coventry City in 1976 before moving to Luton.

Denis Irwin: joined United from Oldham Athletic early in June 1990. He cost United £625,000 with a further £75,000 heading

Oldham's way once he has made three full international appearances for the Republic of Ireland. Born in County Cork, he began his career at Leeds United but after four years and around 100 league and Cup appearances, he was given a free transfer by manager Billy Bremner. Alex Ferguson has no doubts about the versatile left- or right-back making a name for himself at Old Trafford.

Steve Bruce: came to United in a £850,000 deal with Norwich City in December 1987 and was an ever-present in the side. He was the Norwich skipper before his move to Old Trafford, and filled a similar role when playing for England B. Although born in Newcastle, his professional career began at Gillingham, where he stayed for seven years before being sold to Norwich. Scored his first goal for United in the 2–0 win at Chelsea in February 1988 and the first of the 1989–90 season in the 4–1 win over champions Arsenal.

Gary Pallister: cost United a record £2.3 million when bought from Middlesbrough in August 1989. Born in Ramsgate he played non-league football with Billingham Town before being spotted by Middlesbrough. His league debut was at Plough Lane when Middlesbrough played Wimbledon on 17 August 1985, and three years later he won his first England cap playing against Hungary in Budapest. At 6ft 4ins he is one of the tallest players on United's books and is tipped by Alex Ferguson to become an outstanding central defender.

Clayton Blackmore: a full Welsh international and regular choice for his country, he has been unable to command the same treatment at Old Trafford. Made his debut at Nottingham Forest in May 1984 but it was December 1985 before he played a game at Old Trafford. His longest run in the side came after Alex Ferguson included him in his team at the start of the

1988–89 season. A native of Neath, he has a fierce shot and has scored some spectacular goals. As a schoolboy he was capped seventeen times for Wales and played in his country's Under-18 side when he was only fifteen.

Michael Phelan: signed for United a few days before Neil Webb in June 1989. Born in Nelson in North Lancashire, he began his career with Burnley, and was sold to Norwich City after around 200 appearances. Became Norwich skipper and led them to success in 1988–89, their best season in the First Division. Was capped for England at youth level during his Burnley days and had his full England call-up in November 1989 when he replaced Bryan Robson during the friendly against Italy at Wembley.

Bryan Robson: captain of club and country and one of the game's top players. Was spotted by West Bromwich Albion while playing junior football in his hometown of Chester-le-Street and signed in August 1974. Made his first-team debut at the end of that season and played for England Youth. His progress was hit by injury when he broke an ankle, but he finally made his full international debut in 1980. A year later, Ron Atkinson brought him to Old Trafford for £1.75 million. Under Atkinson, he captained United to FA Cup success in 1983 and 1985. After Alex Ferguson took over, he collected the Cup for a historic third time in 1990. Received the OBE in the 1990 New Year's Honours list.

Paul Ince: joined United from West Ham in September 1989 after months of speculation and some unusual happenings. Declared his eagerness to move north by being photographed in a United shirt three months before the deal went through! Alex Ferguson agreed a fee of £2 million with West Ham manager Lou Macari, then the move hit a snag on medical grounds.

Three weeks later, agreement was reached and Paul made his debut in the 5–1 victory over Millwall on 16 September 1989. Scored his first goals for the club when he netted twice at Portsmouth in the Littlewoods Cup four days later. Born in Ilford, West Ham was his first club and he joined them through the Youth Training Scheme. Has played for England at youth and Under-21 levels and a senior call-up looks certain.

Lee Sharpe: few players can claim to have signed for Manchester United in the early hours of the morning, but Lee Sharpe did – and he was still a sixteen year old at the time! Alex Ferguson made a midnight dash to Torquay to sign Lee who had joined the south coast club on YTS terms. A year later, he established himself as a regular in the United first team until an Achilles heel injury sidelined him temporarily. Lee was born in the West Midlands and almost signed for Birmingham City before getting the chance to join Torquay. Played fourteen games for the Seasiders before his move north. He won England Under-21 honours during his first season and scored his first United goal in the 5–1 home win over Millwall on 16 September 1989.

Brian McClair: brought his goalscoring skills south when he joined United in the summer of 1987. At that time he had scored 123 goals in four seasons with Glasgow Celtic and was Scotland's top scorer in 1986–87 with forty-one strikes. That earned him the Scottish Golden Boot award, and a season later he was only just pipped for the English version. Became the first United player for two decades to score more than twenty League goals in a season, hitting the net twenty-four times as the Reds finished First Division runners-up. He scored thirty-one goals in his first season, but a move to midfield caused this to drop to seventeen in his second term. A regular member of the Scotland squad, he studied mathematics but gave up university to become a professional footballer.

Mark Hughes: returned to Old Trafford in June 1988 after two years in Europe. He joined United from school and made his debut in the 1983–84 season in the League Cup, scoring on his first senior outing. It was a similar story on his league debut against Leicester City, and he made it a hat-trick of debut goals when he scored for Wales against England in his first full international. His transfer to Barcelona in August 1986 brought in a club record of £1.8 million. United gave the Spaniards most of their money back two years later to bring Sparky home. He was voted PFA Player of the Year in 1989.

It was obvious right from the start of the final that Alex Ferguson's plan was to take the game to Barcelona and put pressure on their goalkeeper Carlos Busquets, who was making his first-team debut. The twenty-four year old was thrown into the melting pot of a European final because regular keeper Andoni Zubizarreta was suspended after picking up the fateful second yellow card during Barcelona's semi-final against Juventus. Despite the obvious pressure, Busquets looked confident in the opening stages. The Spaniards were also without Hristo Stoichkov, their highly rated Bulgarian striker whose place went to Julio Salinas.

For United, Lee Sharpe made a tremendous start. He attacked Barcelona's right flank, bringing back memories of John Aston's performance in the club's previous European final. Sharpe's speed caused havoc and Barcelona had to pull an extra man over to United's left side to cover the nineteen year old's runs. This meant there was an opportunity to switch play to the opposite flank and there McClair had freedom to operate, helped out by Phelan and Irwin.

The deluge continued throughout the game and thousands of rain-soaked United fans urged their side on. The millions watching on television heard the strains of 'Always look on the

Bright Side of Life' ringing out from the terraces, as the Monty Python song became the theme tune of the Red Army.

Mark Hughes was supported in his front-line battle by McClair's runs. Robson dominated midfield. His strong challenges upset the Spaniards' rhythm, and with Ince alongside him, the England skipper seemed to be enjoying the occasion.

United's first scoring chance fell to Sharpe after Hughes won the ball deep in his own half. Pallister and Robson interchanged passes and the tall central defender carried the ball over the halfway line before finding McClair. The Scot's pass split the Spanish defence but Busquets beat Sharpe to the ball just as he was moving in for the kill.

In defence, Bruce and Pallister seemed to have an answer to everything Barcelona could produce and after twelve minutes McClair found himself in front of goal with a great opportunity to score. Unfortunately, an awkward bounce made him loft his shot higher than intended, and the ball sailed harmlessly over the crossbar.

Moments later, United appealed for a penalty when Hughes fell to the ground, sandwiched between two defenders as he ran towards the Spanish goal. One of his markers, Fernando Munoz, known as Nando, appeared to push him over but Swedish referee Bo Karlsson ignored the incident and waved play on.

Barcelona were being restricted to long-range shooting but shots were either off target or cleared by the United defence. When Michael Laudrup finally did get an effort on target, it was easily dealt with by Sealey.

Clayton Blackmore was quick to react to one threatening free kick midway through the first half, hooking the ball over his head and back to Sealey who showed the first signs that he might be having problems with his knee. He rolled awkwardly to collect and clear, his movement hindered by the protective bandage he had been forced to wear. The knee was obviously

Bryan Robson

a handicap and without doubt Barcelona were aware of this. They, too, wanted to put pressure on the opposition goalkeeper but United's defenders protected him efficiently.

Up front Hughes showed there was no love lost between him and his former club as he clashed with Salinas in the centre circle. He followed this with another hard challenge on defender Alberto Ferrer just before half-time but neither side could break the deadlock and at the interval it was 0–0.

Early in the second-half it was Hughes who struck the first blow but again he failed to score. Chesting down a McClair pass, he tried to chip the keeper only to see the ball once again pass over the bar.

United kept up the pressure, forcing Busquets to punch away as Bruce aimed a free kick into the Barcelona box. The pattern of play stayed the same, United taking the game to the Spaniards who relied on the swift breakaway to launch their attacking movements. Their hope was that Alex Ferguson's side would tire from the relentless pressure but United's approach remained positive. After sixty-seven minutes their effort paid off.

Sealey cleared downfield and United won a free kick in the middle of the Barcelona half. Ince and Robson arranged things so that the Spaniards half expected a long-range shot from free-kick specialist Blackmore. Instead, Robson chipped the ball to the right of the Barcelona penalty area and Bruce, running in, met it firmly with his head. It looked a goal all over and Bruce turned to celebrate as Hughes, making sure, followed the ball towards the left-hand post meeting it on the half-volley and forcing it into the empty net. The United fans went wild with delight as they saw their side take the lead, but the Spanish fight was far from over.

Johan Cruyff made a substitution, taking off Jose Alexanco and bringing Antonia Pinilla into the action. Barcelona reorganised and United's answer was to score a second goal within two minutes of the switch. It came after Barcelona pressure and, this time, United hitting them on the break.

The Spaniards won a corner on the right and Robson headed clear. McClair chased the ball as it ran towards the halfway line and appeared to be fouled, but the referee played the advantage. McClair sent a long pass towards Hughes but Ferrer beat him to the ball and it ran to Robson. The United captain chipped a pass forward and Hughes picked up the ball wide on the right. He controlled it with his first touch and ran at the Spanish goal as Busquets came towards him. Hughes dipped his right shoulder and ran towards the goalline, passing the goalkeeper and leaving him stranded, chasing back towards his goal. It seemed Hughes had taken the ball too wide but, still at full stretch, he hit a fierce drive. It passed beyond the reach of two defenders as they chased back to cover, and went inside the far post – United 2 Barcelona 0.

The soaking supporters enjoyed another moment of glory. Mark Hughes's dream had come true. He had scored two crucial goals against his former club, and with sixteen minutes remaining it seemed the Cup was won.

The Spaniards were forced to attack and the pressure led to two corners. Ince and Sharpe combined to clear one dangerous effort from Koeman, then Bakero was booked for a fierce over-the-top challenge on Hughes. Tempers were getting frayed and Robson followed the Spaniard into the referee's notebook after a heavy tackle on Eusebio. A lunging two-footed tackle by the United captain gave away another free kick and Ronald Koeman stepped up to take it.

United formed a five-man wall of Bruce, Hughes, Robson, Ince and McClair which was directed into position by Sealey but even with every angle seemingly covered, the powerful Dutchman showed why he had earned the reputation as one of the best free-kick exponents in the game. He hit a fierce shot from all of thirty yards which went under Sealey's desperate dive and into the net.

The United keeper was beaten not just by the pace of the shot, but by the bounce of the ball. His restricted movement had not helped because he was unable to get down quickly. Perhaps with more mobility he might have palmed the ball away but all he could do was turn the shot on to the inside of the post from where it went spinning into the back of the United net.

Barcelona were back in the game. With less than ten minutes to go United were rocked when the Spaniards seemed to have scored the equaliser. Laudrup carried the ball down the left wing and Pinilla, coming in on the right, beat the defence and forced the ball home. Barcelona celebrated but the linesman had raised his flag for offside. United had escaped.

Watching from the crowd, Jordi Cruyff, son of the Barcelona coach, had a different opinion. 'I thought it was a perfectly good goal, but I was only fifteen and of course I wanted my father's club to win. I could not see why Pinilla was ruled offside, but that's football,' was the view of the player who would join United five years later.

Before the end, more Barcelona pressure from Salinas and Laudrup forced United on to the back foot. Time was running out for the Spaniards and their anxiety turned into frustration as Hughes broke forward, threatening their goal once again. He evaded one challenge before Nando brought him down with a tackle which would not have looked out of place on a rugby field. The full-back wrapped an arm around the Welsh star's neck and hung on. Out came the red card and Barcelona were forced to finish the game with ten men.

Barca won a late corner which Sealey failed to punch clear; a Laudrup cross almost caught United out; and twice Sealey had to throw himself at the feet of the Spanish attackers to prevent them getting the equaliser. As the United supporters screamed for the final whistle, Blackmore cleared from his own goalline under intense pressure as Barcelona launched do-or-die attacks. Ten men or not, they refused to give up and there was relief on the United bench when McClair got in a shot on the Spanish goal which was turned for a corner.

From the cross Busquets saved as McClair tried to put the issue beyond doubt. In the final minute, Sharpe lost possession, Barcelona poured into the United half and Irwin cleared. The kick downfield from the full-back – a decade later he became the club's most successful player of all time – was the final moment of the game. As the ball went out of play the referee blew his whistle and United had won their second European trophy.

The crowd hailed its heroes and the muddied winners acknowledged the magnificent support given by the rain-soaked masses. A scene which was to become a regular occurrence in the coming years ensued as Manchester United paraded with their trophy, pausing occasionally for photographs, players collecting scarves and hats from fans and enjoying their moment in the spotlight. Steve Bruce summed up the feeling in the United camp once the on-the-field celebrations had ended.

'It's quite unbelievable,' he said. 'It's the first season I've ever played in Europe and I'm thirty-one this year. The memory will stay with me. It's a great occasion for us all and I'm obviously very delighted.'

Delight was the key word. Chairman Martin Edwards said, 'I'm absolutely shattered. It was a superb performance. Barcelona just crept back into the game towards the end, but I felt on the night we were by far the better side. We played in the tradition of Manchester United.

'Mark Hughes is delighted with his two goals but he has just told me that he has given the first one to Steve Bruce. I have seen the goal replayed on television and I know Mark helped the ball over the line but it was going in from Steve's header. Now it's time to celebrate. We have a party organised at our hotel and I'm sure it's going to be a fairly noisy celebration. I'm delighted.'

Despite his sporting offering, Hughes was officially credited with both goals and his second was United's one hundredth of the season, taking his personal tally to twenty-one.

For Alex Ferguson it was another trophy and another place in football history as he became the first British manager to win the Cup-Winners' Cup with two different clubs, having lifted the trophy while with Aberdeen. He summed up the feeling of déjà vu by saying, 'This is why we do it. With the support that we have, we have got to win things. The atmosphere tonight was incredible, the supporters were superb. It was the first European experience for a lot of the players and there were understandably some nerves in the first half, but they settled well in the second. They got about their job and I think they deserved to win. I know there was nervousness in the last part of the match, but you can't expect anything else. As I said to them, you have to go through some pain in a European final, and they did. But it is worth it.'

Entering the debate about the first goal the manager added, 'Who claims the goals doesn't really matter but what is important is that the second was our hundredth of the season.

'The supporters who were in Rotterdam were out of this world. The ones back home who have supported us all season will know that this win was for them. That is what this club is about. It is based on the wonderful support that we have, and on the traditions Sir Matt Busby brought to the club. Tonight that was cemented.

'Now we have to have more success. We have to use this as a platform to get more because that is what we want.'

United did party that night at their exclusive hideaway hotel, and the following day flew home to a rapturous welcome. They carried the European Cup-Winners' Cup through miles of cheering fans as they travelled by open-topped bus to Old Trafford.

A second European trophy had finally been won by England's pioneers and the victory signalled the start of great times under Alex Ferguson.

Mark Hughes

Rotterdam was a great night for me, for Manchester United and for British football. It was a difficult game for us because they were a very good side, but I think on our second-half performance we deserved to win.

I said before the final that I felt I had something to prove to Barcelona and after the game I knew I had made my point. I must stress that I had no axe to grind with them. I had a chance when I was at the club and I didn't take it. That's history now.

To win the Cup-Winners' Cup for Manchester United meant a lot. To do it in front of so many of our supporters who had gone across to Holland made it a great moment. It was a very emotional night.

The lads could hardly believe we had gone out and won because we were under a lot of pressure before the competition started. We were the first English club allowed back into the competition and as it went on we knew we were carrying the flag for British football. To get to the final was a great achievement and we knew if we could win it, it would be such a boost for British football following all the set-backs.

As for the goals, I was delighted to claim them both. The first came from Steve Bruce. It was definitely going in but I made sure by kicking the ball over the line. The record books will show that I scored, but really it should go down as one for Steve.

I said before the game that my ideal would be to score a special goal against Barcelona and while I am not claiming the second fitted the bill, it meant a lot to me. Some of the lads thought I had hit it too wide, some were expecting a cross but I could see a lot of the goal and I was confident in what I was trying to do. I made good contact, and in it went.

It's one game I will never forget. It was a special night and the beginning of some great times at Old Trafford.

19

BIENVENUE, M. CANTONA

FOOTBALL entered yet another period of change in the summer of 1991, but it was not unexpected. For some time the top tier had threatened to breakaway from the Football League and on 16 August 1991, the split widened as the twenty-two clubs in the First Division took the unprecedented step of tendering their resignation. They announced that the following year they would join forces with the game's other governing body in English football, the Football Association, and form a Premier League. The 1991–92 season would mark the end of an era.

There was confusion. It was difficult to imagine Manchester United, Liverpool, Arsenal, Everton, Tottenham Hotspur and the other major members of the First Division suddenly walking away from tradition. The Football League had been responsible for running professional, competitive football in the country for more than a century.

The main reason behind the breakaway appeared to be money. The big clubs wanted the lion's share of television revenue arguing – and with good reason – that it was their games that were being screened. A deal was struck with satellite television BSkyB for an incredible £304 million but there were many opposed to it, including Alex Ferguson. In his book *Six Years at United* (Mainstream) the manager said:

How the football people negotiating the contract did not have the savvy to know that once the agreement was signed the Sky people would fleece the fans, I will never know.

The agreement sells supporters right down the river and hits the hardest and most vulnerable part of society, the old people. Pensioners and thousands of people who can ill afford it, must now buy a satellite dish to see football on television and then, after the initial outlay, they will also have to pay £2.99 to watch the sports channel. I understand it is likely to go up to £6 a month before very long.

Some of the clubs opposed to the breakaway wanted the League to exile the rebels forever. By moving under the umbrella of the FA, those forming the new set-up knew they would be outside the jurisdiction of the Football League so this was an empty threat. Those who saw the folly of such a proposal said that the seventy clubs outside the Premier League would be 'shooting themselves in the foot'. If the top section became a closed shop and there remained strong opposition from the clubs in the lower divisions, the Premier League could simply decide to stay that way – one division made up of twenty-two clubs with no promotion from the old Second Division and certainly no relegation.

The opposition came mainly from the clubs who saw themselves being left behind by the breakaway but the League also made changes. With the old First Division clubs becoming the Premier League, they promoted the Second Division clubs *en masse*, changing the title of their division to First. The Third Division became the Second and the Fourth was forgotten. No wonder the United manager described the goings on as 'a piece of nonsense'.

There were many of the scheme's opponents who felt the threat of the breakaway was simply a bluff, claiming the big boys would be back cap in hand when it all went terribly wrong.

Supporters of the idea saw it as a new dawn, a football revolution to take the game into a new era – a whole new ball game, according to the promotional campaign of the satellite television company.

While this was going on in the English League, changes were also being planned by UEFA. Anxious to extend the Champions Cup, the European body drew up a blueprint for a new-style tournament. Combined with the moves in England, this brought predictions that it was the first step towards the inevitable, the formation of a European league.

In the wake of the mass resignation, the 1991–92 season began with uncertainty. No one quite knew what lay ahead and at the end of the campaign, when the First Division trophy was handed to Leeds United, few really believed this was the last time the famous prize would be awarded to the country's top team.

United almost won the title in the last season the winners of the First Division would be known as the League champions, but were narrowly beaten to first place, failing at Liverpool as Leeds tied things up in their game against Sheffield United.

Alex Ferguson's side stepped into the FA Premier League as the last true runners-up in the Football League, beaten in the end by injuries and fixture congestion as well as by Leeds. The League forced them to play five of their closing six games in an eleven-day period at the end of a gruelling campaign, and it was little wonder they staggered breathlessly to the finishing line. Was this the League's revenge against United's involvement in the breakaway talks? It looked like it to Ferguson whose plea for an extension to the season, not just for his club but for others with similar fixture problems, fell on deaf ears.

New players had been added to the squad at the start of the 1991–92 season. England full-back Paul Parker was signed from

Queen's Park Rangers for £1.7 million and Ukrainian forward Andrei Kanchelskis became a regular after being introduced towards the end of the previous campaign.

The final season of First Division football began with Kanchelskis partnered by young discovery Ryan Giggs, who had been unveiled in the derby win over Manchester City three months earlier. The two were devastatingly fast and it was hardly surprising United topped the table for most of the run-up to Christmas.

Another new player also made a major contribution to the success. At 6ft 4ins Peter Schmeichel was one of the tallest goalkeepers to play for the club, and the first to hail from Denmark. From the start he was outstanding. Eight clean sheets marked his first ten appearances, one of those coming as the defence of the Cup-Winners' Cup began.

Even with the new faces there were problems in Europe and this time they were caused by red tape. The British clubs found themselves handicapped by the introduction of a new rule which stipulated the number of foreign players a team could field. Each side was allowed four. The ruling had serious implications within the British Isles.

Each home nation was regarded as a separate country. Simply being 'British' meant nothing. According to UEFA, players were either English, Scottish, Irish or Welsh. A team from England might be allowed three Scots and an Irishman or any other combination from the home nations but that would exhaust its foreign player quota. The side Ferguson was forced to select for the opening game against Greek club Athinaikos illustrated the handicap and was certainly not the team he would have named given freedom of choice.

English reserves Russell Beardsmore and Mark Robins were in the starting line-up; Welshmen Giggs and Clayton Blackmore, Irish defender Mal Donaghy and Kanchelskis were all sidelined. Even the manager's own son Darren, a useful mid-fielder, was unable to play because like his father he was a Scot and under the rules that meant he was foreign. Schmeichel, Irwin, Hughes and McClair made up the non-English contingent of the team, which drew 0–0 in the first leg in Athens.

What of the other Englishmen? Bryan Robson missed the game because of suspension and Parker was injured, but Neil Webb found himself back in favour and Danny Wallace was used as one of the substitutes.

In the return leg Kanchelskis played, but because of his inclusion manager Ferguson had to leave out Denis Irwin. Under such farcical conditions it was no surprise United were knocked out in the second round.

They only just managed to get past the first obstacle, a side they could easily have beaten had they been allowed to play at full strength. The home leg against the Greeks actually went into extra time before goals from the Foreign Legion of Hughes and McClair clinched victory. In round two against a powerful Atletico Madrid side, they stood no chance. The UEFA ruling coupled with the skill of the Spaniards took its roll. Atletico romped home 3–0 in the opening game in Spain and United knew they were up against it in the second leg.

The ruling had far-reaching repercussions. Since professional football began, players from other parts of the British Isles had earned a living playing in England. Would that now end? Would clubs be reluctant to take on juniors from Scotland, Wales and Ireland?

According to Alex Ferguson they would, and he instructed his scouts to concentrate on finding a higher percentage of English players. The ruling was also seen as internal politics with pressure being put on the British from beyond their shores. For many years FIFA and UEFA had regarded the British nations as a problem. England, Scotland, Ireland and Wales each had individual football associations. So despite being seen within Europe as one country, Great Britain, they had four voices at international level.

What the World and European football authorities wanted was for the British domestic bodies to disband to form one nation within the game. This would mean one British team would be able to play in the European Championship and World Cup rather than any or all four of them. The four British nations each had a vote and used it to stand firm.

Counter objections were raised about Spain, which was allowed to field teams made up of Catalans, Basques and Andalusians. UEFA's response was simple. The players were all Spanish. Each player carried a Spanish passport and played international football under the Spanish Football Association. The English, Scots, Welsh and Irish players may have held British passports but played for different international associations. Touché!

United disappointingly bowed out of the Cup-Winners' Cup after drawing the second leg with Atletico. This time Schmeichel was dropped under the foreigner rule, and Gary Walsh took over in goal. Kanchelskis also watched reluctantly from the grandstand.

Ferguson's side did, however, manage to win another European trophy in 1991. The European Super Cup was introduced in 1972 and played for annually by the winners of the Champions Cup and the Cup-Winners' Cup. Nineteen years on it had admittedly lost a little of its gloss but this time it had nothing to do with UEFA's restrictive new rules.

Red Star Belgrade had won the European Cup by beating Olympique Marseille, the final being decided by a penalty shoot-out, but the outbreak of civil war in Yugoslavia ripped the country apart and it seemed the authorities would have no alternative but to abandon the Super Cup. It was certainly impossible to stage the game on a two-legged basis with Belgrade on the edge of a war zone, so UEFA decided on a one-off match to be played at Old Trafford.

On 19 November 1991, Manchester United beat Red Star 1–0 to win their third European trophy. What should have been a memorable occasion – it was United's one hundredth competitive European game – was very much a non-event. Brian McClair scored the goal but only 22,110 supporters were at Old Trafford to see it. It was sad that the European dream should be reduced to this.

It is at this point that a Frenchman comes into the Manchester United story; only fate had prevented Eric Cantona from featuring before.

Cantona had helped Montpellier to win the French Cup in 1990 but had left the club before they faced United in the quarter-final of the Cup-Winners' Cup the following year. He joined Olympique Marseille and was in the side that clinched the French championship and with it qualification for the Champions Cup. He did not play in the 1991 European Cup final and later moved on to Nîmes. By the time United played Red Star he had decided on life in England. A month after the Super Cup, Cantona joined Sheffield Wednesday for a trial period. His travels were bringing him closer to Manchester but he had not crossed paths with United up to that point.

While he was at Hillsborough, United played Leeds three times with each game staged at Elland Road. They drew 1–1 in the League, then knocked the champions elect out of both Cup competitions, winning 3–1 in the fifth round of the League Cup, and 1–0 in the FA Cup third round. A fortnight after the second Cup game, Cantona turned his back on Wednesday, joined Leeds and played an influential role in their championship success.

Also in that side was Gordon Strachan who two seasons earlier had left Old Trafford. At the time of his transfer, Strachan had said he felt he needed a new challenge and he certainly responded to it, helping Leeds to win promotion from the Second Division before sweeping to the top of the old First Division in grand style. There was delight for Strachan, but despair for the man who had transferred him twice, Alex Ferguson!

It had been a quarter of a century since Manchester United last won the league championship and with it the right to enter the European Cup. The pain of letting the title slip away was only too obvious. It hurt everyone at Old Trafford from the humblest supporter up to Ferguson himself. Before the abortive run-in to the championship, United had won a trophy, the League Cup, picking up the award for the first time in the club's history. While providing little consolation for losing out on the major prize, it at least guaranteed European football during the first season of the new Premier League.

So came the 1992–93 season and English football took its giant stride. The cynics still predicted failure. They believed the Premier League would die an early death, and those involved would perish with it. Despite the warning cries, nineteen of the twenty-two clubs who had tendered their resignation a year earlier plus the three promoted from the Second Division – under the agreement reached between the two governing bodies – became founder members of the FA Premier League.

The Football Association had offered to combine forces with the Football League to run the new set-up but the invitation was declined. The League feared a loss of power but to neutral observers it seemed this had already gone. With most of the country's big clubs now in the Premier League, there was little concern for the thoughts of those left behind.

Graham Kelly, who had been secretary of the League for many years, had changed camps and was established in his new post as Chief Executive of the FA. Rick Parry held a similar post with the Premier League and these would be the men to guide English football forward, ignoring those whose empty threats of failure and its consequences continued to make headline news.

At one point it seemed the Premier League was going to make that complete breakaway they had threatened, drawing a line across football, the clubs in the top section staying there with no relegation or promotion at the end of a season. Eventually it was agreed that there would be a link between the two organis- ations, three sides stepping up from the Football League and three going down. The financial implications of relegation and promotion were obvious for all to see with vast wealth from television revenue for those in the top flight.

The original members of the Premier League included giants such as Arsenal, Liverpool, Aston Villa and, of course, Man- chester United but there were lesser mortals, too – Oldham Athletic, Wimbledon and Blackburn Rovers, a club beginning to emerge from the shadows after years in the lower sections.

United's start in the Premier League was far from impressive. They lost their opening game to Sheffield United at Bramall Lane, 2–1. If that was bad there was worse to follow with a 3–0 defeat against Everton in the first home game of the season followed by a draw with Ipswich at Old Trafford. This was hardly the stuff of potential champions and there were rumblings that the title could be forgotten once again – not from Alex Ferguson, though. He had made just one major signing during that summer, adding the powerful striker Dion Dublin to his squad.

Dublin had not been the main target. The manager had tried to sign Alan Shearer from Southampton but instead he opted for Blackburn, where steel magnate Jack Walker was making his intentions clear. Multi-millionaire Walker hoped to build a club in keeping with the new high profile of the Premier League. Rich beyond question and a passionate Blackburn supporter, Walker spent heavily on players, ready to outbid any offer to secure Shearer, especially one from Manchester United.

Dublin was introduced slowly. He was used as a substitute for the first three games then made his first start at Southampton where he scored. But like Neil Webb and others before him, he was struck down by injury before his United career really took off. In the home clash with Crystal Palace, which followed wins over Southampton and Nottingham Forest, he broke a leg and did not start another game all season.

It was a major blow. Mark Robins, the young hero of the FA Cup run in 1990, had been allowed to leave the club and was sold to Norwich for £800,000. He and Shearer began to haunt United. With twelve games gone, Shearer had scored twelve times and Robins six. The player who turned down United and the player the club turned away had between them scored more goals than the sixteen outfield players Ferguson had used.

Again there was disappointment in Europe, coming this time in a penalty shoot-out in Russia. United were paired with Torpedo Moscow in the first round of the UEFA Cup, and although their stay in the competition was brief there is some significance to the games against the Russians.

In the opening leg when Schmeichel was once again dropped because of his nationality, the five substitutes included players who would play a leading role in the club's future success. Seventeen-year-old Gary Neville, a central defender in the youth team, found himself taking the field for the last three minutes to replace full-back Lee Martin. Neville left his teenaged friends David Beckham and Nicky Butt on the bench as he stepped into the action.

Some of the disappointing crowd of 19,998 – with Old Trafford's capacity restricted by building work – never even saw the youngster's debut as they made an early exit after watching eighty-seven minutes of a frustrating game.

The other substitutes were goalkeeper Kevin Pilkington and Russell Beardsmore, the only one of the quintet with any first-team experience albeit limited.

Ferguson used Denis Irwin as one of his non-English contingent. He partnered Martin at full-back; Bruce and Pallister were the two central defenders. Andrei Kanchelskis was given the rare opportunity to play a European game but only at the expense of Giggs. Hughes and McClair took up the remaining foreign places.

Kanchelskis was left out for the return leg as Schmeichel returned to chalk up his seventh clean sheet of the season, even though he was on the losing side.

The second leg on 29 September 1992, will probably be remembered for two things – the penalty shoot-out which cost United their place in the second round, and the sending off of Mark Hughes. There was something else anyone who made the long trip to Moscow will also recall and that was the weather. It might have been September, but any signs of a late summer failed to materialise as incessant rain fell on the Russian city.

It poured all morning, it poured all afternoon and it was still pouring as United made their way back to the airport after a dismal end to their European hopes. A single goal might have put them through and they went close more than once, but at the end of ninety minutes it was still 0–0. In extra time, Hughes's frustration showed and he picked up a second booking from Danish referee Jan Damgard and trudged from the field. Three Russians were also booked along with Steve Bruce and Brian McClair, who collected his only yellow card of the entire season.

When the final whistle came, McClair knew he would be called upon to take one of the penalties in the decisive shoot-out. He had been the regular penalty taker following his move from

Celtic, but had stepped down following a much publicised miss at Highbury. Steve Bruce replaced him and during the 1990–91 season converted no fewer than eleven spot kicks out of the impressive tally of nineteen goals he scored in all competitions.

Bruce also showed the way in Russia and hopes were raised as United took a 2–1 lead. But McClair and Pallister failed to score from their spot kicks and United bowed out, the manager more convinced than ever that he had to improve the side's goal power.

With fifteen league fixtures completed United were tenth in the table. Arsenal, Blackburn Rovers and Aston Villa were setting the pace. Not surprisingly, Alex Ferguson was on the hunt for a striker.

Sheffield Wednesday's David Hirst was targeted but there was a major row when the news of United's interest leaked out. Wednesday put a block on any move by the striker and it was back to the drawing board for the manager.

United were due to play Arsenal on Saturday, 28 November. Forty-eight hours before the game, Ferguson pulled off what will probably be the transfer coup of his career. It is fair to say that if he continued as manager of Manchester United for another fifty years, it is doubtful he would land as significant a catch as Eric Cantona.

The Frenchman had expressed a wish to leave Leeds and Ferguson found out by chance when the Yorkshire club made a tentative inquiry about Denis Irwin. They were told Irwin was not for sale but the conversation got round to Cantona and Leeds hinted the Frenchman was available. Ferguson quickly agreed a £1.2 million move and so came the turning point.

Just a few days after Neil Webb was re-sold to Nottingham Forest, the tall, dark Cantona arrived at Old Trafford. Quiet, and apparently shy of publicity, he responded to a friendly 'bienvenue', stating in what became recognised as true Cantona style, 'I am very happy to be here. If I was not happy, I would not be here. Now together we must win at Manchester United.' French logic and the promise of Eric Cantona.

Alex Ferguson revealed to a hastily arranged press conference why the deal had been tied up in record time:

> We didn't allow any leaks to come out because you know what this club can be like, there's no secrets in this place at all. The clubs agreed on Wednesday night and the next thing was for Eric to come across and sign.
>
> I'm delighted. I see Eric as a Manchester United player, the kind of player that we want at this club. He's got style, he's got class and his goalscoring was instrumental in the success of Leeds last year. That's why I'm happy to bring another striker to the club, one who has a good reputation and won't in any way be overawed by playing here.

If Cantona was the man for Manchester United, he had the perfect setting in which to demonstrate it when he made his debut, coming on as a substitute during the derby game against Manchester City at Old Trafford. It was nine days after his move from Leeds and he played the whole of the second half as a replacement for Giggs. His vision and touch were obvious to all who watched the 2–1 win.

It was not his first appearance at the United ground. He had played there for Leeds two months earlier and tasted the atmosphere as his former club lost 2–0. That day perhaps he saw what United might have to offer, which may have influenced his decision to move across the Pennines when the chance came.

After City, United beat leaders Norwich with Cantona impressive throughout his first ninety minutes for the club. The gap at the top was cut to six points.

Cantona became the new hero. Fans flocked to buy T shirts

bearing his picture. A chant of 'Ooh-Aah Cantona!' was the theme of the masses and his first goal in front of his home fans was heralded with deafening cheers. It came as Coventry were beaten 5–0, the goal famine that had worried Ferguson was finally over.

They moved into second place and, after beating Tottenham 4–1 – Cantona getting his fourth goal in as many games – tasted life at the top of the Premier League for the first time. It was 9 January 1993 and with nineteen games remaining, the championship became a possibility.

Aston Villa, managed by Ron Atkinson, were United's main rivals. They had to come to Old Trafford on Sunday, 14 March for a game that satellite television – fast winning over an audience – promoted as 'the championship decider'. If that was the case, it would be a race to the final day. The game ended 1–1, Mark Hughes scoring an equaliser after Steve Staunton put Villa in front.

Cantona had scored six goals up to this point but his presence in the side was of even greater importance. With him laying off precise passes, Kanchelskis and Giggs were able to use their speed to run opponents dizzy. Ince became more dominant in midfield and confidence oozed through the whole side.

With six matches remaining, Sheffield Wednesday, the club rejected by Cantona because manager Trevor Francis wanted him to extend his trial period, stood between United and a clear lead at the top. They shocked Old Trafford by taking a one-goal lead after replacement referee John Hilditch awarded them a penalty.

The game is remembered for what happened in the dying minutes – Hilditch allowed for changeover time between him and the original referee, Michael Peck, who had pulled a muscle, and Wednesday employed delaying tactics. With six minutes to go, skipper Steve Bruce scored the equaliser; possibly as long into stoppage time he got the winner, sending Ferguson and his assistant Brian Kidd dancing for joy.

The result was significant to United's success. Much was made of the stoppage time allowed by the stand-in referee but perhaps little would have been said had it been Wednesday who had scored the late goal.

United went on to the championship winning all their remaining games and completing an unbeaten run from March to May with seven successive victories. They became the first club to receive the new FA Premier League trophy but there was more to the success than that. It meant they had also qualified for the European Cup for the first time since the 1968–69 season.

As for Eric Cantona's contribution, it is impossible to say whether the title would have been won had he not been signed, but there are many reasons to believe that his influence turned the side from one which could take the honours, into one which seemed certain to do so.

He was a striking figure both on and off the field. Tall and straight backed like a Guards' officer he seemed to have an aloofness about him, but in fact he was exactly the opposite. He had time for the ordinary man and became immensely popular with any supporters who met him.

On the field he stroked the ball around like an artist painting a canvas – one of his hobbies. He mixed delicacy with power, a flick with the side of his boot would lob the ball over an advancing defender then in an instant he would fire home a shot of such ferocity it would seem to threaten a goalkeeper's life should he try to stop it.

Cantona's influence on the younger players also became apparent. He was held in awe by the juniors at the club yet he would train with them, teaching by example. Anyone watching a youth team game before and after the arrival of Cantona could see the change. The young players had talent, but Cantona helped to bring out vision and style. It is perhaps no coincidence that during his time at the club there should be a season when every team won its respective championship – four teams, four titles from juniors to first eleven. If it is coincidence, why, with Cantona in the side, did Olympique Marseille become champions in France? Why did Leeds win the First Division championship with him, yet nothing after he had left?

Alex Ferguson summed up the Frenchman by paying him the ultimate compliment.

'He was always the perfect professional,' he said. 'His influence on the team was marvellous. He came at the right time. He gave us vision we maybe lacked in terms of winning the championship. I think we possibly could have done it, but he just made the final piece that gave us the composure at important times. He was the scorer of important goals, so it just gelled together after that.'

Cantona created a bond between player and supporter. He went out of his way to satisfy the demands of fans hungry for autographs and snapshots of him. If a hundred asked for autographs, Cantona would sign for each of them. If they asked him to hold their children for a photograph, he obliged. If they waited in the rain at the training ground, he would never pass them by. He signed every autograph book, posed for every picture and shook every hand. He was the perfect ambassador for the game, but there was another side to the Frenchman.

He was a law unto himself. If he felt he was the victim of ungentlemanly behaviour, he would seek revenge. He would do this in the open, not behind the referee's back, and more often than not would land himself in hot water because of it. If Eric Cantona felt he had been fouled and the offender was escaping punishment, it was within his right to retaliate. Unfortunately, the authorities did not follow the same philosophy.

Eric Cantona

Cantona was a great believer in speaking his mind and this too led to problems. He did not suffer fools gladly and made this abundantly clear. He is reported to have vented his true feelings at the end of a French disciplinary hearing by walking up to each member of the committee and one by one calling them an idiot. No sitting on the fence for M. Cantona!

He was also a warm, friendly, family man, with a love of art and poetry and a great sense of humour.

Eric Cantona helped United bridge that twenty-six year gap by winning the championship and was as eager as anyone that they should succeed in Europe the following season.

The Champions Cup is the ultimate club prize but in 1992–93 UEFA made changes to the format of the competition which meant it would be a more arduous route for any clubs hoping to get to the final. Using a format which was a blend of the old and the new, the Champions League became a reality at the start of that season.

Eight clubs played in a preliminary round under the original home and away, winner-goes-through rules. The four winners joined clubs that had been nominated for the first round by their football associations, because of past performances. Again games were played under the original rules with sixteen getting through to the second round. The eight winners were split into two groups with each club playing the other three home and away under league conditions. The sides finishing at the top of each group met in the one-off final.

As 1992 First Division champions, Leeds were England's first representatives. They entered the competition in round one and stumbled into the second. They beat VfB Stuttgart but only after a struggle, losing the first leg 3–0 in Germany, then winning at home 4–1. Technically they should have gone out under the away goal ruling, but salvation came when it was discovered the Germans had fielded a fourth foreign player. UEFA declared the result null and void and ordered a play-off in Barcelona, which Leeds won 2–1.

In round two the Yorkshire club was drawn against Glasgow Rangers and were knocked out, losing both legs 2–1. This meant that Rangers became the first British club to play in the Champions League proper, and they just failed to make it to the final, finishing runners-up to the eventual European champions, Olympique Marseille, Cantona's former club.

Now it was Manchester United's turn to try their luck in the new-style competition.

20

A WHOLE NEW BALL GAME

IGNORING UEFA's restrictive rule on foreign players, Alex Ferguson added another non-English member to his squad before Manchester United began their first assault on the Champions League. Roy Keane, the Republic of Ireland midfield star, was signed from Nottingham Forest for £3.75 million. It signalled the beginning of a new era. It was obvious the manager was preparing to fill the void which would be left when Bryan Robson stepped down.

Robson had missed a considerable number of games during the championship campaign as he recovered from a hernia operation, and Ferguson felt the years were catching up on the veteran midfielder. His number seven shirt had been inherited by Eric Cantona, and the captain's armband passed to Steve Bruce, but Robson (now wearing the number twelve shirt) felt he still had a part to play. Both he and Bruce went to the rostrum to collect the Premier League trophy after Old Trafford's closing game of the 1992–93 season, and when the new campaign began, Robson was in the side. He even scored in a 2–0 win at Norwich, but this turned out to be his last league goal for the club.

Before a ball was kicked, Robson revealed the target of the squad was to 'do the double', to win both the League and the

FA Cup in the same season, something no Manchester United side had done.

'You always need a target in life and even though winning the championship has taken a millstone from around our necks, the feeling among the players is that we all want to leave our own mark,' he said.

Alex Ferguson had a target too – success in Europe. He realised it would be difficult because the rules prevented him from playing his championship-winning side in the Champions Cup.

United set the early pace in the League – now dubbed the FA Carling Premiership, following a hyped-up re-launch by its lager-producing sponsors – and were leading the table when the first European game came up.

The competition had been extended with twenty clubs meeting in the preliminary round and the ten winners joining twenty-two others in the first-round draw. United were given a bye to the second phase, as were their first opponents, Hungarian side Kispest Honved.

Two goals from new boy Keane and a third from Eric Cantona gave United a 3–2 win in the first leg in Budapest; Steve Bruce headed home twice for a 2–1 win at Old Trafford in the return fixture.

There were sixteen clubs in the second round. AC Milan, Barcelona, FC Porto, Feyenoord and United were among the past European Cup winners to get through. Beaten 1993 finalists Milan were drawn to play FC Copenhagen, Barcelona met Austria Vienna, Porto and Feyenoord were paired together, and United were to play little-known side Galatasaray. The champions of Turkey stood between United and qualification for the Champions League. This would be the first time Manchester United had faced a side from Istanbul and while it would not be the last, the confrontation proved eventful, to say the least.

Firstly the Turks came to Old Trafford where United defended their unbeaten home record. It remained intact by the end of the game but only because of a goal from Cantona eight minutes from time. Before this, Galatasaray had stunned the 39,396 crowd by coming from 2–0 down to take a 3–2 lead.

Ferguson had selection problems before the game. Paul Parker went down with 'flu and with Roy Keane, Peter Schmeichel and Eric Cantona using up the three non-English places and Hughes and Giggs qualifying as assimilated players, Lee Sharpe was switched to left full-back.

'Assimilated' was the term given to players who would normally fall into the foreign classification but had come through a club's youth system and played all their football under that country's football association. By using assimilated players, a team's quota of non-domestic players could be increased to five.

Englishman Lee Martin was drafted in but Denis Irwin, Brian McClair and Andrei Kanchelskis were forced to stand down.

Robson reached another milestone in this game. His last European goal came in the third minute when he finished off a move involving Keane and Cantona.

Ten minutes later Ryan Giggs floated in a corner, Gary Pallister pressurised centre-forward Sukur Hakan and the Turk turned the ball into his own net. Then Arif Erdem ran through and hit a shot from twenty-five yards out. It was a speculative effort but the ball flew into the top corner beyond Schmeichel. Galatasaray were back in the game and it proved the turning point of the tie.

In the thirty-second minute the Turks equalised. This time, Lee Martin turned to pass back to Schmeichel but miskicked. The ball ran beyond the keeper who had come to the edge of his area. It was on its way into the net when Kubilay Turkyilmaz pounced and made sure. At least the Turk saved Martin's embarrassment as memories of a similar mix-up against Montpellier in 1991 came flooding back.

Galatasaray had the upper hand and in the sixty-third minute, Turkyilmaz scored his second. After leading 2–0, United were now 3–2 behind.

The game was then disrupted. Two Turkish supporters ran on to the pitch and the United players reacted thinking it was an attempt to waste time. Schmeichel took his own action and what ensued caused political uproar. Bryan Robson describes the incident:

> They were carrying what we thought was a burning torch, and play stopped. We could see the police getting ready to move in when big Peter came out of his goal and grabbed one of them. He didn't mess about. He wrestled him to the ground, picked him up and carried him to the side of the pitch and threw him into the advertising hoardings.

It turned out that the 'torch' was in fact a Turkish flag being burned in protest by two Kurdish students. They had come from London to use the televised game for a political demonstration, fully aware it was being seen throughout Europe. While their actions had nothing to do with football, Schmeichel found himself the target not only of criticism for the way he dealt with the intrusive 'fan', but for opposing the Kurds fight for human rights!

After the interruption play re-started and Cantona equalised as a cross came into the packed Turkish goalmouth at the Stretford End. He forced the ball home and the game ended 3–3, the Turks somehow surviving tremendous pressure from United.

So to Istanbul and a European encounter that will be remembered for many years to come by United players and supporters alike. It began sensationally. Hundreds of chanting

Turkish fans staged a riotous welcome for the United players when they arrived at Istanbul airport. Publicity about the Schmeichel incident, plus the Galatasaray supporters' fanaticism, ensured a big turn out. Many held banners proclaiming 'Welcome to The Hell', and declaring the English were 'Barbarians'. The players were forced to run the gauntlet of the mob but it was just a taste of what was to come when they arrived at 'The Hell' itself, Galatasaray's Ali Sami Yen stadium.

Ahead of the game there was a major problem involving United fans when police raided an hotel and rounded up all those staying there. Apparently the trouble began with an incident in a bar when some English fans cheered the foreign opposition when a Turkish side played in a televised game. The locals took exception and a group of youths followed the United supporters back to their hotel. Stones were thrown, windows broken and the police were called.

They turned on the English. Everyone was hauled out of the hotel, even elderly supporters who had been asleep in bed and unaware of the rumpus. Most of the party were held in jail overnight and sent back to England next morning with the word 'deportee' stamped across their passports. Others were detained and faced prison sentences until the British government intervened. An all-party group of MPs raised support, gathered information from all those who had stayed at the Tansa Hotel in Istanbul, and the charges were dropped.

However, once claims for compensation were lodged, the Turks again changed course. The trial was re-opened and in their absence, each English supporter was found guilty. Eventually, the Home Office arranged for new passports to be issued to each of the innocent 'deportees' who at least had this stain on their character erased.

The players learned of the trouble as they went down for breakfast on the morning of the game. They knew they were walking on thin ice as they stepped out at the Ali Sami Yen. Would they be kicked out of the competition even if they won? No one knew the full extent of the previous night's troubles. Problems in Istanbul were to haunt other English clubs visiting the Turkish capital, culminating in the murder of two Leeds United supporters in 2000.

The game itself turned out to be clouded by controversy. United started well but a goal from Lee Sharpe was disallowed. Television later proved it should have stood and had it done so there might have been a different outcome. Instead, the second leg finished 0–0 and United were out before reaching the new league stage, but the troubles were far from over.

At one point during the second half, the ball had bounced out of play and finished close to the Galatasaray bench. Eric Cantona went to retrieve it, but one of the Turks refused to hand it over. Cantona grabbed the ball with one hand and pushed the man away with the other. The Turk made the most of the situation, staggering back and falling to the ground as if injured. This angered the fans and some of the Turkish squad. When referee Kurt Rothlisberger blew for time, Cantona became a target.

Bryan Robson led the players into the centre circle to applaud the United fans who had made the trip out to Turkey:

We noticed during the game they had been unusually quiet. We thought it might have had something to do with the result, but discovered later they had been warned that chanting for the opposition might cause problems.

He continues his version of the events which followed:

I noticed that Eric Cantona had gone up to the referee and thought I saw him make a gesture with his finger and thumb as he spoke. I thought he formed a circle telling the ref he was getting 'Zero points'. He claimed Eric gave him a V sign and pulled out his red card. Then all hell broke out.

There were Turkish fans running on to the pitch so I got hold of Eric's arm and led him towards the dressing-room steps. A policeman came up and got on the other side. We thought he was there to help. When we got to the steps which went down to the changing areas there were about twenty or thirty policemen with riot shields gathered round the entrance.

Some faced inwards, others had their backs to us, watching the Turkish fans swarming on to the running track. I paused to let Eric go down the steps first and turned to thank the policeman for helping us when suddenly the Turk swung a punch. He hit Eric fully on the back of the head knocking him down the steps.

Eric grabbed at the handrail to regain his balance and prevent himself falling several feet, then turned to see what had happened. I swung round to grab the policeman but his mates waded in and I was hit with a shield. It gashed my hand and I was pushed backwards down the steps.

Other United players were also attacked according to Robson, and the team was forced to retreat to the dressing-room as the riot police swarmed into the corridors outside. Afterwards they revealed they wanted to arrest Cantona for assault! That never happened but Cantona still found himself in trouble with UEFA. It was not his dismissal that caused the problem but an off-the-cuff remark made later when things had quietened down.

In the first round of the competition, Dinamo Tiblisi had been disqualified for allegedly trying to bribe a referee. There were also allegations of similar happenings in France. With this in mind, Cantona is alleged to have said, when speaking to a

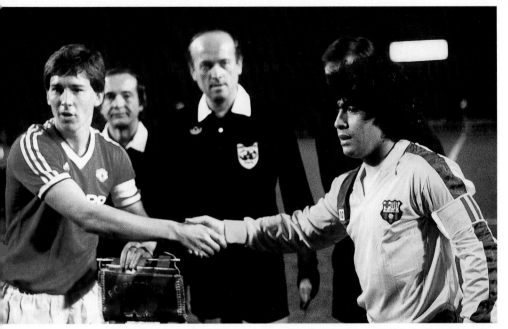

Bryan Robson shakes the 'Hand of God'! Two years before Diego Maradona's infamous goal against England in the World Cup, the United skipper welcomes Barcelona to Old Trafford ahead of the 1984 Cup-Winners' Cup clash. This was the night United pulled off a remarkable comeback, winning 3–0 to overturn a 2–0 deficit from the first leg.

Substitute Alan Davies scores the equaliser against Juventus in the 1984 Cup-Winners' Cup semi-final first leg. The goal was the highlight of the young Welshman's life which was to end tragically when he committed suicide in 1992.

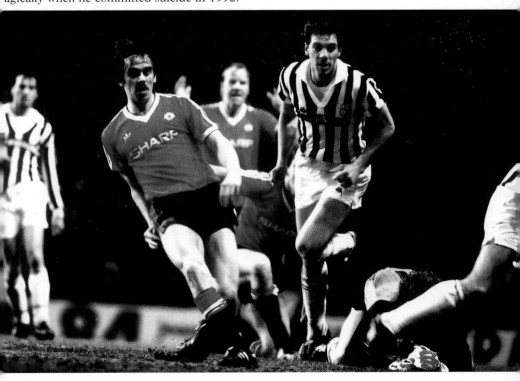

Lee Martin started it all when his goal won the 1990 FA Cup final replay to give Sir Alex Ferguson his first trophy as manager of Manchester United. The rest is history.

They took Manchester United to Europe's pinnacle. Sir Alex and Sir Matt pose with the Cup-Winners' Cup, the morning after the victory in Rotterdam.

They came, they saw, and they sang their hearts out as United conquered. Torrential rain throughout the 1991 Cup-Winners' Cup final failed to dampen the spirits of the hordes who followed the Reds to Rotterdam.

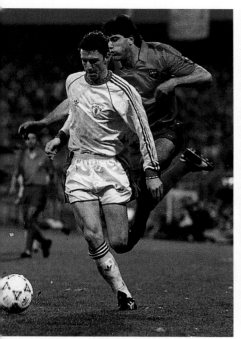

ee Sharpe's pace was a constant threat
to the Barcelona defence during the
1991 Cup-Winners' Cup final.

Another season, another trophy. Skipper Steve
Bruce parades the European Super Cup at
Old Trafford after victory over Red Star
Belgrade.

Mark Hughes follows up Steve Bruce's goal-bound header to force home United's opening
goal against former club Barcelona in Rotterdam.

Brian McClair scores a close-range equaliser against Legia Warsaw to put United on the road to their first Cup-Winners' Cup final.

Steve Bruce's second-half shot ties up a 3–1 win in Poland and United book their ticket for the final in Rotterdam.

ondon-based Kurdish students stage an anti-Turkish demonstration during the 1993 Champions League game with Galatasaray at Old Trafford. Goalkeeper Peter Schmeichel elped end the incident, during which a Turkish flag was set alight, by throwing one of the rotesters from the pitch. His actions were strongly criticised in Istanbul.

Welcome to The Hell'. Bryan Robson leads United out at Galatasaray's Ali Sami Yen Stadium n Istanbul. There were even more fireworks after the final whistle!

Peter Schmeichel saves from Fenerbahce striker Elvir Bolic during the Champions League game at Old Trafford in October 1996. It was Bolic's second-half goal that brought United's first home defeat in over forty years of European football.

Manchester United's greatest goalkeeper of all time. Statistics put Peter Schmeichel ahead of all Old Trafford predecessors, but Fabien Barthez may challenge for his crown.

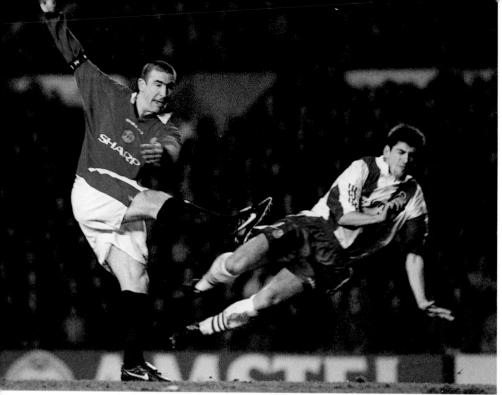

What a night! Eric Cantona slams home the second of United's four goals in the rout of FC Porto who started the game favourites to win the 1997 Champions League quarter-final.

What a night! They think it's all over . . . and it is. Andy Cole and David Beckham cannot hide their disappointment after the 1-0 defeat by Borussia Dortmund in the second leg of the 1997 Champions League semi-final at Old Trafford.

Paul Scholes, scorer of the second goal in the 3–2 win over Juventus in October 1997.

Ryan Giggs *en route* for the Juventus goal. At the time he rated his match winner against the Italians as 'the best I have ever scored'.

French journalist who he was friendly with, 'When you see a display of refereeing like that you can understand all this talk about bribery in the game.' The remark was off the record but a television sound crew picked up the conversation and it was broadcast throughout Europe. That was that.

The incident came to light the day after the game and eventually Cantona was suspended for four European games for making remarks about the referee. No action was taken with regard to the alleged after-match gesture to the official and as far as the treatment of the United players was concerned, this was ignored by UEFA. As Bryan Robson says, 'If that had happened to the Turks in Manchester, we would have been kicked out of Europe and banned for years!'

The disappointment of failing to reach the Champions League was forgotten as United led the Premiership into the New Year, but it was not a time for celebration at the club. On 20 January 1994, Sir Matt Busby died. He was eighty-four and had been in hospital for some time but his death came as a great shock for everyone connected with the club. Sir Matt achieved many things during his time as manager but winning the European Cup in 1968 will be remembered as the pinnacle. It was a fitting tribute to the great man that in the year of his death, Manchester United should complete the elusive Premiership and FA Cup double. It was almost a treble but they lost to Aston Villa in the League Cup final at Wembley.

The run-in was eventful – twice in three days Cantona was in trouble and sent off. The first was at Swindon, the second at Arsenal, and he was suspended for five games returning in time to help United win their second successive Premiership title. He scored his twenty-fourth and twenty-fifth goals of the season, each from the penalty spot, as Chelsea were beaten 4–0 in the FA Cup final.

As for Bryan Robson, it was a season tinged with success and sadness. He collected his second championship medal, but was left out of the Cup final side. Alex Ferguson felt he should turn to the players who would be with the club the following season, and Robson, who had enjoyed a successful career at Old Trafford, moved on to become player-manager of Middlesbrough.

As champions again, Europe beckoned once more in 1994–95, but this time UEFA made adjustments to the Champions League that were to United's advantage. It now truly was a league of champions. Under the new format, clubs entered four qualifying groups. The top two sides from each section went through to the two-legged quarter-finals, with the winners meeting in the semi-final. These later games were played under the old knock-out rules.

Clubs were graded using coefficients – points gained from previous successes in European competitions. A club that had rarely played in Europe, or got no further than the early stages of a competition, was given a lower coefficient than one that had succeeded. With 106 European games to their credit, the legacy of Sir Matt's days in charge, Manchester United were justifiably regarded as one of the top clubs.

They were put into Group A along with Barcelona, the previous season's runners-up. The third and fourth teams for each section had to qualify in a preliminary round before entering the draw. Sweden's Gothenburg got through after beating Sparta Prague and became the third side in United's section, while the last place went to Galatasaray!

The new format meant United were guaranteed six European games, but four would be without the suspended Cantona. They knew it would not be easy.

Gothenburg came first on 14 September 1994, with United winning 4–2 at Old Trafford. Kanchelskis for once got a game after being the player seemingly worst hit by the foreigner ruling. He was left out more than any other because there was cover for his position, but he had the satisfaction of scoring against the Swedes in a game that was more evenly balanced than many predicted.

Ferguson drafted in more of his young players and with summer signing David May playing right full-back, Nicky Butt made his full debut in midfield. Butt's first taste of senior football had come the previous season in an exciting FA Cup semi-final against Oldham when he was used as a late substitute at Wembley.

As well as Butt there was David Beckham, a Londoner who had been on United's books since his school days. Beckham caught the club's eye when he won the Bobby Charlton Soccer School's top award, and with it a trip to Barcelona. He was on the bench together with Paul Scholes and Gary Neville, two local youngsters.

After the Swedes came the Turks but the trip to Istanbul was nothing like that controversial first visit. There was the same reception committee, but this time it was seen as high-spirited fans rather than life-threatening fanatics. The game produced a professional performance from United and the 0–0 scoreline was more to their advantage than Galatasaray's.

Two games played three points collected, United were in pole position following the shock defeat of Barcelona in Gothenburg. The Spaniards were next and before the game at Old Trafford, United chalked up two Premiership wins, but lost at Sheffield Wednesday where David Hirst scored the only goal. They slipped to fifth place in the League, but were through to the third round of the League Cup after beating Port Vale with a team comprising mostly the new young players.

The game against Barcelona was United's first encounter with the Spanish club since the 1991 Cup-Winners' Cup final, and the 40,000 crowd at Old Trafford was filled with optimism. United played with spirit and Mark Hughes scored against his former club, putting Ferguson's side in front in the nineteenth minute, but Barcelona's foreign stars shone brightly. Romario hit a low shot through Schmeichel's legs in the thirty-fourth minute and the Spaniards came at United sensing an opportunity to succeed away from home.

Using the skills of Stoichkov and Romario and looking solid in defence thanks to Nadal and Ronald Koeman, the score stayed 1–1 until half-time. Five minutes after the re-start, Jose Maria Bakero was left unmarked as Koeman crossed and his strike put Barcelona ahead. United were up against it and once again trailed in a European game at home.

The Spaniards flooded back in defence and slowed the game down using substitutions. Coach Johan Cruyff sent on his son Jordi in the sixty-sixth minute, and he impressed with a fine touch of speed, playing wide and switching to both flanks.

United fought for an equaliser but left it late, levelling through Lee Sharpe in the eightieth minute. He stepped over a Roy Keane cross and flicked the ball home, sending the crowd home happy and keeping the home record intact. It had been a close call and was a warning of what was to come.

Paul Ince assessed the performance saying, 'We started very well and for twenty-five minutes looked the better side. We could have gone two up in that period. Sparky scored a good header and we were on top of our game, but with them scoring close to half-time it knocked us back a bit.

'We were disappointed with their second goal because we were left with four against one at the back, but all credit to the lads, we worked hard and got ourselves back into it.

'It's going to be hard for us in Barcelona but there won't be any surprises. We feel that if we can get our wingers working in the Nou Camp, we are in with a chance.'

Brave words. As it turned out, the game at Nou Camp virtually ended United's hopes of reaching the closing stages of the competition. Injuries coupled with the foreign player ruling became a greater burden than manager Ferguson anticipated.

United found themselves facing one of the strongest sides in the world with reserve keeper Gary Walsh in goal, youngster Nicky Butt in midfield and a half-fit Ryan Giggs. The bench looked like a line-up from the youth team with David Beckham, Gary Neville, Kevin Pilkington, Simon Davies and Paul Scholes sitting there.

Scholes replaced Giggs in the seventy-eighth minute, stepping out for his first taste of European football. By that time, United trailed 3–0 and Barcelona added a fourth before the final whistle. It was a comprehensive defeat. The home side showed its class and the up-and-coming Cruyff junior was outstanding.

'In games like that you have to hold your hand up and say that you were beaten by a better team,' said a despondent Steve Bruce afterwards. 'They were better than us in all quarters. In a big game like this, you have got to start well and I don't think we did and got a good beating for it. We know they are good but I don't think that we played the way we can play. It is going to be very difficult for us now.'

United were still in the Champions League, but only just. Barcelona had fought back after a disappointing start. They had been expected to walk into the quarter-finals. Gothenburg were the surprise package and led the group after four games. United had to beat them in Sweden to qualify.

A fortnight after the disappointment of Barcelona, the Nya Ullevi Stadium, scene of Alex Ferguson's Cup-Winners' Cup triumph with Aberdeen, staged the decisive fixture. Cantona returned from the shackles of suspension, but United's defence seemed to be wearing the ball and chain as Gothenburg took a crucial lead after just ten minutes. Left winger Jesper Blomqvist ran through to score and set the scene for a dramatic finale.

Mark Hughes equalised after sixty-three minutes, building

false hopes – a minute later Magnus Erlingmark scored with a close-range shot after another Blomqvist run.

The game ended in turmoil. The Swedes scored a third decisive goal from the penalty spot, Paul Ince was sent off for arguing with the referee and United lost 3–1.

They were out of the competition with still a game to play and a 4–0 victory over Galatasaray at Old Trafford was nothing more than consolation. In this match David Beckham scored his first senior goal for the club, after another young blood, Simon Davies, opened the scoring in the third minute. The others came from Roy Keane and an own goal from Korkmaz Bulent. The first true taste of the Champions League had been too much for United's digestion.

With Europe behind him, Alex Ferguson added to his strike force early in the New Year, setting a new transfer record in buying Andrew Cole from Newcastle United. The deal was estimated at £6.25 million, with Irish youngster Keith Gillespie moving to the north east as part of the agreement. Cole and Cantona were supposed to be Ferguson's dream duo but there was a long wait before he had the opportunity of playing them together regularly.

United ended the season runners-up in both major domestic competitions, beaten to the Premiership title by Blackburn on the final day, and losing 1–0 to Everton in the FA Cup final.

From United's point of view, the decisive day of the season came not at its closure but four months earlier during a game at Crystal Palace. It was Wednesday, 25 January 1995 when Eric Cantona was once again sent off. As referee Alan Wilkie held high the red card and Cantona turned to walk from the pitch, no one at Selhurst Park could have anticipated the drama about to unfold. As he left the pitch, the home supporters jeered and goaded him. One went a step too far in Cantona's eyes. Matthew Simmons had left his seat at the rear of the crowd and made his way to the front of the grandstand to hurl abuse from a gangway. He waved a clenched fist at Cantona who was a few yards away walking ahead of United kit-man Norman Davies who was accompanying him to the dressing-room.

Suddenly Cantona stopped, turned and made eye-to-eye contact with Simmons. He mouthed the response, 'What did you say?' and walked towards Simmons who was beyond his reach still shouting abuse from behind the perimeter fencing. Cantona stepped over a tarpaulin sheet used for covering the pitch which was rolled along the running track as the tirade continued. He leapt at Simmons kung-fu-style and kicked him in the chest. Punches were exchanged before they were separated. Other players piled in, Peter Schmeichel pulled his colleague away, leading him from the scene, and the police moved in.

The following morning the tabloids demanded Cantona's head. The world witnessed the incident time and again on television. Cantona's expulsion from English football seemed certain, even his deportation from England! The Football Association called a press conference and chief executive Graham Taylor announced:

Eric Cantona of Manchester United and France has been charged with misconduct that has brought the game into disrepute. What happened last night was a stain on our game. If any offence is proved, the player concerned is bound to face a severe punishment.

We are confident that Manchester United will meet their responsibility, not just to their own club, but to the widest interests of the game. The Football Association believes last night's incident was unprecedented. It brought shame on those involved, and worst of all, on the game itself. We especially deplore the appalling example set to young supporters who are the game's future.

The FA did not have the power to ban Cantona immediately but United did, and they suspended their star until the end of the season, fining him a maximum two weeks' wages. As for expulsion, chairman Martin Edwards wrote:

> I realised that something had to be done and the first thing the club had to decide was do we keep Eric or not?
>
> The board decided that anybody is worth a second chance, but in granting that second chance we had to decide the severity of the punishment. Manchester United is bigger than Eric Cantona, and the game of football is bigger than Manchester United. We felt we had to set an example and make the punishment fit the crime.

When Cantona attended the Football Association's hearing at Sopwell House Hotel, St Albans, United's end of season ban was extended until 30 September 1995, the disciplinary commission thus adding its own punishment to that imposed by the club. Martin Edwards was angry.

'People have different views on the case,' he said, 'and all I can say is that we felt we had punished Eric heavily. The FA felt they had to add to that ban and we are disappointed they felt that they needed to go further than we had already gone. What is on our minds is that if we had banned Eric for, say, ten games, then the FA may just have doubled that and he would have been available for the start of next season. It is going to make clubs think twice when they are punishing players.'

It is understood a deal had been struck with a representative of the Football Association that if United banned Cantona until the end of that season this would be seen as sufficient punishment. The commission had either been unaware of the arrangements or had reneged, and Manchester United were far from pleased.

The weeks that followed were some of the most dramatic

in the club's history. Cantona faced Croydon magistrates on Thursday, 23 March amid strong speculation that he might quit the country if the court handed him a severe sentence. After fifty minutes' deliberation, Mrs Jean Peach the senior magistrate announced:

> You have pleaded guilty to common assault and the facts that we have heard show that this is a serious offence. We have heard from your counsel that you deeply regret your actions. We have taken this into account together with your previous good character and your guilty plea. We do feel, however, that you are a high-profile public figure with undoubted gifts and as such, you are looked up to by many young people. For this reason the only sentence that is appropriate for this offence is two weeks' imprisonment forthwith.

Jail for Eric Cantona? United responded with an immediate appeal and a week later the punishment was reduced to one of community service. The judge who heard the appeal said that Simmons, who later appeared in the Croydon court for his part in the affray, had indulged in conduct which would 'provoke the most stoic'.

At the ensuing press conference, Eric Cantona stunned the media when summing up the situation. 'When the seagulls follow the trawler, it is because they think, perhaps, sardines will be thrown into the sea.' Many laughed but it was Cantona who was inwardly laughing loudest. The remarks were directed at those media seagulls who had followed him for weeks, hoping a mistake would offer them a sardine of a story.

Later club solicitor and director Maurice Watkins summed things up wryly when he said, 'Eric could have expressed his true feelings in two other words, but felt it would have been inappropriate!'

In a magazine interview, the French star later revealed the extent to which the incident and its repercussions had affected him:

The hardest thing was having to put up with the endless comments, the swift judgements, the resounding criticism. My family were quite shocked but they were also there. Every time I go through this kind of experience, I react in the same way. First I feel like going away, forgetting it all, escaping. Very quickly pride, and maybe even a deep sense of honour, urges me to take action. Then I can stand tall and face up to it. Then you have the kids to keep in mind, they are my strength.

His punishment was to complete 120 hours' community service and he was ordered to coach schoolchildren for the next month. Punishment? Cantona enjoyed it so much he continued beyond the period imposed by the courts. He left a lasting impression.

In December 1997, Salford Probation Service announced that because of the Cantona coaching sessions, juvenile crime in the area had dropped. The time the children spent with their hero had become a regular topic of conversation, even two years on, and many of the underprivileged youngsters who passed through the scheme continued their interest in sport.

Even so, during the spring of 1995 speculation continued that Cantona would be driven out of England by the media. United wanted to keep him and on Friday, 28 April 1995, a press conference announced that Cantona had agreed a new three-year deal.

'I am staying here because Manchester United is the biggest club in England, maybe in Europe, maybe in the world. I am very pleased to have the opportunity to win again many trophies with them. Everybody at this club deserves it and all the fans too,' the player said.

Alex Ferguson was relieved, even though aware of the problems there would be when Cantona eventually returned to football.

'We were never going to win no matter what we did,' he said. 'I think what we have done has pleased our own fans and pleased Manchester United, the players and everybody associated with the club. In doing that, we have taken a giant step towards winning things, by sealing Eric's future for the next three years. Watching the situation since January, how he had handled the whole thing, we know that he has always wanted to stay here. I think that was important for Eric as much as it was for us.'

It was obvious that the club remained angered by the FA's decision to increase the suspension when the manager added, 'I don't think there will be any player in the history of football who will get the sentence that he got. I think it is so severe.'

Cantona admitted his tolerance had been stretched to the limit and there were times when he felt he might leave.

'Yes, I thought about it. It was a difficult moment for me when I thought that, but it was a very short moment. Now I would like to spend the rest of my career here. The support of the manager and everybody who loves Manchester United was important. It is a compliment for me when people speak about me, even when it is hard. You fear me much more than I fear you,' he told the 'seagulls'.

Cantona ended the conference on a light note. Looking at his watch, he said, 'You will have to forgive me. I must go, we have got the training, and I need to be fit for my next game . . . in October!'

He made a smart exit, speaking only to Tom Tyrrell in a brief radio interview in which he explained his relationship with

Manchester United and the club's supporters. 'It's a love story,' he said. 'It's a love story. I cannot say more than that. It is very strong. That, and the level of the club. It is one of the biggest clubs in the world and I couldn't leave.'

The 1995–96 season was five weeks old when Eric Cantona stepped back into the spotlight. By then, Rotor Volgograd had ended United's hopes of a run in the UEFA Cup in the first round by scoring twice at Old Trafford following a goalless first leg in Russia. They went out under the away goals rule with the second leg ending in sensational style. Goalkeeper Peter Schmeichel ran the length of the field to head an equaliser in the 2–2 draw.

Schmeichel had decided it was all or nothing when United won a corner in the eighty-eighth minute. To cheers of expectancy, the Dane sprinted into the opposition penalty area. His presence created havoc in the Russian defence and his unexpected goal preserved the club's record. United had played their first-ever European game on 26 September 1956 and thirty-nine years later to the day, on the anniversary of that memorable 10–0 win over Anderlecht by the Busby Babes, they remained unbeaten in a home game.

United had played thirty-two games since the Selhurst Park incident and without Cantona success had slipped through their fingers. Stunned at losing the championship and by defeat in the FA Cup final, there had been more shocks for United supporters during the summer of 1995. Paul Ince was sold to Inter Milan, who also tried to persuade Cantona to move to Italy. Mark Hughes decided his days at Old Trafford were over and joined Chelsea, and as the new season began an unhappy Andrei Kanchelskis paid little regard to a new five-year contract signed months earlier and joined Everton.

The exodus caused a sensation. Some claimed that Alex Ferguson was putting a noose around his own neck. Hughes and

Ince left on the same day with chairman Martin Edwards stating, 'If we were to lift a trophy next year, people would say that it was not so bad after all. If, however, things turn sour, they will point to this particular issue as being the start of it.'

Was Edwards covering himself against possible failure when he added it was the manager who would 'stand or fall' by those transfer decisions?

The most successful manager in the country suddenly found his judgement being questioned. Comments from the tabloid press caused a few ripples but the actions of the local newspaper, the *Manchester Evening News*, created a tidal wave. Ferguson was deeply hurt when the newspaper asked its readers to phone in and vote on the question 'Should Fergie go?' It was totally unprecedented. The telephone poll severely damaged relationships between the manager and his local newspaper. Its outcome – that Ferguson should remain – was of little relevance; it was the decision to hold such a poll in the first place which caused ructions. It is something Alex Ferguson will never forget, or forgive.

United's supporters demonstrated their loyalty to the manager by chanting his name at pre-season games and his response to events was, 'I think we have listened to a lot of diatribe in the summer and I have absolutely no feeling of having let anyone down, and the supporters must know that about me. That is the last thing I would want.

'I have made one decision which I felt was in the interests of Manchester United and that is what I will always do. Alex Ferguson is not important, it is the supporters and the club that are important.'

That decision was to part with Ince; Hughes and Kanchelskis went of their own accord.

In an attempt to strengthen his squad and replace Kanchelskis, the manager made a bid for Tottenham and England winger Darren Anderton but was rejected. It meant that United would go into the campaign without any new faces in the side, without three key players and with Eric Cantona still weeks away from his comeback. In the season's opening game at Aston Villa, United were beaten 3–1 and the knives were out. 'Forget it!' said one tabloid. 'You will never win anything with kids,' television pundit Alan Hansen declared. Like the *Manchester Evening News* poll, those words would not be forgotten.

A new era was beginning. David Beckham, Nicky Butt, brothers Gary and Philip Neville, Paul Scholes, Simon Davies and John O'Kane were all included in the squad for the opening game. Beckham scored the consolation goal when the manager changed the pattern of play for the second half, and when victories over West Ham and Wimbledon at Old Trafford were followed by a creditable 2–1 win over champions Blackburn at Ewood Park, people began to have other ideas.

The kids went to Goodison Park and beat Everton 3–2 in a game in which Andrei Kanchelskis faced his former club for the first time. Then came a 3–0 win over Bolton and an away draw at Sheffield Wednesday before Cantona returned on 1 October, scoring a penalty in the 2–2 home draw against Liverpool.

Two days after his comeback, Cantona played in the second leg of a Coca-Cola Cup tie at York, which United won 3–1. They went out of the competition following a giant-killing 3–0 defeat at Old Trafford two weeks earlier.

As part of his build-up to full match fitness, Cantona played in a reserve game which attracted a crowd of 21,502 to Old Trafford, but he was injured and as a result missed the following Premiership fixture against Manchester City. He returned for the trip to Chelsea and the first real test of how he would be treated by hostile supporters. But it was more than that – Mark Hughes faced his former club and the referee was none other than Alan Wilkie, the official who had sent off Cantona at Selhurst Park. There were three bookings and Chelsea's Frank Sinclair was sent off two minutes from time. Hughes scored, but United won 4–1.

In the Premiership, the gap between United and leaders Newcastle widened as winter set in. Two points had separated the sides after a win over Bryan Robson's Middlesbrough at Old Trafford, but the difference grew to five following defeat at Arsenal.

December was a disaster. The squad was depleted by injuries and suspensions. Peter Schmeichel was out after having an operation on his elbow, and Gary Pallister was sidelined after injuring his back. Roy Keane had been sent off against Middlesbrough and had a hernia operation during his suspension. Nicky Butt accumulated twenty-one disciplinary points and was given a three-match ban, and to add to this Steve Bruce picked up a hamstring injury. It was no surprise form slumped. There seemed little hope of winning the championship and a place in the Champions League. Newcastle were in the driving seat, swept along by a run of victories which opened the gap to ten points.

Ferguson searched for a defender to bridge the gap left by Pallister's absence and turned to another Frenchman, William Prunier, a friend of Cantona's. Prunier watched from the wings as United beat Newcastle 2–0, reducing the gap between the clubs to seven points. It was the second game Keane had played following his operation and he gave a superb performance, scoring the second goal after Andy Cole had got the first against his former club.

Prunier made his debut against QPR and United won 2–1 with the trialist doing enough to be included in the side for the New Year's day game at Tottenham. That was the last we saw of Prunier who made a swift return to his homeland following a 4–1 defeat, which at the time was the heaviest United had endured since the Premiership was launched. The defeat might have been seen by many as the end, but it turned out to be the making of the season.

Inspired by a burst of goals from Cantona, United went on a run which started with a somewhat fortunate 2–2 home draw against Sunderland in the third round of the FA Cup. A draw with Aston Villa was followed by ten consecutive wins. United clawed back Newcastle's lead and at the same time reached the quarter-finals of the FA Cup.

Cantona was in explosive form, scoring the only goal at West Ham, two on his media-hyped return to Selhurst Park, and Cup goals against Reading in round four plus a penalty as Manchester City were beaten.

Still nine points adrift of Newcastle, the Tynesiders were favourites for the title but there were signs the pressure was getting to them and their form started to slip.

Cantona had chalked up ten goals since his return. Four had come from penalties and he had hauled himself to within one goal of leading scorer Paul Scholes. Perhaps the most important strike came at Newcastle. By 4 March, the gap at the top had been reduced to four points when the sides met at St James' Park.

After a first half in which United were forced to defend and Schmeichel was in superb form, their attack opened up. With fifty-one minutes gone, Andy Cole forced the ball out to Philip Neville on the left flank. The young full-back ran forward and crossed. Cantona met the ball on the right-hand edge of the penalty area. He took it in his stride and hit a low half-volley which bounced beyond the reach of Srnicek in the Newcastle goal. United won 1–0 and the gap at the top was down to one point.

United knew they could do it. The Premiership title was

within reach and the task which had seemed impossible at Christmas became a probability by Easter.

The goal at Newcastle sparked off another scoring run from King Cantona. He and Lee Sharpe scored in the 2–0 victory over Southampton in the FA Cup quarter-final and he followed this with one in each of the next three Premiership games – a 1–1 draw with QPR, and single goal wins over Arsenal and Tottenham.

In the semi-final of the FA Cup, United beat Chelsea 2–1 thanks to goals from Cole and Beckham, booking a Wembley final against Liverpool. The double-double of League and FA Cup for a second time – a feat that had not been achieved by any club during the twentieth century – was a possibility.

By Easter Monday, United had turned the ten-point Christmas deficit into a six-point lead over Newcastle, two more Cantona goals helping United earn maximum points.

The Frenchman was a changed character. When Steve Bruce was injured he was given the captaincy, leading his young comrades by example. His behaviour earned him praise from all quarters, including the Football Writers' Association. The week before United beat Nottingham Forest 5–0 in the closing home game of the season, Cantona was voted Footballer of the Year. It was another amazing turnaround. The seagulls honoured their trawler!

The following Sunday, 5 May 1996, United were away to Middlesbrough in the closing league game of the season while Newcastle were at home to Tottenham Hotspur. Earlier in the week, Newcastle had drawn at Nottingham Forest. Now the only way they could prevent United from winning the championship was by beating Tottenham, and Alex Ferguson's side losing to Bryan Robson's new club.

With Steve Bruce out of the side because of a hamstring injury and Cantona once again captain, United won 3–0. David

May began the victory with his only goal of the season, a far post header from a thirteenth minute corner; the others came from Andy Cole (fifty-four minutes) and Ryan Giggs (eighty minutes). United were champions once more.

It was a great achievement for a side that had been given little chance at the start of the season, and there was more success to come. The championship cheers had hardly died as preparations for the following Saturday's FA Cup final moved into full swing.

With the game just a few hours away, there was strong speculation that Alex Ferguson would not risk playing regular skipper Steve Bruce who was under treatment for the injury which kept him out at Middlesbrough. It was déjà vu for Ferguson. In 1994 he had left out Bryan Robson, and in 1990 dropped Jim Leighton for the replayed final against Crystal Palace. A manager's life is never an easy one.

The game itself was not the showpiece many hoped for, but with extra time four minutes away United made history, thanks to Eric Cantona. They won a corner on the right and as the cross came over, David James, the Liverpool keeper, misjudged his jump. He collided with one of his team-mates and could only palm the ball out of the penalty area. It ran to Cantona. Leaning back to get into the correct position, the Frenchman hit a powerful right-foot volley through the ruck of players. That was it, and the Cup was won.

The double-double was completed a week after United secured their passport into the Champions League and Cantona, who had remained silent since his return to football, finally pledged, 'We know that it is very important for us and everybody in England that we try to win the European Cup next season. We will try our best, and with the young players and the experienced players we have got, we have a very good chance.

'Winning the Cup is different from the championship. That is a long run so in the end it is normally the best one who wins. In the Cup, you have to perform on the day of the game, but we have proved that in the past three years we can handle that situation.

'What is important is the last game and the last victory. We have won today and we are the first team to win the double twice. Maybe today was more important than when we won the double two years ago, but it was also important two years ago.'

La philosphie de Cantona.

Steve Bruce

While the defeat in Barcelona was a great disappointment to us, I didn't read as much into it as some people did. There were claims that it showed the gap between English football and the game played on the Continent, but that was not my viewpoint.

You have to remember that a fortnight earlier, after the first game at Old Trafford, people were raving about our performance. When we went over to Barcelona, I think the answer was that on the night we just did not play to the best of our capabilities. It was as simple as that. We allowed them to dictate the game and when you do that to a side which had the quality of players they had, then you pay the penalty.

Their possession at times was fantastic and all credit to them. They played a patient ball game, a different type of game from our approach in those days, and for many of our players it was a vital part of the learning process that night.

We had never lost as heavily in Europe but when you get beaten like that you have to take a look at what happened, get a grip of yourself, and bounce back. I was sure we would, and we did. We beat Aston Villa at Villa Park, Manchester City 5–0 at Old Trafford then Crystal Palace. Altogether we scored ten times and conceded just one goal, not a bad reaction.

What we did learn at the Nou Camp was that in big games you must start right. You must set out your stall, and try to impose yourself on the opposition from the first minute. What happened that night was that we gave Barcelona too much possession of the ball, and that made it easier for them. When you do that with quality players they get confident and they punish you. We were punished for our mistakes, but at least in defeat some of the younger players added to their experience and all that has come in handy since then.

21

CLOSER EVER CLOSER

J EAN-MARC BOSMAN makes only a brief appearance in this European history of Manchester United, but his role is of major importance. Like the actor murdered in the opening scene of an Agatha Christie mystery, Bosman is essential to our plot.

He will not be remembered for his contribution as a player, but for his actions off the field. When standing up for his rights, he sent shock waves reverberating throughout the game. On 15 December 1995, Bosman won a ruling from the European Court of Justice.

His argument was that players should be allowed to become free agents once their contract with a club had terminated. He argued it was wrong that they should be the subject of transfer deals once a contract had ended, and objected to clubs holding on to a player's registration for this purpose. He also fought for footballers to have the same freedom of movement within the European Community as any other worker. If it was possible for German bricklayers to work in France, and English electricians in Spain, why should there be restrictions on footballers. Were those in the EEC Europeans or not?

The Bosman ruling forced UEFA to re-think its foreigner rule and in February 1996 it was scrapped. Clubs were told they could field as many players from within the European community as they wished and a wind of change blew throughout the game.

With England staging the European Championships that summer, it seemed perfect timing for many managers. Out came the chequebooks and in came the no-longer-foreign stars. Fabrizio Ravanelli from Juventus went to Middlesbrough, and his Italian international team-mates Gianluca Vialli, Gianfranco Zola and Roberto di Matteo joined Chelsea, who also signed French defender Frank Leboeuf from Racing Club Strasbourg.

Alex Ferguson bought a Dutch goalkeeper Raimond Van der Gouw, plus two Norwegians, Ronny Johnsen, a versatile all-rounder from Turkish club Besiktas, and the unknown Ole Gunnar Solskjaer from Molde. Solskjaer, a young striker, cost £1.5 million and was seen as an investment for the future. Jordi Cruyff was bought from Barcelona where his father had been replaced as coach, and Karel Poborsky who starred for the Czech Republic, runners-up in Euro '96, became the costliest newcomer. United paid Slavia Prague £3.5 million for his services. Poborsky was the only foreigner in the squad, his homeland being beyond the bounds of the EEC.

Ferguson also made a second move for Alan Shearer and was willing to pay up to £10 million for the England star. United's approach was rejected, even though Shearer, through his agent, had made it clear that he was interested in joining the champions. Blackburn refused to do business with United, yet opened talks with Newcastle and sold them the player for £15 million!

Martin Edwards reacted to the Blackburn dealings by saying, 'I was disappointed because we had set our stall out to buy Alan. I think circumstances went against us and feel with hindsight we were never going to get him. Blackburn were in the driving seat, he was their player, he had three years of his contract to go. They could dictate whether he came to United or not.

'I can also understand Newcastle stretching themselves. They have come a long way in a very short space of time. They just lost out to us last year and there must have been tremendous disappointment. I think their feeling was that if Manchester United got Shearer then everybody else could forget the championship for the next five years.'

There were also departures from Old Trafford that summer. Steve Bruce had been a regular in the side until his hamstring problems hampered his season. David May had been outstanding in his place, as had Eric Cantona as captain. Bruce was left out of the Cup final. He found it all too much to take and when the opportunity came, he joined Birmingham City.

Paul Parker was allowed to leave at the end of his contract under the Bosman ruling. He was a free agent because his agreement had terminated and there was no offer of an extension. Stand-in goalkeeper Tony Coton, signed from Manchester City as back-up for Schmeichel, moved to Sunderland for £400,000.

Perhaps the most surprising sale was that of Lee Sharpe who was transferred to Leeds United for £4.5 million. Because of the arrival of Cruyff and Poborsky together with the emergence of Giggs, Sharpe felt his chances of a regular first-team place had diminished and accepted the move to Elland Road.

The curtain-raiser to the new season sent an ominous shudder down the rest of the Premiership as United beat Newcastle – Shearer, David Ginola *et al* – 4–0 in the Charity Shield. Cantona, Butt, Keane and Beckham scored in the Wembley showpiece. By now the United youngsters were being recognised as the new stars of the game and a week later on the opening day of the 1996–97 season, Beckham scored a sensational goal. The midfielder shot from inside his own half sending the ball fifty-five yards before it passed over the head of Wimbledon keeper Neil Sullivan and into the net. The Dons were beaten 3–0 at Selhurst Park and it was abundantly clear that Manchester United would be the team to make the headlines once again.

Two games into the new season, the draw for the Champions League was made and United were placed in Group C along with Italian giants Juventus. They were joined by Austria's Rapid Vienna who had impressively beaten Dynamo Kiev 6–2 over the two legs of the preliminary round, and once again a Turkish club, Fenerbahce. Many saw it as a tough group but reigning champions Juventus and United were expected to qualify for the knock-out stage.

United's opening fixture, away to Juventus, was to be their toughest. Alex Ferguson's reaction to the draw was, 'It's going to be quite a challenge right away, but playing Inter Milan a couple of times during our pre-season build-up [as part of the deal that took Paul Ince to Italy] gives us an insight into the type of game we will get.

'Overall, I am satisfied. They look difficult games, but they all are in this competition so I am looking forward to it.'

As for the return to Turkey he added, 'That's an interesting one, but the experience we have had on the last two occasions will serve us well. I don't think there will be any problems for us, the second time we went to Turkey it was fine; there were no problems at all.

'Rapid Vienna knocked out Dynamo Kiev to qualify and did well in Europe last year so they are obviously a very competent side. It is an interesting and exciting group.'

Could United get beyond that stage of the competition and into the quarter-finals? That was Ferguson's aim.

The opening game in the new Stadio del Alpi in Turin was a disappointment. They lost by a single goal scored in the thirty-fourth minute by Croatian striker Alen Boksic, but staged a tremendous fight-back and felt they deserved at least a draw.

Martin Edwards summed up, saying, 'I think we matched

them in the second half but it is a six-game league and we have got to make sure that over those games we do enough to get in the top two places. The other sides in our group have drawn, so that doesn't make this result look too bad. This was always going to be the hardest game of the six.'

Unbeaten in the Premiership after seven games, they were in fourth place after drawing four times. Norwegian signing Solskjaer had become the surprise newcomer. He was drafted into the side as a substitute against Blackburn and scored the equaliser in a 2–2 draw after just eight minutes on the field. In his first start, against Nottingham Forest, he scored again and his third goal for the club came in Europe.

With the return game against Juventus two months away, United faced Rapid Vienna at Old Trafford on 25 September 1996. In the twentieth minute, Solskjaer ran on to a Keane cross and coolly struck the ball home. Seven minutes later Beckham added a second and United moved into second place in the group thanks to the 2–0 win. Juventus were top after beating Fenerbahce in Istanbul, the venue of United's next game.

Domestically, things improved. A 2–0 win over Tottenham, in which Solskjaer scored both goals and completed his first full ninety minutes, was followed by a 1–0 win over Liverpool at Old Trafford. The victory was the perfect send-off for the trip to Turkey, but Eric Cantona was far from pleased with his own performance.

Perhaps giving the first clue about events to follow, Cantona said, 'I forgot that I could play so bad. I am very unhappy because I am very disappointed about my performance. If people say I played badly, it is true. I realise that myself and I can tell you I am not happy. I am very disappointed.'

Cantona was no doubt happier four days later when in the intimidating surroundings of Fenerbahce's stadium he scored United's second in a comfortable 2–0 win over the Turks. Again a visit to Istanbul provided those present with unforgettable moments. As the United players took the field to warm up before the kick-off, the crowd held flaming torches aloft. The floodlights went out, either by choice or through electrical failure, and the blazing background from the terracing provided the only source of illumination for a few minutes. When play started, a screaming cheerleader howled encouragement to the home side over the public address system until a UEFA official was called on to end his antics.

United ignored the distractions. David Beckham scored the first goal and his third in Europe.

'Olly [Solskjaer] got the ball just inside our half and I started to run to the left, but I couldn't see a way through so I cut over to the right and he played it in to me. I thought the defender was going to come through me at one point so I just tried to hit it and I scuffed it in,' said the rising star after the game. They all count.

Schmeichel enjoyed the pre-match floodlight incident. 'I thought it was very cosy,' he said afterwards. 'I could do all my stretching and watch the scene, it was beautiful! I loved every minute of it. As for the loudspeaker encouraging the fans, you know that they are going to try that sort of thing but if you pay too much attention, you can lose concentration and perhaps lose the game. You have to ignore it, and we did.'

Rapid and Juventus drew in Vienna and Schmeichel added, 'We know how important this win was. We have got six points now and nine can take us through. We have got three games to get another three points. The most important thing is getting through to the next stage.'

United may have been on a high after the win in Turkey but they were brought back to earth quickly when they returned to Premiership action. Four days after Fenerbahce, Newcastle took revenge for that Charity Shield defeat and the disappointment of the previous season by winning 5–0 at St James' Park. Six days later Southampton won 6–3 at the Dell. Two games and an 11–3 deficit – if that was bad, there was even worse to come.

On Wednesday, 30 October 1996, forty years and forty-eight days after the first-ever European Cup game played in Manchester, United lost their home record. After fifty-seven European home games, the club finally tasted defeat.

It came not at the hands of one of Europe's giants, but Fenerbahce. The Turks won thanks to a lone goal and somehow survived a bombardment from United both before and after taking a surprise lead.

The decisive goal came in the seventy-seventh minute as the Turks broke away and found themselves with four attackers against United's three-man defence. Elvir Bolic chipped the ball over the advancing Schmeichel, silencing a packed Old Trafford, and hundreds of travelling Turks celebrated.

Elvir Bolic may have earned his place in Manchester United history but it was a bitter pill for Sir Bobby Charlton to swallow.

'I suppose the record had to go some time and I could perhaps accept it more easily if we had lost it to a club like Real Madrid, Barcelona, Juventus or AC Milan,' he said. 'I don't mean to be disrespectful to Fenerbahce, but it is a pity that it had to go in the way it did.'

The run of defeats continued. In the next Premiership game, Chelsea became the first side to take maximum points at Old Trafford that season, and it was not the way Alex Ferguson would have planned to mark the tenth anniversary of his appointment as United's manager. He refused to let the slump dampen his spirits.

'It's a tremendous achievement, ten years as manager of Manchester United. It has been a fantastic experience and hopefully this is the start of another good decade. When I came I never thought that I would still be here ten years on. You never think that way. It's a long time. I was eight and a half years at Aberdeen so eighteen and a half years with two clubs is quite extraordinary. Now I'm looking forward to the next ten.'

The poor form was temporary but there was another European home defeat before the Champions League games were completed. Juventus came to Old Trafford on 20 November and won 1–0 thanks to a Del Piero penalty. Once again United felt they had done enough to earn a draw against the Italians and the result left Ferguson saying, 'It was a great game of football and I think they proved why they won the European Cup last season and why they are the best. They are a very good side. They have good experience in the right places, good composure and are always a threat.

'We felt there were areas where they were not defending well and tried to exploit them in the second half. We stretched them and it became a really fantastic game of football. I thought it was a sporting game, both sets of players were honest, and it was an entertaining match for everyone.'

Once more United's fate in the Champions League hung in the balance. Fenerbahce had beaten Rapid Vienna on the night of the Juventus upset, and had seven points from their five games. United had six. The Turks' final group game was in Turin while United travelled to Vienna. Juventus had already qualified for the quarter-finals and rumours spread that the Italians might not put maximum effort into their game knowing they could get rid of a future threat from United should they clash again in the competition. The English side had proved tougher than any other but Ferguson dismissed the speculation.

'Juventus are a team of habit and have a great work ethic. I cannot see them going into a game not wanting to win and I think we can be safe in the knowledge that they will be doing their best,' he said.

He was right. On 4 December 1996, United took another

giant stride forward, becoming the first British side to reach the quarter-finals of the new-style European competition. Juventus beat the Turks 2–0 in Italy and Rapid Vienna were overrun on their own ground by a spirited Manchester United led by Eric Cantona. Giggs and Cantona got the goals midway through each half and the Austrians were outclassed in the 2–0 win. United finished runners-up to Juventus and were to face FC Porto, winners of Group D in the two-legged quarter-final.

That stage of the Champions Cup was three months away and Ferguson planned to use the winter break to clear the club's injury problems and turn his attention to the push for the Premiership. He had outlined his plans at the start of the season. His aim was to be in touch with the league leaders when European football reached its interval period and United lay sixth in the table. Now it was time to begin the assault.

'December has always proved a very important month. Last year our December form caused us a real headache. It put us so many points behind Newcastle but fortunately we made it up. We can't take that for granted and a good December would help,' he said as the run-in to Christmas began.

United then beat Sunderland 5–0 at Old Trafford, Nottingham Forest 4–0 away from home and completed their three holiday games by beating Leeds 1–0 in front of 55,256 supporters. By New Year they were second to Liverpool with Arsenal behind them.

The set-backs continued. No sooner had Andy Cole returned after fracturing both legs during a reserve game at Liverpool, than Philip Neville was struck down with glandular fever. Ferguson was forced to use twenty-seven players in the first five months of the 1996–97 season with senior debuts for teenaged full-back Michael Clegg and midfielder Michael Appleton.

He tried to strengthen his squad but his efforts to land Blackburn's Henning Berg met the same reaction as the earlier bid for Shearer. With David May out of action following his second hernia operation in a year, Ferguson spent two weekends in Spain watching Real Betis star Roberto Rios, but the cheque-book remained firmly closed when the Spaniards asked for a fee of £6 million.

United also lost interest in the FA Cup a little earlier than usual. A home tie against Wimbledon seemed over when Paul Scholes scored in the eighty-ninth minute but Robbie Earle equalised and two weeks later the Dons won the replay 1–0. Between the Cup games, United beat Wimbledon and Southampton in the Premiership to go top, where they remained for the rest of the season.

By the time the quarter-final date arrived, May was fit again, Cole was back in action and Philip Neville had recovered from his illness.

The Portuguese were hot favourites to go through to the semi-finals after overcoming the might of AC Milan in their group. Porto had won five of their six qualifying matches including the game at the San Siro, and were the only unbeaten side in the competition. Because of this, and the struggle to reach second place in their group, United went into the quarter-final as underdogs.

They were also handicapped when Roy Keane was injured and ruled out of the first game against Porto. Remarkably, the influential midfielder was not really missed and although he was a reluctant spectator he must have enjoyed seeing his colleagues in action on what proved another memorable night at the Theatre of Dreams.

With Schmeichel in goal, Gary Neville and Irwin were the full-backs on either side of May and Pallister. Beckham played on the right of midfield but with Nicky Butt injured, Ronny Johnsen was switched to midfield with Giggs on the left. Cole and Solskjaer led the attack with Cantona tucked behind, and the Portuguese did not know what had hit them. United went on all-out attack from the start and ripped Porto apart.

David May scored the first after twenty-two minutes. It was a brilliant opportunist goal. Pallister headed down a corner and the defender turned striker to force the ball home from close range.

Cantona made it 2–0 twelve minutes later, picking up a loose ball from a defender and shooting home from inside the penalty area. Giggs got a third with the game just over an hour old, forcing home a near-post shot after a move involving Cantona and Cole. Andy Cole got the fourth, Cantona taking the ball into the penalty area and picking him out with a pass. The underdogs had shown their teeth!

The tennis-style format of the Champions League made it possible for clubs to plot a course to the final. In the quarter-finals, the winner of group A met the runner-up from group B, with the first club in Group D facing the second side from Group C. The same pattern was followed in the bottom half, so it seemed that unless there was a disastrous second leg in Portugal, United would play Borussia Dortmund in the penulti-mate round. The Germans had beaten Auxerre 3–1 in Germany on the night of the Porto game, while the other games ended in stalemate. Ajax and Atletico Madrid drew 1–1 in Amsterdam, while dark horses Rosenborg of Norway were held to the same score by Juventus.

Meanwhile, with eight Premiership games remaining, United had a three-point lead at the top of the table despite losing at Sunderland, their first upset since Chelsea won at Old Trafford four months earlier.

So came the return leg against Porto and another European fixture remembered not for the football but for what happened to United's supporters before and after the game. Many were beaten by baton-wielding police and others injured when plastic bullets and tear gas canisters were fired at them as they tried to leave the stadium. According to Greater Manchester Police officers, the problems were caused by an overreaction from the local force and a misunderstanding between both factions. The inquiry into the crowd problems at Stadio Dad Antas reached the conclusion that over-zealous policing was to blame, coupled with a lack of organisation and understanding.

United fans had been herded into one area of the stadium even though their tickets were clearly for another and at kick-off, many were still outside the stadium. A small group of supporters anxious to get in had rushed at an entrance and the police held them back. Scuffles broke out and the innocent were caught in the fray as police used batons on those they thought had been to blame.

The Portuguese claimed fans with forged tickets were responsible for the fracas saying many United fans had arrived with non-valid tickets. The English response was that fans with tickets for Gate 3 were ushered to Gate 5, which was why the tickets were invalid, and it was when they got to that entrance the trouble began.

The scenes at the end of the game were the worst. A line of riot police faced the United followers. Announcements made within the stadium fell on deaf ears, either drowned out by celebratory chanting or misunderstood. As a result, instead of remaining inside the stadium for instructions to leave, fans tried to get out, only to find the exits blocked by police. With hundreds pushing from behind, those at the front took the brunt of the reprisals. Choking tear gas filled the air and plastic bullets were fired, injuring many fans. It was yet another example of the problems faced by English fans travelling abroad and dampened the enjoyment of a successful night for United.

Domestically, they increased their lead at the top of the Premiership to six points in the game that followed the trip to

Portugal, a 2–0 win at Everton. They were knocked back on their heels a week later when Derby County won 3–2 at Old Trafford.

An even greater disappointment was in store before the first leg of the semi-final against Borussia Dortmund. Peter Schmeichel injured his back in training and did not respond to treatment. Reserve keeper Raimond Van der Gouw was called in. His only previous appearances in the first team had been at Aston Villa in a goalless league match, and two Coca-Cola Cup ties.

Van der Gouw found himself keeping goal in the most important European game United had played in twenty-eight years as he faced the Germans in the Westfalenstadion. The Dutchman did well, holding out against a Dortmund side that included Scottish defender Paul Lambert, German star Andreas Möller, Paulo Sousa of Portugal and midfielder Stefan Reuter.

The game remained goalless until the seventy-sixth minute when the stand-in keeper was beaten by a shot from midfielder Rene Tretschok which took a wicked deflection *en route* for goal.

All was not lost, European hopes were still alive and at home the championship was virtually won when United followed up a 3–2 win at Blackburn by beating Liverpool 3–1 at Anfield.

In the Blackburn game Eric Cantona missed a penalty for only the second time since joining the club. The first miss came at Leeds earlier that season, but just as he had done at Elland Road, the Frenchman went on to score a crucial goal later in the game. At Leeds he got United's last in a 4–0 rout of their Yorkshire rivals while at Ewood Park he hit the ball home following Andy Cole's by-line run and cross. It was the Frenchman's eightieth goal for United. It was also his last.

At the time, there was no indication Cantona was planning to leave. He seemed to be enjoying his football surrounded by United's talented youngsters, Beckham, Butt, Scholes and the

Neville brothers, all of whom were about to establish themselves as regular members of the England squad.

Cantona's contribution to the club's success was beyond question. They were about to win their fourth Premiership title in five seasons and had progressed further in Europe's leading competition than any other squad for almost three decades. Despite this he had privately decided on a future away from the game.

When the first leg of the Champions League semi-final was played, Dortmund had been without their mainstay defender Matthias Sammer. He was banned, and United were similarly restricted for the return game when Roy Keane was ruled out. He had been booked during the game in Germany and, after picking up a first yellow card four months and four days earlier during the game in Vienna, he had to serve an automatic one-match suspension.

Schmeichel returned in goal but plans to pull back the Germans' lead as quickly as possible went sadly wrong. United were caught by a counterattack and Lars Ricken scored. Once again the ball was deflected past the keeper, this time striking Gary Neville and flying beyond Schmeichel's reach. United, fighting for their European future, kept Dortmund under sustained pressure for the rest of the game but somehow the Germans held out. As in the opening game, they won the second leg by a single goal. After playing for more than forty years without suffering a home defeat, United had lost three European games within the space of six months. Alex Ferguson and his players had moved closer to the dream but not quite close enough.

The season ended with United securing the Premiership title for a fourth time and ensuring a place in the Champions League for 1997–98.

Regardless of the set-back in Europe, Alex Ferguson was now on the verge of becoming United's most successful manager.

He was within one championship of the five achieved by Sir Matt Busby. He had won the European Cup-Winners' Cup, taken the FA Cup three times – one more than his legendary predecessor – and achieved two league and FA Cup doubles. He had won the League Cup and produced a side filled with young talent which was envied throughout Europe. Only one prize eluded him, the European Cup.

'I think it goes without saying that Europe is our aim. Our experience this year has been a good one and it was the type of experience that gives the players the confidence to know that they can do it,' were his words at the end of the 1996–97 campaign. 'I think it will be tough next year but it's always tough. People are saying that we are not good enough to win the Premiership again but that's a bit silly. In a League where there are going to be a lot of challengers, it is very difficult to imagine that we cannot be there.

'There is going to be a dog-eat-dog situation and we have proved with our experience and the ability of our players that we are equipped for that. We will be there or thereabouts.'

Anyone doubting the manager's view that United's supremacy would continue needed to look no further than Old Trafford on the closing day of the 1996–97 season. United were crowned champions not once but four times. As well as the Premiership, the reserve side won the Pontin's Premier League, and the A and B teams took the First and Second Divisions of the Lancashire League. It was a clean sweep of every competition the club entered, a marvellous achievement and surely an indication of more to come under Ferguson. There was also a major shock a week later.

On Sunday, 18 May, seven days after Eric Cantona had been handed the Premiership trophy, manager Ferguson and chairman Edwards faced the media at a hurriedly arranged Old Trafford press conference. The chairman broke the news:

'Manchester United today announced that Eric Cantona has advised the chairman and manager that it is his wish to retire from football with immediate effect. I am extremely sorry Eric has arrived at this decision, but understand and respect his reasons. Many of us believe Eric has been the catalyst for the most successful period in our history. It has truly been a magical time.'

Alex Ferguson looked sad as he added, 'Eric has had a huge impact on the development of our younger players. He has been a model professional in the way he conducted himself and a joy to manage. He is certainly one of the most gifted and dedicated players I have had the pleasure of working with. He leaves with our best wishes and will always be welcome at Old Trafford. He has given us so many wonderful memories.'

It was the end of another era at Old Trafford.

Eric Cantona

This is the brief statement issued by Eric Cantona on the day he announced his retirement from football:

I have played professional football for thirteen years, which is a long time. I now wish to do other things. I always planned to retire when I was at the top and at Manchester United I have reached the pinnacle of my career.

In the last four and a half years I have enjoyed my best football and had a wonderful time. I have had a marvellous relationship with the manager, coach, staff and players and not least the fans.

I wish Manchester United even more success in the future.

22

SO NEAR

I T ' S N O T E A S Y to conquer Europe, as the challenge in season 1997–98 bore out. Bad luck had been considered the main factor in United's failure to get past the semi-final stage the previous year, so hopes were high again. There was a mood in the camp suggesting that this time they were capable of going all the way to win the one trophy that would confirm Alex Ferguson's place in the history of Manchester United as a legend sitting comfortably on the right hand of Sir Matt Busby.

The fans were optimistic, too. Enthusiasts pointed out the omens involving the number eight along the European trail – a team destroyed in Europe in 1958, Busby's crowning glory winning the European Cup in 1968. Surely, they argued, the year 1998 would bring Ferguson's finest moment.

The early stages in the qualifying group looked more than promising, especially after they beat Juventus at Old Trafford in their first home fixture. The result seemed to confirm that United's young team were quick learners and had made tremendous progress following their naive displays against the Italian champions the previous season.

But in the quarter-finals it all came to nought, French with tears. A goalless draw in Monaco and then a 1–1 draw at Old Trafford sent the champions of France through to the semi-finals on the strength of scoring an away goal.

329

It was a devastating blow for supporters, players and manager, who confessed, 'Immediately after the match I felt wretched with a sadness shared just as keenly, I'm sure, by everyone associated with Manchester United. I have got to admit that it hit me hard. I don't ever remember being quite so down following a defeat. To a certain extent, as a manager you get used to set-backs and take them in your stride because by the very nature of football you are bound to get them. Nobody wins every match.

'But in this never-ending supply of disappointments, some are worse than others, and our European disaster with the semi-finals beckoning was a very deep one for me. I'm sure I haven't been on my own. I know that the hopes and expectations of our supporters were just as high as mine and that they, too, came back to earth with an almighty bump. Losing such an early goal in the first five minutes was a real killer. It left us chasing the game for another eighty-five minutes and it was too much for the players.

'I went through everything with them at half-time but the reality was that they just did not have the legs for it. The number of injuries we had bit deeper than merely putting a number of important players out of the team. They meant that others had to play who had been spending more time under treatment than training, and at European level in the circumstances of that particular game it eventually showed. Only one or two were able to live with it. Too many found it difficult to summon up the drive to force themselves over the line.

'It emphasised just how difficult it is to succeed in Europe. I felt we had a fantastic chance this season. Normally I am confi-dent of success if I can just get eleven of our players on the pitch, but the one key element which let us down was losing the early goal. It was a bad one to concede.'

Ferguson was undoubtedly lifted in the immediate aftermath

of defeat by the fact that his team were still involved in the Premiership title race. Their league form had slumped but after Monaco they still held a six-point lead at the top of the table, albeit with Arsenal in the driving seat with three games in hand on their northern rivals.

The United manager was soon back to his aggressive best rallying his troops and dismissing suggestions that the European disappointment would trigger his retirement or perhaps prompt a move to the board of directors. Ferguson wasted no time in putting the record straight as he announced his intention to stay at the helm of Manchester United and steer the club into the next century.

'I intend to stay as manager,' he declared. 'I say that because there has been another round of speculation about when I might retire, which frankly, bugs me. I am fed up with people trying to pigeonhole me for retirement. I'm fifty six, feel as fit as I ever did and have a lot more to achieve. I intend to work into my sixties because Manchester United is my life.

'I think my record entitles me to say when it is time for me to step aside and not other people, and this is certainly not the time to be talking about quitting. There is important work to do. We have to put our European nightmare behind us and come out even more determined to become champions again.

'We have taken a buffeting and a lot of criticism but we are through all that and I want to see our team refreshed, strong and eager to make their mark again. We may have had a very commanding lead eroded, but the fact is that we are still in with a great chance of winning the League and I know we can do it. This is no time for doubters or fainthearts, either on or off the field.'

It was fighting talk, but it was not to be. The injury blitz in March had knocked the stuffing out of them, and although they beat Wimbledon in their first league fixture after the Monaco tie, they dropped more points and watched in agony as Arsenal slowly but surely narrowed the gap to nose ahead and take the title.

At least United finished in second place, which with the Champions League format extended, meant they would have another crack at Europe. They would have to play in an early preliminary round at the start of the season in order to qualify for the competition proper.

So a season that had promised so much ended in tears, something of a shock after such sparkling form in the first half of the season and some masterly displays in their European group. The bookmakers had quoted them as favourites to take the Cup. Right from the start they had looked well prepared to take on the cream of the Continent after being paired in Group B with Feyenoord of Holland, the Slovakian side Kosice and Juventus again.

The enlarged competition meant that winners of the six groups would qualify along with the two best runners-up. Ferguson spelt out his strategy. 'We have to win the group, nothing less will do, but my lads know what they are facing and they have nothing to be afraid of. Last season was like going down a street not knowing which door to knock on because there is no name on the door. This time we know what's what,' he declared.

United were not fazed by the prospect of being pitted against Juventus again, the team that had beaten them twice the previous season. As skipper Roy Keane said, 'Juventus are one of the best teams in the world. We'll respect them but we are not scared of them. We have a year's more experience under our belts and we'll be stronger than when we faced them last season. We are aiming to finish top of our group.'

Ferguson welcomed the opportunity to measure themselves against the best, and the chance to put the record straight. 'Life doesn't always give people a second chance,' he said, 'but that's exactly what this year's draw has given us.'

His confidence was justified in the way his team opened their campaign against Kosice in Slovakia. It was a textbook operation after a tentative opening. Kosice created a couple of chances. Right in the opening minute Rusian Ljubarskij whipped a header just outside the United post as the home team pressed particularly hard down the flank against Denis Irwin. The Irishman had the last laugh in the twenty-ninth minute – he raced clear behind the home defence and scored from Andy Cole's cross.

United had a scare early in the second half when Gary Pallister hauled Albert Rusnak back by the shirt and was fortunate to escape not just a penalty but a red card. Referee Leif Sundell from Sweden gave him the benefit of the doubt and United went on to win at a canter. Henning Berg scored just after the hour after the Kosice keeper had failed to hold David Beckham's free kick and Andy Cole made up for two missed chances by making the score 3–0 with just a couple of minutes to go.

The scoreline was probably better than the display, as Pallister later admitted. 'It was a decent performance but nothing to write home about,' he said. 'To win 3–0 away in Europe is a great result, though, which we would certainly have settled for before the match.'

Pallister was perhaps mindful of the penalty he had almost given away and like everybody else in the United camp knew the real test was coming up in the next fixture with the visit of Juventus, who had enjoyed a 5–1 victory over Feyenoord in Turin in their opening game.

United made the worst possible start against the Italian team, conceding a goal to Alessandro del Piero in the very first minute. It was a complete stunner and not at all in the script envisaged for the Reds. Many a heart sank among the watching United supporters. They had already been shattered by the news about

Roy Keane following his knee injury playing against Leeds at the weekend. Rumours had spread like wildfire that the United captain's despairing tackle on Alfe-Inge Haaland in the closing stages of the match had left him needing a cruciate ligament operation. Although it wasn't confirmed until the day after the Juventus match, most people seemed to know that Keane was likely to be sidelined for the rest of the season. The early goal by Juventus seemed the final straw, but the players didn't panic and by the thirty-sixth minute they had fought back on to level terms with a fine goal from Teddy Sheringham.

Paul Scholes, who had replaced an injured Nicky Butt in the first half, put United ahead in the seventieth minute and the home team underlined their command in the last minute when Ryan Giggs, who had been in electric form, scored to make it 3–1. Zinedine Zidane scored in injury time for the Italians to make the final score 3–2 but there was no doubting United's superiority.

As a delighted Ferguson said later, 'Their hearts were in the right place for the big one against Juventus and it showed in the attitude and determination of every player who took part in one of the great nights of European football at Old Trafford. It was a great victory achieved after a horror start of going a goal down in the opening minute of the match.

'Maybe scoring so early lured the Italians into thinking it was going to be easy, but at the same time, it still required great courage and composure for our players to force their way back into the game with such stunning success. They knew the importance of winning our home game against Juventus and every man of them was up for it. As we have seen before, when the pot starts to boil at Old Trafford, there is no way you can keep the lid on.

'It wasn't just about fighting spirit, though, it was about maturity, patience, discipline and tactical awareness, and I think we can say that our football earned a deserved victory which has changed the shape of our group league. The players have proved not just to us, but importantly to themselves, that they have nothing to fear about playing in Europe. We overcame injury problems because simply everybody was ready for the challenge.

'The downside was the injury to Roy Keane who will not play again this season. He will have a cruciate operation in four weeks' time, but I must stress that such is the development of the procedure for this type of knee problem that we know he will make a full and complete recovery. The seriousness of the injury was a depressing background for our preparations, but we kept the news to ourselves until after the Juventus match. It was important for the rest of the players and indeed our supporters to be fully upbeat for the European challenge.'

The victory put United at the head of the group with a maximum six points; Juventus and Feyenoord trailed with three points each. United were undoubtedly helped by the dismissal of Didier Deschamps in the sixty-sixth minute, but Marcello Lippi, the Juventus coach, was generous in his appreciation of United's performance.

'Both teams played very well,' he said, 'and the Old Trafford crowd was very strong. They helped their side and in the end we couldn't do what we had to do. Giggs is a truly superb player. He played well in the same game last season but this time there was more reward for him. Sheringham also stood out. Neither side managed to create a host of chances but Sheringham was at the heart of all that they did. United are a strong side and judging by the result, it's clear they have improved in the last year, while Juventus have deteriorated.'

Peter Schmeichel kept his feet on the ground and said, 'It was a good night but I don't think we can start saying this is a famous victory because if we don't qualify this means nothing.'

Peter Schmeichel

Nobody begrudged Ryan Giggs feeling pleased with himself after his startling run and immaculate finish for his goal.

'Purely because of the occasion, it has to go down as one of my best goals ever,' he said later. 'It turned out to be doubly important because Juventus hit back with a second goal in injury time. We've proved we are the best in Britain and we wanted to take it a step further. We wanted to prove something and I think we did. We're in a strong position and we mustn't let it slip,' he warned.

It seemed at this stage as if concentration on the European scene was sapping efforts on the domestic front. Defeat at Leeds after draws against Bolton and Chelsea were relieved by beating Crystal Palace but you knew where Ferguson's priorities lay when he sent a young squad to Ipswich for the Coca-Cola Cup and lost 2–0.

This was followed by a draw with Derby County but the strategy of focusing on Europe paid off with a 2–1 victory over Feyenoord at Old Trafford. Ferguson went to see the Dutch champions play just before the United match against them and came home feeling quietly sure that if his team did nothing silly they would win. His confidence was not misplaced and United won with a more impressive display than the scoreline might suggest. Indeed, the only criticism afterwards was that United should have scored more goals, but the issue never looked in doubt.

Jerzy Dudek, the Dutch team's Polish goalkeeper, held United at bay in a hectic opening spell, saving goal attempts from Andy Cole and Ryan Giggs. He had no chance in the thirty-second minute, though, when Cole headed a cross from Denis Irwin back across goal for Paul Scholes to curl in a goal with the outside of his right boot. It was a brilliant effort and United carved out several more chances, some well saved by Dudek but others missed because of weak finishing.

Peter Schmeichel had little to do, but rose to the occasion by smothering a shot from Petricio Graff with his legs. Otherwise it seemed a matter of waiting for United's next score. Scholes, Irwin and Teddy Sheringham all made heavy weather in front of goal until the seventy-second minute when Graff dumped Sheringham, conceding a penalty.

Usually Sheringham would have picked up the ball to take the spot kick, but two misses had brought a change of plan and Irwin stepped up to take his first United penalty for nearly three years. He made no mistake, but confessed afterwards that he had slipped slightly on his run-up. Henk Vos pulled a late goal back for Feyenoord, and there was regret about the missed chances, but the points were in the bag.

Alex Ferguson summed up, 'We are on course in Europe, and though one can quibble that we should have scored a few more goals against Feyenoord, we came out OK. It is very nice to be sitting at the top of our group table with maximum points at the halfway stage.

'There were periods against Feyenoord when the speed of our play was excellent and once again demonstrated the maturity that has developed in the side. The quality of play was good, which is always encouraging, and overall it was a fine perform-ance. If we keep performing as we are doing in Europe, I don't think we need to worry about reaching the quarter-final stage and we won't even have to be concerned with the safety net of finishing as one of the best second-placed teams.

'Our aim is to go to Turin for the final game in our group in a strong position. That means we will need maximum concen-tration when we play in Rotterdam in ten days' time. It will be hard but then they are all hard in the European Champions League and as Feyenoord showed at Old Trafford, they are quite capable of scoring. Having said that, I don't think they opened us up enough to have won the game or get anything out of it. Certainly we weren't ruthless enough. You always hope to kill off teams when you get the number of chances we had, but our nature is not like that.'

Jordi Cruyff had been restricted to the substitutes' bench, a situation which no doubt disappointed his father who had watched the match from the stand and had been impressed by United's performance. Johan Cruyff, who won the European Cup three times with Ajax, gave his verdict afterwards.

'United are capable of winning the Champions League. They are playing very well. They are strong enough, so why not? Winning three games and getting nine points mean that already the best second place is very near. I'll be supporting them,' he said.

The European success seemed to trigger a scoring resurgence in the Premiership with United beating Barnsley 7–0 and then accounting for Sheffield Wednesday 6–1. The period was a personal triumph for Andy Cole, pilloried so often for missing chances, but now seemingly scoring for the sheer fun of it. He scored a hat-trick against Barnsley, got two against Sheffield Wednesday to speed David Pleat to the managerial exit door, and then took his red-hot form to Feyenoord to blast out another hat-trick for a 3–1 victory.

His opener came after half an hour when he chased a ball hoisted over the home defence by Gary Neville. He was neck and neck with Schuiteman but managed to stretch out a foot to lift the ball over Dudek's head. His second came just before the interval and followed an excellent passing movement between David Beckham and Teddy Sheringham. Beckham's final pass was confidently side-footed home by Cole. The third was the result of a surge forward by Gary Pallister who released Ryan Giggs for the winger to cross from the by-line and give Cole a well-earned third goal.

Igor Korneev scored for Feyenoord three minutes from the

end, but by that time United's concentration had been distracted by some surprisingly shocking behaviour by the Dutch team. A series of provocative incidents, including Gary Neville being elbowed and later spat at, culminated in a disgraceful tackle by Paul Bosvelt on Denis Irwin. It was a wild and spiteful lunge which caught the Irishman on the side of the knee and kept him out of action for a month.

The Dutch later claimed that the bad feeling was the result of David Beckham's challenges in the Old Trafford tie, but Ferguson dismissed that as ludicrous. Feyenoord were quick to react to Bosvelt's tackle, substituting him before referee Sandor Puhl could take disciplinary action. The Hungarian official was hoodwinked. After an inquiry, UEFA announced that he would not be given any further Champions League appointments that season.

Irwin subsequently received an apology from Bosvelt and said, 'The player wrote a fax to me to say he was sorry it had happened. From what I have heard, he's not usually the sort of lad who does that kind of thing. At least he's held up his hands and got in touch. It wasn't a nice tackle but it is finished as far as I'm concerned.'

United were upset by the incident but couldn't contain their joy over both the result and the performance. As skipper Peter Schmeichel declared, 'I'm really pleased for Andy Cole. Inside Old Trafford we have all seen the contribution Andy makes to our game and that's been good enough for us. As far as we're concerned, it has never been a problem. It's the guys in the media who keep bringing up the seven million tag and go on about missed goals. He's certainly answered the press, and that's great.'

Gary Neville also paid tribute to his scoring team-mate. 'Coley is absolutely on fire and long may it continue. The criticism he has had has been unjust.'

The victory meant United were the only side left in the Champions League with 100 per cent winning record. Real Madrid had drawn in Greece, and Bayern Munich had lost in Paris. The Reds were confident of qualifying for the quarter-finals, needing just one point from two games to do so.

Then went down 3–2 at Arsenal four days after the Feyenoord match, but winning 5–2 at Wimbledon sent their spirits soaring again and it was a very chipper Alex Ferguson who prepared for their match against Kosice at Old Trafford.

'We are turning into the home straight of our qualifying group and we could hardly ask to be in a better position. Four games played with maximum points has left us in a two-horse race with Juventus, and while nothing can be taken for granted at this level of football, we have a great chance now to move on to the quarter-final stage.

'A win against Kosice would almost guarantee our qualification, if only as one of the two best group runners-up, and irrespective of how we fare in the final fixture in Turin next month. Talk is easy though, and first we have to do the business against a team we beat 3–0 in Slovakia at the start of the competition. Our performance in Kosice makes us feel very confident of course, but it is significant that our opponents held Juventus to 3–2 in Italy in the last round of matches. To me, that suggests this newly established nation are starting to find their feet in the football world.

'So there will be no complacency on our part. Over the years I think we have been guilty at times of taking too much for granted. It's been the nature of the beast, but not, I feel, on this occasion because it has been clear all season that the players have had a great focus on Europe and nothing has been allowed to stand in the way of making a sustained assault on this most challenging of trophies.

'There was a little caution on our part in our first game against

Kosice but that was understandable because it was something of a step into the unknown and we didn't quite know what to expect. They gave us a few early problems but the boys held their nerve and got a good result. Against Juventus at Old Trafford we went up a few notches and I have got to say we were superb in the victory which catapulted us into the driving seat of our group and underlined the progress we have made on the European front since last season.

'Beating Feyenoord home and away emphasised the steps we have taken in terms of confidence, patience and resilience. We were sorely tested in Rotterdam when the game turned ugly and I have nothing but admiration for the team. They kept their discipline and refused to be provoked. I can always understand players who from time to time do silly things born out of frustration and dislike of being beaten, but there was no excuse for the way Feyenoord behaved. I imagine that even their players must have asked themselves afterwards how they had come to lose their control to such an extent.

'Denis Irwin is still counting the cost, but we mustn't let one bad experience spoil things because we have had some excellent matches in Europe this season.'

United clinched their place in the last eight of the competition with a 3–0 win over Kosice at Old Trafford. David Lacey in the *Guardian* said they looked like a team capable of winning the Champion League whereas last season they were simply grateful to be still taking part. But the goals didn't flow quite so easily as in their first meeting, although the scores were the same. Until the eighty-fifth minute they were held to the slender one-goal lead established by Andy Cole – who else? – shortly before half-time. Cole had scored from David Beckham's pass with a shot through the legs of the goalkeeper.

The second goal came with a rebound off Faktor after Molnar had parried a shot from Karel Poborsky. Sheringham added the third with a beautifully curling shot just inside the post from Beckham's prompt, winning the forgiveness of the home crowd following a shocking miss in the first half.

The victory installed United as 2–1 favourites to become the first English club to win Europe's top trophy since Liverpool won it for a fourth time in 1984. Their final fixture in Turin was an irrelevance as far as United were concerned, but it mattered very much to Juventus, who had lost 2–0 in Rotterdam and who were fighting to qualify as one of the two best runners-up.

It seemed United could do nothing wrong as they roared back into Premiership action. They put Blackburn out of the title hunt by beating them 4–0 at Old Trafford, followed by a similarly important 3–1 win at Liverpool. The bookmakers were quoting United at 1–4 favourites for the championship and Ferguson seemed to be spending a lot of his time refuting the idea that the league race was as good as over.

Everything was going fine on both fronts until the final European group game against Juventus in Italy proved to be a damp squib for the Reds. Filippo Inzaghi scored six minutes from time and the match ended in a 1–0 defeat. It was hardly an anti-climax for Juventus, though. Their snatched victory coupled with Rosenborg being held to a draw meant they squeezed into the quarter-finals as a group runner-up.

'Now we hope to meet you in the final,' said the delighted Juventus coach, Marcello Lippi.

Peter Schmeichel reflected United's disappointment when he said, 'We weren't as good as we have been but you cannot play well in every match. Juventus kept us under pressure and they were very determined. All credit to them, they never gave up, and they kept believing that they could go through.

'They probably deserved their win, but it is a very big dis-appointment to lose. The fact we had already qualified wasn't a problem. It was never mentioned in the dressing-room. What we have done in this campaign is good enough for me. I am confident that no matter who we play in the knock-out stages, we have got a chance.'

Alex Ferguson, however, thought that the lack of pressure was the reason they had lost. 'We didn't play well,' he said. 'We gave the ball away too much and the players seemed to take the attitude that it didn't matter. I suppose that came of knowing that whatever the result we had already qualified.'

Overall, though, he was delighted with the progress his team had made both on the home front and abroad, but he was alarmed at the way the bookmakers had made his team odds-on favourites for the League and at the way the critics reckoned, even before Christmas, that it was a one-horse race. He had nightmare memories of 1992 when they seemed to be coasting but hit an end of season bad patch to let Leeds in as champions; also of the slip-up in 1995 when Blackburn pipped them. So he tried to ignore the hymns of praise threatening to engulf his men, but he did concede, 'I cannot speak too highly of the efforts of the players in Europe this season. Certainly we were disappointed to lose our final group game to Juventus in Turin and the Italians gave us a sharp reminder of what can happen if you lose your concentration and edge. But the way the players have put the lessons they learned last season to such good use has been so impressive. We didn't just qualify, we came through with a sense of power and purpose, which I am sure has thrilled our supporters, and all this has been achieved while setting a hot pace in the Premiership on the back of one of the most sustained and highest scoring sprees I have ever enjoyed.'

But he warned against self-congratulation when he added, 'We must remind ourselves that nothing has actually been won yet this season. We must not pay any attention to the kind of stuff we have been reading in the newspapers following our success at Liverpool. I just don't buy all the nonsense about Manchester United being home and dry for the championship. If the players take that idea on board, we are in trouble.

'It's so easy to throw away the League and see things fall apart. It happened to us not so long ago. We seemed to have the title in our pockets and then suddenly it all went wrong. There is nothing to say it couldn't happen again like that – particularly if we start to believe everything that is being written about us at the moment.'

Handing out a warning is one thing, heeding it is another. United supporters watched their team slither into trouble in the Premiership early in the New Year. Their rivals' poor results enabled them to stay at the top of the table but their league form had been far from convincing when they went to Monaco for the first leg of the quarter-final on 4 March.

The Reds played out a goalless draw with tactics that were new for United in Europe. Ferguson later explained, 'I'm sure our supporters suffered a culture shock when we played in Monte Carlo and they saw a rather cautious Manchester United after years of watching our more cavalier approach.

'But you can get very fed up when people keep telling you how unlucky you have been and I lost count of the number of times sympathy was expressed after our defeat in Germany against Borussia Dortmund in last season's semi-final of the Champions League. Everyone recognised that we deserved to win that first leg – and, indeed, the return match as well – but sympathy doesn't change results and the more I thought about our tie with Monaco the more I could see a repeat scenario of the 1–0 defeat we suffered in the first leg in Dortmund.

'If you remember, we were hammering the Germans to pieces but then towards the end of the match we had become spread in midfield so that Rene Tretschok was allowed to shoot from twenty-five yards. His effort took a deflection off Gary Pallister's boot, looped over Raimond Van der Gouw and gave Borussia a win against the run of play.

'I didn't want to come home from Monaco a goal down this time, and with the German experience in mind I thought long and hard about our tactics. The fact that the Monaco pitch has a car park underneath which means the grass has a concrete base and is therefore very hard was the final argument which decided me that we would play with more emphasis on safety. As it turned out, I wanted my wide players to give the strikers more support than they were able to supply, and this part didn't work as well as I expected, but defensively we were very tight and gave nothing away.

'An experience like the previous season introduces a certain caution in you and reminds you that we have young players who always have the tendency to express themselves without too much thought, and they are that way simply because they are young. There is nothing wrong with that. You want players who have that kind of ability and courage, but at certain stages of Europe you have to guard against being carried away. We must always search to make progress, and though I know we are capable of winning this round, I had to leave nothing to chance.

'Bad luck cost us dearly last season and sometimes you have to make sure you make your own luck! We could have been more adventurous and some will say I was over-cautious, but uppermost in my mind was a determination that we wouldn't leave ourselves open to anything silly. You will see a much more open game in the second leg and I believe we now have a very good chance of going through to the semi-finals again.'

He added, 'It was very significant that all four first-leg games in the quarter-finals were drawn with 0–0 or 1–1 results. It's the nature of European football once you get to the two-

legged stage and it is something we had to take on board. Hopefully the game at Old Trafford will repay the patience of our
supporters.'

Alas, Ferguson's plans didn't work out. There was nothing
wrong with the strategy; he simply lost too many key personnel
to make his tactics work, and then had the bad luck to concede
a goal after only five minutes. And what a goal!

United were initially at fault, making a hash of trying to
clear the ball, allowing David Trezeguet to break through.
He ran like an arrow for goal and beat Raimond Van der
Gouw with a rocket measured by Sky television as travelling
at 96 miles per hour. This wasn't a case of missing Peter Schmeichel – it was an unstoppable shot. It immediately conjured up
the difficulties United had experienced in previous European
games when they had conceded a goal to Juventus after twenty-
three seconds and similarly suffered against Borussia Dortmund by letting in a goal after eight minutes. They had
recovered to win against Juventus but the goal against the
Germans in the previous season's semi-final at Old Trafford
had crushed them.

This time United responded bravely enough and drew level
in the fifty-third minute. David Beckham whipped the ball into
the path of Ole Gunnar Solskjaer who scored with a well-hit
volley. Beckham worked hard to supply a creative spark but the
pace and penetration of Ryan Giggs was missed up front, just
as the experience and steadiness of Gary Pallister was lacking
at the back. Gary Neville and Paul Scholes both carried injuries
into the match and the Reds looked weary as they ran out of
time in their search for a winner.

Denis Irwin, captain in the absence of Schmeichel and
Pallister, said, 'It was bitterly disappointing because we just
couldn't turn our late pressure into more chances. We didn't
have the legs to do it. We had so many big-game players missing

and it knocked us out of our stride. Also, when it came to the crunch, we again didn't have the luck. Maybe we can do it next year.'

23

THE INCREDIBLE TREBLE

IN THE BEGINNING, even Alex Ferguson thought the historic treble was out of reach, and although his ambition and confidence grew as his team gathered momentum towards the end of the season, it still seemed a tall order.

The season boiled down to eleven momentous days in which the Premiership, the FA Cup and the European Champions League would be decided. Which would be the priority?

Manager and players alike insisted that each competition on its final day would be the principal objective, but that didn't stop Ferguson juggling his players to make sure that he had his strongest possible side out in pursuit of the prize that had eluded Manchester United for thirty-one years. It meant that Nicky Butt was left out of the FA Cup final team and Jaap Stam was given a late walk-on role from the substitutes' bench, but we shouldn't have been surprised because right from the start of the season the manager had operated his squad rotation system to keep his troops fit and fresh to fight on three fronts.

He denied it at the time but the focus was always on Europe. When asked during the early rounds if the European championship had become an obsession, he bridled and denied it, saying that he considered that his overall record made it clear he had competed successfully in a number of competitions. The point was emphasised when he went on to land the grand slam of League, FA Cup and Europe!

Nevertheless, his planning for the season seemed to revolve round the European campaign. He believed that his players were ready for the ultimate challenge, convinced that they had failed the previous year only because they had been hit by an above average level of injuries.

He succeeded in bringing his team to a peak for the testing knock-out stages against Inter Milan and Juventus, and there was no question about their incredible fitness, mentally and physically, when they produced their late victory against Bayern Munich.

Earlier in the competition there had been nervousness, as if the weight of expectation was becoming increasingly hard to bear. The fact that they came into the Champions League because UEFA had decided to broaden the competition and admit runners-up was hardly conducive to confidence.

As Ferguson said when he welcomed LKS Lodz for the pre-liminary round, which second-placed teams had to enter, 'It's a touch ironic because I was originally against the idea of inviting a number of second-placed finishing teams to qualify for the competition proper. I felt that the UEFA Champions League should be for what it said – champions!

'But now here we are taking advantage of the expansion of the tournament. I thought of declining to take part on principle, but only for a millisecond. Europe figures too prominently in our list of priorities for there to be any other decision than a grateful acceptance for a small mercy. We are in by the back-door, but no matter. The chance of a reprieve was too good to miss and I am just glad of the opportunity to have Europe on our agenda again.'

The first leg against Lodz was at Old Trafford on 12 August three days before the opening Premiership fixture, and supporters wondered if there had been enough time for proper preparation. New signing Jesper Blomqvist, the Swedish international who had played against United for Gothenberg in an earlier life, wasn't fit following his transfer from Parma; Jaap Stam, the £10 million summer signing from Eindhoven, replacing Gary Pallister, was ready for his debut. But it was one of the established players, Ryan Giggs, who caught the eye more than the new centre-half. United were in attacking mode and Giggs, perhaps conscious of missing the previous season's unsuccessful later stages through injury, was in dynamic form. With the help of Paul Scholes, he scored superbly after sixteen minutes, and though it wasn't until nine minutes from the end that Andy Cole was able to make it 2–0, it was a good result which gave the fans some peace of mind after watching their team destroyed 3–0 by Arsenal in the FA Charity Shield the previous weekend.

A dour but disciplined goalless draw in Poland a fortnight later eased United successfully through the qualifying round to put them into a demanding group with Barcelona, Bayern Munich and Brondby, the Danish club.

The opening fixture brought Barcelona to Old Trafford and left the home supporters not knowing whether to laugh or cry! United's first-half performance against the Spanish superstars was so good that Europe seemed there for the taking, but in the second half the Old Trafford team collapsed. It was a painful experience after watching the Reds race into a two-goal interval lead with marvellous strikes by Ryan Giggs and Paul Scholes, followed by David Beckham's superb free-kick goal after the interval.

For the first forty-five minutes Giggs was electric on the left, Beckham produced a stream of quality crosses from the right and Roy Keane was the heartbeat in midfield while Jaap Stam looked invincible at the back. But then United's beautiful game disintegrated, Barcelona took control and ran the home team ragged. You could argue about the merit or otherwise of the two penalties awarded to the visitors, but there was no denying that Barcelona had pulled themselves together to produce a tremendous fight-back and earn a deserved 3–3 draw.

On reflection, it should not have been a big surprise. The European Champions League represents the highest form of football, even better than the World Cup because the leading clubs, with players drawn from around the world, produce more subtle team-work and more practised tactics. Even the less fashionable teams are capable of producing a high calibre of game, as the results of the opening round of matches emphasised. Juventus, for instance, finalists for the past two seasons, were held to a 2–2 draw on their own ground by Galatasaray, the Turkish team which keeps throwing spanners in the works, as United fans know all too well. Mighty Inter Milan, whose star turn Ronaldo flopped, crashed 2–0 at Real Madrid, and then in United's Group D came the big shock of Brondby beating Bayern Munich 2–1.

As Barcelona manager Louis van Gaal said after the game at Old Trafford, 'Brondby are our next opponents and we will have to be alert. They are very dangerous and comparable with Dynamo Kiev of last season. Nobody talked about Kiev but they finished winning their group.'

In other words, get set for another rollercoaster ride. The Champions League was clearly more competitive than ever and with that in mind Alex Ferguson struck a positive note after the disappointment of seeing his team hanging on with ten men, following the dismissal of Nicky Butt for hand-ball on the goalline.

'When you consider we lost two penalties and had a man sent off, it wasn't perhaps too bad a result,' he declared, and looked at from that point of view, he was probably right. They could easily have lost when they were playing a man short with their backs to the wall for the last twenty minutes.

It was a hard lesson, but at least they had shown in the first half what they were capable of and it was clear that if they could hit that level consistently there was no need to fear anyone. As Ferguson said, 'You just didn't want the first half to finish.'

The next fixture took United to Munich for another agonisingly drawn game, remembered for a rare error by Peter Schmeichel which presented Bayern with an equaliser for a 2–2 finish. The draw left the Reds third in their group and facing a giant task to qualify for the knock-out stages.

Alex Ferguson stoutly defended his goalkeeper after watching in horror as Schmeichel came out for a corner only to fail to reach the ball and leave Giovane Elber able to score his second goal of the game, following successful strikes by Dwight Yorke and Paul Scholes.

'It was an error of judgement but no one is pointing a finger at him because overall he had a magnificent game and didn't deserve to be punished for his one mistake,' he said.

There was to be no quick way back for Schmeichel to wipe out the memory of his nightmare moment; he dropped out of action to recover from a stomach muscle injury. Naturally enough, Schmeichel didn't want to talk about his rash decision to come for the corner but skipper Roy Keane said, 'Nobody is blaming him. Just minutes before he had made two great saves to keep us in the game.'

Ferguson was philosophical about the draw which left Barcelona topping Group D on four points with Bayern on three, United two and Brondby one. United desperately needed two wins over Brondby while hoping that Barcelona and Bayern would draw with each other. That way, United could perhaps force a showdown in their final group game against Barcelona in Spain.

The trip to Germany underlined the complications that can arise when travel arrangements don't go smoothly. A fault with the emergency lighting on the plane due to pick up the team in Munich straight after the match meant an unexpected stop-over in Germany with players not getting to bed until the early hours and not back in Manchester until the afternoon of the following day, Thursday. United were due to fly to Southampton on the Friday and training had to be cancelled to give the team time to rest. It was not the best preparation for an always difficult fixture. The failure to get away from Munich as planned had an uncanny undertone reflecting the persistent attempts by the Busby Babes to take off in 1958 after a refuelling stop in Munich on the way home from a European Cup tie in Belgrade. On that occasion, the need to get back in time for the weekend league fixture undoubtedly influenced the captain's decision to make the third fatal dash down the runway which ended with the crash.

At least there was no attempt to press a faulty plane into service on this occasion, but the resulting chaos as the travel company hunted round for hotel beds and a place to eat brought home the difficulties of trying to marry an intensive European fixture list with an already busy domestic programme.

United, of course, were competing in a strong section quickly tagged the 'group of death' and Brondby must have felt suicidal after finding themselves on the receiving end of a 6–2 hammering by Manchester United in front of their own fans. United blasted away the worries left by their drawn games with Barcelona and Bayern and wasted no time getting down to business. Ryan Giggs picked up an easy goal after only two minutes, courtesy of the goalkeeper dropping a centre, and got a second in the twenty-first with a header from Jesper Blomqvist's cross.

Giggs was making Danish pastries of the opposition in his new role as a central striker and before the half-hour he sent

Andy Cole in for an interval 3–1 lead. Roy Keane, Dwight Yorke and substitute Ole Solskjaer piled in three goals in the space of seven blistering minutes early in the second half to leave Alex Ferguson saying, 'I wasn't overly impressed by our performance. We gave away the ball too often for my liking, though I must not be churlish and I acknowledge the manner of our goals. For me the scoring was the big feature of our game and you cannot dismiss that aspect. To score six goals away from home is a record in the Champions League and it sends out good messages from us to our rivals. It's no bad thing to establish a reputation for scoring goals.'

With Bayern Munich winning against Barcelona in Germany, United's fortunes were dramatically changed. The Reds now topped the group. Ferguson was at pains to stress that they still needed the points against Brondby in the next fixture because he worried that when his team got complacent they didn't perform. But the manager's fears proved groundless as he watched another whirlwind display for a 5–0 win at Old Trafford, which not only kept them top of their group but made them the bookmakers' favourites to go all the way and win the Champions League.

Again they wasted no time finding the net. David Beckham worked one of his spectacular free kicks to score after only seven minutes and by half-time they were four up with goals from Andy Cole, Phil Neville – his first in Europe – and Dwight Yorke. Paul Scholes added the fifth in the second half.

The group had become a two-horse race with Barcelona and Brondby out of it. Ferguson was naturally delighted and said, 'It was stunning, probably the best performance in the first half that I have seen in my time at Old Trafford. The goals were superb, well created and brilliantly executed. The movement and imagination were fantastic.

'We have also got back into the Premiership groove and I am

pleased with our form. The players are enjoying their game and playing with the kind of enthusiasm, as well as the hunger, you need to make this a successful season with something to show for it at the end.

'You can never be complacent of course, but it is helping that our new players are settling much quicker than one is perhaps entitled to expect. Some do, of course – Eric Cantona marched into Old Trafford and immediately took centre stage. Dwight Yorke has been much the same, playing with an infectious zest that is good to see. I am pleased, too, with the way Jesper Blomqvist has come into his own. He arrived with a foot injury but has overcome that and has done very well since getting into the team.

'It goes without saying that we are much better equipped to deal with the loss of key players such as Ryan Giggs. Indeed, I believe that if we had had Jesper last season when Ryan had to drop out, we would have won the championship.

'Jaap Stam has also impressed, especially considering that he had a long and busy World Cup playing for Holland all the way to the match for third place. It can have a draining effect, and with the kind of limited break Jaap enjoyed, can reach into the following season. Jaap Stam is going to get even better as he builds an interesting partnership with Gary Neville in central defence.'

The manager's confident words were backed up by his team when they achieved a 3–3 draw in the Nou Camp Stadium, putting paid to Barcelona's bid to reach the quarter-finals. So the group came to a grand finale between Manchester United and Bayern Munich to decide which of them should have automatic entry as group winners to the knock-out stage.

Ferguson's major concern at that point of the season was in trying to maintain a challenge in the Premiership alongside the demands of playing in Europe.

England full-back Gary Neville starts an attack in the 3–0 win over Kosice in Poland in the opening game of the 1997 Champions League campaign.

A youthful David Beckham wins a midfield tussle with Monaco's Martin Djetou at the Stade Louis II during the first leg of the 1998 Champions League quarter-final.

Hat-trick hero Andy Cole is congratulated by Teddy Sheringham and David Beckham as United celebrate a return to Rotterdam with a 3–1 over Feyenoord. The fourth successive victory put United firmly on top of their group in the 1997–98 Champions League.

Barcelona here we come. Roy Keane takes the plaudits after scoring United's fourth goal of the 6–2 romp over Danish side Brondby in the opening phase of the 1998–99 Champions League.

Jesper Blomqvist in action against Barcelona in the 3–3 draw at the Nou Camp in November 1998. On United's next visit to the famous Spanish stadium they were crowned European Champions.

Brazilian superstar Ronaldo is thwarted by Henning Berg during the second leg of the Champions League quarter-final against Inter Milan.

Outstanding French midfielder Zinedine Zidane of Juventus, finds his way to goal blocked by Denis Irwin during the 1999 Champions League semi-final second leg in Turin.

Ole Gunnar Solskjaer gets straight into the action after coming on as a late substitute during the 1999 Champions League final against Bayern Munich. His arrival proved crucial to the outcome of the game.

England versus Germany. David Beckham, the man who would later become England captain, tries to hold off a challenge from Bayern midfielder Jens Jeremies, the German international.

The camera captures what many claim to be the greatest moment in Manchester United history. Ole Gunnar Solskjaer flicks home the decisive stoppage-time goal and Bayern Munich are beaten. The European Cup is won and the treble completed after a sensational fight-back by the Premiership champions.

An ecstatic Teddy Sheringham turns after scoring his late equaliser. With ninety minutes played, Bayern Munich thought the European Cup was theirs but United had other ideas. Just four days earlier, Sheringham opened the scoring as United beat Newcastle 2–0 in the FA Cup final.

A night to remember. David May *(third from left)* leads the celebrations as United are crowned Champions of Europe for the second time in the club's history.

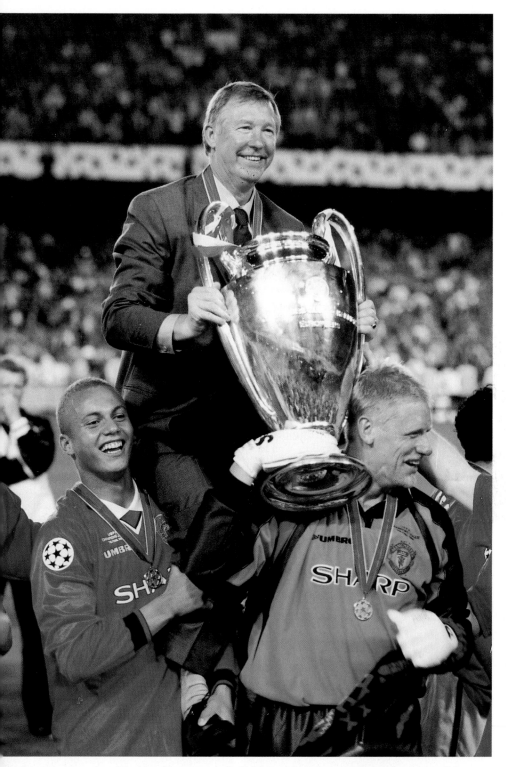

. knight to remember. Sir Alex Ferguson is held high as he becomes the most successful Manchester United manager, surpassing the feats of the legendary Sir Matt Busby. Wes Brown *eft)* and skipper for the night Peter Schmeichel carry off 'The Gaffer' as well as the European *:up.*

It's a deal. David Beckham agrees to swap shirts with Real Madrid full-back Roberto Carlos following the 0–0 draw in the Champions League quarter-final first leg at the Bernabeu Stadium in April 2000.

United's French international full-back Mika Silvestre leaves Maksim Shatskikh flat on his back as he skips over a challenge during the 0 draw with Dynamo Kiev in September 2000

Fabien Barthez had plenty to celebrate after his move to Old Trafford in the summer of 2000. As well as helping France add the European Championship to the World Cup they won in 1998, he topped his first season in the Premiership by collecting another champions' medal. Here he welcomes the final whistle as Sturm Graz are beaten 2–0 in Austria.

Right Spot the ball. Jaap Stam heads clear under pressure from Markus Schopp as United chalk up a 3–0 win over Sturm Graz Old Trafford in March 2001.

Roy Keane wins the ball from Valencia midfielder Gaizka Mendieta at the Mestalla Stadium. The game ended in a 0–0 stalemate and after a 1–1 draw at Old Trafford both United and the Spaniards progressed to the 2001 Champions League quarter-finals.

Manchester United paid a record price for a defender when they bought Jaap Stam from PSV Eindhoven in the summer of 1998. The £10.75 million proved to be money well spent as they went on to win three successive Premiership titles, which included the treble of 1999. Here the big Dutchman uses his strength to thwart Bayern Munich's Giovane Elber in the second leg of the 2001 Champions League quarter-final.

Bayern Munich captain Stefan Effenberg holds off his United counterpart Roy Keane during the Champions League quarter-final first leg at Old Trafford in April 2001. Bayern won 1–0 thanks to a late goal from substitute Paulo Sergio and went on to win the trophy.

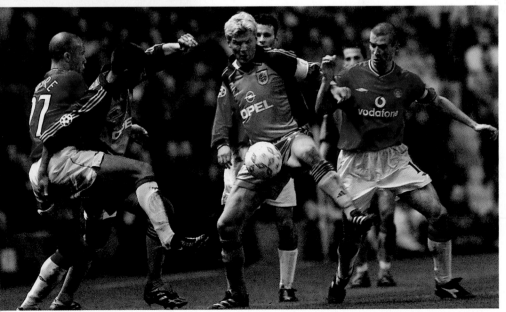

European Coach of the Year 2000, Sir Alex Ferguson receives his award from former German national team boss Berti Vogts. Sir Alex collected his prize at the UEFA Soccer Gala in Monaco

Manchester United look to the future in signing £19 million Dutch striker Ruud Van Nistelrooy in April 2001. Sir Alex had targeted the player a year earlier but the deal fell through when the PSV Eindhoven star failed a medical. After undergoing cruciate ligament surgery, Van Nistelrooy made a successful return for club and country before his move to Old Trafford.

'We are not handling the two competitions of Champions League and Premiership at all well. A pattern has emerged indicating that we don't take in our stride the demands of switching from one to the other. There have been some notable exceptions, but overall, our hiccups in the League have nearly all come on one side or another of a European tie,' he explained.

'This is simply unacceptable at our club and it is something that the players must take on board. Our squad is big and has quality. It has been built to cope with the demands of competing at the top level, which of course is what being a Manchester United player is all about.

'Perhaps some of our new players have not quite adjusted to this basic fact of football life, maybe some of our younger players are struggling to come to terms with the pressure, but what is crystal clear, in my mind at any rate, is that the players have got to get to grips with these expectations.

'We simply cannot afford – or tolerate – the under-performing displays at places like Derby County and Sheffield Wednesday which have cost us valuable points and let us all down.

'We have a challenge on our hands if we are going to win the Premiership this season and I want to see a big improvement with the problem. I know Europe looms large in all our minds, and it is no secret that we would dearly like to go all the way this year after the near-misses, injuries and other set-backs of recent seasons. But it must not be at the expense of our challenge for the home championship.'

Naturally, he was delighted with his team's performance in Barcelona.

'Any manager would be very proud to have a team going so boldly to the attack in the Nou Camp Stadium as to score three goals, picture goals, too. It's a very impressive and intimidating arena, and I was delighted with the way they set about their task.

'Obviously, we would have liked a win rather than a draw but in a game of that nature both sides were capable of scoring more goals and so I think we can be satisfied with what I thought was a reasonable and fair result,' he said.

United impressed with the way they shrugged off the blow of conceding a goal from Anderson in the very first minute. There were not many United fans who did not immediately recall the four-goal hammering they received in the Nou Camp in 1994. This time, though, they hit back hard and quickly with a goal from Dwight Yorke in the twenty-fifth minute before taking the lead through Andy Cole early in the second half. Rivaldo equalised for Barcelona four minutes later, but Yorke struck again in the sixty-eighth minute, raising hopes of a win only for Rivaldo to make it 3–3 with an impressive bicycle kick over his shoulder. The Brazilian went close when he hit the bar but United survived and moved into the last eight of the competition by drawing 1–1 with Bayern at Old Trafford on 9 December.

It was an achievement to celebrate but there was an air of anti-climax because, as the news of the scores in the other groups filtered through, it became clear that a win was no longer necessary to qualify. A draw would be good enough to take them through to the next phase as one of the two best group runners-up. United's reaction was to waste time and knock it around at the back to play out time. This suited the Germans because a draw was also sufficient to put them through as the winners of Group D. It meant a pretty sterile finish to a game that had pulsed with so much excitement and drama in the first half.

The United fans were passionate with joy when their hero, Roy Keane, shot them into the lead just before half-time after a marvellous piece of play by Ryan Giggs who cut the ball back to his skipper. The tension went up a notch when Hasan

Salihamidzic equalised ten minutes into the second half and both teams went flat out for a winner, but the last quarter of an hour was a let-down as all the players relaxed in the knowledge that if the score stayed the same they were both going to figure in March after a mid-winter break.

Ferguson himself acknowledged that the game, in his words, had petered out, and it must have hurt for him to order his players to slow down. That's just not United's style but there was still much to please him.

'There are some big names left in the competition. All eight, including ourselves, are good enough to win it. All the teams have the kind of history and tradition you associate with success in Europe.'

Manchester United lined up in the last eight with Bayern Munich, Olympiakos, Juventus, Inter Milan, Real Madrid, Dynamo Kiev and Kaiserslautern with the draw in Geneva giving the Reds the daunting task of meeting Inter Milan in the quarter-final. United rose magnificently to the challenge, winning 2–0 at Old Trafford in the first leg on 3 March, and leaving an abiding memory of the way David Beckham's crosses continuously threw the Italians into a panic. After only six minutes he crossed perfectly from the right for Dwight Yorke to glance in a header. They repeated the move just before half-time and again the Italians had no answer.

There were some anxious moments in the second half as Inter turned up the heat. Diego Simeone headed in from a corner but the goal was disallowed for pushing; and Henning Berg, who had replaced the injured Ronny Johnsen at half-time, appeared from nowhere to clear off the line just before the final whistle.

Ferguson was pleased to be taking a two-goal lead to the San Siro, but that did not stop him criticising his team's performance.

'Our concentration was first-class and I was pleased with the tempo we set for much of the game. I was also delighted with the result, which I would happily have settled for before the match, but I thought the general team performance was fragmented. We can play a lot better than that and take our game to a much higher level, he insisted.

Ferguson was striving for the standard required to win the European Cup.

'People still occasionally criticise me for making changes and resting players but I think now is the time you will see its value,' he said. 'David Beckham is a case in point. He had a three-week break around Christmas, along with Paul Scholes and Gary Neville, and I think he has come to a peak at just the right time. His game has come together again, as we saw with those marvellous crosses for Dwight Yorke's goals against Inter.

'People ask me which is David's best position, central midfield or on the wing. Well, he's a very good player in midfield but I also happen to think he is the best crosser of a ball in Europe, and if he can continue to put in the kind of crosses we saw against Inter Milan then he can jolly well stay on the wing!

'I think we have got some key players coming together at the right time. They are playing very well and have done for some time. This time last year we had injuries but now everyone is fit and it's a bonus.

'Our skill and belief is not a problem. The concentration worries me at times but it was fine against Inter Milan, so we are in good shape for the big matches to come and we are really confident about our chances in Milan,' he said.

The second leg went perfectly to plan with a disciplined 1–1 draw for an aggregate 3–1 victory. Even Mircea Lucescu, the Romanian manager of the Italian club, backed Alex Ferguson's team to go all the way.

'Manchester United will play in the final,' he declared.

Ronaldo, his world star, quit after an hour as he continued to struggle with the knee injury that had dogged him since the World Cup in France.

A disappointed Lucescu blamed the French referee, Gilles Veissiere, for turning down three penalty claims and said that Alex Ferguson had put him under pressure by suggesting before the match that Inter, like a typical Italian team, would be 'scheming, diving and referee-baiting'. The United manager has become quite famous for his 'mind games' but at this level you need every trick in the book, and this was by no means an easy match.

United and their 10,000 travelling fans were sweating when substitute Ventola put Inter ahead on the night and they stayed on the edge of their seats until Paul Scholes, on for Ronny Johnsen for the last quarter of an hour, scored in the eighty-eighth minute. A super cross from full-back Gary Neville towards the far side of goal was headed back and down by Andy Cole for the little guy to beat Gianluca Pagliuca from close range.

This was United's best result on Italian soil for forty years and it convinced them that they are ready to take on anyone in pursuit of what has become their holy grail. As Ferguson explained, 'The facts tell you that to succeed in Europe you have got to advance beyond the Italian clubs, and until this unforgettable night it was something that had eluded us.

'We have been close, and honours were even last season when we met Juventus in the qualifying group of the Champions League, beating them at Old Trafford only to lose in Turin. But actually to win over two legs in a knock-out situation is something new for Manchester United, going back a long time. Our record in European competition involving six games on Italian soil was a stark six defeats, which tells you something about the difficulty of overcoming their major clubs.

'Even in this match we had to settle for a draw but at least it was a score draw thanks to Paul Scholes joining Norman Whiteside as the only United players to get a goal in serious competition in Italy.

'So while we all celebrate the success, I take even more satisfaction, if that's possible, from the knowledge that this is an important and key breakthrough. It's a coming of age in European terms, though I've got to say I've felt it coming for some time. I was very positive in our approach to the tie and always considered that the splendid two-goal win in the first leg at Old Trafford would be enough to see us finish off the job successfully.

'We knew we were capable of scoring, and though we left it longer than is good for my nerves, we did just that. We arrived in Milan in good heart, in tip-top condition and enjoying a great groove of form. We had to ride our luck at times, but I thought that over the two legs we deserved to go through.

'My confidence lay in the fact that this team has grown in stature over the last year or two. It's a young side in terms of Europe, certainly not as experienced as the Inter Milan team, but even the younger ones have now played twenty matches or so in Europe and, most importantly, learned from them.

'There were things we can still do better but the players showed great composure and the belief in their passing was good. I was also grateful that my call for a strong referee was answered by a fantastic performance from Gilles Veissiere who, in my opinion, called everything correctly. The San Siro Stadium is a fearsome place for a referee as well as for visiting players, but the penalty claims were not penalty kicks and he stood no nonsense.

'We had good fortune at times but I certainly wouldn't say we were lucky because we also created and missed chances.

'We defended well and knocking an Italian team out of Europe is a major step forward for us. I see the Italian big guns as a barometer of our progress and I think we are entitled to feel that, with Inter Milan out of the way, we can go all the way and become champions.'

United needed to think boldly because the semi-final paired them with Juventus, another Italian giant. Dynamo Kiev met Bayern Munich in the other semi.

The first leg at Old Trafford on 7 April was the match in which Teddy Sheringham reminded everyone of his qualities. He came on as a substitute for the last quarter of an hour and changed the course of the game. United needed a saviour after struggling in the first half, falling behind to a twenty-fifth minute goal from Antonio Conte. The score seemed destined to stay that way until Sheringham spurred a series of raids for Ryan Giggs to score a last-minute equaliser.

Kevin Keegan, the England manager, was at the game and he described the substitution as a masterstroke.

'Who would have thought before the match that putting Sheringham on for Dwight Yorke would have proved such a good move?' he asked afterwards. 'It wasn't happening for Yorke and when Sheringham came on he turned the game. Ryan Giggs got the goal but it was Sheringham who put United on top in that last phase and now at least they have a chance when they play the second leg.'

Sheringham, dogged by injury and then kept out of the team by the brilliant, high-scoring partnership of Yorke and Andy Cole, had made only three Premiership starts that season and just two in Europe. It seemed a desperate gamble when Ferguson put him on with United a goal down and looking as if they wouldn't score in a month of Sundays.

Perhaps it was the sight of the normally stylish Sheringham going into a full-blooded clattering tackle with Zinedine Zidane and coming out with the ball that prompted the revival.

Certainly the tempo suddenly shot up. The Reds had un-doubtedly improved on their first-half display after the interval, but their most effective spell came in the final fifteen minutes.

For a moment, it looked as if Sheringham had got an equaliser himself when he got his head to a fierce shot from Roy Keane and steered the ball past the goalkeeper, but he was ruled offside and television later confirmed that the linesman had been right, even if he had been slow with his flag.

Sheringham was also a key figure in the equaliser that counted, heading on a cross from David Beckham for Giggs to score for the 1–1 result, which gave United a lifeline for the return game.

'Juventus will feel they are not the favourites and rightly so. It was a great result for them but they may live to regret us scoring our late goal. I have a gut feeling that we can reproduce the form we showed in the second half when we created three or four chances. Something tells me that we are going to win,' said Alex Ferguson.

He was right, too. His team went to Turin and produced a performance that will live long in the memories of United supporters. Juventus went into the game knowing that scoring an away goal at Old Trafford had given them an enormous advantage, and the situation became even more grim for United when Filippo Inzaghi scored twice in the opening eleven minutes. United were clearly shocked; everything pointed to the end of their glorious adventure. The situation called for an inspired revival and it came via the most obvious source, their captain, Roy Keane – a player who does not give in easily. Leading from the front as usual, the Irishman stormed forward to pull a goal back with a header from a David Beckham corner in the twenty-fourth minute.

Not long after that, Keane brought Zidane down and got a yellow card which he knew would keep him out of the final, if they got there, but it didn't stop him trying his utmost to pull the game round. Sure enough, in the thirty-fourth minute Yorke dived in to head home a centre from Cole.

United were back in business and on the strength of scoring two away goals, were now heading for the final. Twice United hit the woodwork, and the Italians also had their moments with Inzaghi denied a hat-trick by Peter Schmeichel.

Paul Scholes came on as a substitute and wished he hadn't because after just eight minutes he was booked. The second yellow card of the competition put him out of the final, with Keane.

On a happier note, United underlined their superiority on the night when Yorke, going through, was pulled down by the goalkeeper. The referee allowed advantage and Cole put the ball in for a triumphant and memorable 3–2 victory.

Martin Edwards summed up the drama when he said, 'I was nervous at 2–2 because it needed just one break by Juventus and they would be in the final, and when we hit the post twice I began to think is it really going to happen.

'But, in the end, we did it with style and now of course we wonder about the treble. Obviously it would be fantastic if it happened but I still think it would be a miracle.

'It certainly goes down already as a great year because it has not been easy. There have been some tough FA Cup ties, the League is always testing and we came through arguably the hardest group in the Champions League to knock out two major Italian teams.

'I have seen the team grow in stature in the past few years and already it's a dream come true.'

But there was more to come and the chairman's miracle happened as the team gathered momentum to clinch the League from Arsenal by a point, crush Newcastle United at Wembley in the FA Cup and, on 26 May, snatch victory from the jaws of defeat against Bayern Munich in Barcelona to claim the club championship of Europe.

Fortune favours the bold, and it favoured United in Barcelona. They made a dreadful start with a mix-up in the fifth minute that let Mario Basler in to score. He rocketed a free kick through the defensive wall. Even allowing for the shock and distress of conceding such an early goal, United weren't playing particularly well. Beckham justified his midfield role, at times carrying the team's attacking responsibility single-handed, and looking every inch a world-class player, but as a team they were under-performing. They eventually got their game together but still didn't look like scoring. That was the time for Ferguson to step into the action with his masterplan involving the use of substitutes.

With twenty-three minutes to go he put Sheringham on for Jesper Blomqvist and was rewarded by Andy Cole trying a spectacular overhead kick which flew wide. United were dominating now but in their eagerness to push up on attack they were leaving their defence exposed. It took a great save by Schmeichel to push a chip from Stefan Effenberg over the bar and every United fan gulped with relief when substitute Mehmet Scholl hit the post after a piercing run from midfield by Basler.

Still no goal for the Reds, so Ferguson ordered up another substitute with Solskjaer on for Cole – and even bigger gaps appeared in the United defence. Schmeichel made another fine save from Scholl, this time diving full length to push the shot round his post, and two minutes later the woodwork saved them again when Carsten Jancker blazed against the bar. By this time, as Ferguson later admitted, he was ready to accept defeat.

'I started to adjust to losing the game. I was reminding myself that the important thing in defeat would be to keep my dignity and accept that it was just not our year,' he explained.

His players, though, were not ready to accept defeat and in the last few minutes they flung themselves forward. They won a corner which brought Schmeichel pounding up into opposition territory to try to get on the end of Beckham's kick. He said later he was trying to cause some confusion in the Bayern goalmouth and that's exactly what he did. The clock was showing ninety minutes as Giggs helped the ball on for Sheringham to sweep home in a repeat of the rescue act he had performed in the FA Cup final against Newcastle after coming on as a sub.

Now in the injury time allowed by Italian referee Pierluigi Collina, the game seemed to be heading for extra time and the possibility of a golden goal decider. Coach Steve McClaren had started to talk tactics with Ferguson for the extra half-hour, but again the players had other ideas. Three minutes on, they forced another corner which this time was helped on by Sheringham for Solskjaer to lash into the roof of the net.

Basler, who had been substituted by the Germans just a minute from the end of normal time, had been feted by his coach and his team-mates on the bench as he left the field – the scoring hero who seemed to have won the match for Bayern. But then, like the rest of the Bayern team, he watched helplessly in utter amazement as United stepped up the pressure for their super subs to sink their opponents. It was a victory for United's never-say-die spirit and their refusal to accept a defeat that had been staring them in the face.

It was arguably the most sensational finish at this level in the history of English football and it was impossible not to feel a twinge of sympathy for the Germans. Peter Schmeichel said, 'Of course you have to feel a little sorry for Bayern in that situation – but that's the beauty and cruelty of football.' It was Schmeichel's last game for United before he left to play in Portugal.

Ferguson was not in the mood to feel so sympathetic.

'We were the team trying to attack all the time. Nobody can deny that our team plays with a spirit to attack and will to win. We were prepared to take risks and in football when you are prepared to be like that, you deserve to succeed.

'We rode our luck in one spell when they hit the post and the bar but towards the end they were tired out. I am so very proud of my players and my heritage. This is the greatest moment of my life,' he declared.

The stunning 2–1 victory was summed up the next day by a Spanish newspaper under the headline 'Increible'. That's incredible in anyone's language and they went on to explain that it would be 'a minute which would pass into history'.

Sir Matt Busby would have been ninety on the day of the match. The man hailed as the founding father of United had been dead for five years but the fact that his birthday fell on the day of the European Cup final seemed somehow appropriate. Even Ferguson said, 'I think Sir Matt must have been kicking for us up there tonight.' It's not difficult to imagine Busby, the man who last won the European Cup for Manchester United, smiling down on the fellow Scot taking his club to fresh glory.

For United followers who span both games it was a fantastic feeling to see the great European feat achieved again. In 1968, Busby, Sir Bobby Charlton, Harry Gregg and Bill Foulkes, all survivors of the Munich air crash, were inspired by the memory of those who had died. They made no secret of the fact that winning in Europe was a tribute to those who had gone. They were also a team on the point of breaking up because most of the players were at the end of their careers.

Ferguson's players are a much younger team with their futures ahead. The football world lies at their feet. On the evening after the match, thousands turned out to pack the streets of Manchester and welcome home their returning heroes. They sang and shouted themselves hoarse because they knew they had experienced, be it in Barcelona or on television, one of the great sporting occasions of our time.

David Beckham

David Beckham

I was thrilled when I first saw Old Trafford dressed up for a big night in the Champions League. There is definitely a different atmosphere for a European match.

Everything in the build-up helps make it all the more special. Walking to the centre circle with the opposition team, the music, the shaking hands with your opponents, all give you a tingle and I think the fans love it as well.

I shall never forget my debut in Europe because I had the good fortune to mark it with a goal. It was against Galatasaray at Old Trafford in December 1994. The ball was rolled back to me, and although I didn't hit it as cleanly as I might, it went in to crown a great night. We won 4–0. It was a good start in Europe for me.

The game I remember most, though, has got to be the night we came back from two goals down in Turin to beat Juventus 3–2 and go on to become European champions. I am tempted to choose the final but that would be obvious and we wouldn't have been there but for that astonishing performance in the semi-final second leg. I guess everyone wrote us off when we went two down so early in the game. It's certainly not what you want, but we got a first goal, then a second and took command to score a winner. I shall never forget it.

The final itself was, of course, also unforgettable. It was difficult at first to take in, but the atmosphere soon convinced me that we had done it. It was the most exciting atmosphere I have ever experienced and the first thing I did at the end was to run to our supporters in the crowd. I like to celebrate with the fans because I think they deserve a piece of the action.

From a purely personal point of view, one of my best performances was probably the 3–3 draw against Barcelona at Old Trafford in the early group stage of the competition. What made it special was the goal I scored from a free kick. It's always satisfying when one of my free kicks goes in, especially in a big match like this one.

The other game I'll never forget was the quarter-final that season at Old Trafford against Inter Milan, if only for all the hype before the match. Everyone was going on about me being up against Simeone, the player involved in my sending off in the World Cup in France. I don't know exactly what people were expecting, but it didn't happen. He didn't say sorry to me and I definitely didn't apologise to him, but at the end we swapped shirts. We are both professionals. Life goes on and you have to move on with it.

The most impressive ground in my view is the Nou Camp Stadium at Barcelona. Its size, the way it's shaped and the atmosphere of the crowd make playing there something amazing. Playing in the European final there added something to make it the most impressive ground for me outside Old Trafford.

It's always special to play for your club in Europe. It's why you play for a club like Manchester United. Getting into the Champions League is the target every year, and you need the experience it gives you if you are to progress as an international player.

I think that everyone at Old Trafford is aware of the tradition involved in Europe for Manchester United. You know what has happened in the past and you want to be part of it in the future. The attraction for me is playing against the world's best players, as well as giving you a lot more high-level matches.

German teams are always hard to play against and Bayern Munich are particularly difficult. Their players are physically tough and they are well organised.

Individually the most difficult opponent for me has been Roberto Carlos, the Brazilian full-back who plays for Real

Madrid. He is a really great defender with astonishing pace. He likes to get forward which makes it difficult because I am not a very good defender. I just pass him on to our full-back, Gary Neville! I also respect Roberto because he is a nice bloke with a great attitude to the game.

I also like playing against Zidane, Del Piero, Rivaldo and Ronaldo because they are the best.

24

CHASING THE
DREAM

I T WAS soon clear that achieving the elusive treble and
becoming the masters of Europe would be no guarantee of
future success, at least on the foreign front. With the cheering
from Barcelona perhaps still ringing in their ears, United were
brought back down to earth with a bump when they met Lazio in
Monaco at the start of the 1999–2000 season in the Super Cup.

The UEFA showpiece between the European Champions
League winners and the Italian winners of the Cup-Winners'
Cup on 27 August was sandwiched between Premiership fixtures, two days after playing at Coventry and three days before
entertaining Newcastle.

It seemed the occasion meant more to the Romans than
United and Lazio notched a 1–0 win with a thirty-fifth minute
goal from Salas. Sir Alex Ferguson made little effort to hide
his attitude to this interruption to his preparations for the new
season.

'We were tired performers and Lazio were much better than
us,' he said. 'Once they went into the lead, I wasn't prepared
to risk anything in the sense of using other players, Yorke and
Giggs for instance. Lazio showed great commitment but we
were looking at other things. If we had to lose a game, it had
to be this one. The Super Cup doesn't determine anything. The

Champions League is a better barometer. That's the best test.'

United's opening match in Group D of the Champions League, involving Croatia Zagreb, Sturm Gratz and Olympique Marseille, did not produce any fireworks either. A goalless draw against the Croatians at Old Trafford emphasised Ferguson's view that UEFA's decision to extend the competition by introducing a second group phase would make it even more difficult to win again. The visitors illustrated exactly the point he was making with a determined, defensive display that showed how easy it is for the minnows to frustrate the big fish. The extended tournament was full of tiddlers looking for shock results.

Ferguson commented ruefully, 'You have got to give credit to Croatia. They sat in midfield and made it difficult for us. They got the result they were looking for. They were disciplined at the back. They took no chances and were looking for an away draw. We perhaps face a different kind of challenge now and we must find another way to play against this kind of team before we meet the clubs who have the same ambitions as ourselves.'

The next fixture put them up against more underdogs in the shape of Sturm Gratz, but this time United played like true reigning European champions, coming home from Austria with an impressive 3–0 win. The fact that Sturm had lost their opening match against Marseille worked in United's favour because it meant that to stand any chance at all, the Austrians had to try to win the game. And try they did, especially in the second half. With either a little more luck or better finishing, depending on your point of view, they could have had five goals. It was an edgy period for the champions, but they kept their composure and after changes to tighten up in midfield, they secured a better share of possession and Sturm faded. The whole game fell away, but that suited United who had done the job in the first half by scoring three goals through Roy Keane, Dwight Yorke and Andy Cole.

As Ferguson summed up, 'I was pleased to see not just the three points but the response from the players, who are well aware of the importance of establishing a presence in the competition if we are to get anywhere near repeating last season's success.

'At this stage, the standard of the teams in a group can vary, but as Sturm demonstrated in the second half and as Zagreb showed with their difficult-to-beat approach in Manchester, you cannot take anything for granted.'

Gradually picking up momentum, United made their presence felt against the stronger opposition of Marseille, a 2–1 win at Old Trafford putting them at the top of their group, one point ahead of their French rivals.

The outlook didn't look too promising just before the interval when Henning Berg slipped and lost the ball for Ibrahim Bakayoko to race clear and beat Raimond Van der Gouw with a fierce drive. United picked themselves up after the interval to do more of the pressing and step up their strikes on goal. It looked for a time as if it would be one of those non-scoring nights as Cole, Yorke and Solskjaer all squandered chances.

But as well as perseverance, United revealed their capacity once more for producing magic moments late in a game. Ten minutes from the end, David Beckham lofted a free kick to the far post where Jaap Stam climbed to head the ball back across goal. Although caught with his back to the target, Cole hit an overhead shot which flew past Stephane Porato, the French goalkeeper. Shortly after that, Paul Scholes ran in the winner.

Afterwards, the United manager said, 'It took something special to beat Marseille. Andy Cole provided it with the kind of instinctive finish that he is so good at. His reflexes are razor sharp and he hit the ball so cleanly that it took the keeper by surprise. Then Scholes dug out the winner from nothing. He has such quick feet he took the ball clean through on his own.'

Henning Berg finished the match a mightily relieved player because it was a key win, especially in the light of their return in France the following week when they lost 1–0, ending an unbeaten run of eighteen games in the Champions League. Mark Bosnich, making his Champions League debut, just had no answer to a piercing thrust from defence by William Gallas. In the seventieth minute, Gallas took a return from Stephane Dalmat and hit his shot beyond Bosnich's reach. United fought back spiritedly, and in injury time Ole Gunnar Solskjaer headed in a Beckham free kick only for Jaap Stam to be ruled offside. What had seemed an equaliser was disallowed.

Sir Alex was in a grim mood on the flight home after setting his heart on a win, which would have virtually clinched qualification for the second phase. As it was, United had to hit the road again to play in Croatia, though at least Sturm Gratz had done them a massive favour by beating Zagreb to maintain a gap between the top two and the bottom two. Marseille were now top on 9 points with United on 7, Zagreb 4 and Gratz 3.

Ferguson said, 'We couldn't deny Marseille their victory. There wasn't much between the two teams, but we can play better. We lost a bad goal and I wish it had been earlier to have had more time to get back at them because once we were behind we raised our game. In fact, we played well and were a shade unlucky not to have snatched an equaliser.

'At least we showed we are capable of raising our game and that's always an important quality. We are a good team and we are still there. The name of the game at this stage is to qualify and we are capable of going through. I can indeed see a light at the end of the tunnel.'

It was as if the manager had talked himself round into a more hopeful mood, an optimism justified in the next game. A 2–1 win in Croatia hoisted his team to the top of the group and assured them of a place in the second stage with a fixture to spare. The champions could breathe again and as Sir Alex said, 'Suddenly our whole position has been transformed and a big black cloud has been blown away.'

David Beckham set United on their way with one of his free-kick specials after Paul Scholes had been brought down in the thirty-second minute. His viciously swerving kick from just outside the penalty area left Tomislav Butina grabbing fresh air. Just into the second half Roy Keane made sure of victory when he fired in a twenty-five-yard volley after a centre from Denis Irwin had been headed into his path. Robert Prosinecki's goal in the last minute was too late to influence the outcome.

Qualification for the second phase confirmed that there would be no change of mind following the controversial decision to pull out of the FA Cup in order to compete in the World Club Championship in Brazil. This was to back up England's bid to stage the World Cup of 2006. There had been a slim hope that if they had been knocked out of Europe, they might have been able to cope with the FA Cup, as well as the January trip to South America. But there was no chance now of a late switch back into the domestic cup competition. It was full steam ahead in Europe with just the final fixture of Group D to play against Sturm Gratz at Old Trafford.

It was hardly a spectacular celebration with a low-tempo display by the Reds until they found more pace and purpose after the break. Ten minutes into the second half Ole Gunnar Solskjaer rounded off a spell of sustained pressure involving two corners by scoring with a cracking shot from the edge of the box. Roy Keane settled matters twelve minutes later when he smacked in a rebound from the bar following an effort from Henning Berg.

Ivica Vastic scored a late penalty for the visitors after he had been pulled back by Ryan Giggs, which prompted a late flurry of attacks, but Bosnich stood firm. The United goalkeeper made a particularly fine full-length save from Hannes Reinmayr in injury time to ensure his team finished group winners on 13 points, three in front of Marseille who went through as runners-up.

Ferguson concluded, 'It was a difficult group for us. At first there is relief that you have avoided the major clubs from Italy, Germany and Spain, but it can lull you into a false sense of security.'

There was no doubting the strength of Group B with Fiorentina, Valencia and Bordeaux their next opponents. Fiorentina emphasised the more acute challenge by opening with a 2–0 win against the Reds in Florence, a defeat which came as a huge shock to players and fans alike, and for a while, memories of all those humiliating losses over the years against Italian clubs came vividly to life.

It seemed at first as if Sir Alex Ferguson's pre-match words about United having caught up with the skills and techniques practised in Italy were just so much whistling in the dark. Knocking Inter Milan and Juventus out of the Champions League the previous season had suggested perhaps that Fiorentina would be there for the taking, but the reality was quite different. Gabriel Batistuta and Abel Balbo, their two Argentinian stars, blasted in goals, leaving United stunned and facing an enormous task to qualify from the second group phase.

United were undone by two horrendous errors. Roy Keane, of all players, was the culprit in the twenty-fourth minute. The captain fluffed an attempted clearance and Gabriel Batistuta pounced to give the Italians the lead. Keane explained afterwards, 'I just made a blind pass and I'm devastated by it. We were dominating the game until my mistake and then everything changed. We could have won if I hadn't blundered. This is the European Cup and what do you expect when you make mistakes like that?' he asked.

The second goal after fifty-two minutes came courtesy of Henning Berg whose weak clearance on the right flank was picked up by Batistuta for a cross which Balbo hammered home.

Ferguson remained upbeat because, defensive howlers apart, there was little wrong with their general form, as they showed when they flew to Tokyo the following week to become the first British club to win the Inter Continental trophy in the form of the Toyota Cup, and earn the perhaps slightly enhanced title of World Champions. They beat Palmeiras 1–0 to win this trial of strength between the respective league champions of Europe and South America, and ironically the hero for United was none other than Roy Keane who scored at the far post from a cross by Ryan Giggs after thirty-five minutes. Mark Bosnich also had a fine game but Ferguson kept a lid on the celebrations.

'The World Championship is very special and I was both proud and thrilled for my players when they lifted the Cup, but we won't let ourselves be carried away. This was a one-match occasion and we won't be strutting around on the strength of winning just one game, however prestigious it might be.

'The folly of setting too much store by one match or perform-ance was never better illustrated than by the experience of Roy Keane. Before we went to Japan, he was cursing his luck after an out-of-character pass which opened the door for Fiorentina to beat us in the Champions League. Nobody on the bench could believe it but at the same time there was no anger because this is a man who has made a million passes without involving an error like that.

It must have been a particularly sweet moment for our captain when he scored the winning goal against Palmeiras. Not only did he resume his normal immaculate service, he collected a trophy on a world stage after missing the European final against Bayern Munich through suspension after doing so much to get us to Barcelona.'

Keane stayed in the news and ended weeks of speculation by announcing that he would be signing a new contract to play on with the Reds. He told his team-mates just before they went out against Valencia at Old Trafford, a boost that might go a long way towards explaining a decisive 3–0 victory, which put them level on points with Valencia and just a point behind Fiorentina, the leaders.

With Keane safely in the fold for the future, the captain emphasised his value by scoring the opening goal after thirty-eight minutes, his fourth in Europe of the season. It was a magnificent performance against the fancied Spanish team. Ole Gunnar Solskjaer, enjoying one of his rare starts after his four goals against Everton, sidefooted United's second goal home from David Beckham's cross a couple of minutes after the interval. Paul Scholes neatly headed in Beckham's seventieth minute free kick to make the result safe and warn their rivals that the sluggish start to the season was now behind them.

As Sir Alex Ferguson put it, 'We have had a ropey spell but the confidence is back. There is no disguising my delight because it was a game we had to win. We will certainly be ready for it in March. We are always better in the springtime and now everything is looking good for us.'

The Reds kept in touch with foreign fields during the Champions League hibernation by flying to Brazil in January to take part in FIFA's stylishly named World Club Championship along with Corinthians, Raja, Al Nassr, Real Madrid, Necaxa, Vasco de Gama and South Melbourne representing various global areas. Many critics said the trip was an unmitigated disaster. The results were nothing to boast about – a draw against Necaxa, defeat against Vasco de Gama and a modest 2–0 win against the part-timers of South Australia put them out of the competition. That was not the end of it. There was another well-publicised dismissal for David Beckham, and a barrage of criticism claimed that United scored an own-goal with a poor public relations effort. All this was on top of pulling out of the FA Cup to take part in the Rio de Janeiro jamboree, an action felt keenly even by United fans who had wanted their team to defend the title.

At least it was a sunshine break, and as Andy Cole, made captain for their final game against the Australians, declared on arriving back in Manchester, 'We have come home to win the championship. Results have gone our way while we were away. We are just a point behind Leeds [the leaders] with two games in hand. We are in a healthy position and confident of what we can do.'

Gary Neville pointed out, 'Some people were worried about the effect going to Brazil at this time of the year might have had on us physically, but it has not been a problem. We have had some fantastic training sessions, and in the matches we have proved that our stamina is as good as anyone's.'

The team, continuing to do well in the Premiership, eagerly looked forward to picking up the European challenge in March with back-to-back fixtures against Bordeaux. The first match against the Frenchmen brought a 2–0 victory. The United manager said he was still waiting for his men to explode into better form, but moving up the group table to second place just one point behind Fiorentina didn't seem bad to most observers.

Ryan Giggs, who had been the star man in a 2–2 draw at Wimbledon at the weekend, simply carried on from where he had left off at Selhurst Park. Scoring the first goal and crossing for Teddy Sheringham to score the second was a good contribution and put the team in good heart for the fixture in France.

It takes more than heart to win at Champions League level, and the return match wasn't going too well when Raimond Van der Gouw made a rare error. He allowed a shot from Michel Pavon to slip through his gloves, which gave the home team a ninth-minute lead. But when Bordeaux had Lilian Laslandes sent off in the twenty-third minute for two yellow cards collected within the space of a minute, United bucked up their ideas. Roy Keane forced home a thirty-third minute equaliser at the second attempt after Ulrich Rame had blocked his initial shot.

The ten men of Bordeaux put up a stiffer resistance than might have been expected but Ole Gunnar Solskjaer found the answer. He was brought on to replace Denis Irwin with eight minutes of the match left and within sixty seconds he had slotted home the winner.

It hadn't been United at their best, but they were still good enough to bring about Bordeaux's second home European defeat in nine years. They knew, though, that even with home advantage, they faced a tough challenge against Fiorentina in their next match. But they shook off their stuttering inconsistencies at Old Trafford, swept away all the uncertainties and established themselves once again as a team playing like true European champions.

They beat the Italians 3–1 and booked their place in the quarter-finals with a game to spare and they did it in the most resilient of ways. After fifteen minutes Gabriel Batistuta stunned them with a wonder goal, a rocket from thirty yards which flew past Mark Bosnich. Ferguson said later that it had taken his breath away! United took just four minutes to equalise, Andy Cole controlling David Beckham's cross, turning and delivering the perfect reply.

United stepped up the tempo and in the thirty-third minute Roy Keane was in the right place to latch on to a rebound from Henning Berg's header against the bar. They made the game safe after Fabio Rossitto had been sent off for tripping Dwight Yorke from behind. Yorke took advantage a few minutes later by stealing in to head home a cross from Ryan Giggs.

'I always prepare my teams to come strongly around March

and April because that is when the moment of truth arrives and you have to win the big games. We do a lot of hard stamina work in training around New Year time and I think this pays off in the final two or three months,' explained Ferguson.

'It was our best performance of the season, no doubt about that, and if we maintain that level we can go on to win the European Cup again. Up to that point we had been playing in fits and starts but against Fiorentina we rekindled the form and spirit of last season's achievements,' he added.

Sir Bobby Charlton believed it would prove a turning point.

'We don't often beat the big Italian teams,' he said, 'but we didn't just beat Fiorentina, we humiliated them. Even before they had a man sent off, I didn't feel we were in any trouble.

'The Italians have tough defenders and they don't give you much space, but our boys were terrific with crisp, fast passing. It is very encouraging for what lies ahead. It looks now as if the team have picked up the challenge and I think they are fully capable of winning both the Premiership at home and at the same time successfully defending their title as champions of Europe.'

Ferguson added, 'I think you will see a different United now. The big occasion seems to suit my players and they are all big occasions now until the end of the season. They were focused and I think that is how it will be from now on.'

First though, they had to complete their group fixtures and play Valencia in Spain. The match was important to Valencia because there was still the possibility that Fiorentina could pip them for second place. The only issue for United was trying to win the group so that they would meet a second-placed team in the quarter-finals.

The first half in Spain was an excellent exhibition with both sides producing some cracking football. Mark Bosnich pulled off several good saves, notably from Kily Gonzalez. At the other end, Canizares was equally agile, stopping a fierce header from Teddy Sheringham. United breathed a sigh of relief when Jocelyn Angloma smashed a shot against the post, but after an hour the game petered out. Valencia realised Fiorentina were losing against Bordeaux, which meant a draw would be sufficient to see them through. United were quick to catch on. A draw would be good enough for them to win the group. Both teams eased up and the match finished in a tame goalless draw. United had 13 points, three ahead of Valencia.

The first leg of the quarter-final against Real Madrid was played in Spain, and most critics considered the 0–0 draw a good result in the Bernabeu Stadium, but Sir Alex Ferguson was not at all satisfied. The manager described United's performance as their worst in a big game for a long time. He said his players had failed to tackle, especially in the first half, and he was disappointed with the amount of possession they had needlessly given away.

'We expect our players to be perfect in these things,' he declared. 'Mark Bosnich kept us in the game. It was a relief to get a draw.'

What went wrong? Ferguson reckoned that the runaway 7–1 victory over West Ham three days earlier had lulled his men into complacency. The display against the Hammers had been awesome, and a ten-point lead at the top of the table with just seven games remaining looked good for the championship, but Ferguson had the retention of their European crown firmly in his sights as well. He had desperately wanted the reassurance of scoring an away goal.

The atmosphere for the second leg at Old Trafford was tremendous and expectations were high, but their luck ran out. With a cruel twist of irony, their hero captain, Roy Keane, put the skids under his team with an own-goal. He slid the ball past Bosnich, trying to cut out a cross from Michel Salgado at the near post. The twenty-first minute blunder knocked the Reds groggy, while at the same time giving the Spanish team a lift. They went on to produce the level of football which entitled them to go through to the semi-finals to meet United's old rivals, Bayern Munich.

As Sir Alex said, 'Sometimes it goes for you, and sometimes it doesn't.'

You know what he means when you consider the hand-ball by a Real player as Andy Cole jumped in the goalmouth, which went unnoticed by the referee.

United staged a tremendous bid to pull the game round, but were so gung-ho, with caution thrown to the wind, that they got caught on the break and punished by Raul who scored twice in three minutes in the second half, putting the visitors a daunting three goals up.

Still United fought back with a marvellous goal from David Beckham who jinked through cleverly in the sixty-fourth minute and a penalty by Paul Scholes after Keane had been brought down by Steve McManaman. It added up to a hard-fought 3–2 defeat and was a match to remember. The Reds played some brilliant attacking football in the second half with Ryan Giggs in bewitching form, and at least with the league title as good as in the bag, they knew they would be back the following season.

Keane was in a defiant mood.

'We are bitterly disappointed, but we'll be back next year and put it right,' he declared. 'My own-goal changed the whole complex of the match. They knew we had to score twice after that, and that they could afford to sit back and pick us off. They did that very well. They were bad goals we gave away. We've done that a couple of times this year. You can't concede three goals at home in the quarter-finals of the European Cup against a good team and expect to go through. That says it all.

'We kept going but to score four goals in the second half was always going to be difficult. We gave it our best shot but it wasn't to be. We hoped a comeback would be on when we got the first goal, but it was too much for us. Last year we had a bit of luck winning the treble, but we didn't get that luck against Real Madrid.

'We are disappointed for everyone but we have no divine right to win. In football you get highs and lows and unfortunately this is a low for Manchester United. We have still got a league championship to win so it won't be too difficult to pick ourselves up. Hopefully, we can win the title now and then next year we'll come back in this competition and win it.'

Bold words from skipper Keane, but he got at least one half of his plan for the future right. While Real Madrid went on to beat Valencia 3–0 in the final in Paris, United did indeed go on to win the championship, and by a record 18 points, to book themselves another tilt at Europe, still chasing the dream!

25

THE NEXT STEP

U nited returned to the European trail in even more determined mood after the Real Madrid disaster, but it proved
to be a rocky road. Qualifying in the two group stages was
erratic and they again came to grief at the quarter-final stage,
ironically against Bayern Munich, the team they had beaten to
become European champions in 1999.

Sir Alex Ferguson was deeply hurt and responded with the
£19 million acquisition of the Dutch international striker, Ruud
van Nistelrooy, and the promise of further reinforcements
designed to produce a squad better equipped for Europe.

After securing the Premiership by Easter with another sub-
stantial margin of points, their continued domination of domestic football was once more evident. What concerned those
within the club and the following outside was the apparent
inability of the team to lift themselves to the level needed for a
consistent challenge in Europe.

Roy Keane pulled no punches in his analysis of the situation
and what needed to be done after losing to Bayern 1–0 at Old
Trafford and then crashing to a 2–1 defeat in the second leg in
Munich. He declared, 'Maybe it is the end of the road for this
team, I'm not sure. Maybe it is time to move on. We have given
our all and we are just not good enough. You have to face
the facts. The signs have been there this season against PSV

Eindhoven, Anderlecht, and Panathinaikos. We were lucky to get through the first group stage even. It's all very well and good winning the Premiership but we need to step up another level. Some of the teams in Europe, like Real Madrid, are the benchmark for us. Teams like Real seem to be going further away and we seem to be going further behind. They have proved themselves a great team and are through to another semi-final. It's very hard to take. The great teams get back to finals and win them again and again. It just goes to show we are not a great team but an average team. We're not good enough in a lot of areas. It's hard to admit that we are not good enough, but it is a fact.

'It's time to bring in new faces. Everybody knows now that a few new faces would freshen things up. A lot of players, including myself, should be worried because we just haven't performed. It's not just this match, it's been throughout the season. But that's not my department, it's up to the manager and the rest of the staff.

'Before the game we all thought we would get through, despite the disappointing result at Old Trafford. But to go two goals down left us too much to do. You have to defend as a team and to lose two goals was a disastrous start for us. We had a go in the second half but that is the least you would expect from us. I don't think they were the better team. I don't think there are many better teams than us when we actually perform. But it is no good standing here and saying that – you have to go and do the business, and we have not done it this season or even last season.'

Harsh words from the skipper for which he later apologised, saying he hadn't meant any disrespect to his team-mates, the manager or the club. Curiously, nobody had accused him of talking out of turn because everyone appreciated that while disappointment doubtless coloured his views, basically what he was saying was right.

There was no doubting the disappointment of the manager either, although he did urge a sense of perspective, saying that the European misery should not be allowed to diminish in any way the achievement of winning three successive league titles.

After the Munich defeat against a manager he both likes and respects, Ottmar Hitzfeld, Sir Alex said, 'We look at Europe to measure our progress as a football team and we failed, which is a big disappointment. The experience leaves you in reflective mood, wondering what should be the next step forward. We want to swing on that star and we are within touching distance without being quite there yet. It was the kind of set-back which cuts right through you and leaves you stunned. One of the big problems is that you feel you have let so many people down.

'I can assure all our supporters that everything is under review and that I know exactly what needs to be done. It's not a time for hasty decisions because first we must drag ourselves out of the depths.'

Sir Alex had plenty to think about. Roy Keane was right when he said that the signs of failure had been there almost from the start of the campaign. The opening group brought United up against Anderlecht, Dynamo Kiev and PSV Eindhoven with the curtain going up at Old Trafford against the Belgian club United had beaten 10–0 in their very first European Cup round in 1956. This tie didn't present any problems either. Andy Cole celebrated his return to the England team by scoring a hat-trick in the 5–1 win. That gave him his fifteenth goal in the European championship, one better than Denis Law's record which had stood for thirty-two years.

Cole opened the scoring after fifteen minutes, and with a penalty from Denis Irwin, and a goal from Teddy Sheringham, United were three up at half-time. Ryan Giggs was in devastating form as Cole completed his hat-trick in the second half, the lanky Anderlecht centre-forward Jan Koller scoring in between.

It was an impressive onslaught that had the Belgian coach, Aime Anthuenis, saying, 'United are one of the best teams in Europe, if not the best. And they are quite possibly the best side in the world. At times tonight, their football was from another planet. It is true we found it very difficult to handle Giggs but there again we found it difficult to control the rest of their team.'

The trip to Kiev for the next game brought the high-flying Reds back down to earth. The manager was satisfied with a point from a goalless draw, but not overjoyed with the performance.

Raimond Van der Gouw, enjoying a rare appearance in the absence of the injured Fabien Barthez, said, 'I was very happy with a clean sheet and it was nice to be playing again. We should have scored in the first half but realistically we should be happy to be top of our group with four points.'

It had been a satisfactory start, but then came the first big jolt of the competition – a 3–1 defeat against Eindhoven in Holland that slid them down the group table to third. With a big Premiership match at Arsenal coming up at the weekend, Sir Alex left David Beckham, Ryan Giggs and Andy Cole on the bench, but this time his famous rotation policy didn't work out in the way he anticipated. Paul Scholes shot United into an ideal opening lead with a penalty after only three minutes, but Wilfred Bouma, Van Bommel and Mateja Kezman gave PSV a deserved win.

Roy Keane warned, 'We need to get our finger out now. There is no need to panic. We are not going to get too heavy about this one. We have enjoyed success over the last few years and we want that to continue. There is still a lot to play for.

'We have PSV at home next and we will be aiming to dominate at Old Trafford. They showed they had a fighting spirit in the first game and you have to give them credit. They battled hard and took their goals well, but hopefully it will be a different story in our next game.'

And indeed it was with United back on course with a 3–1 win and heading the group table again. Things could easily have gone wrong for although Teddy Sheringham gave United a ninth-minute lead, Mark van Bommel equalised with just a quarter of an hour to go and the Reds were staring at a draw. However, Paul Scholes and Dwight Yorke, replacing Sheringham, each scored in the last eight minutes as the team rounded off the match in fine style. Ryan Giggs was again a top man and summed up the mood well when he said, 'It has been a strange group so far and just goes to prove there are no easy games.'

For strange read nearly calamitous as United crashed 2–1 against Anderlecht in Belgium and left themselves with a win-or-bust situation for their final group game against Dynamo Kiev at Old Trafford. Tomasz Radzinski, a Polish-born naturalised Canadian, was the man who did the damage with goals in the fifteenth and thirty-third minutes. United's only reply was a penalty from Denis Irwin in the thirty-sixth minute. United did better in the second half but as Irwin summed up, 'I have not played in a United side for a long time that gifted so many chances. We could easily have been four or five goals down in the first half.'

It was United's second away defeat, a worrying statistic at this early stage of the competition. There had been nothing wrong with their home form, however, and although there were anxious spells against Kiev in the Old Trafford decider, a goal from Teddy Sheringham, his twelfth of the season, after seventeen minutes for a 1–0 win was enough to see them through to the second stage.

It probably wasn't the right time for Roy Keane to launch his 'prawn sandwich' attack on fat-cat supporters. Stung by the failure of the crowd to get behind the team, and no doubt still sweating after George Demetradze had let them off the hook by missing an open goal for an equaliser five minutes from the end, he said, 'Our fans away from home are as good as any, but at Old Trafford you sometimes wonder if they understand the game of football. We are 1–0 up and then there are a couple of stray passes and they are getting on the players' backs. It's just not on. Away from home our fans are fantastic, but at home they have a few drinks and probably their prawn sandwiches and they don't realise what's going on out on the pitch. These people want fantasy football but they should get in the real world.'

The skipper later apologised but the real issue was their stuttering form as they looked at the next group made up of Valencia, Sturm Gratz and Panathinaikos. So it was heartening for United supporters to see their team beat Panathinaikos 3–1 at Old Trafford in their Group A opener.

United saluted Teddy Sheringham for his goal three minutes after the interval after a goalless first half. The team desperately needed a breakthrough and not for the first time the Londoner rose to the occasion with a blistering finish after Dwight Yorke had flicked on a massive goalkick from Fabien Barthez. As Sir Alex Ferguson said afterwards, 'Teddy keeps scoring vital goals for us and it sums up his season. He is having a fantastic time.'

It was Sheringham's fourteenth goal of the season, equalling his best in the three years he had played for United, following his transfer from Spurs – a convincing achievement for a thirty-four-year-old who had been in two minds about signing a new contract.

It wasn't exactly plain sailing, though, because Giorgios Karagounis equalised with a Beckham-type free kick in the sixty-fifth minute, and it needed two great goals from Paul Scholes to see the Reds home. For his first, Mikael Silvestre, after a great run, found him in the right place at the right time. His second, a cheeky chip, left the manager purring, 'It was the best-quality game seen on this ground for two or three years. It was the ideal way to start the group, just everything was perfect.'

A trip to Austria to play Sturm Gratz brought not only a satisfying 2–0 win but relief that the team had at last put on a convincing display away from home following the Eindhoven and Anderlecht defeats. As Gary Neville said, 'We have struggled away from home in Europe this season and to win this tournament you have to play well away, score goals and look like you are going to hurt teams. We did that when we won the competition in 1999. We didn't do it for a large part of last season and neither have we in this campaign until tonight. It was important against Sturm Gratz that we put a marker down to say we are back. We needed to do that. It was the game in which we had to re-invent ourselves. We had to look like we were going to score and we did. That was more pleasing for me than the clean sheet.'

Paul Scholes gave United the lead in the eighteenth minute after being set up by Sheringham, and Ryan Giggs, coming on for the last ten minutes, raced in from the left to score the other. So United went into the winter break with a maximum six points from three games, leading the group.

Valencia, as expected, provided a more searching examination in the back-to-back games in February. A good disciplined performance in the Mestalla Stadium for a point from a goalless game kept the campaign on track. Sir Alex Ferguson was pleased and said, 'When you have a defence playing like that it breeds confidence through the whole team. We were up against a good attacking side in front of their own fans but we stood strong and performed well. We were tremendous and we were up against two top strikers in Aimar and Carew. That helped us to a point that has put us so close to the quarter-finals. We now aim to get the result at Old Trafford next week that could put us through with two second phase fixtures still to go.'

United were bubbling, indeed English football generally was enjoying a good moment on the European front, following victories for both Arsenal and Leeds in the Champions League and with Liverpool also going well in the UEFA Cup. So expectations were high for the visit to Valencia the following week, perhaps unreasonably so, because this was the team which last year had gone all the way to the final.

Even so, the prospects looked good when Ryan Giggs opened up the Spanish defence with a thrust down the left flank, and a neat exchange of passes enabled Andy Cole to give United a twelfth minute lead. Unfortunately, five minutes later a recurrence of his hamstring problem forced Giggs out of the game and without him United lost their touch of special magic. Slowly but surely, Valencia came back into the game and equalised for a 1–1 result just three minutes from the end of normal time. The Spaniards needed help with Wes Brown the luckless victim of an own-goal. Trying to intercept a cross from Vicente he could only stab the ball past Fabien Barthez. It was a cruel misfortune for the youngster because up to that point he had not put a foot wrong in an immaculate partnership with Jaap Stam.

The manager had nothing but sympathy for him and said, 'The own-goal was unfortunate but these things happen. Fortunately, Wes is not that young now so he will recover OK. He knows he is playing in a man's game. There's nothing unusual about the players qualifying the hard way. Happily, they invariably respond to the last call.'

The feeling was that while United, with a two-point lead, were still on track to qualify for the knock-out stage, they would have to be on their guard against Panathinaikos in Athens and even at home to Sturm Gratz who, thanks to two wins over the Greeks, were now level on six points with Valencia.

Panathinaikos did indeed surprise the Manchester men who turned in one of their most disappointing displays for a long time. Giorgios Seitaridis gave the Greeks a twenty-fifth minute lead and it wasn't until injury time that Paul Scholes grabbed an equaliser. The point gave United one foot in the quarter-finals. Only a three-goal defeat against Sturm Gratz in the final game could stop them qualifying, but the matter which concerned both the captain and the manager was the poor performance.

Roy Keane was in critical mood again when he said, 'We could have been three or four goals down if it hadn't been for Fabien Barthez. We have to step it up and we're not through yet.'

Sir Alex was even more scathing. 'If we play like that we could lose heavily next week. It was a poor performance. We got off to a bad start. The concentration and passing were not there and we gave them an edge.'

To a man, they knew that they would have to improve dramatically to stand a chance of getting anywhere near their European triumph of two years ago, and Ferguson demanded an improvement against the Austrians.

'We need a top performance, not just to wrap up a place in the last eight, but because there are other considerations. I am insisting that we win in a manner that will reveal the true capability of the team. I want a performance in keeping with the standards we have set ourselves over the past few years. It's a matter of not only returning to that level for our own sense of pride but in order to send out the right messages to the rest of the teams who have reached the knock-out stage. We really let ourselves down against Panathinaikos and the only way to get it out of our system it to get back quickly to normal service,' he said.

To make sure everybody got the point, he dumped David Beckham, Dwight Yorke, Andy Cole, Wes Brown and Phil

Neville on the substitutes' bench. Something certainly seemed to make a difference as his team romped home 3–0 against the Austrians at Old Trafford with goals from Nicky Butt, Teddy Sheringham – his twentieth of the season – and Roy Keane.

Sir Alex was in a much happier frame of mind as he explained, 'The performance illustrated perfectly where we had been going wrong. Our concentration level had been wayward in our previous attempts for the win that would have moved us into the last eight of the competition with no messing about, but against the Austrians it was clear early in the game that there was a resolution and focus to make sure there was no slip-up this time.

'We attacked from the start in a positive way and it took only five minutes for Nicky Butt to put us ahead. It was pleasing to see Luke Chadwick figuring in the build-up and again in the third goal scored by Roy Keane. He played with a lot of promise and has a good future.

'But it was the overall approach of the team that really pleased me as we made up for our lapses and not only qualified in a convincing way but sent out the right message to the other teams left in the competition.

'Of course, it would have been nice to have won the group but that was the price we had to pay for letting ourselves down in a couple of the other group games. Obviously the standard goes up another notch now because everyone left in has real quality, but again anyone who draws us will know they are in for a tough tie, especially as we have reminded everyone that when we concentrate properly we are as good as the next guy.'

Brave words, but unfortunately the quarter-finals against Bayern Munich found the Reds struggling again. The team were beaten 1–0 at Old Trafford in the first leg and 2–1 in the return.

United played well in the first half of the opening leg but Ryan Giggs, who early on had looked capable of winning the match on his own, tired and Bayern had much the better of the

Fabien Barthez

second half. Stefan Effenberg took over the running of the game and Fabien Barthez came under fierce fire. He knew little about a cracking effort from Alexander Zickler which rattled the bar and he was helpless when their other substitute, Paulo Sergio, rammed in an eighty-sixth minute winner. The Reds were devastated. It was exactly the scenario they wanted to avoid with an away goal counting double in the event of a drawn tie. The Germans were firmly in the driving seat.

Ferguson rallied his troops and insisted, 'It won't be easy but we have players capable of opening up the game in Munich. They have a good appetite and the tie is still open. We have got to score over there, and if we do, then the game changes. We simply have to do ourselves justice in the return. It was a similar situation against Juventus two years ago and we can draw on it. Let's get the bandwagon rolling again.'

Ottmar Hitzfeld refused to talk in terms of revenge for the 1999 final defeat in Barcelona, but it was soon evident that his players were in no mood to see victory snatched from them a second time. By half-time Bayern were two goals up and it could easily have been twice as many. Giovane Elber struck the first goal after only five minutes and Mehmet Scholl got the other five minutes before the break.

Ryan Giggs put United back into the game early in the second half with a clever lob over Oliver Kahn from a nicely weighted ball forward from Paul Scholes. Immediately there were hopes of another famous late recovery but this time there was no way back. Luke Chadwick, a late substitute, caught the eye with one tricky run but Bayern had no intention of repeating their Nou Camp collapse and Manchester United were out.

However, another championship success put them straight back into the Champions League, and in his final season as manager of Manchester United Sir Alex Ferguson will be more intent than ever on a further taste of European glory.

STATISTICS

Manchester United Against the Rest

A club by club guide to the sides United have met in Europe since 1956 (in 1956–57, home games were played at Maine Road because Old Trafford did not have floodlights).

The European Cup and Champions League

Anderlecht	12 September	1956	A	W	2–0	
Anderlecht	26 September	1956	H	W	10–0	
Anderlecht	13 November	1968	H	W	3–0	
Anderlecht	27 November	1968	A	L	1–3	
Anderlecht	13 September	2000	H	W	3–1 Champions League	
Anderlecht	24 October	2000	A	L	1–2 Champions League	
Barcelona	19 October	1994	H	D	2–2 Champions League	
Barcelona	2 November	1994	A	L	0–4 Champions League	
Barcelona	16 August	1998	H	D	3–3 Champions League	
Barcelona	25 November	1998	A	D	3–3 Champions League	
Athletic Bilbao	16 January	1957	A	L	3–5	
Athletic Bilbao	6 February	1957	H	W	3–0	
Partizan Belgrade	13 April	1966	A	L	0–2 Semi-final (1)	
Partizan Belgrade	20 April	1966	H	W	1–0 Semi-final (2)	
Red Star Belgrade	14 January	1958	H	W	2–1	

Red Star Belgrade	5 February	1958	A	D	3–3	
Benfica	2 February	1966	H	W	3–2	
Benfica	9 March	1966	A	W	5–1	
Benfica	29 May	1968	N	W	4–1	(aet) FINAL
Bordeaux	1 March	2000	H	W	2–0	Champions League
Bordeaux	7 March	2000	A	W	2–1	Champions League
Brondby	21 October	1998	A	W	6–2	Champions League
Brondby	4 November	1998	H	W	5–0	Champions League
Borussia Dortmund	17 October	1956	H	W	3–2	
Borussia Dortmund	21 November	1956	A	D	0–0	
Borussia Dortmund	4 April	1997	A	L	0–1	Semi-final (1)
Borussia Dortmund	23 April	1997	H	L	0–1	Semi-final (2)
PSV Eindhoven	26 September	2000	A	L	1–3	Champions League
PSV Eindhoven	18 October	2000	H	W	3–1	Champions League
Fenerbahce	16 October	1996	A	W	2–0	Champions League
Fenerbahce	30 October	1996	H	L	0–1*	Champions League
Feyenoord	22 October	1997	H	W	2–1	Champions League
Feyenoord	5 November	1997	A	W	3–1	Champions League
Fiorentina	23 November	1999	A	L	2–0	Champions League
Fiorentina	15 March	2000	H	W	3–1	Champions League
Galatasaray	20 October	1993	H	D	3–3	
Galatasaray	3 November	1993	A	D	0–0	
Galatasaray	28 September	1994	A	D	0–0	Champions League
Galatasaray	7 December	1994	H	W	4–0	Champions League
Gomik Zabrze	28 February	1968	H	W	2–0	
Gomik Zabrze	13 March	1968	A	L	0–1	
IFK Gothenburg	14 September	1994	H	W	4–2	Champions League
IFK Gothenburg	23 November	1994	A	L	1–3	Champions League
Sturm Graz	22 September	1999	A	W	3–0	Champions League
Sturm Graz	2 November	1999	H	W	2–1	Champions League
Sturm Graz	6 December	2000	A	W	2–0	Champions League
Sturm Graz	13 March	2001	H	W	3–0	Champions League
Honved	15 September	1993	A	W	3–2	
Honved	29 September	1993	H	W	2–1	

*First home defeat in European competition

400

HJK Helsinki	22 September	1965	A	W	3–2	
HJK Helsinki	6 October	1965	H	W	6–0	
Hibernian (Malta)	20 September	1967	H	W	4–0	
Hibernian (Malta)	27 September	1967	A	D	0–0	
Dynamo Kiev	19 September	2000	A	D	0–0	Champions League
Dynamo Kiev	8 November	2000	H	W	1–0	Champions League
Juventus	11 September	1996	A	L	0–1	Champions League
Juventus	20 November	1996	H	L	0–1	Champions League
Juventus	1 October	1997	H	W	3–2	Champions League
Juventus	12 December	1997	A	L	0–1	Champions League
Juventus	7 April	1999	H	D	1–1	Semi-final (1)
Juventus	21 April	1999	A	W	3–2	Semi-final (2)
Kosice	17 September	1997	A	W	3–0	Champions League
Kosice	27 November	1997	H	W	3–0	Champions League
LKS Lodz	12 August	1998	H	W	2–0	Champions League
LKS Lodz	26 August	1998	A	D	0–0	Champions League
Real Madrid	11 April	1957	A	L	1–3	Semi-final (1)
Real Madrid	25 April	1957	H	D	2–2	Semi-final (2)
Real Madrid	24 April	1968	H	W	1–0	Semi-final (1)
Real Madrid	15 May	1968	A	D	3–3	Semi-final (2)
Real Madrid	4 April	2000	A	D	0–0	Quarter-final (1)
Real Madrid	19 April	2000	H	L	2–3	Quarter-final (2)
Olympique Marseille	29 September	1999	H	W	2–1	Champions League
Olympique Marseille	19 October	1999	A	L	0–1	Champions League
AC Milan	8 May	1958	H	W	2–1	Semi-final (1)
AC Milan	14 May	1958	A	L	0–4	Semi-final (2)
AC Milan	23 April	1969	A	L	0–2	Semi-final (1)
AC Milan	15 May	1969	H	W	1–0	Semi-final (2)
Inter Milan	3 March	1999	H	W	2–0	Champions League
Inter Milan	17 March	1999	A	D	1–1	Champions League
Monaco	5 March	1998	A	D	0–0	Quarter-final (1)
Monaco	18 March	1998	H	D	1–1	Quarter-final (2)
Bayern Munich	30 September	1998	A	D	2–2	Champions League
Bayern Munich	9 December	1998	H	D	1–1	Champions League
Bayern Munich	26 May	1999	N	W	2–1	FINAL

Bayern Munich	3 April	2001	H	L	0–1	Quarter-final (1)
Bayern Munich	18 April	2001	A	L	1–2	Quarter-final (2)
Panathinaikos	21 November	2000	H	W	3–1	Champions League
Panathinaikos	7 March	2001	A	D	1–1	Champions League
FC Porto	5 March	1997	H	W	4–0	Quarter-final (1)
FC Porto	19 March	1997	A	D	0–0	Quarter-final (2)
Dukla Prague	20 November	1957	H	W	3–0	
Dukla Prague	4 December	1957	A	L	0–1	
Sarajevo F.K.	15 November	1967	A	D	0–0	
Sarajevo F.K.	29 November	1967	H	W	2–1	
Shamrock Rovers	25 September	1957	A	W	6–0	
Shamrock Rovers	2 October	1957	H	W	3–2	
Valencia	8 December	1999	H	W	3–0	Champions League
Valencia	21 March	2000	A	D	0–0	Champions League
Valencia	14 February	2001	A	D	0–0	Champions League
Valencia	20 February	2001	H	D	1–1	Champions League
Rapid Vienna	26 February	1969	H	W	3–0	
Rapid Vienna	5 March	1969	A	D	0–0	
Rapid Vienna	25 September	1996	H	W	2–0	Champions League
Rapid Vienna	4 December	1996	A	W	2–0	Champions League
ASK Vorwaerts	17 November	1965	A	W	2–0	
ASK Vorwaerts	1 December	1965	H	W	3–1	
Waterford	18 September	1968	A	W	3–1	
Waterford	2 October	1968	H	W	7–1	
Croatia Zagreb	14 September	1999	H	D	0–0	Champions League
Croatia Zagreb	27 October	1999	A	W	2–1	Champions League

UEFA Cup (originally named the Inter-Cities Fairs Cup)

Ajax (Amsterdam)	15 September	1976	A	L	0–1	
Ajax (Amsterdam)	29 September	1976	H	W	2–0	
Djurgaarden	23 September	1964	A	D	1–1	
Djurgaarden	27 October	1964	H	W	6–1	
Borussia Dortmund	11 November	1964	A	W	6–1	
Borussia Dortmund	2 December	1964	H	W	4–0	

Dundee United	28 November	1984	H	D	2–2	
Dundee United	12 December	1984	A	W	3–2	
PSV Eindhoven	24 October	1984	A	D	0–0	
PSV Eindhoven	7 November	1984	H	W	1–0	
Everton	20 January	1965	H	D	1–1	
Everton	9 Febuary	1965	A	W	2–1	
Ferencvaros	31 May	1965	H	W	3–2	Semi-final (1)
Ferencvaros	6 June	1965	A	L	0–1	Semi-final (2)
Ferencvaros	16 June	1965	A	L	1–2	Semi-final play-off
Raba Gyor	19 September	1984	H	W	3–0	
Raba Gyor	3 October	1984	A	D	2–2	
Juventus	20 October	1976	H	W	1–0	
Juventus	3 November	1976	A	L	0–3	
Widzew Lodz	17 September	1980	H	D	1–1	
Widzew Lodz	1 October	1980	A	D	0–0	
Torpedo Moscow	16 September	1992	H	D	0–0	
Torpedo Moscow	29 September	1992	A	D	0–0	Lost on penalties
Racing Strasbourg	12 May	1965	A	W	5–0	
Racing Strasbourg	19 May	1965	H	D	0–0	
Valencia	15 September	1982	H	D	0–0	
Valencia	29 September	1982	A	L	1–2	
Videoton (Hungary)	6 March	1984	H	W	1–0	
Videoton (Hungary)	20 March	1984	A	L	0–1	Lost on penalties
Volgograd	12 September	1995	A	D	0–0	
Volgograd	26 September	1995	H	D	2–2	

The European Cup-Winners' Cup

Athinaikos	18 September	1991	A	D	0–0	
Athinaikos	2 October	1991	H	W	2–0	(aet)
Barcelona	7 March	1984	A	L	0–2	
Barcelona	21 March	1984	H	W	3–0	
Barcelona	15 March	1991	N	W	2–1	FINAL
Juventus	11 April	1984	H	D	1–1	Semi-final (1)
Juventus	25 April	1984	A	L	1–2	Semi-final (2)

Sporting Lisbon	26 February	1964	H	W	4–1
Sporting Lisbon	18 March	1964	A	L	0–5
Atletico Madrid	23 October	1991	A	L	0–3
Atletico Madrid	6 November	1991	H	D	1–1
Montpellier	6 March	1991	H	D	1–1
Montpellier	19 March	1991	A	W	2–0
Pecsi Munkas	19 September	1990	H	W	2–0
Pecsi Munkas	3 October	1990	A	W	1–0
FC Porto	19 October	1977	A	L	0–4
FC Porto	2 November	1977	H	W	5–2
Dukla Prague	14 September	1983	H	D	1–1
Dukla Prague	27 September	1983	A	D	2–2
St Etienne	14 September	1977	A	D	1–1
St Etienne	5 October	1977	H†	W	2–0
Tottenham Hotspur	3 December	1963	A	L	0–2
Tottenham Hotspur	10 December	1963	H	W	4–1
Spartak Varna	19 October	1983	A	W	2–1
Spartak Varna	2 November	1983	H	W	2–0
Legia Warsaw	10 April	1991	A	W	3–1
Legia Warsaw	24 April	1991	H	D	1–1
Willem II (Holland)	25 September	1963	A	D	1–1
Willem II (Holland)	15 October	1963	H	W	6–1
Wrexham	23 October	1990	H	W	3–0
Wrexham	7 November	1990	A	W	2–0

European Super Cup
(Champions' Cup winners v Cup-Winners' Cup winners)

| Lazio | 27 August | 1999 | N | L | 0–1 |
| Red Star Belgrade | 19 November | 1991 | H | W | 1–0 |

†played in Plymouth

Manchester United in Europe 1956–2001

The complete countdown of all United's games in UEFA competitions.

European Cup

1	Anderlecht	12 September	1956	A	W	2–0	
2	Anderlecht	26 September	1956	H	W	10–0	
3	Borussia Dortmund	17 October	1956	H	W	3–2	
4	Borussia Dortmund	21 November	1956	A	D	0–0	
5	Athletic Bilbao	16 January	1957	A	L	3–5	
6	Athletic Bilbao	6 February	1957	H	W	3–0	
7	Real Madrid	11 April	1957	A	L	1–3	Semi-final
8	Real Madrid	25 April	1957	H	D	2–2	Semi-final

European Cup

9	Shamrock Rovers	25 September	1957	A	W	6–0	
10	Shamrock Rovers	2 October	1957	H	W	3–2	
11	Dukla Prague	20 November	1957	H	W	3–0	
12	Dukla Prague	4 December	1957	A	L	0–1	
13	Red Star Belgrade	14 January	1958	H	W	2–1	
14	Red Star Belgrade	5 February	1958	A	D	3–3	
15	AC Milan	8 May	1958	H	W	2–1	Semi-final
16	AC Milan	14 May	1958	A	L	0–4	Semi-final

Cup-Winners' Cup

17	Willem II	25 September	1963	A	D	1–1	
18	Willem II	15 October	1963	H	W	6–1	
19	Tottenham Hotspur	3 December	1963	A	L	0–2	
20	Tottenham Hotspur	10 December	1963	H	W	4–1	
21	Sporting Lisbon	26 February	1964	H	W	4–1	
22	Sporting Lisbon	18 March	1964	A	L	0–5	

UEFA (Fairs) Cup

23	Djurgaarden	23 September	1964	A	D	1–1	
24	Djurgaarden	27 October	1964	H	W	6–1	
25	Borussia Dortmund	11 November	1964	A	W	6–1	
26	Borussia Dortmund	2 December	1964	H	W	4–0	

27	Everton	20 January	1965	H	D	1–1	
28	Everton	9 February	1965	A	W	2–1	
29	Racing Strasbourg	12 May	1965	A	W	5–0	
30	Racing Strasbourg	19 May	1965	H	D	0–0	
31	Ferencvaros	31 May	1965	H	W	3–2	Semi-final (1)
32	Ferencvaros	6 June	1965	A	L	0–1	Semi-final (2)
33	Ferencvaros	16 June	1965	A	L	1–2	Semi-final play-off

European Cup

34	HJK Helsinki	22 September	1965	A	W	3–2	
35	HJK Helsinki	6 October	1965	H	W	6–0	
36	ASK Vorwaerts	17 November	1965	A	W	2–0	
37	ASK Vorwaerts	1 December	1965	H	W	3–1	
38	Benfica	2 February	1966	H	W	3–2	
39	Benfica	9 March	1966	A	W	5–1	
40	Partizan Belgrade	13 April	1966	A	L	0–2	Semi-final (1)
41	Partizan Belgrade	20 April	1966	H	W	1–0	Semi-final (2)

European Cup

42	Hibernian (Malta)	20 September	1967	H	W	4–0	
43	Hibernian (Malta)	27 September	1967	A	D	0–0	
44	Sarajevo F.K.	15 November	1967	A	D	0–0	
45	Sarajevo F.K.	29 November	1967	H	W	2–1	
46	Gornik Zabrze	28 February	1968	H	W	2–0	
47	Gornik Zabrze	13 March	1968	A	L	0–1	
48	Real Madrid	24 April	1968	H	W	1–0	Semi-final
49	Real Madrid	15 May	1968	A	D	3–3	Semi-final
50	Benfica	29 May	1968	N	W	4–1	(aet) FINAL

European Cup

51	Waterford	18 September	1968	A	W	3–1	
52	Waterford	2 October	1968	H	W	7–1	
53	Anderlecht	13 November	1968	H	W	3–0	
54	Anderlecht	27 November	1968	A	L	1–3	
55	Rapid Vienna	26 February	1969	H	W	3–0	
56	Rapid Vienna	5 March	1969	A	D	0–0	
57	AC Milan	23 April	1969	A	L	0–2	Semi-final
58	AC Milan	15 May	1969	H	W	1–0	Semi-final

UEFA Cup

59	Ajax	15 September	1976	A	L	0–1	
60	Ajax	29 September	1976	H	W	2–0	
61	Juventus	20 October	1976	H	W	1–0	
62	Juventus	3 November	1976	A	L	0–3	

Cup-Winners' Cup

63	St Etienne	14 September	1977	A	D	1–1	
64	St Etienne	5 October	1977	H†	W	2–0	
65	FC Porto	19 October	1977	A	L	0–4	
66	FC Porto	2 November	1977	H	W	5–2	

UEFA Cup

67	Widzew Lodz	17 September	1980	H	D	1–1	
68	Widzew Lodz	1 October	1980	A	D	0–0	

UEFA Cup

69	Valencia	15 September	1982	H	D	0–0	
70	Valencia	29 September	1982	A	L	1–2	

Cup-Winners' Cup

71	Dukla Prague	14 September	1983	H	D	1–1	
72	Dukla Prague	27 September	1983	A	D	2–2	
73	Spartak Varna	19 October	1983	A	W	2–1	
74	Spartak Varna	2 November	1983	H	W	2–0	
75	Barcelona	7 March	1984	A	L	0–2	
76	Barcelona	21 March	1984	H	W	3–0	
77	Juventus	11 April	1984	H	D	1–1	Semi-final (1)
78	Juventus	25 April	1984	A	L	1–2	Semi-final (2)

UEFA Cup

79	Raba Gyor	19 September	1984	H	W	3–0	
80	Raba Gyor	3 October	1984	A	D	2–2	
81	PSV Eindhoven	24 October	1984	A	D	0–0	
82	PSV Eindhoven	7 November	1984	H	W	1–0	
83	Dundee Utd	28 November	1984	H	D	2–2	

†played in Plymouth

84	Dundee Utd	12 December	1984	A	W	3–2	
85	Videoton	6 March	1984	H	W	1–0	
86	Videoton	20 March	1984	A	L	0–1	Lost on penalties

Note: English clubs were banned from European competitions from 1985 until 1990 following rioting at the 1985 European Cup final between Juventus and Liverpool. Thirty-nine Juventus fans were killed at the Heysel Stadium. During the ban, as FA Cup winners in 1985 United would have qualified for the Cup-Winners' Cup. In 1986 they were fourth in Division One and in 1988 they were runners-up. They would have qualified for the UEFA Cup on both occasions.

Cup-Winners' Cup

87	Pecsi Munkas	19 September	1990	H	W	2–0	
88	Pecsi Munkas	3 October	1990	A	W	1–0	
89	Wrexham	23 October	1990	H	W	3–0	
90	Wrexham	7 November	1990	A	W	2–0	
91	Montpellier	6 March	1991	H	D	1–1	
92	Montpellier	19 March	1991	A	W	2–0	
93	Legia Warsaw	10 April	1991	A	W	3–1	
94	Legia Warsaw	24 April	1991	H	D	1–1	
95	Barcelona	15 May	1991	N	W	2–1	FINAL

Cup-Winners' Cup

96	Athinaikos	18 September	1991	A	D	0–0	
97	Athinaikos	2 October	1991	H	W	2–0	aet
98	Atletico Madrid	23 October	1991	A	L	0–3	
99	Atletico Madrid	6 November	1991	H	D	1–1	

UEFA Cup

| 100 | Torpedo Moscow | 16 September | 1992 | H | D | 0–0 | |
| 101 | Torpedo Moscow | 29 September | 1992 | A | D | 0–0 | Lost on penalties |

European Cup

102	Honved	15 September	1993	A	W	3–2	
103	Honved	29 September	1993	H	W	2–1	
104	Galatasaray	20 October	1993	H	D	3–3	
105	Galatasaray	3 November	1993	A	D	0–0	

Champions League

106	IFK Gothenburg	14 September	1994	H	W	4–2
107	Galatasaray	28 September	1994	A	D	0–0
108	Barcelona	19 October	1994	H	D	2–2
109	Barcelona	2 November	1994	A	L	0–4
110	IFK Gothenburg	23 November	1994	A	L	1–3
111	Galatasary	7 December	1994	H	W	4–0

UEFA Cup

112	Volgograd	12 September	1995	A	D	0–0
113	Volgograd	26 September	1995	H	D	2–2

Champions League

114	Juventus	11 September	1996	A	L	0–1	
115	Rapid Vienna	25 September	1996	H	W	2–0	
116	Fenerbahce	16 October	1996	A	W	2–0	
117	Fenerbahce	30 October	1996	H	L	0–1	
118	Juventus	20 November	1996	H	L	0–1	
119	Rapid Vienna	4 December	1996	A	W	2–0	
120	FC Porto	5 March	1997	H	W	4–0	Quarter-final (1)
121	FC Porto	19 March	1997	A	D	0–0	Quarter-final (2)
122	Borussia Dortmund	4 April	1997	A	L	0–1	Semi-final (1)
123	Borussia Dortmund	23 April	1997	H	L	0–1	Semi-final (2)

Champions League

124	Kosice	17 September	1997	A	W	3–0	
125	Juventus	1 October	1997	H	W	3–2	
126	Feyenoord	22 October	1997	H	W	2–1	
127	Feyenoord	5 November	1997	A	W	3–1	
128	Kosice	27 November	1997	H	W	3–0	
129	Juventus	10 December	1997	A	L	0–1	
130	Monaco	5 March	1998	A	D	0–0	Quarter-final (1)
131	Monaco	18 March	1998	H	D	1–1	Quarter-final (2)

Champions League

132	LKS Lodz	12 August	1998	H	W	2–0
133	LKS Lodz	26 August	1998	A	D	0–0

134	Barcelona	16 September	1998	H	D	3–3	
135	Bayern Munich	30 September	1998	A	D	2–2	
136	Brondby	28 October	1998	A	W	6–2	
137	Brondby	4 November	1998	H	W	5–0	
138	Barcelona	25 November	1998	A	D	3–3	
139	Bayern Munich	9 December	1998	H	D	1–1	
140	Inter Milan	3 March	1999	H	W	2–0	Quarter-final (1)
141	Inter Milan	17 March	1999	A	D	1–1	Quarter-final (2)
142	Juventus	7 April	1999	H	D	1–1	Semi-final (1)
143	Juventus	21 April	1999	A	W	3–2	Semi-final (2)
144	Bayern Munich	26 May	1999	N	W	3–2	FINAL

Champions League

145	Croatia Zagreb	14 September	1999	H	D	0–0	
146	Sturm Graz	22 September	1999	A	W	3–0	
147	Marseille	29 September	1999	H	W	2–1	
148	Marseille	19 October	1999	A	L	0–1	
149	Croatia Zagreb	27 October	1999	A	W	2–1	
150	Sturm Graz	2 November	1999	H	W	2–1	
151	Fiorentina	23 November	1999	A	L	0–2	
152	Valencia	8 December	1999	H	W	3–0	
153	Bordeaux	1 March	2000	H	W	2–0	
154	Bordeaux	7 March	2000	A	W	2–1	
155	Fiorentina	15 March	2000	H	W	3–1	
156	Valencia	21 March	2000	A	D	0–0	
157	Real Madrid	4 April	2000	A	D	0–0	Quarter-final (1)
158	Real Madrid	19 April	2000	H	L	2–3	Quarter-final (2)

Champions League

159	Anderlecht	13 September	2000	H	W	3–1	
160	Dynamo Kiev	19 September	2000	A	D	0–0	
161	PSV Eindhoven	26 September	2000	A	L	1–3	
162	PSV Eindhoven	18 October	2000	H	W	3–1	
163	Anderlecht	24 October	2000	A	L	1–2	
164	Dynamo Kiev	8 November	2000	H	W	1–0	
165	Panathinaikos	21 November	2000	H	W	3–1	
166	Sturm Graz	6 December	2000	A	W	2–0	
167	Valencia	14 February	2001	A	D	0–0	
168	Valencia	20 February	2001	H	D	1–1	

169	Panathinaikos	7 March	2001	A	D	1–1	
170	Sturm Graz	13 March	2001	H	W	3–0	
171	Bayern Munich	3 April	2001	H	L	0–1	Quarter-final (1)
172	Bayern Munich	18 April	2001	A	L	1–2	Quarter-final (2)

How They Lined Up

1956–57 European Cup

12 September	Pre(1)	Anderlecht	A	W	2–0	Wood	Foulkes	Byrne	Colman
26 September	Pre(2)	Anderlecht	H	W	10–0	Wood	Foulkes	Byrne	Colman
17 October	1(1)	Borussia Dortmund	H	W	*3–2	Wood	Foulkes	Byrne	Colman
21 November	1(2)	Borussia Dortmund	A	D	0–0	Wood	Foulkes	Byrne	Colman
16 January	2(1)	Athletic Bilbao	A	L	3–5	Wood	Foulkes	Byrne	Colman
6 February	2(2)	Athletic Bilbao	H	W	3–0	Wood	Foulkes	Byrne	Colman
11 April	S/F(1)	Real Madrid	A	L	1–3	Wood	Foulkes	Byrne	Colman
25 April	S/F(2)	Real Madrid	H	D	2–2	Wood	Foulkes	Byrne	Colman

*own goal by Burgsmueller

1957–58 European Cup

25 September	Pre(1)	Shamrock Rovers	A	W	6–0	Wood	Foulkes	Byrne	Goodwin
2 October	Pre(2)	Shamrock Rovers	H	W	3–2	Wood	Foulkes	Byrne	Colman
20 November	1(1)	Dukla Prague	H	W	3–0	Wood	Foulkes	Byrne	Colman
4 December	1(2)	Dukla Prague	A	L	0–1	Wood	Foulkes	Byrne	Colman
14 January	2(1)	Red Star Belgrade	H	W	2–1	Gregg	Foulkes	Byrne	**Colman 1**
5 February	2(2)	Red Star Belgrade	A	D	3–3	Gregg	Foulkes	Byrne	Colman
8 May	S/F(1)	AC Milan	H	W	2–1	Gregg	Foulkes	Greaves	Goodwin
14 May	S/F(2)	AC Milan	A	L	0–4	Gregg	Foulkes	Greaves	Goodwin

1963–64 Cup-Winners' Cup

25 September	1(1)	Willem II	A	D	1–1	Gregg	Dunne	Cantwell	Crerand
15 October	1(2)	Willem II	H	W	6–1	Gregg	Dunne	Cantwell	Crerand
3 December	2(1)	Tottenham Hotspur	A	L	0–2	Gaskell	Dunne	Cantwell	Crerand
10 December	2(2)	Tottenham Hotspur	H	W	4–1	Gaskell	Dunne	Cantwell	Crerand
26 February	Q/F(1)	Sporting Lisbon	H	W	4–1	Gaskell	Brennan	Dunne	Crerand
18 March	Q/F(2)	Sporting Lisbon	A	L	0–5	Gaskell	Brennan	Dunne	Crerand

1964–65 Inter-Cities Fairs Cup (UEFA Cup)

23 September	1(1)	Djurgaarden	A	D	1–1	P. Dunne	Brennan	A. Dunne	Crerand
27 October	1(2)	Djurgaarden	H	W	6–1	P. Dunne	Brennan	A. Dunne	Crerand
11 November	2(1)	Borussia Dortmund	A	W	6–1	P. Dunne	Brennan	A. Dunne	Crerand
2 December	2(2)	Borussia Dortmund	H	W	4–0	P. Dunne	Brennan	A. Dunne	Crerand
20 January	3(1)	Everton	H	D	1–1	P. Dunne	Brennan	A. Dunne	Crerand

412

Jones	Blanchflower	Berry	Whelan	**Taylor 1**	**Viollet 1**	Pegg
Jones	Edwards	**Berry 1**	**Whelan 2**	Taylor 3	**Viollet 4**	Pegg
Jones	Edwards	Berry	Whelan	Taylor	**Viollet 2**	Pegg
Jones	McGuinness	Berry	Whelan	Taylor	Edwards	Pegg
Jones	Edwards	Berry	**Whelan 1**	**Taylor 1**	**Viollet 1**	Pegg
Jones	Edwards	**Berry 1**	Whelan	**Taylor 1**	**Viollet 1**	Pegg
Blanchflower	Edwards	Berry	Whelan	**Taylor 1**	Viollet	Pegg
Blanchflower	Edwards	Berry	Whelan	**Taylor 1**	**Charlton 1**	Pegg

Blanchflower	Edwards	**Berry 1**	**Whelan 2**	**Taylor 2**	Viollet	**Pegg 1**
Jones	McGuinness	Berry	Webster	Taylor	**Viollet 2**	**Pegg 1**
Blanchflower	Edwards	Berry	Whelan	**Taylor 1**	**Webster 1**	**Pegg 1**
Jones	Edwards	Scanlon	Whelan	Taylor	Webster	Pegg
Jones	Edwards	Morgans	**Charlton 1**	Taylor	Viollet	Scanlon
Jones	Edwards	Morgans	**Charlton 2**	Taylor	**Viollet 1**	Scanlon
Cope	Crowther	Morgans	**E. Taylor 1**	Webster	**Viollet 1**	Pearson
Cope	Crowther	Morgans	E. Taylor	Webster	Viollet	Pearson

Foulkes	Setters	**Herd 1**	Chisnall	Sadler	Law	Charlton
Foulkes	**Setters 1**	Quixall	**Chisnall 1**	Herd	**Law 3**	**Charlton 1**
Foulkes	Setters	Quixall	Stiles	Herd	Law	Charlton
Foulkes	Setters	Quixall	Chisnall	Sadler	**Herd 2**	**Charlton 2**
Foulkes	Setters	Herd	Stiles	**Charlton 1**	**Law 3**	Best
Foulkes	Setters	Herd	Chisnall	Charlton	Law	Best

Foulkes	Setters	Connelly	Charlton	**Herd 1**	Stiles	Best
Foulkes	Stiles	Connelly	**Charlton 2**	Herd	**Law 3**	**Best 1**
Foulkes	Stiles	Connelly	**Charlton 3**	**Herd 1**	Law 1	**Best 1**
Foulkes	Stiles	**Connelly 1**	**Charlton 2**	Herd	Law 1	Best
Foulkes	Stiles	**Connelly 1**	Charlton	Herd	Law	Best

413

9 February	3(2)	Everton	A	W	2–1	P. Dunne	Brennan	A. Dunne	Crerand
12 May	Q/F(1)	Racing Strasbourg	A	W	5–0	P. Dunne	Brennan	A. Dunne	Crerand
19 May	Q/F(2)	Racing Strasbourg	H	D	0–0	P. Dunne	Brennan	A. Dunne	Crerand
31 May	S/F(1)	Ferencvaros	H	W	3–2	P. Dunne	Brennan	A. Dunne	Crerand
6 June	S/F(2)	Ferencvaros	A	L	0–1	P. Dunne	Brennan	A. Dunne	Crerand
16 June	S/F(3)	Ferencvaros	A	L	1–2	P. Dunne	Brennan	A. Dunne	Crerand

1965–66 European Cup

22 September	Pre(1)	Helsinki JK	A	W	3–2	Gaskell	Brennan	A. Dunne	Fitzpatrick
6 October	Pre(2)	Helsinki JK	H	W	6–0	P. Dunne	Brennan	A. Dunne	Crerand
17 November	1(1)	ASK Vorwaerts	A	W	2–0	Gregg	A. Dunne	Cantwell	Crerand
1 December	1(2)	ASK Vorwaerts	H	W	3–1	P. Dunne	A. Dunne	Cantwell	Crerand
2 February	2(1)	Benfica	H	W	3–2	Gregg	A. Dunne	Cantwell	Crerand
9 March	2(2)	Benfica	A	W	5–1	Gregg	Brennan	A. Dunne	**Crerand 1**
13 April	S/F(1)	Partizan Belgrade	A	L	0–2	Gregg	Brennan	A. Dunne	Crerand
20 April	S/F(2)	Partizan Belgrade	H	W	*1–0	Gregg	Brennan	A. Dunne	Crerand

*own goal by Soskic

1967–68 European Cup

20 September	1(1)	Hibernians (Malta)	H	W	4–0	Stepney	Dunne	Burns	Crerand
27 September	1(2)	Hibernians (Malta)	A	D	0–0	Stepney	Dunne	Burns	Crerand
15 November	2(1)	Sarajevo	A	D	0–0	Stepney	Dunne	Burns	Crerand
29 November	2(2)	Sarajevo	H	W	2–1	Stepney	Brennan	Dunne	Crerand
28 February	Q/F(1)	Gornik Zabrze	H	W	*2–0	Stepney	Dunne	Burns	Crerand
13 March	Q/F(2)	Gornik Zabrze	A	L	0–1	Stepney	Dunne	Burns	Crerand
24 April	S/F(1)	Real Madrid	H	W	1–0	Stepney	Dunne	Burns	Crerand
15 May	S/F(2)	Real Madrid	A	D	†3–3	Stepney	Brennan	Dunne	Crerand
29 May	Final	Benfica	N	W	4–1	Stepney	Brennan	Dunne	Crerand

*own goal by Florenski
†own goal by Zoco
N – neutral venue, Wembley Stadium

1968–69 European Cup

18 September	1(1)	Waterford	A	W	3–1	Stepney	Dunne	Burns	Crerand
2 October	1(2)	Waterford	H	W	7–1	Stepney	Dunne	**Burns 1**	Crerand
13 November	2(1)	Anderlecht	H	W	3–0	Stepney	Brennan	Dunne	Crerand
27 November	2(2)	Anderlecht	A	L	1–3	Stepney	Kopel	Dunne	Crerand
26 February	Q/F(1)	Rapid Vienna	H	W	3–0	Stepney	Fitzpatrick	Dunne	Crerand

Foulkes	Stiles	**Connelly 1**	Charlton	**Herd 1**	Law	Best	
Foulkes	Stiles	**Connelly 1**	**Charlton 1**	**Herd 1**	**Law 2**	Best	
Foulkes	Stiles	Connelly	Charlton	Herd	Law	Best	
Foulkes	Stiles	Connelly	Charlton	**Herd 2**	**Law 1**	Best	
Foulkes	Stiles	Connelly	Charlton	Herd	Law	Best	
Foulkes	Stiles	**Connelly 1**	Charlton	Herd	Law	Best	

Foulkes	Stiles	**Connelly 1**	**Law 1**	**Herd 1**	Charlton	Aston	
Foulkes	Stiles	**Connelly 3**	**Best 2**	**Charlton 1**	Law	Aston	
Foulkes	Stiles	Best	**Law 1**	Charlton	Herd	**Connelly 1**	
Foulkes	Stiles	Best	Law	Charlton	**Herd 3**	Connelly	
Foulkes 1	Stiles	Best	**Law 1**	Charlton	**Herd 1**	Connelly	
Foulkes	Stiles	**Best 2**	Law	**Charlton 1**	Herd	**Connelly 1**	
Foulkes	Stiles	Best	Law	Charlton	Herd	Connelly	
Foulkes	Stiles	Anderson	Law	Charlton	Herd	Connelly	

Foulkes	Stiles	Best	**Sadler 2**	Charlton	**Law 2**	Kidd	
Foulkes	Stiles	Best	Sadler	Charlton	Law	Kidd	
Foulkes	Sadler	Fitzpatrick	Kidd	Charlton	Best	Aston	
Foulkes	Sadler	Burns	Kidd	Charlton	**Best 1**	**Aston 1**	
Sadler	Stiles	Best	**Kidd 1**	Charlton	Ryan	Aston	
Sadler	Stiles	Fitzpatrick	Kidd	Charlton	Best	Herd	
Sadler	Stiles	**Best 1**	Kidd	Charlton	Law	Aston	
Foulkes 1	Stiles	Best	Kidd	Charlton	**Sadler 1**	Aston	
Foulkes	Stiles	**Best 1**	**Kidd 1**	**Charlton 2**	Sadler	Aston	

Foulkes	Stiles	Best	Sadler	Charlton	**Law 3**	Kidd	Rimmer for Stepney
Foulkes	**Stiles 1**	Best	Sadler	**Charlton 1**	**Law 4**	Kidd	
Sadler	Stiles	Ryan	**Kidd 1**	Charlton	**Law 2**	Sartori	
Foulkes	Sadler	Fitzpatrick	Stiles	Charlton	Law	**Sartori 1**	
James	Stiles	**Morgan 1**	Kidd	Charlton	Law	**Best 2**	

5 March	Q/F(2)	Rapid Vienna	A	D	0-0	Stepney	Fitzpatrick	Dunne	Crerand
23 April	S/F(1)	AC Milan	A	L	0-2	Rimmer	Brennan	Fitzpatrick	Crerand
15 May	S/F(2)	AC Milan	H	W	1-0	Rimmer	Brennan	Burns	Crerand

1976-77 UEFA Cup

15 September	1(1)	Ajax	A	L	0-1	Stepney	Nicholl	B. Greenhoff	Buchan
29 September	1(2)	Ajax	H	W	2-0	Stepney	Nicholl	B. Greenhoff	Buchan
20 October	2(1)	Juventus	H	W	1-0	Stepney	Nicholl	B. Greenhoff	Houston
3 November	2(2)	Juventus	A	L	0-3	Stepney	Nicholl	B. Greenhoff	Houston

1977-78 Cup-Winners' Cup

14 September	1(1)	St Etienne	A	D	1-1	Stepney	Nicholl	B. Greenhoff	Buchan
5 October	1(2)	St Etienne	H	W	2-0	Stepney	Nicholl	B. Greenhoff	Buchan
19 October	2(1)	FC Porto	A	L	0-4	Stepney	Nicholl	Houston	Buchan
2 November	2(2)	FC Porto	H	W	*5-2	Stepney	**Nicholl 1**	Houston	Buchan

*two own goals by Murca

1980-81 UEFA Cup

17 September	1(1)	Widzew Lodz	H	D	1-1	Bailey	Nicholl	Jovanovic	Buchan
1 October	1(2)	Widzew Lodz	A	D	0-0	Bailey	Nicholl	Jovanovic	Buchan

1982-83 UEFA Cup

15 September	1(1)	Valencia	H	D	0-0	Bailey	Duxbury	Buchan	McQueen
29 September	1(2)	Valencia	A	L	1-2	Bailey	Duxbury	Moran	Buchan

1983-84 Cup-Winners' Cup

14 September	1(1)	Dukla Prague	H	D	1-1	Bailey	Duxbury	Moran	McQueen
27 September	1(2)	Dukla Prague	A	D	2-2	Bailey	Duxbury	Moran	McQueen
19 October	2(1)	Spartak Varna	A	W	2-1	Bailey	Duxbury	Moran	McQueen

416

ames	Stiles	Morgan	Kidd	Charlton	Sadler	Best	
Foulkes	Stiles	Morgan	Kidd	Charlton	Law	Best	
Foulkes	Stiles	Morgan	Kidd	**Charlton 1**	Law	Best	
Houston	Coppell	Daly	McIlroy	Pearson	Macari	Hill	McCreery for Daly
Houston	Coppell	Daly	**McIlroy 1**	McCreery	**Macari 1**	Hill	Albiston for Daly, Peterson for Hill
Albiston	Coppell	Daly	McIlroy	Pearson	Macari	**Hill 1**	McCreery for Daly
Albiston	Coppell	Daly	McIlroy	Pearson	Macari	Hill	McCreery for McIlroy, Peterson for Macari
Albiston	McGrath	McCreery	McIlroy	Pearson	Coppell	**Hill 1**	Grimes for McIlroy, Houston for B. Greenhoff
Albiston	**Coppell 1**	J. Greenhoff	McIlroy	**Pearson 1**	Macari	Hill	McGrath for Pearson
Albiston	McGrath	McCreery	McIlroy	Coppell	Macari	Hill	Forsyth for Houston, Grimes for McGrath
Albiston	McGrath	**Coppell 2**	McIlroy	Pearson	McCreery	Hill	
Albiston	Coppell	Grimes	**McIlroy 1**	J. Greenhoff	Macari	Thomas	Duxbury for Nicholl
Albiston	Coppell	Grimes	McIlroy	Jordan	Duxbury	Thomas	Moran for Buchan
Albiston	Wilkins	Robson	Grimes	Stapleton	Whiteside	Coppell	
Albiston	Wilkins	**Robson 1**	Grimes	Stapleton	Whiteside	Moses	Macari for Buchan, Coppell for Moses
Albiston	**Wilkins 1**	Robson	Muhren	Stapleton	Macari	Graham	Moses for Muhren, Gidman for Robson
Albiston	Wilkins	**Robson 1**	Muhren	**Stapleton 1**	Whiteside	Graham	
Albiston	Wilkins	**Robson 1**	Muhren	Stapleton	Whiteside	**Graham 1**	

2 November	2(2)	Spartak Varna	H	W	2–0	Bailey	Duxbury	Moran	McQueen
7 March	3(1)	Barcelona	A	L	0–2	Bailey	Duxbury	Moran	Hogg
21 March	3(2)	Barcelona	H	W	3–0	Bailey	Duxbury	Moran	Hogg
11 April	S/F(1)	Juventus	H	D	1–1	Bailey	Duxbury	Moran	Hogg
25 April	S/F(2)	Juventus	A	L	1–2	Bailey	Duxbury	Moran	Hogg

1984–85 UEFA Cup

19 September	1(1)	Raba Gyor	H	W	3–0	Bailey	Duxbury	Moran	Hogg
3 October	1(2)	Raba Gyor	A	D	2–2	Bailey	Duxbury	Moran	Hogg
24 October	2(1)	PSV Eindhoven	A	D	0–0	Bailey	Gidman	Moran	Hogg
7 November	2(2)	PSV Eindhoven	H	W	1–0	Bailey	Gidman	Moran	Hogg
28 November	3(1)	Dundee Utd	H	D	2–2	Bailey	Gidman	McQueen	Duxbury
12 December	3(2)	Dundee Utd	A	W	*3–2	Bailey	Gidman	McQueen	Duxbury
6 March	4(1)	Videoton	H	W	1–0	Bailey	Gidman	McGrath	Hogg
20 March	4(2)	Videoton	A	LP	0–1	Bailey	Gidman	McGrath	Hogg

LP – lost on penalties
*own goal by McGinnis

1990–91 Cup-Winners' Cup

19 September	1(1)	Pesci Munkas	H	W	2–0	Sealey	Irwin	Bruce	Pallister
3 October	1(2)	Pesci Munkas	A	W	1–0	Sealey	Anderson	Bruce	Pallister
23 October	2(1)	Wrexham	H	W	3–0	Sealey	Blackmore	**Bruce 1**	**Pallister 1**
7 December	2(2)	Wrexham	A	W	2–0	Sealey	Irwin	**Bruce 1**	Pallister
6 March	3(1)	Montpellier	H	D	1–1	Sealey	Blackmore	Donaghy	Pallister
19 March	3(2)	Montpellier	A	W	2–0	Sealey	Irwin	**Bruce 1**	Pallister
10 April	S/F(1)	Legia Warsaw	A	W	3–1	Sealey	Irwin	**Bruce 1**	Pallister
24 April	S/F(2)	Legia Warsaw	H	D	1–1	Walsh	Irwin	Bruce	Pallister
15 May	Final	Barcelona	N	W	2–1	Sealey	Irwin	Bruce	Pallister

N – neutral venue, Feyenoord Stadium, Rotterdam

Albiston	Moses	Robson	Macari	**Stapleton 2**	Whiteside	Graham	Dempsey for Moran, Hughes for Whiteside
Albiston	Wilkins	Robson	Muhren	Stapleton	Hughes	Moses	Graham for Hughes
Albiston	Wilkins	**Robson 2**	Muhren	**Stapleton 1**	Whiteside	Moses	Hughes for Whiteside
Albiston	McGrath	Graham	Moses	Stapleton	Whiteside	Gidman	**Davis 1** for Gidman
Albiston	Wilkins	McGrath	Moses	Stapleton	Hughes	Graham	**Whiteside 1** for Stapleton
Albiston	Moses	**Robson 1**	**Muhren 1**	**Hughes 1**	Whiteside	Olsen	
Albiston	Moses	Robson	**Muhren 1**	Hughes	**Brazil 1**	Olsen	Gidman for Robson
Albiston	Moses	Robson	Strachan	Hughes	Brazil	Olsen	
Albiston	Moses	Robson	**Strachan 1**	Hughes	Stapleton	Olsen	Whiteside for Stapleton, Garton for Moran
Albiston	Moses	**Robson 1**	**Strachan 1**	Hughes	Whiteside	Olsen	Stapleton for Whiteside
Albiston	Moses	Robson	Strachan	**Hughes 1**	Stapleton	**Muhren 1**	
Albiston	Duxbury	Strachan	Whiteside	Hughes	**Stapleton 1**	Olsen	
Albiston	Duxbury	Robson	Strachan	Hughes	Stapleton	Whiteside	Olsen for Robson
Blackmore 1	Phelan	**Webb 1**	Ince	McClair	Robins	Beardsmore	Hughes for Robins, Sharpe for Ince
Donaghy	Phelan	Webb	Blackmore	**McClair 1**	Hughes	Martin	Sharpe for Martin
Martin	Sharpe	Webb	Ince	**McClair 1**	Hughes	Wallace	Robins for Wallace, Beardsmore for Ince
Blackmore	Phelan	Webb	Ince	McClair	**Robins 1**	Wallace	Donaghy for Ince, Martin for McClair
Martin	Phelan	Robson	Ince	**McClair 1**	Hughes	Sharpe	Wallace for Martin
Blackmore 1	Phelan	Robson	Ince	McClair	Hughes	Sharpe	Martin for Ince
Blackmore	Phelan	Webb	Ince	**McClair 1**	**Hughes 1**	Sharpe	Donaghy for Phelan
Blackmore	Phelan	Robson	Webb	McClair	Robins	**Sharpe 1**	
Blackmore	Phelan	Robson	Ince	McClair	**Hughes 2**	Sharpe	

1991–92 Cup-Winners' Cup

18 September	1(1)	Athinaikos	A	D	0–0	Schmeichel	Phelan	Bruce	Pallister
2 October	1(2)	Athinaikos	H	W	2–0	Schmeichel	Phelan	Bruce	Pallister
23 October	2(1)	Atletico Madrid	A	L	0–3	Schmeichel	Parker	Bruce	Pallister
6 November	2(2)	Atletico Madrid	H	D	1–1	Walsh	Parker	Bruce	Phelan

1992–93 UEFA Cup

16 September	1(1)	Torpedo Moscow	H	D	0–0	Walsh	Irwin	Bruce	Pallister
29 September	1(2)	Torpedo Moscow	A	LP	0–0	Schmeichel	Irwin	Bruce	Pallister

LP – lost on penalties

1993–94 Champions League

15 September	1(1)	Kispest Honved	A	W	3–2	Schmeichel	Parker	Bruce	Pallister
29 September	1(2)	Kispest Honved	H	W	2–1	Schmeichel	Parker	**Bruce 2**	Pallister
20 October	2(1)	Galatasaray	H	D	*3–3	Schmeichel	Martin	Bruce	Pallister
3 November	2(2)	Galatasaray	A	D	0–0	Schmeichel	Parker	Bruce	Pallister

*own goal by Hakan

1994–95 Champions League

14 September	Grp A	Gothenburg	H	W	4–2	Schmeichel	May	Bruce	Pallister
28 September	Grp A	Galatasaray	A	D	0–0	Schmeichel	May	Bruce	Pallister
19 October	Grp A	Barcelona	H	D	2–2	Schmeichel	Parker	May	Pallister
2 November	Grp A	Barcelona	A	L	0–4	Walsh	Parker	Bruce	Pallister
23 November	Grp A	Gothenburg	A	L	1–3	Walsh	May	Bruce	Pallister
7 December	Grp A	Galatasaray	H	W	*4–0	Walsh	G. Neville	Bruce	Pallister

*own goal by Korkmaz

Irwin	Webb	Ince	McClair	Beardsmore	Hughes	Robins	Wallace for Beardsmore
Martin	Robson	Ince	**McClair 1**	Kanchelskis	**Hughes 1**	Wallace	Robins for Wallace, Beardsmore for Martin
Irwin	Robson	Ince	McClair	Webb	Hughes	Phelan	Martin for McClair, Beardsmore for Phelan
Blackmore	Robson	Robins	McClair	Webb	**Hughes 1**	Giggs	Pallister for Robins, Martin for Phelan

Martin	Kanchelskis	Blackmore	McClair	Webb	Hughes	Wallace	G. Neville for Martin
Phelan	Wallace	Ince	McClair	Webb	Hughes	Giggs	Parker for Phelan, Robson for Wallace

Irwin	**Keane 2**	Robson	Ince	Sharpe	**Cantona 1**	Giggs	Phelan for Giggs
Irwin	Hughes	Robson	Ince	Sharpe	Cantona	Giggs	Martin for Irwin, Phelan for Ince
Sharpe	Keane	**Robson 1**	Ince	Hughes	**Cantona 1**	Giggs	Phelan for Robson
Irwin	Keane	Robson	Ince	Sharpe	Cantona	Giggs	Dublin for Keane, G. Neville for Phelan

Irwin	**Kanchelskis 1**	**Sharpe 1**	Butt	Ince	Hughes	**Giggs 2**	
Sharpe	Kanchelskis	Keane	Butt	Ince	Hughes	Giggs	Parker for Giggs
Irwin	Kanchelskis	Keane	Butt	Ince	**Hughes 1**	**Sharpe 1**	Bruce for May, Scholes for Sharpe
Irwin	Kanchelskis	Keane	Butt	Ince	Hughes	Giggs	Scholes for Giggs
Irwin	Kanchelskis	McClair	Cantona	Ince	**Hughes 1**	Davies	G. Neville for May, Butt for Davies
Irwin	**Beckham 1**	**Keane 1**	Cantona	Butt	McClair	**Davies 1**	

1995–96 UEFA Cup

12 September	1(1)	Rotor Volgograd	A	D	0–0	Schmeichel	G. Neville	Bruce	Pallister
26 September	1(2)	Rotor Volgograd	H	D	2–2	**Schmeichel 1**	O'Kane	Bruce	Pallister

1996–97 Champions League

11 September	Grp C	Juventus	A	L	0–1	Schmeichel	G. Neville	Johnsen	Pallister
25 September	Grp C	Rapid Vienna	H	W	2–0	Schmeichel	G. Neville	Johnsen	Pallister
16 October	Grp C	Fenerbahce	A	W	2–0	Schmeichel	G. Neville	May	Pallister
30 October	Grp C	Fenerbahce	H	L	0–1	Schmeichel	G. Neville	May	Johnsen
20 November	Grp C	Juventus	H	L	0–1	Schmeichel	G. Neville	May	Johnsen
4 December	Grp C	Rapid Vienna	A	W	2–0	Schmeichel	G. Neville	May	Pallister
5 March	Q/F(1)	FC Porto	H	W	4–0	Schmeichel	G. Neville	**May 1**	Pallister
19 March	Q/F(2)	FC Porto	A	D	0–0	Schmeichel	G. Neville	May	Pallister
9 April	S/F(1)	Borussia Dortmund	A	L	0–1	van der Gouw	G. Neville	Johnsen	Pallister
23 April	S/F(2)	Borussia Dortmund	H	L	0–1	Schmeichel	G. Neville	May	Pallister

1997–98 Champions League

17 September	Grp B	Kosice	A	W	3–0	Schmeichel	G. Neville	**Berg 1**	Pallister
1 October	Grp B	Juventus	H	W	3–2	Schmeichel	G. Neville	Berg	Pallister
22 October	Grp B	Feyenoord	H	W	2–1	Schmeichel	G. Neville	P. Neville	Pallister

Irwin	Beckham	Keane	Butt	Sharpe	Scholes	Giggs	Davies for Keane, Parker for Scholes
P. Neville	Beckham	Keane	Butt	Sharpe	Cole	Giggs	**Scholes 1** for O'Kane, Cooke for Beckham
Irwin	Beckham	Keane	Butt	Cruyff	Cantona	Giggs	McClair for Giggs, Solskjaer for Cruyff, Cole for Poborsky
Irwin	**Beckham 1**	Keane	Poborsky	**Solskjaer 1**	Cantona	Giggs	May for Johnsen, Cole for Solskjaer, Butt for Poborsky
Irwin	**Beckham 1**	Poborsky	Butt	Solskjaer	**Cantona 1**	Johnsen	Poborsky for Cruyff
Irwin	Beckham	Keane	Butt	Poborsky	Cantona	Cruyff	Scholes for Poborsky, Solskjaer for Cruyff, P. Neville for G. Neville
P. Neville	Beckham	Cruyff	Butt	Solskjaer	Cantona	Giggs	McClair for P. Neville, Cruyff for Solskjaer
Irwin	Beckham	Keane	Butt	Solskjaer	**Cantona 1**	**Giggs 1**	McClair for Keane, Poborsky for Butt, Casper for G. Neville
Irwin	Beckham	**Cole 1**	Johnsen	Solskjaer	**Cantona 1**	**Giggs 1**	
Irwin	Beckham	Keane	Butt	Solskjaer	Cantona	Johnsen	Scholes for Solskjaer, Poborsky for Beckham, P. Neville for Irwin
Irwin	Beckham	Keane	Butt	Solskjaer	Cantona	Giggs	Cole for Solskjaer, Scholes for Giggs
P. Neville	Beckham	Cole	Butt	Solskjaer	Cantona	Johnsen	Giggs for Solskjaer, Scholes for May
Irwin 1	Beckham	Keane	Butt	**Cole 1**	Scholes	Poborsky	McClair for Beckham
Irwin	Beckham	Johnsen	Butt	Solskjaer	**Sheringham 1**	**Giggs 1**	**Scholes 1** for Butt, P. Neville for Solskjaer
Irwin 1	Beckham	**Scholes 1**	Butt	Cole	Sheringham	Giggs	Solskjaer for Cole

5 November	Grp B	Feyenoord	A	W	3–1	Schmeichel	G. Neville	Berg	Pallister
26 November	Grp B	Kosice	H	W	*3–0	Schmeichel	G. Neville	Berg	Pallister
30 November	Grp B	Juventus	A	L	0–1	Schmeichel	G. Neville	Berg	Pallister
4 March	Q/F(1)	Monaco	A	D	0–0	Schmeichel	Irwin	Berg	G. Neville
18 March	Q/F(2)	Monaco	H	D	1–1	Van der Gouw	Irwin	Johnsen	G. Neville

*own goal by Faktor

1998–99 Champions League

12 August	Qual(1)	LKS Lodz	H	W	2–0	Schmeichel	G. Neville	Stam	Johnsen
26 August	Qual(2)	LKS Lodz	A	D	0–0	Schmeichel	P. Neville	Stam	Johnsen
16 September	Grp D	Barcelona	H	D	3–3	Schmeichel	G. Neville	Stam	Berg
30 September	Grp D	Bayern Munich	A	D	2–2	Schmeichel	G. Neville	Stam	P. Neville
21 October	Grp D	Brondby	A	W	6–2	Schmeichel	G. Neville	Stam	Brown
4 November	Grp D	Brondby	H	W	5–0	Schmeichel	G. Neville	Stam	**P. Neville 1**
25 November	Grp D	Barcelona	A	D	3–3	Schmeichel	G. Neville	Stam	Brown
9 December	Grp D	Bayern Munich	H	D	1–1	Schmeichel	G. Neville	Stam	Brown
3 March	Q/F(1)	Inter Milan	H	W	2–0	Schmeichel	G. Neville	Stam	Johnsen
17 March	Q/F(2)	Inter Milan	A	D	1–1	Schmeichel	G. Neville	Stam	Berg
7 April	S/F(1)	Juventus	H	D	1–1	Schmeichel	G. Neville	Stam	Berg
21 April	S/F(2)	Juventus	A	W	3–2	Schmeichel	G. Neville	Stam	Johnsen
26 May	Final	Bayern Munich	N	W	2–1	Schmeichel	G. Neville	Stam	Johnsen

N – neutral venue, Nou Camp Stadium, Barcelona

Irwin	Beckham	Scholes	Butt	**Cole 3**	Sheringham	Giggs	P. Neville for Irwin, Poborsky for Scholes, Solskjaer for Cole
P. Neville	Beckham	Scholes	Butt	**Cole 1**	**Sheringham 1**	Giggs	Solskjaer for Butt, Poborsky for Giggs, Berg for P. Neville
P. Neville	Beckham	Johnsen	Poborsky	Solskjaer	Sheringham	Giggs	Cole for Solskjaer, McClair for Poborsky
P. Neville	Beckham	Johnsen	Butt	Cole	Sheringham	Scholes	McClair for Irwin
P. Neville	Beckham	**Solskjaer 1**	Butt	Cole	Sheringham	Scholes	Berg for G. Neville, Clegg for Scholes

Irwin	Beckham	Keane	Scholes	Butt	**Cole 1**	**Giggs 1**	Solskjaer for Scholes
Irwin	Beckham	Keane	Scholes	Butt	Sheringham	Giggs	Solskjaer for Giggs
Irwin	**Beckham 1**	Keane	**Scholes 1**	Yorke	Solskjaer	**Giggs 1**	Butt for Solskjaer, P. Neville for Irwin, Blomqvist for Giggs
Irwin	Beckham	Keane	**Scholes 1**	**Yorke 1**	Sheringham	Blomqvist	Cruyff for Blomqvist
P. Neville	Blomqvist	**Keane 1**	Scholes	**Yorke 1**	**Cole 1**	**Giggs 2**	**Solskjaer 1** for Cole, Cruyff for Giggs, Wilson for Yorke
Irwin	**Beckham 1**	Keane	**Scholes 1**	**Yorke 1**	**Cole 1**	Blomqvist	Cruyff for Blomqvist, Solskjaer for Cole, Brown for P. Neville
Irwin	Beckham	Keane	Scholes	**Yorke 2**	**Cole 1**	Blomqvist	Butt for Beckham
Irwin	Beckham	**Keane 1**	Scholes	Yorke	Cole	Giggs	Butt for Cole
Irwin	Beckham	Keane	Scholes	**Yorke 2**	Cole	Giggs	Berg for Johnsen, Butt for Scholes
Irwin	Beckham	Keane	Johnsen	Yorke	Cole	Giggs	Butt 1 for Johnsen, P. Neville for Giggs
Irwin	Beckham	Keane	Scholes	Yorke	Cole	**Giggs 1**	Johnsen for Berg, Sheringham for Yorke
Irwin	Beckham	**Keane 1**	Butt	**Yorke 1**	**Cole 1**	Blomqvist	Butt for Blomqvist
Irwin	Beckham	Blomqvist	Butt	Yorke	Cole	Giggs	**Solskjaer 1** for Blomqvist, **Sheringham 1** for Cole

425

1999–2000 Champions League

14 September	Grp D(1)	Croatia Zagreb	H	D	0–0	Van der Gouw	Clegg	Berg	Stam
22 September	Grp D(1)	Sturm Graz	A	W	3–0	Van der Gouw	Irwin	Berg	Stam
29 September	Grp D(1)	Marseille	H	W	2–1	Van der Gouw	Irwin	Berg	Stam
19 October	Grp D(1)	Marseille	A	L	0–1	Bosnich	Irwin	Berg	Stam
27 October	Grp D(1)	Croatia Zagreb	A	W	2–1	Bosnich	Irwin	Berg	Stam
2 November	Grp D(1)	Sturm Graz	H	W	2–1	Bosnich	G. Neville	Berg	May
23 November	Grp B(2)	Fiorentina	A	L	0–2	Bosnich	G. Neville	Berg	Stam
8 December	Grp B(2)	Valencia	H	W	3–0	Van der Gouw	Irwin	Stam	G. Neville
1 March	Grp B(2)	Bordeaux	H	W	2–0	Van der Gouw	G. Neville	Stam	Silvestre
7 March	Grp B(2)	Bordeaux	A	W	2–1	Van der Gouw	G. Neville	Stam	Silvestre
15 March	Grp B(2)	Fiorentina	H	W	3–1	Bosnich	G. Neville	Berg	Stam
21 March	Grp B(2)	Valencia	A	D	0–0	Bosnich	G. Neville	Berg	Stam
4 April	Q/F(1)	Real Madrid	A	D	0–0	Bosnich	G. Neville	Berg	Stam
19 April	Q/F(2)	Real Madrid	H	L	2–3	Van der Gouw	G. Neville	Berg	Stam

P. Neville	Beckham	Wilson	Scholes	Cole	Yorke	Giggs	Fortune for Clegg, Sheringham for Wilson
P. Neville	Beckham	**Keane 1**	Scholes	**Cole 1**	**Yorke 1**	Cruyff	Sheringham for Cruyff, Wilson for Keane, Solskjaer for Cole
P. Neville	Beckham	Butt	**Scholes 1**	**Cole 1**	Yorke	Solskjaer	Sheringham for Berg, Clegg for Cole, Fortune for Solskjaer
P. Neville	Beckham	Keane	Scholes	Cole	Yorke	Giggs	Solskjaer for Berg
P. Neville	**Beckham 1**	**Keane 1**	Scholes	Cole	Yorke	Giggs	Solskjaer for Yorke, Cruyff for Cole, Greening for Scholes
Irwin	Greening	**Keane 1**	Wilson	Cole	**Solskjaer 1**	Giggs	P. Neville for Wilson, Cruyff for Greening, Higginbotham for Irwin
Irwin	Beckham	Keane	Scholes	Cole	Yorke	Giggs	Sheringham for Cole, P. Neville for Berg, Solskjaer for Yorke
P. Neville	Beckham	**Keane 1**	**Scholes 1**	Cole	**Solskjaer 1**	Giggs	Butt for Scholes, Yorke for Cole
Irwin	Beckham	Keane	Butt	Cole	**Sheringham 1**	**Giggs 1**	P. Neville for Cole, Solskjaer for Giggs, Fortune for Keane
Irwin	Beckham	**Keane 1**	Butt	Cole	Sheringham	Giggs	**Solskjaer 1** for Irwin
Irwin	Beckham	**Keane 1**	Scholes	**Cole 1**	**Yorke 1**	Giggs	
Irwin	Butt	Keane	Scholes	Solskjaer	Sheringham	Fortune	Cruyff for Solskjaer
Irwin	Beckham	Keane	Scholes	Cole	Yorke	Giggs	Butt for Scholes, Sheringham for Yorke, Silvestre for Irwin
Irwin	**Beckham 1**	Keane	**Scholes 1**	Cole	Yorke	Giggs	Sheringham for Berg, Silvestre for Irwin, Solskjaer for Cole

427

2000–01 Champions League

13 September	Grp G(1)	Anderlecht	H	W	5–1	Barthez	**Irwin 1**	G. Neville	Johnsen
19 September	Grp G(1)	Dynamo Kiev	A	D	0–0	Van der Gouw	Irwin	G. Neville	Johnsen
26 September	Grp G(1)	PSV Eindhoven	A	L	1–3	Van der Gouw	P. Neville	G. Neville	Brown
18 October	Grp G(1)	PSV Eindhoven	H	W	3–1	Barthez	Irwin	G. Neville	Johnsen
24 October	Grp G(1)	Anderlecht	A	L	1–2	Barthez	**Irwin 1**	G. Neville	Johnsen
8 November	Grp G(1)	Dynamo Kiev	H	W	1–0	Barthez	Irwin	G. Neville	Brown
21 November	Grp A(2)	Panathinaikos	H	W	3–1	Barthez	P. Neville	G. Neville	Brown
6 December	Grp A(2)	Sturm Graz	A	W	2–0	Barthez	Irwin	G. Neville	Brown
14 February	Grp A(2)	Valencia	A	D	0–0	Barthez	G. Neville	Stam	Brown
20 February	Grp A(2)	Valencia	H	D	1–1	Barthez	G. Neville	Stam	Brown
7 March	Grp A(2)	Panathinaikos	A	D	1–1	Barthez	G. Neville	Stam	Brown
13 March	Grp A(2)	Sturm Graz	H	W	3–0	Barthez	Irwin	Stam	G. Neville
3 April	Q/F(1)	Bayern Munich	H	L	0–1	Barthez	G. Neville	Stam	Brown
18 April	Q/F(2)	Bayern Munich	A	L	1–2	Barthez	G. Neville	Stam	Brown

Silvestre	Beckham	Keane	Scholes	**Cole 3**	**Sheringham 1**	Giggs	P. Neville for Irwin, Yorke for Cole, Solskjaer for Giggs
Silvestre	Beckham	Keane	Butt	Cole	Yorke	Giggs	Sheringham for Yorke, Solskjaer for Cole
Silvestre	Greening	Keane	Butt	Solskjaer	Yorke	**Scholes**	Beckham for Greening, Giggs for Scholes, Wallwork for Silvestre
Silvestre	Beckham	Keane	**Scholes 1**	Cole	**Sheringham 1**	Giggs	Butt for Beckham, **Yorke 1** for Sheringham, Brown for Irwin
Silvestre	Beckham	Keane	Scholes	Cole	Yorke	Giggs	Solskjaer for Irwin, Brown for Silvestre
P. Neville	Beckham	Keane	Butt	Cole	**Sheringham 1**	Giggs	Yorke for Sheringham, Fortune for Giggs, Silvestre for Fortune
Silvestre	Beckham	Keane	Butt	Yorke	**Sheringham 1**	**Scholes 2**	
Silvestre	Beckham	Keane	Butt	Yorke	Sheringham	**Scholes 1**	**Giggs 1** for Butt, P. Neville for Irwin, Solskjaer for Yorke
Silvestre	Beckham	Keane	Scholes	Cole	Sheringham	Giggs	Butt for Beckham, Solskjaer for Cole
Silvestre	Beckham	Keane	Scholes	**Cole 1**	Sheringham	Giggs	Butt for Giggs, Solskjaer for Sheringham
Silvestre	Beckham	Keane	**Scholes 1**	Cole	Yorke	P. Neville	Sheringham for P. Neville, Solskjaer for Cole, Chadwick for Silvestre
Silvestre	Chadwick	**Keane 1**	Scholes	Solskjaer	**Sheringham 1**	**Butt 1**	Greening for Scholes
Silvestre	Beckham	Keane	Scholes	Cole	Solskjaer	Giggs	Yorke for Beckham
Silvestre	Scholes	Keane	Butt	Cole	Yorke	**Giggs 1**	Sheringham for Yorke, Solskjaer for Butt, Chadwick for Brown

Appearances

Who has played the most games for Manchester United in Europe?
From the pioneering years of the Busby Babes to today's Champions
League, this is the complete list:

	Player	Seasons played	European Cup/ Champions League	UEFA Cup	Cup-Winners' Cup	Total
1	Denis Irwin	1990–91 to 2000–01	54	3	8	65
2	David Beckham	1994–95 to 2000–01	56(1)	2	0	59
3	Gary Neville	1993–94 to 2000–01	55(2)	11	0	59
4	Roy Keane	1993–94 to 2000–01	54	2	0	56
5	Ryan Giggs	1993–94 to 2000–01	49(3)	2	0	54
6	Bill Foulkes	1956–57 to 1968–69	35	11	6	52
7	Paul Scholes	1994–95 to 2000–01	39(9)	1(1)	0	50
8	Nicky Butt	1994–95 to 2000–01	36(11)	2	0	49
9	Andy Cole	1996–97 to 2000–01	41(4)	0	0	45
10	Bobby Charlton	1956–57 to 1968–69	28	11	6	45
11	Ole Gunnar Solskjaer	1996–97 to 2000–01	19(25)	0	0	44
12	Peter Schmeichel	1991–92 to 1998–99	36	3	3	42
13	Pat Crerand	1963–64 to 1968–69	24	11	6	41
14	Tony Dunne	1963–64 to 1968–69	23	11	6	40
15	Gary Pallister	1990–91 to 1997–98	23	4	16	40
16	Nobby Stiles	1963–64 to 1968–69	23	11	2	36
17	George Best	1963–64 to 1968–69	21	11	2	33
18	Denis Law	1963–64 to 1968–69	18	10	5	33
19	Phil Neville	1996–97 to 2000–01	22(11)	0	0	33
20	Dwight Yorke	1998–99 to 2000–01	27(6)	0	0	33
21	Jaap Stam	1998–99 to 2000–01	32	0	0	32
22	Mark Hughes	1983–84 to 1994–95	7	10	12(3)	32
23	Teddy Sheringham	1997–98 to 2000–01	20(11)	0	0	31
24	Arthur Albiston	1976–77 to 1984–85	0	14(1)	12	27
25	Bryan Robson	1982–83 to 1993–94	4	9(1)	13	27
26	Steve Bruce	1990–91 to 1995–96	9(1)	4	12	26
27	Ronny Johnsen	1996–97 to 2000–01	24(2)	0	0	26
28	David Herd	1963–64 to 1967–68	8	11	6	25
29	Shay Brennan	1963–64 to 1968–69	11	11	2	24
30	Henning Berg	1997–98 to 1999–00	19(4)	0	0	23
31	Brian McClair	1990–91 to 1997–98	2(6)	2	13	23
32	Alex Stepney	1967–68 to 1977–78	15	4	4	23
33	Gary Bailey	1980–81 to 1984–85	0	12	8	20
34	Paul Ince	1990–91 to 1994–95	9	1	10	20
35	John Connelly	1964–65 to 1965–66	8	11	0	19
36	Mike Duxbury	1980–81 to 1984–85	0	9(1)	8	18
37	Mikael Silvestre	1990–00 to 2000–01	15(3)	0	0	18
38	Mike Phelan	1990–91 to 1993–94	1(3)	1	12	17
39	Lee Sharpe	1990–91 to 1994–95	7	2	6(2)	17
40	Eric Cantona	1993–94 to 1996–97	16	0	0	16
41	Brian Kidd	1967–68 to 1968–69	16	0	0	16
42	David Sadler	1967–68 to 1968–69	14	0	2	16
43	Wesley Brown	1998–99 to 2000–01	12(3)	0	0	15
44	Jordi Cruyff	1996–97 to 1999–00	4(11)	0	0	15

Player	Seasons played	European Cup/ Champions League	UEFA Cup	Cup-Winners' Cup	Total
45 Roger Byrne	1956–57 to 1957–58	14	0	0	14
46 Tommy Taylor	1956–57 to 1957–58	14	0	0	14
47 Kevin Moran	1980–81 to 1984–85	0	5(1)	8	14
48 Frank Stapleton	1982–83 to 1984–85	0	6(1)	8	14
49 Eddie Colman	1956–57 to 1957–58	13	0	0	13
50 David May	1994–95 to 1999–00	12(1)	0	0	13
51 Remi Moses	1982–83 to 1984–85	0	7	5(1)	13
52 Norman Whiteside	1982–83 to 1984–85	0	6(1)	5(1)	13
53 Pat Dunne	1964–65 to 1965–66	2	11	0	13
54 Fabien Barthez	2000–01	12	0	0	12
55 Steve Coppell	1976–77 to 1983–84	0	7(1)	4	12
56 Duncan Edwards	1956–57 to 1957–58	12	0	0	12
57 David Pegg	1956–57 to 1957–58	12	0	0	12
58 Dennis Viollet	1956–57 to 1957–58	12	0	0	12
59 Ray Wood	1956–57 to 1957–58	12	0	0	12
60 Johnny Berry	1956–57 to 1957–58	11	0	0	11
61 Clayton Blackmore	1990–91 to 1992–93	0	1	10	11
62 Harry Gregg	1957–58 to 1965–66	9	0	2	11
63 Rai van der Gouw	1996–97 to 2000–01	11	0	0	11
64 Neil Webb	1990–91 to 1992–93	0	2	9	11
65 Liam Whelan	1956–57 to 1957–58	11	0	0	11
66 Lee Martin	1990–91 to 1993–94	1(1)	1	4(4)	11
67 Francis Burns	1967–68 to 1968–69	10	0	0	10
68 Martin Buchan	1976–77 to 1982–83	0	6	4	10
69 Graeme Hogg	1983–84 to 1984–85	0	6	4	10
70 Mark Jones	1956–57 to 1957–58	10	0	0	10
71 Lou Macari	1976–77 to 1983–84	0	5(1)	4	10
72 Sammy McIlroy	1976–77 to 1980–81	0	6	4	10
73 Jimmy Nicholl	1976–77 to 1980–81	0	6	4	10
74 Paul Parker	1991–92 to 1994–95	5(1)	0(2)	2	10
75 Karel Poborsky	1996–97 to 1997–98	5(5)	0	0	10
76 John Gidman	1983–84 to 1984–85	0	6(1)	1(1)	9
77 John Aston	1965–66 to 1967–68	8	0	0	8
78 Gordon Hill	1976–77 to 1977–78	0	4	4	8
79 Arnold Muhren	1983–84 to 1984–85	0	3	5	8
80 Les Sealey	1990–91	0	0	8	8
81 Ray Wilkins	1982–83 to 1983–84	0	2	6	8
82 Noel Cantwell	1963–64 to 1965–66	3	0	4	7
83 Mark Bosnich	1999–00	7	0	0	7
84 John Fitzpatrick	1965–66 to 1968–69	7	0	0	7
85 Andrei Kanchelskis	1991–92 to 1994–95	5	1	1	7
86 Gordon McQueen	1982–83 to 1984–85	0	3	4	7
87 Maurice Setters	1963–64 to 1964–65	0	1	6	7
88 Jesper Blomqvist	1998–99	6(1)	0	0	7
89 Arthur Graham	1983–84	0	6(1)	0	7
90 Jesper Olsen	1984–85	0	6(1)	0	7
91 Mark Robins	1990–91 to 1991–92	0	0	5(2)	7
92 Danny Wallace	1990–91 to 1992–93	0	2	3(2)	7
93 David McCreery	1976–77 to 1977–78	0	1(3)	3	7
94 Brian Greenhoff	1976–77 to 1977–78	0	4	2	6
95 Stuart Pearson	1976–77 to 1977–78	0	3	3	6
96 Gordon Strachan	1984–85	0	6	0	6
97 Gary Walsh	1990–91 to 1994–95	3	1	2	6

	Player	Seasons played	European Cup/ Champions League	UEFA Cup	Cup-Winners' Cup	Total
98	Ashley Grimes	1977–78 to 1982–83	0	4	0(2)	6
99	Jackie Blanchflower	1956–57 to 1957–58	5	0	0	5
100	David Gaskell	1963–64 to 1965–66	1	0	4	5
101	Colin Webster	1957–58	5	0	0	5
102	Russell Beardsmore	1990–91 to 1991–92	0	0	2(3)	5
103	Stewart Houston	1976–77 to 1977–78	0	2	2(1)	5
104	Quinton Fortune	1999–00 to 2000–01	1(4)	0	0	5
105	Phil Chisnall	1963–64	0	0	4	4
106	Gerry Daly	1976–77	0	4	0	4
107	Paul McGrath	1983–84 to 1984–85	0	2	2	4
108	Willie Morgan	1968–69	4	0	0	4
109	Kenny Morgans	1957–58	4	0	0	4
110	Chris McGrath	1977–78	0	0	3(1)	4
111	Mal Donaghy	1990–91	0	0	2(2)	4
112	Jonathan Greening	1999–00 to 2000–01	2(2)	0	0	4
113	Mark Wilson	1998–99 to 2000–01	2(2)	0	0	4
114	Freddie Goodwin	1957–58	3	0	0	3
115	Albert Quixall	1963–64	0	0	3	3
116	Albert Scanlon	1957–58	3	0	0	3
117	Simon Davies	1994–95	2	0	0(1)	3
118	Jimmy Rimmer	1968–69	2(1)	0	0	3
119	Luke Chadwick	2000–01	1(2)	0	0	3
120	Michael Clegg	1997–98 to 2000–01	1(2)	0	0	3
121	Alan Brazil	1984–85	0	2	0	2
122	Ronnie Cope	1957–58	2	0	0	2
123	Stan Crowther	1957–58	2	0	0	2
124	Ian Greaves	1957–58	2	0	0	2
125	Jimmy Greenhoff	1977–78 to 1980–81	0	1	1	2
126	Steve James	1968–69	2	0	0	2
127	Nikola Jovanovic	1980–81	0	2	0	2
128	Wilf McGuinness	1956–57 to 1957–58	2	0	0	2
129	Mark Pearson	1957–58	2	0	0	2
130	Jimmy Ryan	1967–68 to 1968–69	2	0	0	2
131	Steve Paterson	1976–77	0	0(2)	0	2
132	Carlo Sartori	1968–69	2	0	0	2
133	Ernie Taylor	1957–58	2	0	0	2
134	Mickey Thomas	1980–81	0	2	0	2
135	Viv Anderson	1990–91	0	0	1	1
136	Willie Anderson	1965–66	1	0	0	1
137	Joe Jordan	1980–81	0	1	0	1
138	Frank Kopel	1968–69	1	0	0	1
139	John O'Kane	1995–96	0	1	0	1
140	Chris Casper	1996–97	0(1)	0	0	1
141	Terry Cooke	1995–96	0	0(1)	0	1
142	Alan Davies	1983–84	0	0	0(1)	1
143	Mark Dempsey	1983–84	0	0	0(1)	1
144	Dion Dublin	1993–94	0(1)	0	0	1
145	Alex Forsyth	1977–78	0	0	0(1)	1
146	Billy Garton	1984–85	0	0(1)	0	1
147	Dan Higginbotham	1999–2000	0(1)	0	0	1
148	Ronnie Wallwork	2000–01	0(1)	0	0	1

Figures shown in brackets indicate appearances as substitute

Goal scorers

	European Cup/ Champions League	UEFA Cup	Cup-Winners' Cup	Total
Denis Law	14	8	6	28
Bobby Charlton	10	8	4	22
Andy Cole	18	0	0	18
Paul Scholes	15	1	0	16
David Herd	5	6	3	14
Roy Keane	13	0	0	13
Dennis Viollet	13	0	0	13
Ryan Giggs	13	0	0	13
George Best	9	2	0	11
John Connelly	6	5	0	11
Tommy Taylor	11	0	0	11
Dwight Yorke	11	0	0	11
Mark Hughes	2	2	5	9
Teddy Sheringham	9	0	0	9
Bryan Robson	1	3	4	8
David Beckham	7	0	0	7
Ole Gunnar Solskjaer	7	0	0	7
Steve Bruce	2	0	4	6
Eric Cantona	5	0	0	5
Brian McClair	0	0	5	5
Frank Stapleton	0	1	4	5
Liam Whelan	5	0	0	5
Denis Irwin	4	0	0	4
John Berry	3	0	0	3
Steve Coppell	0	0	3	3
Brian Kidd	3	0	0	3
Arnold Muhren	0	3	0	3
David Pegg	3	0	0	3
David Sadler	3	0	0	3
Lee Sharpe	2	0	1	3
Clayton Blackmore	0	0	2	2
Bill Foulkes	2	0	0	2
Gordon Hill	0	1	1	2
Sammy McIlroy	0	2	0	2
Gordon Strachan	0	2	0	2
John Aston	1	0	0	1
Henning Berg	1	0	0	1
Alan Brazil	0	1	0	1
Francis Burns	1	0	0	1
Nicky Butt	1	0	0	1
Phil Chisnall	0	0	1	1
Eddie Colman	1	0	0	1
Pat Crerand	1	0	0	1
Alan Davies	0	0	1	1
Simon Davies	1	0	0	1
Arthur Graham	0	0	1	1
Andrei Kanchelskis	1	0	0	1
Lou Macari	0	1	0	1
David May	1	0	0	1

	European Cup/ Champions League	UEFA Cup	Cup-Winners' Cup	Total
Willie Morgan	1	0	0	1
Phil Neville	1	0	0	1
Jimmy Nicholl	0	0	1	1
Gary Pallister	0	0	1	1
Stuart Pearson	0	0	1	1
Mark Robins	0	0	1	1
Carlo Sartori	1	0	0	1
Peter Schmeichel	0	1	0	1
Maurice Setters	0	0	1	1
Nobby Stiles	1	0	0	1
Ernie Taylor	1	0	0	1
Neil Webb	0	0	1	1
Colin Webster	1	0	0	1
Norman Whiteside	0	0	1	1
Ray Wilkins	0	0	1	1
Totals	211	47	53	311
Own Goals				
Murca (FC Porto)	0	0	2	2
Burgsmuller (Borussia Dortmund)	1	0	0	1
Faktor (Kosice)	1	0	0	1
Florenski (Gornik)	1	0	0	1
Hakan (Galatasaray)	1	0	0	1
Korkmaz (Galatasaray)	1	0	0	1
McGinnis (Dundee Utd)	0	1	0	1
Soskic (Partizan Belgrade)	1	0	0	1
Zoco (Real Madrid)	1	0	0	1
Totals	7	1	2	10
Total goals scored	218	48	55	321

Index